IF YOU THINK Y...
YOU PROBABLY HAVEN'T HEARD THIS . . .

Cindy Jackson has spent over $100,000 on more than 50 cosmetic procedures, including nine full-scale surgical operations since 1988. Her treatments have included everything from facelifts, a nose job, and breast implants to dermal vitamin injections, and tattooed lipstick and eyeliner. She has had the most cosmetic surgery of anyone in the world

The greatest number of bee stings sustained by any surviving human is 2,443 by Johannes Relleke at the Kamativi tin mine, Gwaii River, Wankie District, Zimbabwe (then Rhodesia), on January 28, 1962. All the stings were removed and counted.

London, UK, is the world's most expensive city for dining out. In 2007, the average cost of a three-course meal plus one glass of wine was $79.66—practically double that of New York City, US.

Accreditation

Guinness World Records Limited has a very thorough accreditation system for records verification. However, while every effort is made to ensure accuracy, Guinness World Records Limited cannot be held responsible for any errors contained in this work. Feedback from our readers on any point of accuracy is always welcomed.

Abbreviations & Measurements

Guinness World Records Limited uses both metric and imperial measurements. The sole exceptions are for some scientific data where metric measurements only are universally accepted, and for some sports data. Where a specific date is given, the exchange rate is calculated according to the currency values that were in operation at the time. Where only a year date is given, the exchange rate is calculated from December of that year. "One billion" is taken to mean one thousand million. "GDR" (the German Democratic Republic) refers to the East German state, which unified with West Germany in 1990. The abbreviation is used for sports records broken before 1990. The USSR (Union of Soviet Socialist Republics) split into a number of parts in 1991, the largest of these being Russia. The CIS (Commonwealth of Independent States) replaced it, and the abbreviation is used mainly for sports records broken at the 1992 Olympic Games. Guinness World Records Limited does not claim to own any right, title, or interest in the trademarks of others reproduced in this book.

General Warning

Attempting to break records or set new records can be dangerous. Appropriate advice should be obtained first, and all record attempts are undertaken at the participant's risk. In no circumstances will Guinness World Records Limited have any liability for death or injury suffered in any record attempt. Guinness World Records Limited has complete discretion over whether or not to include any particular records in the book. Being a Guinness World Record holder does not guarantee you a place in the book.

GUINNESS WRLD RECORDS 2009

BANTAM BOOKS
NEW YORK • TORONTO • LONDON • SYDNEY • AUCKLAND

GUINNESS WORLD RECORDS™ 2009
Copyright © 2008 by Guinness World Records Limited.
Published under license.

Bantam edition / May 2009

GUINNESS WORLD RECORDS™ is a trademark of
Guinness World Records Limited and is reproduced under license by
Bantam Dell, a division of Random House, Inc.
New York, New York

Revised American editions copyright © 2009, 2008, 2007, 2006, 2005,
2004, 2003, 2002, 2001, 2000, 1999, 1998, 1997, 1996, 1995, 1994,
1993, 1992, 1991, 1990, 1989, 1988, 1987, 1986, 1985, 1984, 1983,
1982, 1981, 1980, 1979, 1978, 1977, 1976, 1975, 1974, 1973, 1972,
1971, 1970, 1969, 1968, 1966, 1965, 1964, 1963, 1962, 1960
by Guinness World Records Ltd.

For information address: Guinness World Records Ltd.

GUINNESS WORLD RECORDS

EDITOR-IN-CHIEF
Craig Glenday

CONTENTS

★ BRAND-NEW RECORDS are indicated by a solid star, in both the text and record headings

☆ BROKEN OR UPDATED RECORDS are indicated by an open star, in both the text and record headings

INTRODUCTION

The World's Deadliest Cheese, a Giant Gorilla Sculpted from Coat Hangers, an Interview with a Sith Lord, and the Richest Chimpanzee on Wall Street. Think You've Seen It All? Think Again...

Hello and welcome to *Guinness World Records 2009!* The latest edition of our annual compendium is packed solid with the most amazing, inspirational, and quite frankly bizarre world records!

From the farthest corners of the globe to the most intimate corners of people's living rooms, backyards, garages, gyms, and (yes) bedrooms, this year has seen even greater and more exciting records being attempted... and we bring them to you now in this, the all-new *Guinness World Records 2009* book!

Record breaking seems to have gripped the imagination of everyone over the past 12 months, from Dubai to Estonia, from Israel to Uruguay, and from Australia to the United States.... Everyone wants to get into "The Book."

MENTOS-SODA FUN It seems this has been the year of Mentos-soda fountains! The record for the ★ **most soda fountains erupted simultaneously** was first set in May 2007 by Mentos in Cincinnati, Ohio (with 504 fountains), followed by successful attempts by Books Are Fun in Dallas, Texas (above, with 791) in July, Mentos in the Netherlands in September (853), and finally the residents of southeast Missouri (973) in October!

AMERICA'S TALLEST Last year, with the help of *Good Morning America,* we began the search for the tallest man in the U.S.A. Diane Sawyer announced the search, and it took several months of sorting through hundreds of doctors' certificates, photos, and letters, but by the end a truly great big man was found: Sheriff George Bell from Virginia, standing at 7 ft. 8 in. (2.33 m). Congratulations, George!

It would be a perfect world if everyone who broke or set a record last year could make it into print, but unfortunately there just isn't enough room.

But whether you made it in this year or not, we'd like to take this opportunity to thank everyone who wrote, e-mailed, called, faxed, registered, and visited us over the past 12 months. We wouldn't be here without you, so thank you!

Last year's celebration of Guinness World Records Day was our largest ever. Over 20 countries participated, and more than 35 records were attempted. Literally thousands of people joined in from all over the globe, sharing an amazing record-breaking day and having lots of fun as well. If you don't know what this is (where have you been?), you can read all about it on pp. 110–113, where you'll be able to see a selection of the records that were broken and find out how to participate this year. But start planning soon, because this coming year's event already looks like it will be even bigger than last year's!

The special sections this year are of a celebratory nature: to mark the publication of the final book in J. K. Rowling's phenomenal boy

---

FACTS

• Record claims received at GWR during the past year: 35,692

• Records approved: 2,017

• Live and rested records on the GWR database: 40,000

• Number of records in the book: 4,000

PAULA'S PARTY In October, we traveled to Savannah, Georgia, where Queen of Southern Cooking Paula Deen celebrated record-breaking in her own style by having a Guinness World Record–themed episode of her Food Network show *Paula's Party*. It was all happening in her kitchen as she dipped strawberries in chocolate, husked corn, scooped ice cream, and opened oysters all in the name of record breaking! To top it all off, the show ended with the unveiling of the world's ★ **longest crawfish boil**, measuring 96 ft. 4 in. (29.3 m). Eat up, y'all!

SEE US AT X GAMES Since 2004, Guinness World Records has been a presence at the annual ESPN X Games events in Los Angeles and Aspen, chronicling the record-breaking athletes as well as being present at X Fest with our very own booth. Activities in the past have included record-breaking attempts, book raffles, and athlete autograph signings, as well as official presentations of GWR certificates to Tommy Clowers, Fabiola da Silva, Dave Mirra, Lindsey Adams Hawkins, Mat Hoffman, Travis Pastrana, and more!

PLAYING THE GAME When it comes to dominoes, we're more used to toppling them than playing with them. But this year, we accepted a record for the ★ **most people playing dominoes simultaneously.** On March 16, 2008, at Calle Ocho, in the Hispanic quarter of Miami, Florida, U.S.A., the men's brand Old Spice organized 278 players to compete together in the baking Miami sun for a $25,000 prize. At least they had plenty of grooming products on hand to keep them cool!

wizard series, we explore the **Magic of Harry Potter;** we celebrate the 40th anniversary of the **Moon landings,** and have even included an interview with Gene Cernan, the last man to walk on the Moon! And we hope you'll be blown away by our fantastic **dinosaurs** feature.

This year's subject for the **Hall of Fame** is Hollywood, and specifically its greatest record-breaking actors. Turn to pp. 436–438 to find out why the

FALL OUT BOY We literally go to the ends of the Earth to bring you the world's best-selling book—as proved by GWR's Editor-in-Chief Craig Glenday, who was invited to Antarctica for a concert by Fall Out Boy. The Chicago pop/punk/rock band (Pete Wentz, Andy Hurley, Joe Trohman, and Patrick Stump, all U.S.A., above) were hoping to set the record for the **fastest time to perform a gig on every continent.** At the last stage, however, the weather proved too bad, and the band and Craig were left stranded at the southern tip of South America. Better luck next time, guys!

GWR LIVE! Throughout the year, you'll find Guinness World Records out and around at various live events across the U.S.A., staging record attempts and showcasing our favorite record holders.

This year, we paid a visit to the Minnesota Twins (U.S.A.) to award Joe Mauer (U.S.A., left) his certificate for the ★ **first catcher to lead the major leagues in batting average**. He batted .347 playing for the Minnesota Twins in 2006.

And in the summer of 2007, we visited the ESPN X Games to see what tricks *you* could show us from the world of action sports. We set up the GWR BreakFest, an interactive skateboard park where we invited you to show us your stuff and try to get into the *Guinness World Records* book! See what happened when we went West Coast–style on pp. 400–403.

likes of Brad Pitt, Angelina Jolie, Jack Nicholson, and Johnny Depp have been inducted into the prestigious GWR Hall of Fame, and read an extract from our exclusive interview with screen legend Christopher Lee.

The final section is particularly special to us as it welcomes into the

---

FACT

The **tallest man ever** was Robert Pershing Wadlow (U.S.A.), who was 8 ft. 11.1 in. (2.72 m) tall and died on July 15, 1940. In addition to his height, Wadlow also holds the records for the **largest hands** and **largest feet**—see p. 83 for details.

ON THE HUNT We're always looking for fun new Guinness World Records. Got an idea? Then contact us via our website: **www.guinness worldrecords.com.** Simply click on "Break a Record" then follow the instructions and tell us as much as you can about your claim. Left: Guinness World Records' Laura Plunkett and Neil Fingleton, the **tallest man in the UK,** launch the hunt for **tallest man in the U.S.**

Guinness World Records "family" an important new member: He Pingping, the world's ☆**shortest living man!** Guinness World Records Editor-in-Chief Craig Glenday had the experience of a lifetime traveling to Inner Mongolia to meet and measure Pingping, and we hope you enjoy him in all his glory on pp. 439–444!

ROB & BIG From the Hollywood Hills of California, we received a call from two men called Robert and Chris who described themselves as a pro skateboarder and his big friend. "Yes, of course we can help you break a Guinness World Record," we said. Little did we know that we had been contacted by none other than MTV's *The Rob & Big Show!* Over one day, Rob set or broke 21 Guinness World Records, including the ★**highest skateboard ramp jump into water** at 10 ft. 8 in. (3.29 m)! Even Big himself joined in and broke two records, too. Find more skateboard records on p. 392 and 400–403.

100 GREAT MOMENTS In January 2008, NBC aired *Guinness World Records Live: The Top 100*—an unforgettable countdown of our most memorable records. From the **heaviest twins** to the **most kicks to the head**, the show featured 100 of the craziest and most eye-popping moments from our 53-year history of record breaking.

The show culminated in a live record attempt for the No. 1 spot. In probably the most dangerous Guinness World Record attempt ever broadcast on U.S. TV, stunt rider Clint Ewing (U.S.A.) rode his Kawasaki ZX-6R motorcycle through 200 ft. (61 m) of fire—the ☆ **longest motorcycle tunnel of fire** ever.

Alongside British TV personality Fearne Cotton, we were on hand to present Clint with his certificate and welcome him into the GWR family!

This year, we've also added an entirely new section at the back of the book called **The Gazetteer.** This feature explores the record-breaking achievements of all the major countries and territories in which Guinness World Records is available.

It's a cross between a travel guide and a record book, and helpful if you're either visiting somewhere new or investigating a part of the world for a school project.

What else can you expect to see over the next 575 pages? Well, considering we receive over 50,000 letters every year, we can say quite a lot! Our expert team of international adjudicators had been traveling far and wide to make sure we verify as many records as possible. We received over 2,500 enquiries from the U.S.A. alone, more than any other country, and we traveled the length and breadth of the nation in order to chronicle them all.

These ranged from the ★**largest data warehouse** in Dublin, California (p. 241) to the ☆**most 360 kickflips in a minute** in Los Angeles (p. 392),

GWR AND THE NBA Earlier this year we found ourselves in wonderful New Orleans for the **NBA All-Star Jam Session**—a huge basketball event celebrating the best of the sport from the **farthest slam dunk** to the ★**most half-court shots in a minute.** You can read all about it in our NBA All-Star Jam Session feature on pp. 345–348.

and from the ☆**most pancakes made in eight hours** in North Dakota (p. 196) to the ☆**longest baseball marathon** in St. Louis (p. 338).

Finally, this Christmas look out for **Guinness World Records: The Video Game!** It's your chance to attempt records—such as balancing a vehicle on your head (right)—on the Nintendo Wii or the DS. Go head-to-head against friends and family, and compete on a household, national or international level!

So, to all who set, broke, or just asked about Guinness World Records in the U.S., a big thank-you to every single one of you. We wouldn't be here without you. It really has been a brilliant year for Guinness World Records, not only for the variety and volume of records but also because of everyone we worked with—congratulations to you all!

Now turn the page and start enjoying *Guinness World Records 2009.* We think it's our best book ever . . . and we hope you do, too!

REGIS & KELLY A regular feature on the Guinness World Records calendar, 2007 proved no different as we joined Regis "I'm Only One Man" Philbin and Kelly Ripa to kick start a new record-breaking year. Five Guinness World Records were attempted, including ☆ **most skips by a dog in one minute** and ☆ **longest karaoke marathon**. A few of these records have been bettered since August 2007, but those are the breaks of record breaking! As always, the whole week of events was a fantastic celebration and we thank Regis, Kelly, and crew for their continuing support.

HOW TO BE A RECORD BREAKER

1. CONTACT US Got an idea? Then contact us via our website: **www.guinnessworldrecords.com.** Simply click on "Break a Record" and follow the instructions. We need to know as much as possible about your claim, and this is your chance to tell us every detail. LEFT: Robert T. Natoli (U.S.A.) receives his certificate for the ★ **most chin-ups in one minute** (a phenomenal 53!) from GWR's Laura.

2. FOLLOW THE RULES If your application is for an existing record, we'll send you the guidelines that the current record holder followed; if it's for a new record, and we like it, we'll write new guidelines for you. Once you receive these, you're ready to make your attempt. *ABOVE: Sweet-toothed GWR judge Jane gets her job of a lifetime—weighing the* ☆ **largest chocolate (30,540 lb.; 13,852 kg)**!

3. PROVE IT The guidelines we send you will contain details of the evidence we need: expect to film video evidence, take photographs, and collect two written independent witness statements. *LEFT: members of the Scout Association—the world's ★ largest youth organization.*

FACTS

- Last year, we received 35,692 claims—but only 2,017 made it on to our database

- The database holds around 40,000 live and rested records

- The book has room for just 4,000 entries!

How to Be a Record Breaker

4. MAIL IT Next, send us your evidence. If you want a GWR adjudicator present at your event, see p. xxi. Otherwise, we'll get back to you in due course. *LEFT: Câmara Municipal de Gondomar and Montepio (Portugal) achieve the record for the ★ most soccer balls released—an amazing 5,071 balls!*

Is there a cost involved? No! Trying for a Guinness World Record won't cost a thing—just commitment and time. Anyone can apply, but under-18s must get approval from a parent or guardian first.

5. WAIT If you've requested an adjudicator, he or she can ratify your record immediately. Otherwise, once we receive your package of evidence, our researchers will assess it to make sure that you've followed the rules correctly. This process can take a few months, so please be patient! X-ref *GWR's Michael celebrates with the St. Louis Chapter of the Men's Senior Baseball League (U.S.A.) for their record-breaking ☆ longest baseball marathon (see p 338).*

6. CELEBRATE If your attempt is a success, you'll receive your official GWR certificate in the mail. If not, better luck next time! *LEFT: Gary Cole (U.S.A.) celebrates achieving the record for the most faces painted in an hour (217).*

LARGEST PHONE GATHERING *LEFT:* GWR's Kaoru found herself surrounded by giant cell phones at the world's ☆ **largest gathering of people dressed as cell phones**, in San Juan, Puerto Rico, in November 2007. Have you got a few friends who could help you beat this or a similar record? Let us know by visiting our website **www.guinnessworldrecords.com.**

X Games You'll find Guinness World Records out and about at various events throughout the world every year, including the X Games, where we adjudicate records, organize signings with record holders, and stage competitions. *RIGHT: GWR's own Stuart is joined by Danny Way (U.S.A.), holder of several X Games world records (see box p. 402).*

CHOOSING A RECORD? PLEASE AVOID:

- **Non-records**—your claim *must* involve a record! Is it the tallest, longest, smelliest? What is the "-est"? You may be able to lick your own elbow but it's not a record!

- **Animal cruelty**—don't overfeed your pets to make them the heaviest. Not cool.

- **Breaking the law**—driving at high speeds on public roads is dangerous and illegal, so don't do it.

- **Teenage surgery**—teenagers performing medical operations is not OK: you're a danger to society. As are **speedy house builders** who try to erect homes in record time! They come down just as fast....

Marco, Guinness World Records' Director of Records Management, heads up a multilingual team that processes thousands of record claims each year. Here, he gives his advice on getting your name into the records book.

I always recommend looking through the book or watching our TV shows for the kinds of records we like. A record must fulfill four criteria. One, it has to be measureable—that is, you can take a tape measure to it, or weigh it, or count it. So you can't have the ugliest dog or most beautiful girlfriend, but you can have a dog that's won the most "ugly dog" competitions or a girlfriend who's won the most beauty contests. Two, it has to be singularly quantifiable—so, we're looking for just one superlative . . . we're not interested in the fastest tallest man, or the heaviest fastest accordion player. Three, it has to be breakable—unless it's a "significant first," by which we mean it has to be *really* significant, such as **first man on the moon** or **first movie to gross over $1 billion.** Four, it has to be interesting to as wide a range of people as possible. Also, remember that securing a record does *not* guarantee you a place in the book—that decision is the Editor's—but follow these basic pointers and you'll have a much better chance of success.

ADJUDICATIONS

THROUGHOUT THE YEAR, GWR'S ADJUDICATORS TRAVEL THE WORLD TO SEEK OUT NEW RECORDS. HERE'S THE INSIDE STORY ON THEIR UNIQUE ROLE.

Adjudicators at your service! After registering your record idea, you can arrange for a GWR adjudicator to be present at your event. The advantages of this include:

- Instant verification of your record and an official certificate presentation.
- An article about your record on our website. See **www.guinnessworld records.com/register/login.aspx.**
- Support in the build-up to your event.
- International media coverage for your record attempt.
- Availability of the adjudicator for interviews and press conferences.

TOP LEFT: GWR's Patricia Magill celebrates the ★tightest frying pan roll of two pans. TOP RIGHT: Adjudicator Gareth Deaves monitors the ★fastest lap time on Project Gotham 4 (Xbox 360): 47.53 seconds. LEFT: Carlos Martinez takes note of the ★largest chestnut roaster: 16 ft. 4 in. (5 m) in diameter.

★**FASTEST CAR RUN ON DRY-CELL BATTERIES** On August 4, 2007, the *Oxyride Racer* achieved an average speed of 65.83 mph (105.95 km/h) at JARI Shirosato Test Center in Ibaraki, Japan. This dry-cell-battery–powered vehicle was created by the Oxyride Speed Challenge Team, consisting of Matsushita Electric Industrial Co., Ltd., and Osaka Sangyo University (both Japan).

☆ **LARGEST CHOPSTICKS**
Andrea Bánfi and fellow Guinness World Records adjudicator Danny Girton measure the largest chopsticks—22 ft. 1 in. (6.73 m)—manufactured by the Marco Polo Hotel in Dubai and certified at the Dubai Shopping Festival on February 23, 2008.

ANDREA BÁNFI

As Guinness World Records Adjudications Manager, Andrea Bánfi leads a team of multilingual adjudicators located in London, New York, Beijing, and Sydney. So what is it like to attend record-breaking attempts for a living?
People often ask me how I became an adjudicator. Well, it wasn't easy! GWR has a strict recruiting process involving a variety of tests, and successful applicants need to have expertise in a number of different areas, such as sports, music, and science.

After I joined GWR, records that up until then had been just numbers and facts suddenly came alive. Every GWR adjudication is different. Record attempts are always full of emotions and excitement—whether they are successful or not. Some people do extreme sports to get their adrenaline levels going; I get a buzz from record attempts, and not too long after officiating at my first event, I realized I was becoming addicted to them!

Of all the adjudications I've attended, my favorite so far has been the ☆ **most people reading aloud simultaneously in one location**: 13,839 people read a Taoist text together in a rugby stadium in Hong Kong. They were so well rehearsed that they read as if they were one person; when they paused, the silence was stunning.

We officiate at hundreds of record attempts every year and the demand is growing continuously, as a result of our adjudicators' dedication, support, and professionalism. If you are thinking of having us present at your record attempt, get in touch via our website, and I'll get back to you by phone or e-mail.

GWR adjudicators in action! Angela Wu and the ☆ **tallest flower structure**—an 80-ft. 1-in.-high (24.43-m) tower of chrysanthemums; Rob Molloy hands over a certificate for the ★ **longest boom (truck-mounted)**, made by SANY Heavy Industry Co., Ltd., China; our adjudicators are all experienced at working with the media—here, Amarillis Espinoza breaks the news of another GWR record; Kim Lacey and the ★ **largest toilet paper roll**: 5 ft. 6 in. (1.68 m).

Please note: GWR charges a fee for adjudicators to attend record attempts. Visit **www.guinnessworldrecords.com/member** to find out more about this premium service.

We carry out on-site adjudications for corporate activities, charity functions, product launches, marketing and PR events, sports events, and to raise awareness for good causes.

With the publication of ***Guinness World Records: Gamer's Edition,*** GWR now carries out a wide range of PC, console, and arcade game adjudications, from international shows to local arcades. So, if you're aiming for a record-breaking high score, why not have a GWR adjudicator there to make it official?

CHANGING WORLD

RECORD BREAKING IS AS OLD AS HUMANITY ITSELF. IT'S AMAZING TO SEE HOW MUCH SOME WORLD RECORDS HAVE CHANGED OVER THE YEARS—AND HOW LITTLE SOME HAVE ALTERED. . . .

MOST EXPENSIVE PAINTINGS
The Magdalen Reading
Artist: Unknown
Date painted: before 1438
Date of sale: 1746
£6,500
(2008: $1,823,940)

Adoration of the Lamb (above)
Artist: Van Eyck
Date painted: 1432
Date of sale: 1821
£16,000
(2008: $2,232,510)

The Sistine Madonna (above)
Artist: Raphael
Date painted: 1513–14
Date of sale: 1759
£8,500
(2008: $2,269,104)

The Immaculate Conception
Artist: Murillo
Date painted: 1660–65
Date of sale: 1852
£24,600
(2008: $4,083,524)

Garçon à la Pipe*
Artist: Picasso
Date painted: 1905
Date of sale: 2004 (above)
$104,200,000
(2008: $114,372,876)

*In November 2006, it was reported that Jackson Pollock's painting *No. 5* (1948) had been sold by David Geffen (U.S.A.) for $140 million. However, as there has still been no definitive confirmation of the sale, the sale price, or even the buyer, GWR still recognizes *Garçon à la Pipe* as history's most expensive painting.

The Colonna Altarpiece
Artist: Raphael
Date painted: 1503–05
Date of sale: 1901
£100,000
(2008: $15,567,416)

Irises
Artist: Van Gogh
Date painted: 1889
Date of sale: 1987
$53,900,000
(2008: $98,377,938)

FASTEST 100 M
Don Lippincott (U.S.A.)
Date: July 6, 1912
Location: Stockholm,
Sweden
10.6 SEC.

Jesse Owens
(U.S.A., above)
Date: June 20, 1936
Location: Chicago,
Illinois, U.S.A.
10.2 SEC.

Armin Hary
(West Germany)
Date: June 21, 1960
Location: Zürich, Switzerland
10.0 SEC.

Jim Hines (U.S.A., above)
Date: October 14, 1968
Location: Mexico City, Mexico
9.95 SEC.

Leroy Burrell (U.S.A.)
Date: June 14, 1991
Location: New York City, U.S.A.
9.9 SEC.

Carl Lewis
(U.S.A., above)
Date: August 25, 1991
Location: Tokyo, Japan
9.86 SEC.

Donovan Bailey (Canada)
Date: July 29, 1996
Location: Atlanta, Georgia, U.S.A.
9.84 SEC.

Maurice Greene (U.S.A.)
Date: June 16, 1999
Location: Athens, Greece
9.79 SEC.

Asafa Powell
(Jamaica, above)
Date: June 14, 2005
Location: Athens, Greece
9.77 SEC.

Usain Bolt (Jamaica)
Date: May 31, 2008
Location:
New York, U.S.A.
9.72 SEC.

PROGRESSIVE SPEED

Sled
Date: *ca.* 6500 B.C.
Location: Heinola, Finland
25 MPH (40 KM/H)

Horse
Date: *ca.* 1400 B.C.
Location: Anatolia, Turkey
35 MPH (55 KM/H)

Ice yacht
Date: *ca.* 1600 A.D.
Location: The Netherlands
50 MPH (80 KM/H)

Downhill skier
Date: March 1873
Location: La Porte, California,
U.S.A.
Tommy Todd (U.S.A.)
87.8 MPH (141.3 KM/H)

Midland Railway 4-2-2
Date: March 1897
Location: Ampthill, Bedford, UK
90 MPH (144.8 KM/H)

Messerschmitt 163V-1
Date: October 2, 1941
Location: Peenemunde, Germany
Heinz Dittmar (Germany)
**623.85 MPH
(1,004 KM/H)**

USAF Bell XS-1
Date: October 14, 1947
Location: Murdoc Dry Lake,
California, U.S.A.
Capt. C. E. Yeager (U.S.A.)
670 MPH (1,078 KM/H)

North American X-15
Date: March 7, 1961
Location: Murdoc Dry Lake,
California, U.S.A.
Maj. R. M. White (U.S.A.)
**2,905 MPH
(4,675.1 KM/H)**

Vostok 1
Date: April 12, 1961
Location: Earth orbit
Maj. Y. A. Gagarin (USSR)
ca. 17,560 MPH
(28,260 KM/H)

Apollo 10
Date: May 26, 1969
Location: Re-entry into Earth's atmosphere
Crew of *Apollo 10* (U.S.A.)
24,790.8 MPH (39,897 KM/H)

TALLEST STRUCTURES

Djoser Step Pyramid
Location: Saqqâra, Egypt
Built: *ca.* 2650 B.C.
204 FT. (62 M)

Great Pyramid of Cheops
Location: El Gizeh, Egypt
Built: *ca.* 2580 B.C.
480 FT. 10 IN. (146.5 M)

St. Paul's Cathedral
Location: London, UK
Built: 1315–1561
489 FT. (149 M)*

Eiffel Tower
Location: Paris, France
Built: 1887–89
985 FT. 10 IN. (300.5 M)

Chrysler Building
Location: New York City, U.S.A.
Built: 1929–30
1,046 FT. (318 M)

Empire State Building
Location: New York City, U.S.A.
Built: 1929–30
1,250 FT. (381 M)

Warszawa Radio Mast
Location: Plock, Poland
Built: 1974
2,120 FT. (646 M)†

*Original spire destroyed by lightning, June 4, 1561
†Fell during renovation, 1991

**Ursa
Tension Leg
Platform**
Location: Gulf of Mexico
Built: 1998
**4,285 FT.
(1,306 M)**

ALTITUDE
(since 1900)

**248,655 MILES
(400,171 KM)**
Holder/vehicle: crew of U.S.
Apollo 13: Capt. James A.
Lovell Jr.; Frederick W. Haise
Jr.; John L. Swigert Jr. (all
U.S.A.).
Date: April 15, 1970

**234,672 MILES
(377,667 KM)**
Holder/vehicle: crew of U.S.
Apollo 8 command module:
Col. Frank Borman; Capt.
James A. Lovell Jr.; Maj.
William A. Anders (all U.S.A.).
Date: December 25, 1968

**203.2 MILES
(327 KM)**
Holder/vehicle: Maj. Yuri A.
Gagarin (USSR) in *Vostok 1*.
Date: April 12, 1961

**169,600 FT.
(51,694 M)**
Holder/vehicle: Joseph Walker
(U.S.A.) in U.S. *X-15* rocket plane.
Date: March 30, 1961

**126,200 FT.
(38,465 M)**
Holder/vehicle: Capt. Iven
C. Kincheloe Jr. (U.S.A.) in
U.S. *Bell X-2* rocket plane.
Date: September 7, 1956

**79,600 FT.
(24,262 M)**
Holder/vehicle: William
B. Bridgeman (U.S.A.) in U.S.
Douglas D558-11 *Skyrocket*.
Date: August 15, 1951

**72,395 FT.
(22,066 M)**
Holder/vehicle: Capt. Orvill
A. Anderson and Capt. Albert
W. Stevens (both U.S.A.) in U.S.
Explorer II helium balloon.
Date: November 11, 1935

**51,961 FT.
(15,837 M)**
Holder/vehicle: Prof. Auguste
Piccard and Paul Kipfer (both
Switzerland) in *FNRS 1* balloon.
Date: May 27, 1931

**36,565 FT.
(11,145 M)**
Holder/vehicle: Sadi Lecointe
(France) in Nieuport aircraft.
Date: October 30, 1923

BEST-SELLING SINGLE *Although no exact figures are available, it has been estimated that sales of the song "White Christmas," written by Irving Berlin (U.S.A., b. Israel Baline, Russia), exceed 100 million copies worldwide when 78s, 45s, and albums are taken into account.*

"White Christmas" was listed as the world's best-selling single in the first-ever Guinness Book of Records (published in 1955) and—remarkably—still retains the title more than 50 years later.

Bing Crosby (U.S.A., pictured) is the artist most closely associated with the song. He originally recorded it on May 29, 1942, but his re-recording (on March 18, 1947) has become the best-known version. The song has been a Yuletide favorite ever since.

★ LARGEST CONURBATIONS ★

YEAR	CITY/PRESENT LOCATION	POPULATION
ca. 27000 B.C.	Dolní Věstonice, Czech Republic	>100
3000 B.C.	Uruk (Erech; now Warka), Iraq	50,000
2200 B.C.	Greater Ur (now Tell el-Muqayyar), Iraq	250,000
133 B.C.	Rome, Italy	1,100,000
A.D. 900	Angkor, Cambodia	1,500,000
1578	Peking (now Beijing), China	707,000
1801	Greater London, UK	1,117,290
1925	New York City, U.S.A.	7,774,000
1939	Greater London, UK	8,615,050
1985	Tokyo, Japan	11,600,069
2003	Tokyo, Japan	26,546,000
2020 (projection)	Tokyo, Japan	>37,000,000

SPACE

CONTENTS

STARS

☆**Oldest star in the Milky Way** The star HE1327-2326 is located 4,000 light-years from Earth. Its age is measured by its composition. When the Universe was formed, it consisted of hydrogen with some helium. As it evolved, the rest of the chemical elements appeared, formed by nuclear synthesis in stars. HE1327-2326 has almost no metal content in it (just 1/300,000th of the metal content of our own Sun), so it must have formed from clouds of almost pure hydrogen and helium gas when the universe was young. It may date back to just after the very start of the universe, around 13.7 billion years ago.

★**Largest star** Owing to the physical difficulties in directly measuring the size of a distant star, the identity of the largest star is a matter for debate among astronomers. The current most likely candidate is VY Canis Majoris, a red supergiant some 5,000 light-years away. Estimates of its size give it a diameter of 1.55–1.86 billion miles (2.5–3 billion km), or 1,800–2,100 times that of the Sun. If placed at the center of the Solar System, the star's outer surface would reach beyond the orbit of Jupiter.

Largest constellation Of the 88 constellations, Hydra (the Sea Serpent) is the largest, covering 3.16% of the whole sky and containing at least 68 stars visible to the naked eye (to 5.5 magnitude). The constellation Centaurus (Centaur), which ranks ninth in area, embraces at least 94 such stars.

★**Most stars in a star system** The greatest number of stars in a single star system is six. There are a few known examples, but the most famous is Castor, the second brightest star in the constellation of Gemini.

★**Most common type of star** By far the most common class of star in our galaxy and the Universe are red dwarfs. These are weak, dim stars with no more than 40% of the mass of the Sun. The brightest of them shines at only 10% of the Sun's luminosity. Because they burn their fuel so slowly they have life spans much longer than our own star, of at least 10 billion years. Around 80% of all stars in our local neighborhood are red dwarfs.

DENSEST OBJECTS IN THE UNIVERSE

Black holes are the remnants of stars that ended their lives as supernovas. They are characterized by a region of space in which gravity is so strong that not even light can escape. The boundary of a black hole is known as the "event horizon." At its center is the "singularity," where the mass of the dead star is compressed to a point of zero size and infinite density, generating the black hole's powerful gravitational field.

LARGEST DIAMOND Observations of pulsations from the carbon white dwarf star BPM 37093 have allowed astronomers from the Harvard-Smithsonian Center for Astrophysics in Cambridge, Massachusetts, U.S.A., to deduce that it crystallized into a diamond some 2,500 miles (4,000 km) across. BPM 37093 is around 50 light-years from Earth in the constellation of Centaurus.

★**Nearest red supergiant** Betelgeuse, in the constellation of Orion, lies just 427 light-years from the Solar System. Like all red supergiants, it is a massive star nearing the end of its relatively short life span of perhaps just a few million years in total. It has a mass of around 14 times that of the Sun and varies in size between around 400 and 600 times the Sun's diameter.

Nearest star visible to the naked eye. The nearest star visible to the naked eye is the southern-hemisphere binary Alpha Centauri (4.40 light-years distant).

Brightest open star cluster Located in the constellation of Taurus, the Pleiades (M45)—also known as the Seven Sisters—contains approximately 500 individual stars in a region of space roughly 20 light-years across, and at an average distance of around 380 light-years from Earth. Even from a major light-polluted city, around six of the Pleiades can be seen with the naked eye.

Nearest brown dwarf Brown dwarfs are often referred to as "failed stars." Like other stars, they form from clouds of galactic gas and dust that collapse under their own gravity. If the resulting star is less than 0.08 times the mass of the Sun, its core never becomes hot enough to initiate hydrogen fusion and the star is never "born." Brown dwarfs represent the missing link between stars and planets.

The nearest brown dwarf to the Earth is Epsilon Indi B, a companion to the star Epsilon Indi, 11.8 light-years away.

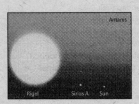

★**SHORTEST-LIVED STARS** With masses of around 100 times that of the Sun, "blue supergiants" (seen left in a computer simulation) burn through their fuel extremely quickly and can last for as little as 10 million years. Their blue color is a consequence of their very high surface temperatures—around 36,032–90,032°F (20,000–50,000°C).

One of the best known is Rigel in the constellation of Orion. It is the sixth brightest star in the sky, even though it is around 900 light-years away.

> *"Equipped with his five senses, man explores the universe around him and calls the adventure Science."*
>
> Edwin Hubble (1889–1953), astronomer

Brightest star viewed from Earth Sirius A (alpha Canis Majoris), located 8.64 light-years from Earth, is the brightest star in the night sky, with an apparent magnitude of -1.46. It has a diameter of 1.45 million miles (2.33 million km), a mass 2.14 times that of the Sun, and is visually 24 times brighter than the Sun.

Brightest supernova In April 1006, the supernova SN 1006 was noted near the star Beta Lupi; it flared for two years and reached a magnitude of -9.5. This titanic cosmic explosion could be seen with the naked eye for 24 months and, at its brightest was 1,500 times brighter than Sirius A.

In 1987, a giant star in the Large Magellanic Cloud, a satellite galaxy of our own Milky Way, exploded in the **brightest supernova of modern times.** Its peak brightness was magnitude 2.3—easily visible without a telescope.

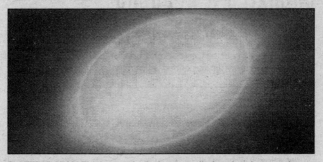

FLATTEST STAR The least spherical star studied to date in our galaxy is the southern star Achenar (Alpha Eridani). Observations made using the VLT Interferometer at the European Southern Observatory's Paranal Observatory in Atacama, Chile, have revealed that Achenar is spinning so rapidly that its equatorial diameter is more than 50% greater than its polar diameter.

DID YOU KNOW?

Neutron stars, which may have a mass up to three times that of the Sun, have diameters of just 6–19 miles (10–30 km), making them the **smallest stars.**

HOTTEST PLACE IN THE SOLAR SYSTEM The temperature at the center of the Sun has been estimated at 28,080,000°F (15,600,000°C). The pressure at the heart of the Sun is huge—around 250 billion times the pressure at sea level on Earth—and it is here that 600 million metric tons of hydrogen are fused into helium every second. This ongoing nuclear reaction is what makes the Sun shine.

★**Most magnetic objects** A magnetar is a type of neutron star (a body created from the remains of a collapsed star) that possesses a stupendously powerful magnetic field of around 10 thousand million teslas. (Earth has a magnetic field of around 50 microteslas.) Measuring around 12 miles (20 km) across, a magnetar should theoretically be able to wipe the data from a credit card at a distance equivalent to halfway to the Moon.

GALAXIES & NEBULAS

★**Largest spiral galaxy** Discovered in 1986, Malin 1 is a spiral galaxy some 1.1 billion light-years away. In terms of its diameter, it is the largest known spiral galaxy in the Universe, measuring around 650,000 light-years across—several times the size of our Milky Way.

SPACE STATS

The Solar System is located in a spiral arm of the Milky Way Galaxy, some 26,000 light-years from the center. The Milky Way is around 100,000 light-years across, 12,000 light-years thick, and contains between 200 billion and 400 billion stars.

The Andromeda Galaxy is similar to our own and, at 2.2 million light-years' distance, is one of the closest galaxies to ours. Because of the time it takes light from the galaxy to reach Earth, we are seeing Andromeda as it was 2.2 million years ago.

The Milky Way and Andromeda galaxies belong to a collection of around 35 galaxies known as the "Local Group." It is part of the Virgo Supercluster of around 100 groups and clusters of galaxies.

It is thought there are about 130 billion galaxies in the Universe, which is around 13.8 billion years old.

It is possible for two galaxies to collide without a single star hitting another.

> *"Our galaxy is only one of some hundred thousand million that can be seen using modern telescopes."*

Professor Stephen W. Hawking

★**Youngest planetary nebula** The Stingray Nebula, located 18,000 light-years away in the southern constellation of Ara, was observed as a star in the 1970s. In 1996, the Hubble Space Telescope imaged it and found that, in the intervening 20 years, its central star had heated up enough to make the ejected gas shells that surround it glow as a planetary nebula.

★**Longest galactic jet** In December 2007, astronomers announced their discovery of an energetic jet of matter that was being emitted from a super-massive black hole in the center of the active galaxy CGCG 049-033. Measuring some 1.5 million light-years long, the high-energy jet happens to be pointed directly at a nearby galaxy. Any planets in that galaxy in the line of fire would have their atmospheres ionized, extinguishing any life there.

Coldest place in the Milky Way The coldest place in the Universe is in the Boomerang Nebula, a cloud of dust and gases 5,000 light-years from Earth. It has a temperature of -457.6°F (-272°C) and is formed by the rapid expansion of gas and dust flowing away from its central aging star.

★**Closest galaxy to the Milky Way** The Canis Major dwarf galaxy was only discovered in 2003 by a team of French, Italian, British, and Australian astronomers. It lies an average of just 42,000 light-years from the center of our galaxy. It was hard to detect because it is behind the plane of our spiral galaxy as seen from Earth. The shape of the dwarf galaxy indicates it is in the process of being ripped apart and absorbed by the gravity of the Milky Way.

The galaxy contains a high percentage of red giant stars and is thought to contain around 1 billion stars in total.

★**LARGEST SATELLITE GALAXY** To date, some 15 minor satellite galaxies have been discovered orbiting our Milky Way Galaxy, the most recent of which was discovered in 2006. Of these, the largest and brightest is the Large Magellanic Cloud, some 160,000 light-years from the center of the Milky Way. It is classed as a dwarf irregular galaxy and measures around 20,000 light-years across, with a mass of around 10 billion solar masses.

★CLOSEST ACTIVE GALAXY Galaxies that contain a compact, highly luminous core that emits intense radiation are known as active galaxies. The source of the radiation is believed to be a vast disc of shredded stars and other matter being swallowed by a central supermassive black hole. At just 11 million light-years away, the enormous elliptical galaxy Centaurus A is the closest of these active galaxies to our own.

BRIGHTEST SUPERNOVA REMNANT The Crab Nebula (M1), in the constellation of Taurus (the Bull), is the brightest supernova remnant in the sky, with a magnitude of 8.4.

SUPERLATIVE SATELLITES

Planet With the Most Moons

As of 2008, astronomers had discovered 63 natural satellites of the planet Jupiter. Saturn has the second greatest number of moons, with 60. Most of these moons are small irregularly shaped bodies of ice and rock, and many are almost certainly captured asteroids.

Closest Moon To a Planet

The tiny Martian moon Phobos orbits Mars at an altitude of 5,827 miles (9,378 km) from the planet's center—or 3,716 miles (5,981 km) above Mars' surface.

Most Distant Moon From a Planet

On September 3, 2003, the International Astronomical Union announced the discovery of the moon S/2003 N1, which orbits Neptune at an average distance of almost 31 million miles (49.5 million km). It has an orbital period of approximately 26 years and measures around 24 miles (38 km) across.

CLOSEST PLANETARY NEBULA
At a distance of around 400 light-years, the Helix Nebula (also known as NGC 7293) is the closest planetary nebula to the Earth. It formed when a dying star threw off its outer layers, which are gradually expanding into space. They are called planetary nebulas because astronomers originally believed they were new planets, due to their often spherical shapes. The Helix Nebula is around 100 times more distant than the nearest stars (excluding the Sun).

★ LARGEST NEBULAS SEEN FROM EARTH As seen from Earth, the vast cloud of molecular hydrogen known as Barnard's Loop is a faintly glowing arc only visible in long-exposure images. At an average distance of around 1,600 light-years and measuring around 300 light-years across, it contains the famous Orion and Horsehead nebulas. If it were visible to the naked eye, Barnard's Loop would fill most of the entire constellation of Orion in the night sky.

HEAVENLY BODIES

Most distant image of Earth On February 4, 1990, NASA's *Voyager 1* spacecraft turned its camera back toward the Sun and the planets. After 12.5 years in space, traveling away from Earth, *Voyager 1*'s camera took a picture of our home planet from a distance of almost 4 billion miles (6.5 billion km).

TALLEST RIDGE IN THE SOLAR SYSTEM Observations of Saturn's moon Iapetus by the NASA/ESA spacecraft *Cassini-Huygens,* on December 31, 2004, revealed an enormous ridge, at least 800 miles (1,300 km) long, which reaches an altitude of around 12 miles (20 km) above the surface. Iapetus is 890 miles (1,400 km) across.

Most volcanically active body When NASA's *Voyager 1* probe passed by the giant planet Jupiter in 1979, its camera imaged Jupiter's moon Io. The photographs revealed enormous volcanic eruption plumes, some reaching hundreds of miles into space. This activity is driven by tidal energy inside Io, created as a result of gravitational interactions between Io, Jupiter, and one of the other moons, Europa.

Deepest crater The largest impact basin on the Moon is the far-side South Pole-Aitken, which is 1,400 miles (2,250 km) in diameter and on average 39,000 ft. (12,000 m) deep below its rim. This is the largest and deepest such crater known in the Solar System.

★Tallest nitrogen geysers When *Voyager 2* encountered Neptune and its large moon Triton in 1989, its cameras discovered active cryovolcanism in the form of geysers of nitrogen gas and snow.

TALLEST NONVOLCANIC MOUNTAINS IN THE SOLAR SYSTEM Boosaule Montes, on Jupiter's active moon Io, are up to 52,493 ft. (16,000 m) tall. Rather than being built up by volcanic eruptions, like Olympus Mons (the tallest mountain in the Solar System—see page 12), they were formed by tectonic activity generated by huge stresses in Io's crust.

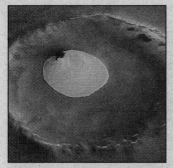

★ LARGEST MARTIAN FROZEN LAKE While scientists are certain that Mars holds vast amounts of frozen water at its poles and under ground, the discovery of a lake of frozen water in 2005 represents a first in the 40-year history of Martian exploration. Sitting in an unnamed crater near the Martian north pole, the lake, which is around 9 miles (15 km) across, was discovered by ESA's *Mars Express* spacecraft.

Reaching heights of up to 5 miles (8 km), these eruptions are believed to be brought about by weak sunlight heating nitrogen ice located just below the moon's surface.

Most reflective body The most reflective body in the Solar System is Enceladus, a small moon of Saturn with a surface composed mainly of icy material. It reflects some 90% of the sunlight that illuminates it, making it more reflective than freshly fallen snow.

★ Largest molten core Relative to its size, the planet Mercury has the largest molten metallic core of all the planets in the Solar System. With a radius of around 1,118 miles (1,800 km), the core takes up around 42% of the planet's volume, compared with just 15% for the Earth's core. Being only around 6% the mass of Earth, Mercury's core was previously believed to have cooled billions of years ago.

NASA's *Messenger* spacecraft, which is currently studying the planet, will hopefully provide data that explain Mercury's molten interior.

★ Least round planet A combination of its low density (less than water) and rapid rotation (once every 10.6 hours) gives Saturn the most oblate shape of all the planets. Its equatorial diameter is 74,897.5 miles (120,536 km); its polar diameter is just 67,560 miles (108,728 km).

★ Largest planetary ring The outermost major ring of Saturn, the E ring, is a tenuous and ethereal sheet of countless tiny particles. It extends from roughly the orbit of the moon Mimas out to roughly the orbit of the

---

DID YOU KNOW?

The NASA/ESA Cassini-Huygens spacecraft was launched on October 15, 1997. At 5,655 kg (12,467 lb.), this unmanned probe is the heaviest ever launched to the outer Solar System.

★TALLEST VENUSIAN MOUNTAIN Maxwell Montes, on the Ishtar Terra plateau (pictured above in a computer simulation) is the highest point on Venus, reaching 6.8 miles (11 km) above the planet's average surface altitude (the Venusian equivalent of sea level). It is named for UK physicist James Maxwell, who devised laws that related electricity to magnetism—the basis for radar.

moon Rhea—a width of around 211,260 miles (340,000 km). Recent discoveries by the *Cassini* spacecraft have revealed that the E ring is being constantly replenished by water ice eruption plumes from the active moon Enceladus.

TALLEST MOUNTAIN IN THE SOLAR SYSTEM The peak of Martian mountain Olympus Mons towers 15 miles (25 km)—nearly three times the height of Mt. Everest—above its base. Because of its shape, it is termed a shield volcano.

LARGEST PLANET IN THE SOLAR SYSTEM Jupiter's Great Red Spot appears as a white oval in this image of the largest planet in the Solar System. The gas giant has an equatorial diameter of 89,405 miles (143,884 km) and a mass of more than 300 Earths. Despite its size, Jupiter also has the shortest day of any planet in the Solar System, completing a full rotation in just 9 hr. 55 min.

In the foreground is the rocky moon Io, complete with blue aurora at its north pole and an orange glow from incandescent molten lava on its surface. This montage was assembled from images taken by NASA's *New Horizons* spacecraft. It passed through the Jupiter system in February 2007 and is now in interplanetary space en route to its encounter with Pluto in July 2015

★**Smallest body with a ring system** In March 2008, scientists announced the discovery of what seems to be a ring along with a debris disc around Saturn's moon Rhea. All four gas giant planets in the Solar System have a ring system but, at just 950 miles (1,530 km) across, Rhea is the smallest world with one.

LARGEST CHAOTICALLY ROTATING OBJECT Saturn's moon Hyperion measures 254 × 161 × 136 miles (410 × 260 × 220 km) and is the largest highly irregularly shaped body in the Solar System. It is one of only two bodies in the Solar System discovered to have completely chaotic rotation, essentially randomly tumbling in its orbit around Saturn. The other is asteroid 4179 Toutatis, measuring 2.7 × 1.5 × 1.8 miles (4.5 × 2.4 × 2.9 km).

Farthest resting place On July 31, 1999, America's *Lunar Prospector* spacecraft crashed into the lunar surface after 18 months of successful mission operations. This orbiter contained a small (1.5-in.; 3.8-cm) polycarbonate container holding one ounce of the remains of planetary science pioneer Dr. Eugene Shoemaker.

ASTEROIDS, COMETS, & METEORS

Brightest asteroid Asteroid 4 Vesta, discovered on March 29, 1807, is the only asteroid visible to the naked eye. This is owing to a combination of the brightness of its surface, its size (357.9 miles, or 576 km, across), and the fact that it can approach Earth as close as 110 million miles (177 million km).

★**First landing on an asteroid** On February 12, 2001, NASA's *NEAR Shoemaker* spacecraft touched down on the asteroid Eros, after 12 months of orbital observations. The landing was considered a mission bonus as the spacecraft had no landing gear but still survived after an impact velocity of between 4 ft. 10 in./sec. and 5 ft. 10 in./sec. (1.5–1.8 m/sec.).

Smallest object landed upon On November 20, 2005, the Japanese spacecraft *Hayabusa* made the first of two touchdowns on asteroid Itokawa in an attempt to collect samples to take back to Earth. Itokawa measures just 1,600 ft. (500 m) across its longest axis.

Greatest number of asteroids discovered by an individual Dr. Eugene Shoemaker (U.S.A., 1928–97) was one of the most eminent geologists of the 20th century. Best known for his work on extraterrestrial impacts, he discovered 1,125 asteroids, many in partnership with his wife, Caroline.

★**Largest source of comets** Beyond the orbit of Neptune lie the Kuiper Belt, the Scattered Disc, and the Oort Cloud, collectively known as Trans-Neptunian Objects. The Oort Cloud is a spherical cloud of thousands of billions of cometary nuclei. It surrounds the Sun at a distance of around 50,000 Astronomical Units (1 AU=the distance from the Earth to the Sun), which is around 1,000 times the distance from the Sun to Pluto. It is believed to be the source of most of the comets that visit the inner Solar System.

X-REF

The story of humanity's sojourns in space is a heady mix of scientific savvy and sheer heroism. Discover the amazing history of the **Moon Landings** for yourself: take off for p. 120 now!

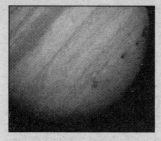

GREATEST RECORDED IMPACT IN THE SOLAR SYSTEM Between July 16 and 22, 1994, more than 20 fragments of comet Shoemaker-Levy 9 collided with the giant planet Jupiter, leaving a series of colossal bruises in its atmosphere. The greatest impact was that of the "G" fragment, which exploded with the energy of roughly 600 times the world's nuclear arsenal, equivalent to 6 million megatons of TNT.

★**Largest Trans-Neptunian object** Sedna, discovered in 2003, is an icy world measuring between 733 miles and 1,118 miles (1,180–1,800 km). It takes an estimated 12,000 years for Sedna to orbit the Sun once.

Greatest impact recorded on Earth An explosion recorded over the basin of the Podkamennaya Tunguska River, Russia, on June 30, 1908, was equivalent to 10–15 megatons of high explosive and resulted in the devastation of an area of 1,500 miles^2 (3,900 km^2). The shock wave was felt up to 620 miles (1,000 km) away. The cause is thought to have been the energy released following the total disintegration, at an altitude of 6 miles (10 km), of a common type of stony meteroid 100 ft. (30 m) in diameter.

The **oldest impact recorded on Earth** was revealed on August 23, 2002. A team of US scientists led by Gary Byerly (Louisiana State University) and Donald Lowe (Stanford University) announced their discovery of a 3.47-billion-year-old asteroid impact on our planet. The scientists had studied ancient rock samples from Australia and South Africa and analyzed

★**FIRST IMPACT WITH A COMET** On July 4, 2005, a 771-lb. (350-kg) copper "bullet" ejected from NASA's *Deep Impact* spacecraft hit the surface of comet Tempel 1 at a velocity of 6.4 miles/sec. (10.3 km/sec.). The impact, which was the equivalent of 10,360 lb. (4.7 metric tons) of TNT, created a huge plume and a crater on the comet around 328 ft. (100 m) wide and 98 ft. (30 m) deep.

★ MOST COMET TAILS ENCOUNTERED BY A SPACECRAFT In February 2007, the NASA/European Space Agency (ESA) spacecraft *Ulysses* unexpectedly flew through the tail of Comet McNaught, some 160 million miles (260 million km) distant from the comet's core. This was the spacecraft's third passage through a cometary tail—in 1996 and 2004, *Ulysses* flew through the tails Hyakutake and McNaught-Hartley, respectively.

spherules (tiny spherical particles) contained within them. They discovered that the impacting body had a diameter of approximately 12 miles (20 km).

★ LARGEST COLLECTION OF ASTEROIDS The main asteroid belt lies between the orbits of Mars and Jupiter. It contains between 700,000 and 1,700,000 asteroids that are at least 0.6 miles (1 km) across, and many millions of smaller bodies.

The total mass of the asteroid belt is equivalent to just 4% of the mass of Earth's Moon, with around half the mass of the whole belt accounted for by the four largest asteroids.

Largest asteroid in the main asteroid belt The largest asteroid is 1 Ceres, discovered by G. Piazzi in Palermo, Sicily, on January 1, 1801. It has an average diameter of 584.7 miles (941 km).

COLOSSAL COMETS

LARGEST COMET

Discovered in May 1977, Centaur 2060 Chiron has a 113-mile (182-km) diameter.

CLOSEST APPROACH TO EARTH BY A COMET

On July 1, 1770, Lexell's Comet, traveling at a speed of 86,100 mph (138,600 km/h) relative to the Sun, came to within 1,360,000 miles (2,200,000 km) of the Earth.

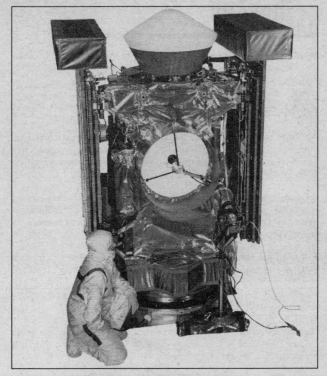

★ **FIRST SAMPLE RETURNED FROM A COMET** An engineer carries out final checks on NASA's *Stardust* spacecraft prior to its launch on January 7, 1999. *Stardust* encountered the comet Wild 2 on January 2, 2004, sweeping up tiny, precious samples of its dust in an aerogel collector.

METEORIC MARVELS

History's **greatest meteor shower** occurred on the night of November 16–17, 1966, when the Leonid meteors (so-called as they appear from the direction of the constellation of Leo) were visible between western North America and eastern Russia (then USSR). Meteors passed over Arizona, U.S.A., at a rate of 2,300 per minute for 20 minutes from 5 a.m. on November 17, 1966.

The Leonids are also the **fastest annual meteor shower:** they enter Earth's atmosphere at a speed of around 44 miles/sec. (71 km/sec.).

ASTRONOMY

Most expensive telescope sold at auction A very rare type of binocular telescope signed and dated in 1720 was sold at Christie's, London, UK, in December 1998 for £155,500 ($256,591).

LARGEST . . .

Airborne telescope NASA's Stratospheric Observatory for Infrared Astronomy has a Boeing 747SP equipped with an infrared telescope bearing an 8-ft. 10-in.-wide (2.7-m) mirror. Its "first light" occurred on August 18, 2004.

★**Cosmic ray telescope** The Pierre Auger Observatory is a vast array of some 1,600 particle detectors arranged across 1,158 miles^2 (3,000 km^2) of western Argentina. It was designed to detect very high-energy cosmic ray particles produced by supermassive black holes.

Fully robotic telescope Owned by the Astrophysics Research Institute (ARI) of Liverpool John Moores University (UK), the Liverpool Telescope

★**LARGEST REFRACTING TELESCOPE** The largest refractor, which uses a lens instead of a mirror to gather and focus light, is at the Yerkes Observatory in Wisconsin, U.S.A. Built in 1897, it has a primary lens diameter of 3 ft. 4 in. (1.02 m).

★ **LARGEST BINOCULAR TELESCOPE** The Large Binocular Telescope comprises two identical telescopes, each with a 27-ft. 6-in.-diameter (8.4-m) main mirror. Working in tandem, they have an equivalent light-gathering power of a single mirror 38 ft. 8 in. (11.8 m) across. The telescope—which is located on a mountain top in Arizona, U.S.A.—became fully functional in March 2008.

is located on La Palma, Canary Islands, Spain, and has a main mirror with a 6 ft. 6 in. (2 m) diameter. It was designed for observing visible and near-infrared wavelengths, and achieved "first light" on July 27, 2003.

Largest land-based telescope The twin Keck Telescopes, on the summit of Hawaii's dormant Mauna Kea volcano, are the world's largest land-based optical and infrared telescopes.

Each Keck telescope is eight stories tall and weighs 600,000 lb. (300 tons), and each has a 32-ft. (10-m) mirror, made up of 36 hexagonal segments which act together to create a single reflective surface. With these telescopes, you would be able to see a golf ball 93.2 miles (150 km) away.

Lens The world's largest refracting optical lens measures 5 ft. 11 in. (1.827 m) in diameter. It was built by a team led by Thomas Peck (U.S.A.), at the Optics Shop of the Optical Sciences Center of the University of Arizona in Tucson, Arizona, U.S.A., and completed in January 2000. It was built as a test for the secondary mirror of the 21-ft. 4-in. (6.5-m) MMT Telescope on Mt. Hopkins, Arizona, U.S.A.

FACT

The Large Binocular Telescope is the world's **highest-resolution and most technologically advanced optical telescope.** It is capable of creating images in the near infrared with 10 times the resolution of the Hubble Space Telescope.

★ **LARGEST SINGLE OPTICAL TELESCOPE** The Gran Telescopio Canarias (GTC) achieved "first light" on July 13, 2007. Located on the island of La Palma, it has a main mirror made up of 36 hexagonal segments and a diameter of 34 ft. (10.4 m). The telescope took seven years to build.

Radio telescope dish The world's largest radio telescope dish is the partially steerable ionospheric assembly built over a natural bowl at Arecibo, Puerto Rico, completed in November 1963. The dish is 1,000 ft. (305 m) in diameter and covers 18.5 acres (7.48 ha) in area—similar to 14 football fields.

★ **Solar telescope** The McMath-Pierce Solar Telescope on Kitt Peak, Arizona, U.S.A., opened in 1962. Light from the Sun is collected via a 498-

---

SPACE TELESCOPES

• The **most powerful gamma ray telescope** was the Compton Gamma Ray Observatory, launched in 1991. After nine years of observations, it re-entered the Earth's atmosphere and burned up on June 4, 2000.

• The Chandra X-Ray Telescope, launched in July 1999, is the world's **most powerful X-ray telescope**. It has a resolving power equivalent to the ability to read a stop sign at a distance of 12 miles (19 km).

• NASA's Spitzer Space Telescope—the **largest infrared space telescope**—was launched into Earth's orbit on August 25, 2003. It is the best tool astronomers have for observing the heat emissions from objects in deep space as well as our own Solar System. The instrument has a total mass of 2,094 lb. (950 kg).

★ **LARGEST LIQUID MIRROR** The Large Zenith Telescope in Canada uses a mirror made from liquid mercury. By spinning the 6,613-lb. (3-metric ton), 19-ft. 8-in.-diameter (6-m) mercury mirror, the liquid forms a concave shape perfect for astronomical observations.

ft. (152-m)-long slanted shaft, which directs sunlight onto a 5-ft. 3-in. (1.6-m) mirror 164 ft. (50 m) below ground. It forms a 33-in.-wide (85-cm) high-resolution image of the Sun.

★ **Submillimeter telescope** Beyond the red end of the visible spectrum of light lies infrared radiation, microwaves, and radio waves. The largest telescope designed to study the Universe at the wavelengths between the far infrared and microwaves—the submillimeter region—is the James Clerk Maxwell Telescope, on Mauna Kea, Hawaii. Rather than an optical mirror, it uses a massive 49-ft. (15-m) dish to collect submillimeter radiation.

★ **LARGEST GATHERING OF MAJOR TELESCOPES** Kitt Peak, a 6,876-ft.-high (2,096- m) mountain in Arizona, U.S.A., is home to the Kitt Peak National Observatory. Its excellent visual conditions and atmospheric clarity have attracted the construction of 23 major telescopes on its summit since 1958.

SPACE TECHNOLOGY

★ **Largest automated European spacecraft** The European Space Agency's (ESA) Automated Transfer Vehicle is an unmanned cargo freighter designed to resupply astronauts on the International Space Station

LARGEST SPACE FUNERAL The ashes of 24 space pioneers and enthusiasts, including *Star Trek* creator Gene Roddenberry (left), were sent into orbit on April 21, 1997, at a cost of $4,900 each. The ashes stayed in orbit for up to five years before burning up in Earth's atmostphere.

(ISS). Its cylindrical body measures 33 ft. 9 in. (10.3 m) long by 14 ft. 9 in. (4.5 m) across with a mass of 44,092 lb. (20 metric tons). Its cargo capacity of 16,534 lb. (7.5 metric tons) is around three times that of the Russian *Progress* unmanned freighter. Its maiden launch was on March 8, 2008.

★**Most durable Mars orbiter** NASA's *Mars Global Surveyor* was launched in 1996 and entered Martian orbit on September 11, 1997. It was due to spend just two years mapping and monitoring the planet, but due to the success of the mission and the quality of the information gathered, it was granted multiple extensions. Contact was lost with the spacecraft on November 2, 2006—after it had sent more than 250,000 images of Mars back to Earth after over nine years in orbit.

☆**LONGEST SPACE TETHER** The *Young Engineers Satellite 2 (YES2)* was launched on September 14, 2007. On September 25, *YES2* unwound an experimental package on a 0.5-mm-thick cable to test the principle of returning payloads to Earth without the use of retrorockets. The cable extended to its full length of 9.6 miles (31.7 km)—the longest man-made structure in space.

SIGNIFICANT SPACECRAFT Since the days of the first satellite, *Sputnik 1,* and the first manned spaceflight, *Vostok 1,* spacecraft have taken on a range of forms and uses. From manned capsules, shuttles, and space stations, to Earth-orbiting satellites, unmanned planetary probes, and landers, spacecraft have provided humankind with global communications and environmental monitoring, as well as being our eyes and ears as we reach out and explore the Universe at large.

VOSTOK 1
Length (of capsule and equipment module): 15 ft. 1 in. (4.6 m)
Mass: 10,427 lb. (4,730 kg)
Launched: April 12, 1961
Duration: 1 hr. 48 min.
Crew: Yuri Gagarin (USSR)
First manned spaceflight

PIONEER 10
Dish diameter: 8 ft. 11 in. (2.74 m)
Mass: 568 lb. (258 kg)
Launched: March 3, 1972
Duration: Last contact on January 23, 2003
First spacecraft to reach the outer Solar System

SPIRIT **MARS ROVER**
Height: 4 ft. 11 in. (1.5 m) with mast up
Mass: 383 lb. (174 kg)
Launched: June 10, 2003
Landed (on Mars): January 4, 2004
Duration: Still operating
Longest-lasting Mars rover

APOLLO 11 **LUNAR MODULE**
Height: 20 ft. 10 in. (6.37 m)
Mass: 36,349 lb. (16,488 kg)
Launched: July 16, 1969
Duration: Five days
First manned lunar landing

CASSINI-HUYGENS
Length: body and dish 22 ft. 3 in. (6.8 m)
Mass: 5,511 lb. (2,500 kg)
Launched: October 15, 1997
Duration: Still operating
First spacecraft to orbit Saturn

HUBBLE
Length: 43 ft. 4 in. (13.2 m)
Mass: 24,250 lb. (11,000 kg)
Launched: April 2, 1990
Duration: Still operating
Most powerful optical space telescope

MOST DURABLE SPACE STATION *Mir,* the central core module of the *Mir* space station (USSR/Russia), was launched into orbit on February 20, 1986. Over the following 10 years, five modules and a docking port for U.S. space shuttles were added to the complex. On March 23, 2001, the space station was deorbited and destroyed in a controlled reentry over the Pacific Ocean. More than 100 people visited the *Mir* space station in its 15-year operational history.

LONGEST SHUTTLE FLIGHT Space shuttle *Columbia* was launched on its 21st mission, STS80, with a crew of five (four men and one woman) on November 19, 1996. The flight lasted 17 days 15 hr. 53 min. 26 sec. to main gear shutdown.

★**Largest military satellite constellation** America's Global Positioning System is a coordinated constellation of at least 24 satellites in orbit around the Earth. They provide, via radio signals, precise 3D navigation data coverage for the whole world, enabling users to quickly pinpoint their location using a receiver. The GPS constellation is operated by the U.S. Air Force 50th Space Wing and was restricted to military use until 1996.

★**Largest combat satellite** The Soviet *Polyus* satellite was a prototype orbital weapons platform measuring 121 ft. 4 in. (37 m) long, 13 ft. 5 in.

FACT

Before the flight, Ham (see p. 25) was trained to push a lever within five seconds of seeing a flashing light. Failure to do so would result in a punishment in the form of a mild electric shock to the soles of his feet, while the correct response was rewarded with a banana pellet.

Space

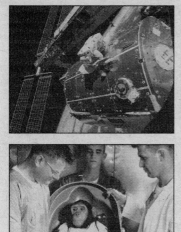

☆ **LARGEST SPACE STATION**
The International Space
Station (ISS) has been under
construction since its first
component, the *Zarya* module,
was launched in November
1998. The latest element to be
added was ESA's *Columbus*
module, on February 11, 2008,
bringing the total mass of the
ISS so far to 541,753 lb.
(245,735 kg).

**EARLIEST HOMINID TO
SURVIVE A SPACEFLIGHT** The
first hominid to survive a
spaceflight was Ham, a four-
year-old chimpanzee who was
launched by NASA on a
suborbital test flight from Cape
Canaveral, Florida, U.S.A., on
January 31, 1961. At its peak,
the rocket he was traveling in
reached 158 miles (254 km)
above Earth, before returning
to land—16.5 minutes after
launch—where Ham was
recovered alive, but with a
bruised nose.

(4.1 m) in diameter, and with a mass of 176,369 lb. (80 metric tons). It was
equipped with an anti-satellite cannon, a sensor-blinding laser to confuse
hostile satellites, and a nuclear space mine launcher. Only one was ever
launched, on May 15, 1987, but it failed to reach orbit and crashed into the
Pacific Ocean.

LIVING PLANET

CONTENTS

OCEANS

Largest area of calm water The Sargasso Sea in the north Atlantic Ocean covers about 2.4 million miles^2 (6.2 million km^2) of relatively still water. Its surface is largely covered by sargassum seaweed.

★**Smallest squid** Currently known only from two specimens, the world's smallest squid is *Parateuthis tunicata,* collected by the German South Polar Expedition of 1901–03. The larger of these two specimens measured 0.5 in. (1.27 cm) long, including its tentacles.

★**Country with the greatest number of seaweed species** With almost 3,000 different species, Australia boasts the greatest number of seaweed species of any country. The majority occur in the more temperate, nutrient-rich southern waters, and a large number of those are endemic to Australia, occurring nowhere else in the world.

★**Rarest penguin** The yellow-eyed penguin *Megadyptes antipodes* is found only in New Zealand. Also claimed to be the most ancient species of modern-day penguin, as well as the world's third largest, its total population probably does not exceed 4,500–5,000 individuals. Its survival is threatened by habitat loss and predation by nonnative mammals, such as ferrets, cats, and stoats.

★**Most marine spider** Spiders are not normally sea-dwelling creatures. *Desis marina* is classed as semi-marine, as it lives on exposed coral reefs and intertidal rocks in Australia and New Zealand. When the tide rises, it hides away inside abandoned seaworm burrows, blocking the water out with a lid woven from silk, and it can survive there underwater for several days.

★**LONGEST RECORDED JOURNEY BY A SHARK** On November 7, 2003, a team of researchers led by Dr. Ramón Bonfil from the Wildlife Conservation Society (U.S.A.) electronically tagged four sharks in South Africa, one of whom was nicknamed Nicole (after actress and shark-lover Nicole Kidman). In August 2004, Nicole was identified off the coast of South Africa, yet her timed-release tag was recovered in Australia six months earlier in February, where a satellite recorded its transmission. Thus, within nine months, this great white had swum 12,400 miles (20,000 km) across an entire ocean, from South Africa to Australia and back, and in doing so completed the longest recorded journey by a shark.

SLOWEST FISH Sea horses (family *Syngnathidae*) are incapable of swimming against the current, and to avoid being swept away, hang on to coral and marine plants with their prehensile tails. Their swimming ability is severely limited by a rigid body structure. The major source of propulsion is the wave motion of the dorsal fin: this makes a ripple, which drives the fish forward in an erect posture. Some of the smaller species, such as the dwarf sea horse (*Hippocampus zosterae*), which reaches a maximum length of only 1.7 in. (4.2 cm), probably never attain speeds of more than 0.001 mph (0.016 km/h).

★**Smallest octopus** Sri Lanka's *Octopus arborescens* has an arm-span of less than 2 in. (5.1 cm).

☆**Smallest shark** Because it is difficult to determine precisely when a small species is sexually mature (i.e., an adult and fully grown), there are three contenders for the smallest species of shark. Adult males of the dwarf lantern shark (*Etmopterus perryi*) measure a total length of 6.3–6.8 in. (16–17.5 cm), with one confirmed male adult specimen collected measuring 7.4 in. (19 cm) long. Mature females are typically 7.4–7.8 in. (19–20 cm) long.

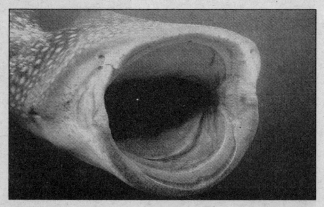

LARGEST FISH The heaviest cartilaginous fish, and also the largest fish, is the whale shark (*Rhincodon typus*). The largest recorded example measured 41 ft. 6 in. (12.65 m) long, 23 ft. (7 m) round the thickest part of the body, and weighed an estimated 33,000–46,200 lb. (15–21 metric tons). It was caught near Karachi, Pakistan, in 1949.

MOST VENOMOUS FISH The most venomous fish in the world are the
stonefish (family Synanceiidae) that inhabit the tropical waters of the
Indo-Pacific. Direct contact with the spines of their fins, which contain a
strong neurotoxic venom, can prove fatal. Pictured is the reed stonefish
(*Synanceia verrucasa*), camouflaged like a rock.

Prior to the discovery of the dwarf lantern shark, the record holder was
the spined pygmy shark (*Squaliolus laticaudus*), males of which measure
6 in. (15 cm), and females 6.7–7.8 in. (17–20 cm). A third rival, the pygmy
ribbontail catshark (*Eridacnis radcliffei*), has males measuring 7–7.4 in.
(18–19 cm). Females might mature at 6–6.3 in. (15–16 cm).

★**First methane-sustained animals** In July 1997, Professor Charles
Fisher led a team of scientists from Pennsylvania State University, Pennsylvania, U.S.A., in a mini-submarine down 1,800 ft. (548 m) to the Gulf of
Mexico's sea floor. Here they observed mushroom-shaped mounds of yellow and white methane ice (gas hydrates), 6–8 ft. (1.8–2.4 m) across. These
mounds were assumed to be too noxious to support any form of animal life,
but Fisher's team discovered large numbers of a hitherto unknown species of
pink, flat-bodied polychaete worms thriving on and burrowing into these
mounds. They have been grazing upon chemosynthetic bacteria growing on
the methane ice.

★**Most common shark** The spiny dogfish (*Squalus acanthias*) lives in
cold and temperate marine waters worldwide. Supporting important fish-
eries in several countries, the record catch for this species probably occurred
in 1904–05, when some 27 million spiny dogfishes were caught off the coast
of Massachusetts, U.S.A., alone.

DID YOU KNOW?

Puffer fish (genus *Tetraodon*) of the Red Sea and Indo-Pacific region
deliver a fatally poisonous toxin called tetrodotoxin. The genus is the
most poisonous fish edible by humans.

DEEPEST DIVE BY A PINNIPED In May 1989, scientists studying
northern elephant seals (*Mirounga angustirostris*, juvenile pictured) off
the coast of San Miguel Island, California, U.S.A., measured a maximum
diving depth of 5,017 ft. (1,529 m).

RIVERS, LAKES, & PONDS

Largest river to dry up The Yellow River (Huang He) is China's second-
longest river. It is known as "China's Sorrow" because of the millions of
people killed in disastrous seasonal floods, while suffering from too little
water the rest of the time. In 1997 and 1998, the Yellow River ran completely dry along its lower section for more than 140 days in each year, leaving farmland parched and threatening the autumn harvest. For several
months a year, the 3,390-mile (5,460-km) river now dries up in the Henan
Province, some 250 miles (400 km) before it reaches the sea.

★ **First animal poisoning by a freshwater blue-green algal bloom**
In the late 19th century, dogs, sheep, pigs, horses, and cattle all died after
drinking water from Lake Alexandrina in South Australia. The cause of
death was poisoning from *Nodularia spumigene*—an alga that had formed
as a layer of scum over the surface of the lake. This blue-green algal species
produces nodularin, a hepatotoxin, which causes blood to collect in the
liver. This, in turn, induces circulatory shock and often brings about the animal's death by internal hemorrhaging (bleeding).

★ **Largest freshwater blue-green algal bloom** The largest recorded
blue-green algal bloom occurred during 1991–92 along the Barwon-Darling
River in Australia. Dominated by *Anabaena circinalis,* which secretes dangerous neurotoxins, the bloom spread for over 620 miles (1,000 km) along
the river, killing domesticated livestock that drank the river's contaminated
water.

★ MOST POISONOUS SALAMANDER The skin, blood, and muscles of the California newt (*Taricha torosa*) all contain tetrodotoxin—an extremely toxic substance that acts as a nerve poison. Laboratory experiments have shown that just a single tiny drop is poisonous enough to kill several thousand mice. The newt itself, however, is immune to even extremely high concentrations of it.

★ Deepest living insect Larvae of the non-biting midge *Sergentia koschowi* have been found thriving at a depth of 4,462 ft. (1,360 m) within Siberia's Lake Baikal, the world's **deepest lake.** This is the greatest water depth recorded for any insect.

★ Insect most tolerant of desiccation Living in small pools on unshaded rocks in northern Nigeria and Uganda, the larvae of *Polypedilum vanderplanki,* a non-biting midge, withstand an environment that is alternately dry and flooded, and are the only insects capable of enduring cryptobiosis. This is defined as the state an organism enters when it shows no visible signs of life, when its metabolic activity comes to a virtual halt and is hardly measurable. Laboratory experiments have revealed that this midge's larvae can survive drying to less than 3% moisture.

Only tree-climbing fish The climbing perch (*Anabas testudineus*), which is found in south Asia, is remarkable for its habit of emerging on land and climbing palm trees. It even walks some distance across country in search of better habitat. The species has a special adaptation of its gills, which allows it to absorb atmospheric oxygen.

LARGEST SPECIES OF RIVER DOLPHIN The largest species of river dolphin is the boto (*Inia geoffrensis*), famed for its striking pink coloration. Inhabiting the Amazon and Orinoco rivers of South America, it attains a total length of up to 9 ft. (2.6 m).

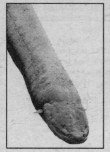

MOST ELECTRIC FISH The electric eel or paroque (*Electrophorus electricus*) that lives in rivers in Brazil and the Guianas, is not an eel at all, but a relative of the piranha. Up to 6 ft. (1.8 m) in length, the fish is "live" from head to tail, with its electrical apparatus consisting of two pairs of longitudinal organs. The shock, which can measure up to 650 volts, is used to immobilize prey and is strong enough to light an electric bulb or to stun an adult human.

MOST PATERNAL AMPHIBIAN The West European midwife toad (*Alytes obstetricans*) takes its name from the behavior of the male. When the female lays her eggs, the male fertilizes them and then winds the string of eggs, which can be 3–4 ft. (1–1.2 m) long, around his thighs. The male—itself only 3 in. (7.5 cm) in length—carries the eggs around in this manner for up to four weeks. When the eggs are ready to hatch, the toad swims into suitable water for the tadpoles to be released.

RIVETING RIVERS

At 4,160 miles (6,695 km) long, the Nile in Africa is officially the planet's **longest river.** Its closest contender is South America's Amazon. The third-longest is the Yangtze in China.

While not in flood (i.e., not including its tidal reaches, where an estuary/delta can be much wider), the main stretches of the **widest river**—the Amazon—can reach widths of up to 7 miles (11 km).

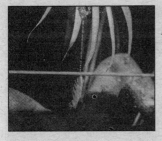

FARTHEST RANGE OF AN ARCHER FISH The archer fish (*Toxotes jaculator*) is found in Thailand's rivers. It lurks near the banks, waiting for a suitable insect to land on a water plant within its amazing 5-ft. (1.5-m) range. The fish shoots a jet of water at the prey from its tubulated (tube-shaped) mouth. If the fish does miss its prey, it is able to attempt again in quick succession.

Largest water lily The gigantic floating leaves of the water lily *Victoria amazonica* measure up to 9 ft. (3 m) across and are held in place on an underwater stalk 23–26 ft. (7–8 m) long. The undersurface of its leaves are supported by a series of rib-like ridges to keep the leaves flat and also prevent them from collapsing. The plant is native to shallow freshwater lakes and bayous in the Amazon basin.

Most energetic animal brain In 1996, scientist Goran Nilsson (Norway) revealed that the brain of the African elephant-trunk fish (*Gnathonomus petersi*) equals 3.1% of its body mass and uses more than 50% of the oxygen that its body takes in. By contrast, the human brain uses a mere 20% of the oxygen that the body takes in.

SHORELINES

★**Largest coastal mangrove forest** The Sundarbans forest stretches for almost 6,000 miles² (15,540 km²) across India and Bangladesh and acts as a natural barrier against tsunamis and cyclones. With saltwater-tolerant roots, this forest's mangrove trees sometimes exceed 70 ft. (21 m) in height above islands of layered sand and gray clay, which have been deposited by

☆**LONGEST SPECIES OF SEAWEED** The giant kelp *Macrocystis pyrifera* lives near rocky shores in the Pacific Ocean. The longest verified specimen measured 197 ft. (60 m) in total, but there are unauthenticated reports of even longer examples.

This kelp is also the ★**fastest-growing seaweed**—it grows up to 13.3 in. (34 cm) per day, a growth speed of 0.0002 mph (0.0003 km/h). Indeed, it is the **fastest-growing marine plant** on Earth. It is also a leading but often overlooked contender for the world's fastest-growing plant of any kind.

DENSEST FUR The sea otter (*Enhydra lutris*) has the densest fur of any mammal, with over 650,000 hairs per 1 in.² (100,000 hairs per 1 cm²). Most of the world's sea otter population is found off the coast of Alaska, U.S.A.

Sea otters are also the **smallest marine mammals.**

rivers that flow for more than 1,000 miles (1,609 km) from the Himalayas to the Bay of Bengal.

★**Largest species of spitting cobra** The giant spitting cobra (*Naja ashei*), discovered in 2004, lives in the coastal region of Kenya. Measuring almost 10 ft. (3 m) long, it is the world's second-longest species of venomous snake (only the king cobra exceeds it) and possesses sufficient poison to kill at least 15 people.

★**Largest mink ever** The sea mink (*Mustela macrodon*) is a scarcely known species that measured up to 2 ft. 8.5 in. (82.6 cm) long—some 50% longer than the longest specimens of the common American mink (*M. vison*) and also much fatter. It inhabited the rocky coasts of New England and Canada's Atlantic coastline as far north as Nova Scotia, but due to its highly prized pale-reddish fur, it was hunted into extinction. The last known specimen was killed on an island off Maine in 1889, but there is an unconfirmed report of a sea mink taken on New Brunswick's Campobello Island during the mid-1890s.

DID YOU KNOW?

Unlike other marine mammals, sea otters do not have a layer of fat to keep them warm. Instead, they rely on their dense, water-resistant fur and an increased metabolism to trap and generate warmth.

☆**ANIMAL WITH THE MOST CHROMOSOMES** Chromosomes are small, thread-like bodies within the nucleus of cells. They contain DNA, the body's hereditary information. Humans have 23 pairs of chromosomes in each cell, but the animal with the most is the hermit crab, of the superfamily Paguroidea, with 254, or 127 pairs per cell.

LARGEST CHELONIAN The widely distributed leatherback turtle (*Dermochelys coriacea*) averages 6–7 ft. (1.83–2.13 m) from the tip of the beak to the end of the tail, with a carapace (shell) around 5–5 ft. 6 in. (1.52–1.67 m) long, and about 7 ft. (2.13 m) across the front flippers. It weighs up to 990 lb. (450 kg).

The largest specimen ever recorded is a male found on the beach in Harlech, Gwynedd, UK, in September 1988. It measured 9 ft. 5.5 in. (2.91 m) in total length over the carapace, 9 ft. (2.77 m) across the front flippers, and weighed 2,120 lb. (961.1 kg). Although most museums refuse to exhibit large turtles because they can drip natural oil for up to 50 years, this specimen was put on display at the National Museum of Wales, Cardiff, UK, on February 16, 1990.

The leatherback is also the **fastest chelonian** in water, with a speed of up to 22 mph (35 km/h) recorded.

★**Most bioluminescent ctenophore** The sea walnut (*Mnemiopsis leidyi*), a species of ctenophore or comb jelly, is native to the waters around the east coast of North America, the Gulf of Mexico, and northeastern South America. (Comb jellies are not true jellyfish, belonging instead to a totally separate phylum, Ctenophora.) It grows to 3.9–4.7 in. (100–120 mm) and features four rows of ciliated combs running along its body, which are iridescent by day and glow green at night.

★**Longest bird's nest burrow** The rhinoceros auklet (*Cerorhinca monocerata*) is a puffin-related seabird. Nesting on small grass-covered islands in the North Pacific, its nest burrows typically measure 6.5–10 ft. (2–3 m) long, but examples twice this length are not unusual, and one exceptional burrow measured 26 ft. (8 m).

Largest gray seal colony Every winter, as many as 100,000 gray seals (*Halichoerus grypus*) arrive on Sable Island off Nova Scotia, Canada, to breed.

LARGEST . . .

Clam Marine giant clam (*Tridacna gigas*): weight 734 lb. (333 kg); length 3 ft. 9.25 in. (115 cm).

Oyster Common oyster (*Ostrea edulis*): weight 8.1 lb. (3.7 kg); length 12 in. (30.5 cm); width 5.5 in. (14 cm).

LARGEST CROCODILIAN The estuarine, or saltwater, crocodile (*Crocodylus porosus*) is found throughout the tropical regions of Asia and the Pacific. The Bhitarkanika Wildlife Sanctuary in Orissa State, India, houses four measuring more than 19 ft. (6 m) in length, the largest being over 23 ft. (7 m) long. There are several unauthenticated reports of specimens up to 33 ft. (10 m) in length. Adult males average 14–16 ft. (4.2–4.8 m) in length and weigh about 900–1,150 lb. (408–520 kg).

★ LARGEST WOODLOUSE The largest species of woodlouse is the common sea slater (*Ligia oceanica*), an aquatic species that is abundant on rocky coasts within the terrestrial and littoral (shoreline) fringe around the UK, particularly in rock pools and crevices and under stones. Up to 1 in. (3 cm) long in total, it has a dorsoventrally flattened body that is twice as long as it is broad, and varies in color from gray to olive.

DESERTS

★ **Rarest cactus** Knowlton's miniature cactus (*Pediocactus knowltonii*) is a tiny pink-flowered species that is critically endangered owing to overexploitation by collectors, and is found only in New Mexico and Colorado, U.S.A.

Longest leaf lifespan The longest-living leaves of all plants belong to the welwitschia (*Welwitschia mirabilis*), named after botanist Dr. Friedrich Welwitsch (Austria), who discovered the plant in 1859 in its native Namib Desert of Namibia and Angola. The welwitschia has an estimated lifespan of between 400 and 1,500 years, with some specimens carbon-dated to 2,000 years old. Each plant produces two leaves per century and never sheds them. Ancient individuals sprawl out over 33 ft. (10 m) in circumference, with enough foliage to cover a 1,312-ft. (400-m) sports field.

★ **Largest modern-day extinct bird** The biggest bird to become extinct in modern times was the Arabian ostrich *Struthio camelus syriacus*, which was common in the desert regions of Syria and Arabia until World War I. After the war it was hunted for its plumes, and was also pursued by

MOST DANGEROUS LIZARD The Gila monster (*Heloderma suspectum*) is a heavily built, brightly colored lizard that lives in the arid parts of Mexico and the southwestern U.S.A., and measures up to 24 in. (60 cm). It has eight well-developed venom glands in its lower jaws and carries enough venom to kill two adult humans. The venom is not injected but seeps into the wound caused when the Gila monster bites its victim with its sharp, fragile teeth. Because of this, a lizard may continue to hang on after it has bitten and actively chew for several minutes. The lizard's teeth may even become embedded in the victim's wound after it has let go. It only attacks when provoked.

hunters in jeeps and shot for sport. The only type of ostrich found outside Africa, the last confirmed specimen of the Arabian ostrich was shot in Bahrain in 1941, but there is a controversial record of one allegedly being discovered drowned in a flash flood as recently as 1966.

★ **Largest population of wild camels** Intriguingly, the world's largest population of camels in the wild, numbering over 200,000 individuals, is

★ **MOST SPECIALIZED LIZARD DIET** Australia's desert-dwelling moloch or thorny devil (*Moloch horridus*) lives exclusively on ants belonging to the genus *Iridomyrmex*.

★ FIRST CAMEL/LLAMA HYBRID On January 14, 1998, at the Camel
Reproduction Center (CRC) in the Arabian desert in Dubai, UAE, a
project headed by chief scientific officer Dr. Julian A. (Lulu) Skidmore
(UK, above) finally came to fruition with the birth of Rama, the world's
first camel/llama hybrid, known as a cama. His father was an Arabian
camel, or dromedary (*Camelus dromedarius*), and his mother was a
South American guanaco (*Lama huanacos*), from which the domestic
llama *L. glama* is descended. They would never have met in the wild.
The camel is over six times heavier than the guanaco, so Rama was
conceived by artificial insemination. This breeding project was funded
by Dubai's crown prince and the defense minister, H.H. Sheik Mohamed
bin Rashed al-Maktoum.

found neither in Arabia nor in Mongolia—the traditional homelands of wild
camels—but instead in the Australian desert. Camels were imported to
Australia from the 1840s until the early 1900s, principally for transportation
purposes in Australia's very hot, arid deserts, but as technology advanced,
the camels were not needed as much. Consequently, many were released or
escaped into the desert and have bred and thrived there ever since.

FASTEST INVERTEBRATE Solifugids
of the genus *Solpuga* inhabit the arid
zones of North Africa and the Middle
East and have a burst sprint capability
estimated at 10 mph (16 km/h),
making them the fastest of all
invertebrates. Despite their
alternative names of camel spider and
sun spider, solifugids are not true
spiders (although they are arachnids),
as their bodies are divided into
separate head, thorax, and abdomen
sections, whereas in spiders the head
and thorax comprise a single section.

MOST DESTRUCTIVE INSECT The single most destructive insect is the desert locust (*Schistocerca gregaria,* pictured above left) from the dry and semi-arid regions of Africa, the Middle East, and western Asia. Individuals are only 1.8–2.4 in. (4.5–6 cm) long but can eat their own weight in food every day. Certain weather conditions induce unimaginable numbers to gather in huge swarms that devour almost all vegetation in their path. In a single day, a "small" swarm of about 50 million locusts can eat food that would sustain 500 people for a year. Pictured above is a man standing in a cloud of these locusts on November 29, 2004, around Corralejo in the north of the island of Fuerteventura, Canary Islands, about 60 miles (100 km) off the Moroccan coast.

Most heat-tolerant land-based animal

The most heat-tolerant animal (thermophile) is *Cataglyphis bicolor,* a desert-dwelling scavenger ant that lives in the Sahara desert and forages at temperatures of over 131°F (55°C).

Largest ground nest

The mallee fowl (*Leipoa ocellata*) constructs huge nests containing up to 8,100 ft.³ (229 m³) of matter and weighing 661,386 lb. (300 metric tons), and are unique in the bird world. Males work on the nest

★**LARGEST INDOOR DESERT** The Desert Dome in Omaha, Nebraska, U.S.A., spreads under the world's **largest glazed geodesic dome,** and spans 84,000 ft.² (7,840 m²) on two levels— with 42,000 ft.² (3,920 m²) on each level. It exhibits flora and fauna from three major deserts—southern Africa's Namib Desert, Mexico's Sonora Desert, and Australia's Red Centre.

most months of the year, digging out a hole, then scraping leaf litter into it and covering it with sandy soil. Alternatively, an existing mound is used year after year and can reach a diameter of 16 ft. (5 m). Once the eggs are laid and covered, they are ignored by both parents, as are the chicks that hatch in 50–90 days.

TALLEST . . .

Wild cactus A cardon (*Pachycereus pringlei*) found in the Sonora Desert, Mexico, by Marc Salak and Jeff Brown in April 1995, measured 63 ft. (19.2 m)—almost the combined height of four giraffes!

☆**Herba cistanches** A herba cistanches (*Cistanche deserticola*) collected from the desert of Inner Mongolia, China, by Yongmao Chen on August 15, 2006, measured 6 ft. 4 in. (1.95 m). This plant is used extensively in Chinese herbal medicine.

WETLANDS

★**Heaviest artiodactyl** The heaviest artiodactyl (even-toed ungulate mammal) is the common hippo *Hippopotamus amphibius* of sub-Saharan Africa, which can weigh up to 8,000 lb. (3,630 kg).

☆**Largest rodent ever** Displacing *Phoberomys pattersoni*, the previous record holder, the world's largest rodent is now a newly named 2 million-year-old fossil species called *Josephoartigasia monesi*. Although it is currently known only from a single skull measuring 21 in. (53 cm) long, scientists estimate from its immense size that the complete animal was probably a massive 2,000 lb. (1 metric ton) in weight. Related to today's much smaller pacarana (*Dinomys branickii*), it lived in coastal Uruguay, in what was then lush forested swampland but is today an arid region, and probably fed upon soft vegetation as its jaws, though huge, lacked much chewing power.

★**Most specialized bird diet** The southern Florida subspecies of the Everglades kite (*Rostrhamus sociabilis plumbeus*) lives exclusively upon a single species of snail, the large freshwater apple snail (*Pomacea paludosa*).

TALLEST FLYING BIRD The tallest of the flying birds are cranes, belonging to the family Gruidae. The largest can stand almost 6 ft. 6 in. (2 m) tall. In the picture left, a sarus crane (*Grus antigone*) is performing a mating dance in the Keoladeo National Park, in Rajasthan, India.

LARGEST DELTA IN ONE COUNTRY The entire Okavango Delta is contained in Botswana, in southern Africa. With a total area of more than 3,861 miles^2 (10,000 km^2), this highly significant area of wetland include a 609-mile^2 (1,578-km^2) wildlife refuge, with over 400 species of birds and 65 species of fish as well a herd of red lechwe antelopes numbering around 20,000. Pictured is one of the delta's male red lechwe (*Kobus leche leche*).

LARGEST SWAMP Located principally in southwestern Brazil, but with small areas within neighboring Bolivia and Paraguay, the Pantanal (which is Spanish for "marshland") covers a surface area of 57,915 miles^2 (150,000 km^2). This is greater than the total surface area of England! During the rainy season (December to May), 80% of the Pantanal is flooded, and it contains the **greatest diversity of water plants in the world.**

SMALLEST HIPPO The pygmy hippopotamus (*Hexaprotodon liberiensis*) found mainly in Liberia, west Africa, has an average head-and-body length of 5–6 ft. (1.5–1.85 m) plus a tail length of approximately 6–8.25 in. (15–21 cm), a shoulder height of 27.5–39.25 in. (70–100 cm), and a weight of 353–606 lb. (160–275 kg).

★**Largest amphibian ever** Far bigger than any modern-day amphibian, the largest amphibian of all time was *Mastodonsaurus*, inhabiting swamplands around 200 million years ago during the late Triassic period. This huge-headed, long-tailed creature vaguely resembled a crocodile and was as big as one too, attaining a total length of 13 ft. (4 m), which included a skull length of 49 in. (1.25 m).

★**Insect with greatest salinity tolerance** The larvae of the brine fly (*Ephydrella marshalli*) inhabit salt lagoons, and under laboratory conditions they have withstood salinities of up to 5,848 mOsm per liter. (By comparison, the salinity of seawater is 1,197 mOsm per liter.) The unit "mOsm" stands for "milliOsmole." An Osmole is the molecular weight of a solute (a

---

DID YOU KNOW?

The Sudd swamp in Sudan has sometimes been referred to as the world's largest. However, even in high flood waters, its total area only slightly exceeds 11,585 miles² (30,000 km²), and thus falls far short of the Pantanal's surface area.

SHORTEST LIFESPAN Mayflies are insects belonging to the order Ephemeroptera. (In Greek, *ephemeros* means "short-lived" and *pteron* means "wing," referring to the short life of winged adults.) Mayflies may spend two to three years as nymphs at the bottom of lakes and streams and then live for as little as one hour as winged adults.

mixture of two or more substances), in grams, divided by the number of ions, or particles, into which it dissociates in solution.

Smallest plants and animals The world's ★ **smallest flowering plants** are the watermeals, species of the genus *Wolffia*. Related to duckweed (*Lemna*), watermeal is an aquatic plant and forms a mat on the surface of ponds and quiet streams. An individual plant is less than 1 mm long and only 0.3 mm wide, and produces a minuscule flower that later develops into the world's **smallest fruit!** Since the entire plant body of the species is less than 1 mm long, the mature fruit takes up a large proportion of its parent plant body. The fruit in the *Wolffia augusta* is only 1/100th of an inch long (0.25 mm) and weighs about 1/400,000 of an ounce (70 micrograms).

The **smallest toad** is the subspecies *Bufo taitanus beiranus* of Africa, the largest specimen of which measured 0.94 in. (24 mm) long.

The **smallest dragonfly** is *Agriocnemis naia* of Burma. One specimen in the British Museum had a wingspan of 0.69 in. (17.6 mm) and a body length of 0.71 in. (18 mm).

SMALLEST RATTLESNAKE The pygmy rattlesnake *Sistrurus miliarius* inhabits wooded areas, preferably close to rivers or lakes, in the southeastern U.S.A. Even adult specimens are less than 18 in. (45 cm) long. The rattle is so tiny that it makes a faint buzzing sound audible only for up to 3 ft. (1 m) or so away. Despite its small size, this species is very venomous and frequently bites humans. Pictured is the red pygmy rattlesnake (*Sistrurus miliarius miliarius*).

TEMPERATE FORESTS

★Largest bioluminescent organism The largest glowing organism is a single gigantic specimen of honey mushroom (*Armillaria ostoyae*)—discovered in the Malheur National Forest, Oregon, U.S.A.—that measures 3.5 miles (5.6 km) across and occupies a total area of 2,200 acres (890 ha): equivalent to 1,220 football fields. The honey mushroom is well known for its glowing surface, caused by bioluminescent bacteria, although most of its tissue is 3 ft. (1 m) underground, in the form of root-like mycelia. Its age is calculated to be at least 2,400 years old, and it also holds the record for the world's **largest fungus.**

Largest living tree The world's largest living tree is General Sherman, a giant sequoia (*Sequoiadendron giganteum*) growing in the Sequoia National Park, California, U.S.A. It stands 271 ft. (82.6 m) tall, has a diameter of 27 ft. 2 in. (8.2); and a circumference of approximately 85 ft. (25.9 m). This tree is estimated to contain the equivalent of 630,096 board feet of timber, enough to make over 5 billion matches, and its red-brown bark may be up to 24 in. (61 cm) thick in parts.

★Insect with the greatest number and range of food plants The insect that feeds on the greatest number of plant species, over the widest range, is the caterpillar of the fall webworm moth (*Hyphantria cunea*), a member of the tiger moth family, Arctiidae. It has been estimated that its caterpillars feed on 636 species of plant worldwide, including over 200 in the U.S.A., 219 in Europe, over 300 in Japan, and 65 in Korea (though some of these plant species are found in more than one of the above regions).

★Largest fern fronds The Australian giant fern *Angiopteris evecta*, which produces an immense woody trunk measuring as much as 3 ft. 3 in. (1 m) in diameter and up to 10 ft. (3 m) tall, grows the world's largest fronds. These can measure up to 26 ft. (8 m) long.

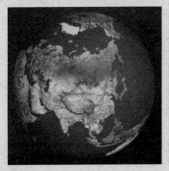

LARGEST CONIFEROUS FOREST
The vast coniferous forests of northern Russia lie between latitude 55°N and the Arctic Circle. The total wooded area covers 1,544,408 miles² (4 million km²). This satellite image shows water, vegetation, arid areas, and snow and ice. The boreal forest "biome," or ecosystem, known as the Taiga, extends across Russia, Scandinavia, Canada, and Alaska.

SMALLEST CARNIVORE The least, or dwarf, weasel (*Mustela nivalis*) has a head-and-body length of 4.3–10.2 in. (110–260 mm), a tail length of 0.5–3.4 in. (13–87 mm), and weighs 1–7 oz. (30–200 g). It is most commonly found in deciduous forests of the northern parts of Europe, Asia, and North America, and usually feed on rodents, moles, and bird's eggs.

Slowest-growing tree The slowest-growing tree is the white cedar (*Thuja occidentalis*), one of which was located on a cliffside in the Great Lakes area of Canada and grew to a height of less than 4 in. (10.2 cm) in 155 years! This same plant weighed only 0.5 oz. (17 g) and averaged a growth rate of 0.003 oz. (0.11 g) of wood each year.

Heaviest fungi A living single clonal growth of the soil fungus *Armillaria bulbosa,* reported on April 2, 1992 to be covering approximately 37 acres (15 ha) of forest in Michigan, U.S.A., was calculated to weigh over 220,462 lb. (100 metric tons)—the weight of a blue whale. The organism is thought to have originated from a single fertilized spore at least 1,500 years ago.

Rarest bird The North American ivory-billed woodpecker (*Campephilus principalis principalis*) is currently the world's most endangered bird. North

★NEWEST TREE The Tahina palm tree (*Tahina spectabilis*) was not officially named and described until January 2008, although it had been discovered accidentally by a family on a picnic in a remote, hilly, wooded area of northwestern Madagascar in 2006. It was only recognized to be a dramatically new species and genus following DNA analysis a year later.

What makes the belated scientific discovery of this species so surprising is its huge size, standing over 58 ft. (18 m) tall—with fan-like leaves 16 ft. (5 m) across—and its bizarre, suicidal life cycle. Taking decades to bloom, when it does it produces an explosion of hundreds of nectar-rich flowers towering above its crown. Each of these develops into fruit, but in so doing the tree's nutrients become so depleted that as soon as it has fruited, the tree collapses and dies.

SMALLEST PRIMATE The smallest true primate (excluding tree shrews, which are normally classified separately) is the pygmy mouse lemur (*Microcebus myoxinus*), discovered in the deciduous forests of western Madagascar in 1993. It has a head-and-body length of about 2.4 in. (62 mm), a tail length of 5.4 in. (136 mm), and an average weight of 1.1 oz. (30.6 g).

America's second biggest woodpecker (only the imperial woodpecker is bigger), it was believed extinct since the 1940s, until a Big Woods Conservation Partnership expedition, led by Cornell University's Cornell Laboratory of Ornithology and the Nature Conservancy, released a video filmed on April 25, 2005, that shows a single male specimen discovered during their intensive year-long search for the species in the Cache River and White River national wildlife refuges of Arkansas, U.S.A.

Diagnostic double-raps and tin-horn–like calls, again characteristic of the

☆ **FASTEST-GROWING TREE** The fastest-growing tree by volume of biomass is a giant sequoia (*Sequoiadendron giganteum*), nicknamed General Grant, in Grant Grove, Kings Canyon National Park, California, U.S.A. The trunk volume increased from 43,038 ft.³ (1,218 ³) in 1931 to 46,608 ft.³ (1,319 m³) in 1976, when it was measured by Wendell Flint (U.S.A.). This amount of wood growth could easily build an average three-bedroomed house. The tree is approximately 1,700 years old, which is quite young for a giant sequoia.

★ LARGEST BADGER SETT The European badger (*Meles meles*) spends more than half its life underground and builds the biggest setts of any badger species. The largest sett on record was estimated to contain a tunnel network 2,883 ft. (879 m) long, containing 50 underground chambers and no fewer than 178 entrances.

ivory-bill, were also recorded there by the expedition, whose team members hope that other specimens exist still undetected in this locality's vast wilderness. The ivory-bill's Cuban subspecies was briefly rediscovered in 1986, but no confirmed sightings have been reported since then, leading to speculation that it is now extinct.

★ LARGEST GROUSE The capercaillie (*Tetrao urogallus*), native to northern European pine forests, became extinct in Scotland during the 17th century, but was successfully reintroduced from Sweden during the 1830s. Adult males of this species weigh up to 8 lb. (4 kg), while adult females weigh up to around 4 lb. (2 kg).

DID YOU KNOW?

A sett is an underground network of tunnels, usually located in pasture or woodland, in soil that is easy to dig. It can take years to excavate. Badgers are nocturnal animals; they usually retreat to their setts at daybreak and emerge at dusk.

RAINFORESTS

★**Highest sound by an arthropod** The highest frequency of ultra-sound of any known arthropod is produced by the male of the *Arachnoscelis* genus of katydids (cricket-like insects) from the family Tettigoniidae, which inhabit the tropical rainforests of Colombia, particularly in the National Park Isla Gorgona. Fernando Montealegre-Z (Colombia/Canada), Glenn K. Morris and Andrew C. Mason (both Canada) of the University of Toronto discovered the source was a "scraper" on the insect's right wing—as it rubs its wings together, the scraper is distorted then springs back into shape, generating the sound. These results were published in the *Journal of Experimental Biology* in December 2006. In November 2007, the "chirp" was measured at 133 kilohertz (133,000 Hz).

★**Smallest artiodactyl mammal** The world's smallest artiodactyl (even-toed hoofed mammal) is the lesser Malay chevrotain, or lesser mouse deer (*Tragulus javanicus*). This tiny ungulate is no bigger than a rabbit, which in the adult male (smaller than the female) has a head-and-body length of 1 ft. 5.3 in.–1 ft. 6.8 in. (44–48 cm), a tail length of 2.5–3.1 in. (6.5–8 cm), and a shoulder height of 7.8–9.8 in. (20–25 cm). It weighs just 3 lb. 12 oz.–6 lb. 9 oz. (1.7–3 kg).

This minuscule mammal inhabits the tropical rainforests and mangrove swamps of southeast Asia.

Largest tropical rainforest The Amazon tropical rainforest is the largest of its kind, covering an area of 2.5 million miles^2 (6.475 million km^2) across nine different South American countries: Brazil, Colombia, Peru, Venezuela, Ecuador, Bolivia, Guyana, Suriname, and French Guiana.

★**SMELLIEST BIRD** Native to the Colombian rainforest, the world's smelliest bird is undoubtedly the hoatzin (*Opisthocomus hoazin*), a bizarre-looking creature variously classified with pheasants, cuckoos, touracos, and even in a taxonomic group entirely of its own. It stinks like cow manure. Even its local name, *pava hedionda*, translates as "stinking pheasant." The noxious odor is believed to derive from a combination of its exclusive diet of green leaves and, for birds, its uniquely bovine digestive system that involves a kind of foregut fermentation.

☆**LARGEST RAT** The largest species of rat is the slender-tailed cloud rat *Phloeomys cumingi* of Luzon, an island in the Philippines. This tree-climbing, densely furred species inhabits Luzon's cloud forests and measures almost 3 ft. 3 in. (1 m) long including the tail.

However, in 2007, during a visit by a scientific team to the remote, scarcely known Foja Mountains in Irian Jaya (Indonesian New Guinea), a huge, previously unknown species of furry rat was observed and captured alive there (picture above). With a head-and-body length of 2 ft. 3.5 in. (70 cm) plus its tail, this newly discovered species is the size of a cat and is already being referred to as the biggest rat known. When further specimens are recorded, it may well dethrone the slender-tailed cloud rat.

VANISHING WORLD

According to data from the United Nations Food and Agriculture Organization's (FAO) *State of the World's Forests 2007* report, of all 44 countries that, combined, represent 90% of the world's forests, the country that pursues the world's ☆ **highest rate of deforestation** is Indonesia, with 4,447,896 acres (1.8 million ha) per year between 2000 and 2005—a rate of 2% of its forests destroyed each year. This equates to an area measuring approximately 20 miles^2 (51km^2) each day or 300 soccer fields every hour!

The **fastest decrease in forested area** is an average rate of 9% every year between 1990 and 2000 in Burundi, Central Africa. If this rate were permanently sustained, Burundi's forested area would be completely cleared in just over 11 years.

★**LARGEST MANTIS** *Toxodera denticulata* (pictured) from Java has a body length of 7.8 in. (20 cm)—making it officially the world's largest mantis. However, a larger, newly discovered and currently undescribed species from the Cameroon jungle has begun to appear in the pet trade, where it has been dubbed the "mega-mantis." Moreover, there are unconfirmed reports of a still longer species inhabiting the rainforests of Bolivia and Peru.

☆**Largest peccary** The giant peccary (*Pecari Maximus*) is native to the Brazilian Amazon rainforest region of the Rio Aripuana basin. Discovered by Dr. Marc van Roosmalen (Netherlands), it is superficially similar to the collared peccary (*Pecari tajacu*) but is notably larger, though slimmer, with much longer legs. It has a total length of about 3 ft. 3 in. (1 m), a shoulder height of 2 ft. 9 in. (0.85 m), and weighs around 88 lb. (40 kg). It has thinly bristled hair, with brown and white fur rather than dark blackish-gray. Until now, the largest recorded peccary species was the Chacoan peccary (*Catagonus wagneri*), discovered alive in 1974 after being known to science only from Ice Age fossil specimens.

DID YOU KNOW?

Mantises (order Mantodea) number around 2,300 species and are popularly referred to as "praying mantises"—from their praying-like stance, not from the word "preying," although they are notorious predators. Captive females are also infamous for biting the heads off male partners during mating!

Tallest orchid A height of 49 ft. (15 m) has been recorded for the orchid *Galeola foliata*, a saprophyte of the vanilla family that grows in the decaying rainforests of Queensland, Australia.

★ **STRONGEST VERTEBRATE** In terms of watts of power generated per pound of muscle, the giant palm salamander (*Bolitoglossa dofleini*) of Central America is the strongest vertebrate species. Its tongue explodes outward at 818 watts per pound (18,000 watts per kg) of muscle. It is believed that the power is stored in the elastic tissue of the tongue, prior to release, much like a rubber band.

GRASSLANDS

Largest grasslands The largest area of natural grasslands is the Great Plains of North America, which stretch through the U.S.A. for 1,158,300 miles² (3 million km²) from southern Canada to northern Mexico. The Great Plains are located inland and experience warm, dry summers. They have a temperate climate, without extremes of heat or cold.

The **largest tropical grasslands**—which grow nearer the coast, have higher rainfall, and often include woodland—are the savannah grasslands of northern Australia, covering 463,320 miles² (1.2 million km²).

HEAVIEST FLYING BIRD The male kori bustard (*Ardeotis kori*) of southern and eastern Africa can weigh up to 40 lb. (18.2 kg)—the weight of the largest confirmed specimen, as documented in 1936 after being shot in South Africa by H. T. Glynn. Pictured is a kori bustard with a carmine bee-eater on its back.

★ **LARGEST EGG FROM A LIVING BIRD** The largest egg from a living bird (pictured) weighed 5 lb. 11 oz. (2.58 kg) and was laid by an ostrich on the farm of Kerstin and Gunnar Sahlin (both Sweden) on August 30, 2007.

The ★ **toughest egg** produced by any extant species of bird is that of the ostrich (*Struthio camelus*), which can withstand the weight of a person weighing 253 lb. 8 oz. (115 kg).

The **largest living bird** is the North African ostrich (*Struthio camelus camelus*). Male examples of this ratite (flightless) subspecies have been recorded up to 9 ft. (2.75 m) tall and weighing 345 lb. (156.5 kg).

The ★ **largest area of dry steppe** land is the Kazakh Steppe of Central Asia, which measures 310,600 miles^2 (804,500 km^2). Steppe land is treeless, savannah grassland with hot, dry summers and cold, snowless winters.

DID YOU KNOW?

The largest species of South American bird is the ostrich-related flightless common rhea (*Rhea americana*), inhabiting the grasslands of Argentina, Bolivia, Brazil, Paraguay, and Uruguay. Adults average 51 in. (129 cm) in length, and 60 lb. (27 kg) in weight.

TALLEST MAMMAL Giraffes (*Giraffa camelopardalis*) live in the dry savannah and open woodland areas of sub-Saharan Africa. An adult bull typically measures 15–18 ft. (4.6–5.5 m) tall. Its long neck has no more than the usual seven vertebrae found in most mammals, but each is greatly elongated. Giraffes have such long legs that they have to spread out their forelegs and bend their knees in order to drink at ground level. They also have long, extensible tongues and lengthy, sensitive lips with which they can delicately pick leaves from the trees and shrubs on which they browse. The horns of giraffes are unique. Present in both sexes, they have a bony core fused to the skull and are covered by skin and hair.

The giraffe is the **tallest artiodactyl** or even-toed ungulate mammal. The **tallest specimen ever recorded** was a 19-ft. (5.8 m) Masai bull (*G. c. tippelskirchi*) measured at Chester Zoo, UK, in 1959.

★**Most common grass** Cogon grass (*Imperata cylindrica*) is a perennial rhizomatous species—meaning a tough, year-round plant with a creeping horizontal stem from which the grass shoots. Native to east and southeast Asia, India, Micronesia, and Australia, it is an aggressively invasive weed and has successfully colonized great swathes of Europe, Africa, the Americas, and northern Asia, as well as numerous islands around the world. The grass's rhizome has become particularly infamous in the U.S.A. for its ability to kill pine seedlings and usurp native plants. The grass is also very flammable in nature, rendering it a major fire hazard and a risk to the habitat of endangered species.

★**Fastest muscle movement** The muscular contraction-expansion cycle of the tiny *Forcipomyia* midge, which occurs in 0.00045 seconds (1/2,218th of a second)—yielding 62,760 wing-beats per minute (1,046 wing-beats per second) under natural conditions—is the **fastest wing-beat** documented for any animal.

★**Most populous bird's nest** Native to southwestern Africa's dry grasslands, the sociable weaver (*Philetairus socius*) builds an immense communal nest that can be up to 26 ft. (8 m) long and 6 ft. 6 in. (2 m) high. Resembling a giant haystack that hangs from a tree or telegraph pole, it contains up to 300 individual nests. Each of these nests in turn houses a pair of weavers and their brood. Not surprisingly, these enormous communal nests can get so heavy that the tree on which they are built sometimes collapses under the weight!

★**Sweetest insects** As many as 5 billion aphids can be supported in a single hectare of vegetation (2.4 acres), and these in turn can saturate the soil each day with 4,410 lb. (2 metric tons) of sugar in the form of honey-dew. This is the **largest sugar secretion by insects.**

FASTEST . . .

Primate The patas monkey (*Erythrocebus patas*) of western and eastern Africa can reach speeds of 34 mph (55 km/h). With their long slender limbs, they are sometimes referred to as "primate cheetahs."

Land snake The aggressive black mamba (*Dendroaspis polylepis*) of southeastern Africa can reach speeds of 10–12 mph (16–19 km/h) in short bursts over level ground.

Caterpillar The larvae of the mother-of-pearl moth (*Pleuroptya ruralis*) can travel 15 in. (38.1 cm) in a second or 0.8 mph (1.37 km/h)—the caterpillar equivalent of 150 mph (241 km/h).

FASTEST LAND MAMMAL (SHORT DISTANCES) When measured over a short distance on level ground, the cheetah (*Acinonyx jubatus*)—found in the open plains of sub-Saharan Africa, Iran, Turkmenistan, and Afghanistan—can maintain a steady top speed of approximately 62 mph (100 km/h). But research by Prof. Craig Sharp of Brunel University, London, UK, in 1965 recorded accurate speeds of 64.3 mph (104.4 km/h) for a 77-lb. (35-kg) adult female over 660 ft. (201.2 m). (For the **fastest mammal on land over long distances**, see p. 459.)

MOUNTAINS

★ **Smallest home range for a bear** The smallest home range of female giant pandas (*Ailuropoda melanoleuca*) studied in the Qinling Mountains, Shaanzi Province, China, is a mere 1.6 miles² (4.2 km²).

The giant panda also has the ★ **most restricted distribution of any bear,** being limited to six small mountainous areas in the Sichuan, Shaanzi, and Gansu Provinces along the eastern rim of the Tibetan Plateau in southwestern China, yielding a total range of only 2,277 miles² (5,900 km²).

★ **Greatest resurrection from extinction for a marsupial** The mountain pygmy. possum (*Burramys parvus*) was known to science only from fossils dating back 10,000–15,000 years until one day in August 1966 when zoologist Dr. Kenneth Shortman discovered an unfamiliar-looking possum, resembling a large dormouse, hiding in a corner of the Melbourne University Ski Lodge, high on the slopes of Mt. Hotham, Victoria, Australia. Studies of this puzzling creature revealed it to be a living mountain pygmy possum, and others have since been found alive elsewhere in Victoria and also in New South Wales, Australia, thereby resurrecting the species from many thousands of years of supposed extinction.

LONGEST TONGUE Relative to body size, the nectar bat (*Anoura fistulata*) of the Andes in Ecuador has the longest mammalian tongue. It has a reach of 3.34 in. (8.49 cm)—that is, 150% of its body length. According to Nathan Muchhala of the University of Miami, Florida, U.S.A., who published these measurements in *Nature* in 2006, it is no coincidence that *A. fistulata* is the sole pollinator of *Centropogon nigricans,* with corolla tubes measuring 3–3.5 in. (8–9 cm) in length. Pictured is a nectar bat drinking from a glass tube.

MOST NORTHERLY PRIMATES
Japanese macaques (*Macaca fuscata*)
live in the mountainous Jigokudani area
of Honshu, Japan, near Nagano (36°40N,
138°10E). Humans aside, they are the
northernmost population of primates.
Also known as snow monkeys, they
survive the 5°F (-15°C) winters by
warming themselves in hot volcanic
springwater.

Highest-living plants and animals

Ermania himalayensis (belonging to the crucifer or cabbage family) and *Ranunculus lobatus* (buttercup family) grow on Mt. Kamet in the Himalayas at 21,000 ft. (6,400 m)—the **highest altitude for flowering plants.**

The large-eared pika (*Ochtona macrotis*) has been recorded at an altitude of 20,100 ft. (6,130 m) in mountain ranges in Asia, making it the **highest-living mammal.** The yak (*Bos mutus*) of Tibet and the Sichuanese Alps, China, climbs to an altitude of 20,000 ft. (6,100 m) when foraging.

The **highest-living fish** is the Tibetan loach (family Cobitidae). It has been found at an altitude of 17,060 ft. (5,200 m) in the Himalayas.

The Himalayan pit viper (*Agkistrodon himalayanus*) is a venomous species that has been found at altitudes up to 16,072 ft. (4,900 m), making it the ★**highest-living snake.**

The vicuña (*Vicugna vicugna*) from South America's high Andes is the ★**highest-living wild camelid.** It lives

HIGHEST MOUNTAIN TABLETOP
Monte Roraima is a sandstone
plateau that marks the border of
Brazil, Venezuela, and Guyana,
although more than 75% of it is
in Venezuela. This tabletop
mountain, or tepui, measures
9,220 ft. (2,810 m) in height. Its
harsh environment has resulted
in about one-third of its plant
species being unique to the
mountain. Monte Roraima is
believed to have been the
inspiration for Arthur Conan
Doyle's novel *The Lost World*.

HIGHEST FLYING INSECT
The greatest altitude reported for migrating butterflies is 19,000 ft. (5,791 m) for a flock of small tortoiseshells *(Aglais urticae)* seen flying over the Zemu Glacier in the eastern Himalayas. This is also the **highest migrating butterfly.**

In comparison, the highest altitude recorded for a bird is 37,000 ft. (11,300 m) for a Rüppell's vulture *(Gyps rueppellii)*, which collided with a commercial aircraft over Abidjan, Ivory Coast, on November 29, 1973.

at altitudes of up to 15,750 ft. (4,80 m), as does the alpaca, a domestic camelid.

The ★ **highest altitude at which trees have been discovered** is 15,000 ft. (4,600 m) for a silver fir *Abies squamata* found in southwestern China. Himalayan birch trees (*Betula utilis*) have also been discovered at this altitude. Specimens of *A. spectabilis*, a species closely related to *A. squamata*, have been found at an altitude of 14,000 ft. (4,267 m) in the Himalayas.

LARGEST SPECIES OF WASP The Asian giant hornet (*Vespa mandarinia)* is native to the mountains of Japan and can grow to be 2.2 in. (5.5 cm) long, with a wingspan of approximately 3 in. (7.6 cm). Its stinger is about 0.25 in. (0.6 cm) long and can inject a venom so powerful that it dissolves human tissue.

"If your tongue were as long as a nectar bat's, you'd be able to lick your own toes while standing upright!"

★**Largest herb** The puya (*Puya raimondii*) is a rare species of giant bromeliad growing high in the Bolivian mountains. Although it is an herbaceous plant, it has a trunk up to 13 ft. (4 m) high.

The puya takes about 150 years to bloom, making it the **slowest plant to flower.**

★**Largest elephant shrew** The gray-faced elephant shrew (*Rhynchocyon udzungwensis*) was discovered in March 2006 in two high-altitude forest blocks in the mountains of south-central Tanzania. Weighing approximately 1 lb. 6 oz. (700 g), it is more than 25% heavier than any previously known elephant shrew (or sengi) species. Confined entirely to Africa and known as elephant shrews on account of their long trunk-like snout and superficial resemblance to true shrews, sengis are now known to constitute a totally separate taxonomic order of mammals more closely related to elephants, sea cows, and aardvarks than to true shrews. With its bright chestnut-red body and gray face, as well as its large size, this new species is very distinctive, making its late discovery by science all the more surprising.

★**HIGHEST-LIVING PREDATOR ON LAND** The range of the snow leopard (*Uncia uncia*) extends across 12 countries in the mountainous regions of central and southern Asia. This rarely seen cat has been photographed by hidden cameras at altitudes as high as 19,000 ft. (5,800 m). Moving footage of a snow leopard hunting a markhor (a species of ibex-related wild goat) was famously captured by a camera crew in remote mountains on the Afghan/Pakistan border for the *Planet Earth* series (BBC, 2006).

SNOW & ICE

★**Largest Antarctic land animal** The biggest—and only—species of Antarctic insect is the Antarctic midge *Belgica antarctica*. At 0.47 in. (12 mm), it is no larger than a rice grain, but is nevertheless the largest animal species that has adapted to live on land in Antarctica all year long. (Seals and penguins spend much of their time in the water.) It lives in penguin colonies, feeding on waste matter and algae.

★**Largest petrel** Native to Antarctica, the world's largest species of petrel is the giant petrel (*Macronectes giganteus*), with a length of approximately 3 ft. (90 cm) and a wingspan exceeding 6.5 ft. (2 m), thus approaching the size of a small albatross. Foraging here both on land and at sea for carrion, these formidable birds will also attack and kill other creatures as large as king penguins and isolated seal pups.

★**Smallest petrel** Also native to Antarctica is Wilson's storm petrel (*Oceanites oceanicus*). It weighs a mere 1.4 oz. (40 g) and is no bigger than a house martin or swallow.

★**Largest crustacean genome** Although only a tiny animal, the genome of the Arctic-dwelling amphipod *Ampelisca macrocephala* contains 63.2 billion base pairs, which is roughly 20 times more than in the human genome.

★**Shortest Arctic tree** The dwarf willow *Salix herbacea* is a tiny species that rarely exceeds 2.5 in. (6.4 cm) tall and has been found growing on frozen tundra in the Arctic.

★LARGEST SPECIES OF FALCON The largest species of falcon is the gyrfalcon (*Falco rusticolus*), indigenous to Arctic and subarctic regions. Adult birds can reach maximum lengths of 25 in. (64 cm), with wingspans of 48 in. (123 cm), and weights of 28–74 oz. (800–2,100 g).

"No plant survives further north than Lat. 83°N or further south than Lat 86°09'S."

Most remote tree The most remote tree is believed to be a solitary Norwegian spruce on Campbell Island, Antarctica, whose nearest companion would be over 119.8 nautical miles (222 km) away on the Auckland Islands.

★**Most southerly tree fern** *Cyathea smithii*, a large species of tree fern with a slender trunk, stands up to 26 ft. (8 m) tall and displays fronds that attain a length of up to 9 ft. (2.5 m) when mature. This species is native not only to the cool mountain forests of New Zealand but also to the subantarctic Auckland Islands. As might be expected, it is one of New Zealand's cold-hardiest tree ferns.

The **southernmost recorded flowering plant** is Antarctic hair grass (*Deschampsia antarctica*), found at Lat. 68°21'S on Refuge Island, Antarctica, on March 11, 1981.

★**Most northerly seal** The common (ringed) seal (*Phoca hispida*) is the most abundant species of seal in the Arctic and also the world's most northerly species. Occurring wherever there is enough open water in the more permanent high Arctic ice, this hardy species has even been recorded as far north as the North Pole itself.

★**Longest fast for a bird** The longest continuous fast on record for any bird was 134 days for a male emperor penguin (*Aptenodytes forsteri*). Once a male emperor penguin arrives on land from the sea, it does not usually eat while traveling overland to the breeding colony, courting a female, incubating their single egg for 62–67 days (a job that the female takes no part in),

LARGEST LAND CARNIVORE The largest of all land carnivores is the polar bear (*Ursus maritimus*). Adult males typically weigh 880–1,320 lb. (400–600 kg) and have a nose-to-tail length of 7 ft. 10 in.–8 ft. 6 in. (2.4–2.6 m). The male Kodiak bear (*U. arctos middendorffi*), a subspecies of brown bear found on Kodiak Island and the adjacent Afognak and Shuyak islands in the Gulf of Alaska, U.S.A., is usually shorter in length than the polar bear and more robustly built.

★**LARGEST POPULATION OF KILLER WHALES** The world's largest population of killer whales, or orcas (*Orcinus orca*), is found in the waters off Antarctica, where there are around 160,000 individuals. (Pictured is a South American sea lion pup being attacked by an orca.)

On October 12, 1958, a bull killer whale was timed at 34.5 mph (55.5 km/h) in the northeastern Pacific, making it the **fastest marine mammal.** Similar speeds have been reported for Dall's porpoise (*Phocoenoides dalli*), but only in short bursts.

waiting for the female to return, and traveling back to the sea. Only when it reaches the sea again does it resume feeding. It is able to survive this enforced fast (during which its body weight falls by half) by surviving on plentiful reserves of subcutaneous fat, which can be 1.2–1.6 in. (3–4 cm) thick.

MOST DANGEROUS PINNIPED The carnivorous leopard seal (*Hydrurga leptonyx*) is the only species with a reputation for apparently unprovoked attacks on people. There are a number of documented cases of leopard seals suddenly lunging through cracks in the ice to snap at human feet. Divers have also been attacked, and there are instances of several people being chased across the ice over distances of up to 330 ft. (100 m). Pictured is a leopard seal resting on the rocky shore at Port Lockroy on Wiencke Island, Antarctica.

★ **LARGEST SPECIES OF PENGUIN** *Anthropornis nordenskjöldi* lived in the Antarctic about 24 million years ago, during the lower Miocene epoch. This human-sized penguin stood approximately 5–5 ft. 10 in. (1.5–1.8 m) tall and may have weighed 198–298 lb. (90–135 kg). By comparison, today's largest penguin species, the emperor penguin (*Aptenodytes forsteri*), stands 3 ft. 3 in. (1 m) tall, has a total length of 3 ft. 9 in. (1.15 m), and weighs up to 95 lb. (43 kg).

The **most southerly bird tracks** ever recorded were those of an emperor penguin, which were happened upon over 248 miles (400 km) from the nearest sea by a team of Antarctic explorers on December 31, 1957.

LOWEST MAMMALIAN BODY TEMPERATURE A body temperature of 26°F (-3°C) was measured for the Arctic ground squirrel (*Spermophilus parryii*) of Alaska and northwest Canada. Its body temperature drops below freezing when in a state of suspended animation during its hibernation period in the Arctic winter. Its normal body temperature in the summer months is 98°F (37°C).

Its hibernation, which can last up to nine months, is the **longest hibernation** by a rodent in the wild.

PENGUINS APLENTY

The **largest penguin colony** in the world is on Zavodovski Island in the South Sandwich Islands. Approximately 2 million chinstrap penguins (*Pygoscelis antarctica*) breed on the slopes of the island, which is an active volcano.

URBAN AREAS

Most legs Despite their names, centipedes do not have 100 legs and millipedes do not have 1,000, although millipedes do have more legs than centipedes. They have two pairs per body segment compared with just one pair per body segment in centipedes. Normally millipedes have about 300 pairs of legs, although a millipede called *Illacme plenipes* found in California, U.S.A., had 375 pairs (equaling 750 legs).

★**Lowest dwelling birds** From the northern hemisphere summer of 1975 to spring 1978, three house sparrows (*Passer domesticus*) lived in Frickley Colliery, Yorkshire, UK, at a depth of 2,100 ft. (640 m), making them the lowest known resident population of wild birds. Two of these three sparrows even nested and raised three chicks, but the chicks died not long afterwards.

★**Largest flock of birds to invade a house** Many people have discovered the odd sparrow or blackbird in their chimney, but the feathered invasion of a house in Pasadena, California, U.S.A., on the evening of May 4, 1998, resembled a scene from Alfred Hitchcock's film *The Birds* (U.S.A., 1963). Luckily, the owners weren't home, because when neighbors called out the Fire Department to investigate, the firefighters discovered that more

HIGHEST FREQUENCY HEARING Bats (order Chiroptera) have the most acute hearing of any non-aquatic animal, owing to their ultrasonic echolocation. Most species use frequencies in the 20–80 kHz range, although some are able to hear frequencies as high as 120–250 kHz, compared to almost 20 kHz for humans and 280 kHz for that of dolphins. Pictured is a parti-colored bat (*Vespertilio murinus*).

LONGEST EARTHWORM In 1967, a giant specimen of the earthworm *Microchetus rappi* was found on the road between Alice and King William's Town, KwaZulu-Natal, South Africa. It was 21 ft. (6.7 m) long when naturally extended and 0.8 in. (20 mm) in diameter. (This was a prize specimen, as the average length of this species is approximately 6 ft. (1.8 m) when naturally extended.)

The shortest earthworm is *Chetogaster annandalei*—it measures less than 0.02 in. (0.5 mm) long.

than a thousand swifts (family Apidae) had flown down the chimney, spreading soot everywhere. Some of the swifts were dead, having apparently flown headlong into the walls in panic, and it took the firefighters at least two hours to shoo the rest of the flock out through windows and doors. It is unclear why the swifts flew down the chimney en masse.

Longest parasitic fasts The common bedbug (*Cimex lectularius*), which feeds on human blood, is able to survive without feeding for more than a year. The soft tick (*Ornithodoros turicata*), which spreads the spirochete causing relapsing fever, can survive without food for periods of up to five years.

★First man-made bioluminescent fish Created in 2001 by Prof. H. J. Tsai of National Taiwan University, the world's first man-made bioluminescent fish (dubbed Frankenfish) are green-glowing specimens of the zebra fish, a popular aquarium species, whose bioluminescence is the result of the introduction of jellyfish DNA.

Smallest spider egg *Oonops domesticus*, a tiny pink spider that lives on the walls of houses in Europe, lays eggs that measure only a fraction of a millimeter across. This spider also lays the **fewest eggs by any spider in a single batch**—only two.

DID YOU KNOW?

Echolocation is a method of sensory perception by which bats orient themselves to their surroundings, detect obstacles, communicate with each other and find food. Bats send out sound waves using their mouth or nose; when the sound hits an object, an echo comes back. The echolocation system is so accurate that bats can detect insects the size of gnats and objects as fine as a human hair.

LARGEST INDOOR SPIDER WEB A cobweb 16 ft. 8 in. (5.08 m) long and 12 ft. 6 in. (3.8 m) wide, covering an area of 208 ft.² (19.3 m²), was discovered in an outbuilding belonging to David Hyde (UK) in Newent, Gloucestershire, UK, in January 1999.

Discovered by Ken Thompson (UK) in 1998, the **largest outdoor web** (made by thousands of black money spiders) covered an entire 11.23-acre (4.54-ha) playing field in Warwick, UK.

★**Oldest marsupial** The longest-living marsupial whose age has been reliably recorded was a common wombat (*Vombatus ursinus*) that was 26 years 22 days old when it died on April 20, 1906, at London Zoo, UK. Although the hypothesis has not been verified, it is possible that the larger species of kangaroo live up to 28 years in the wild.

Most bee stings removed The greatest number of bee stings sustained by any surviving human is 2,443 by Johannes Relleke at the Kamativi tin mine, Gwaii River, Wankie District, Zimbabwe (then Rhodesia), on January 28, 1962. All the stings were removed and counted.

★**FIRST DOMESTICATED ELEPHANTS** The earliest known records of domesticated elephants relate to the Asian elephant (*Elephas maximus*). They tell of tamed elephants being used as beasts of burden at least 4,000 years ago during the Indus Valley civilization in the region of present-day Pakistan and India.

SLEEPIEST MAMMAL In October 2007, University of New England zoologist Dr. Fritz Geiser (U.S.A.) announced a new world record for the sleepiest mammal. After an extensive feed, an Australian eastern pygmy possum (*Cercartetus nanus*) curled up and hibernated for 367 days—the first time any mammal has been known to hibernate nonstop for more than a year. During its marathon sleep, the possum used just one-fortieth of the energy it consumes when awake. Prior to this, the record holder had been a western jumping mouse (*Zapus princeps*) that hibernated for 320 days in a laboratory.

Most dangerous bee The Africanized honey bee (*Apis mellifera scutellata*) will generally attack only when provoked, but is persistent and aggressive in pursuit, and protective of territories. Although its venom is no more potent than that of other bees, because it attacks in swarms the result can be deadly due to the number of stings inflicted.

★Longest yuca root On December 24, 2000, Camilo Outerino (U.S.A.) pulled a yuca (cassava) root from the ground in his garden in Hialeah, Florida, U.S.A. It was a surprising 8 ft. 10 in. (2.46 m) long.

EXTREME HABITATS

★First plant species to flower in space In 1982, the then Soviet Union's Salyut-7 space station grew some *Arabidopsis* on board. During their 40-day life cycle, they became the first plants to flower and produce seeds in the zero gravity of space.

Highest microbe In April 1967, NASA reported that bacteria had been discovered at an altitude of 25 miles (41.13 km).

Deepest plant Algae found by Mark and Diane Littler (both U.S.A.) off San Salvador Island, The Bahamas, in October 1984, grew at a depth of 882 ft. (269 m). These maroon-colored plants survived, despite the fact that 99.9995% of sunlight was filtered out.

LARGEST CAVE DWELLERS Although they do not live there permanently, the salt-mining African elephants (*Loxodonta africana*) of Kitum Cave on Mount Elgon, Kenya, regularly enter the cave and travel underground in search of salt, which they need for dietary purposes. They dig the mineral out with their tusks and have done so for generations.

Most acid-resistant life-form The most acidic conditions in which microbial (or any) life has been discovered to survive is pH O, equivalent to hydrochloric acid. Several organisms are known to thrive in these conditions, including *Cyanidium caldarium,* which lives in volcanic vents.

Most alkali-resistant life-form A bacterium discovered in 2003 near Chicago, Illinois, U.S.A., lives in groundwater contaminated by more than a century of industrial iron-slag tailings, where it can survive pH levels of up to 12.8.

★**Most parasitically controlled mollusk** In January 1998, scientists at Vrije University, Amsterdam, the Netherlands, revealed that specimens of the freshwater snail *Lymnaea stagnalis* parasitized by the digenean fluke *Trichobilharzia ocellata* develop an aversion to sex. Instead, they grow more quickly, allowing their parasites to thrive. Studying this behavioral change in the host species revealed that levels of certain types of a nucleic acid

MOST COLD-TOLERANT TREES The most cold-tolerant trees are the larches (genus *Larix*). These include the tamarack larch *L. laricina* (pictured), native to northern North America—and commonly occurring at the arctic tree line at the edge of the tundra—which can survive winter temperatures down to at least -85°F (-65°C).

MOST HEAT-TOLERANT ANIMAL
The most heat-tolerant multicellular animals are the tardigrades or water bears, a group of tiny, near-indestructible animals that are able to survive temperatures exceeding 302°F (150°C).

(messenger RNA) responsible for producing proteins affecting snail behavior were much higher in parasitized snails than in non-parasitized snails. In other words, *T. ocellata* was directly affecting the gene expression of *Lymnaea*—seemingly the first time that this type of parasite control over its host has been shown.

Largest parasite The broad, or fish, tapeworm (*Diphyllobothrium latum*), inhabiting the small intestine of fish and sometimes humans, too, attains a length of 30–40 ft. (9.1–12.1 m) but can exceptionally reach 60 ft. (18 m). If a specimen survived for 10 years, it could measure almost 5 miles (8 km) long and contain 2 billion eggs!

Another human parasite, the pork tapeworm (*Taenia solium*), can exceed 20 ft. (6 m), while the beef tapeworm (*Taeniarhynchus saginatus*) can reach up to 50 ft. (15.25 m). One extreme *Taeniarhynchus* specimen was 75 ft. (22.86 m) long—three times as long as the entire human intestine!

Most bloodthirsty parasite The indistinguishable eggs of the hookworms *Ancylostoma duodenale* and *Necator americanus* are found in the feces of 1.3 billion people worldwide. Around 2.6 million gallons (10 million liters) of blood is extracted worldwide daily as a result of the worms' feeding.

Most adaptable fluke Most flukes (comprising two classes of flatworms) infect very few different organisms, but the liver fluke (*Fasciola hepatica*) has been found as an adult in the liver, gall bladder, and associated ducts in sheep, cattle, goats, pigs, horses, rabbits, squirrels, dogs, and humans.

DID YOU KNOW?

Parasitism is an association between two different species in which one, the parasite, gains an advantage while the other, the host, suffers. Parasites usually live on or inside their host, which they use as a source of nutrition while reproducing, often causing illness in the host.

★**LARGEST CAVE-DWELLING BAT** The world's largest cave-dwelling bat is Bulmer's fruit bat (*Aproteles bulmerae*), native to Papua New Guinea. Adult females have a wing-span of around 3 ft. 3 in. (1 m) and weigh approximately 21 oz. (600 g). They were known to science only from 9,000-year-old fossils until 1977, when some modern-day preserved specimens were unexpectedly uncovered in a museum. Living specimens were later discovered in a huge cave within western Papua's Hindenburg mountain range.

★**Most heat-tolerant worm** Scientifically described only as recently as 1980, and living in association with deep-sea hydrothermal vents sited on the Pacific Ocean bed just off the Galapagos Islands, the world's most heat-tolerant worm is the Pompeii worm (*Alvinella pompejana*). This small polychete (meaning "many bristled") worm attaches itself to "black smoker" vents and thrives at temperatures of up to 176°F (80°C). Only the tardigrades can tolerate higher temperatures.

★**Deepest bat colony** The world's deepest bat colony—comprising approximately 1,000 little brown bats (*Myotis lucifrugus*)—spends each winter in a New York zinc mine at a record depth for any bat species of 3,805 ft. (1,160 m)—almost six times deeper than their normal roosting depth.

PARASITIC PESTS

Also known as roundworms, the **largest parasitic nematode,** inhabiting the placenta of sperm whales, is *Placentonema gigantissimus*. It can reach a length of 25 ft. (7.62 m).

The **largest parasitic fluke,** a species of didymozoid digenean, encysted in the giant oceanic sunfish *Mola mola,* can attain a length of 20–30 ft. (6–9 m).

BEING HUMAN

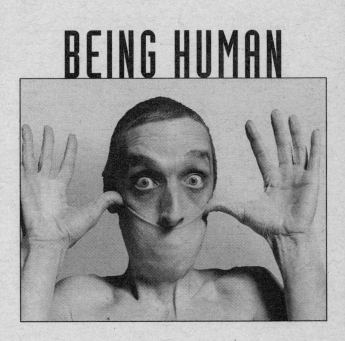

CONTENTS

ANATOMY

LISTEN HEAR

The **smallest muscle** in the body is the stapedius, which controls the stapes (stirrup) bone (see illustration p. 77). It is around 0.05 in. (0.12 cm) long!

Liver The liver can measure up to 8.6 in. (22 cm) long and 3.99 in. (10 cm) wide. Located behind the lower ribs and below the diaphragm, it performs over 100 functions.

Skin An organ is defined loosely as any part of an animal or plant that is adapted for a particular function, such as respiration, digestion, or protection. Skin, therefore, is the **largest organ** in the body.

Bones Excluding a variable number of sesamoid bones, adult humans have 206 bones. Children have about 300—some bones fuse together over time.

Longest bone ever The **longest recorded bone** was a femur measuring 2 ft. 6 in. (76 cm), which belonged to Constantine, a German giant.

BITE MARKS

In August 1986, Richard Hofmann (U.S.A.) achieved a bite strength of 975 lb. (442 kg) for approximately two seconds in a research test using a gnathodynamometer at the College of Dentistry, University of Florida, U.S.A. This is SIX times greater than the average biting strength!

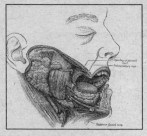

SHOULDER The shoulder is the **most mobile joint** in the body— and as a result is the joint that is easiest to dislocate.

JAW The **strongest muscle** in the human body is the masseter. (There is one masseter on each side of the mouth.) See p. 75 for more notes on jaw strength.

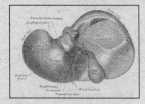

LIVER The **largest internal organ,** the adult liver can weigh 2 lb. 10oz.–3 lb. 4 oz. (1.2–1.5 kg), or about 1/36th of the total body weight.

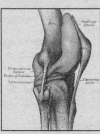

SARTORIUS MUSCLE The **longest muscle in the human body** is the sartorius, which is a narrow ribbon-like muscle running from the pelvis and across the front of the thigh to the top of the tibia below the knee.

PATELLA (KNEE CAP) The patella, or knee cap, is the **largest sesamoid bone** in the human body. Sesamoid bones are only a few millimeters in diameter and are shaped like seeds of the sesame plant. They are usually embedded in tendons close to joints.

FEMUR The **longest bone** is the femur, which normally constitutes 27.5% of a person's stature and may be 19.75 in. (50 cm) long in a man measuring 6 ft. (180 cm) tall.

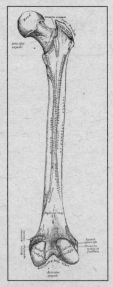

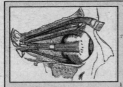

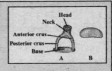

EYE MUSCLES The **most active muscles are** those of the eye, which move an estimated 100,000 times every day.

STAPES (STIRRUP)
The smallest bone in the body is the stapes (or stirrup), found in the ear. It measures just 0.1–0.13 in. (2.6–3.4 mm) long.

HIP The hip joint is the most difficult to dislocate, making it the **strongest joint** in the human skeleton. This is because the head of the femur fits almost perfectly into the socket of the pelvis.

ANATOMICAL ANOMALIES

Heaviest woman Rosalie Bradford (U.S.A., b. August 27, 1943) claimed to have registered a peak weight of 1,200 lb. (544 kg) in January 1987. In August of that year, she developed congestive heart failure and was rushed to a hospital. She was then put on a carefully controlled diet, and by February 1994 weighed 283 lb. (128 kg).

Largest waist Walter Hudson's (U.S.A.) waist measured 119 in. (302 cm) at his peak weight of 1,197 lb. (545 kg).

Tallest woman ever Zeng Jinlian (China, b. June 26, 1964) of Yujiang village, Hunan Province, measured 8 ft. 1.75 in. (2.48 m) when she died on February 13, 1982.

ANATOMICAL MILESTONES

TALLEST MAN EVER

The tallest man in medical history for whom there is irrefutable evidence is Robert Pershing Wadlow (b. 6:30 a.m., on February 22, 1918, in Alton, Illinois, U.S.A.). When last measured, on June 27, 1940, he was found to be 8 ft. 11.1 in. (2.72 m) tall. Robert died on July 15, 1940.

HEAVIEST MAN EVER

Jon Brower Minnoch (U.S.A., 1941–83) suffered from obesity from childhood. He was 6 ft. 1 in. (185 cm) tall and weighed 392 lb. (178 kg) in 1963, 700 lb. (317 kg) in 1966, and 975 lb. (442 kg) in September 1976. In March 1978, Minnoch was admitted to University Hospital, Seattle, U.S.A., where consultant endocrinologist Dr. Robert Schwartz calculated that Minnoch must have weighed more than 1,400 lb. (635 kg), a great deal of which was water accumulation due to his congestive heart failure.

SHORTEST MAN EVER

The shortest mature human of whom there is independent evidence was Gul Mohammed (India, 1957–97). On July 19, 1990, he was examined at Ram Manohar Hospital, New Delhi, India, and found to have a height of just 1 ft. 10.5 in. (57 cm).

TALLEST WOMAN When last measured, Sandy Allen (U.S.A., b. June 18, 1955) was 7 ft. 7.25 in. (2 m 31.7 cm). When she was born, she weighed 6 lb. 7 oz. (2.95 kg) and her abnormal growth began soon after. She stood 6 ft. 3 in. (1 m 90.5 cm) by the age of 10 and was 7 ft. 1 in. (2.16 m) by 16.

TALLEST MAN LIVING Bao Xi Shun (China, b. 1951) is the tallest living man whose height has been fully ratified by GWR. His height, 7 ft. 8.95 in. (2.36 m), was confirmed at Chifeng City Hospital, Inner Mongolia, China, on January 15, 2005. The Ukraine's Leonid Stadnyk, whose height of 8 ft. 5.5 in. (2.57 m) made international news last year, is currently back under investigation, as he continues to reject requests to measure him.

Tallest twins Identical twins Michael and James Lanier (U.S.A.) of Troy, Michigan, both stand 7 ft. 3 in. (2.235 m) in height, making them the **tallest male twins.**

Ann and Claire Recht (U.S.A., b. February 9, 1988) are the ☆ **tallest female twins.** Measured on January 10, 2007, in Oregon, U.S.A., both sisters registered an average overall height of 6 ft. 7 in. (2.01 m).

SHORTEST WOMAN EVER Pauline Musters (Netherlands, b. February 26, 1876) measured 1 ft. (30 cm) at birth. At nine years of age, she was 1 ft. 9.5 in. (55 cm) tall and weighed only 3 lb. 5 oz. (1.5 kg). She died of pneumonia with meningitis on March 1, 1895, in New York City, U.S.A., at the age of 19. A postmortem revealed her to be 2 ft. (61 cm) tall—there was some elongation after death.

HEAVIEST LIVING MAN The heaviest living man is Manuel Uribe Garza (Mexico), who weighed 1,232 lb. (560 kg) in January 2006, when he made a television appeal for help with his condition. Since then, with medical assistance and The Zone diet, he has gradually started to lose weight. As of January 2008, Manuel's weight was down to 660 lb. (299.3 kg). He cannot yet stand up on his own, though, and has remained bed-bound since 2002.

Tallest married couple Anna Hanen Swan (Canada) measured 7 ft. 5.5 in. (2.27 m) in height. On June 18, 1871, she married 7-ft. 2.5-in. (2.2-m) Martin van Buren Bates (U.S.A.), giving the couple a combined height of 14 ft. 8 in. (4.46 m).

Most variable stature Adam Rainer (Austria, 1899–1950) measured just 3 ft. 10.5 in. (1.18 m) at the age of 21 but suddenly started growing at a rapid rate. By 1931, he had nearly doubled to 7 ft. 1.75 in. (2.18 m). But he

★ MANUEL URIBE'S WEIGHT LOSS ★

FEB. 06   **JAN. 08**
1,232 lb.
(558.8 kg)

    1,032 lb.
    (468.1 kg)

        900 lb.
        (408.2 kg)

            844 lb.
            (382.8 kg)

                825 lb.
                (374.2 kg)

                    660 lb.
                    (299.3 kg)

became so weak that he was bedridden for the rest of his life. At the time of his death, he measured 7 ft. 8 in. (2.34 m) and was the only person in medical history to have been both a dwarf and a giant.

Shortest living people Madge Bester (South Africa, b. April 26, 1963) is only 2 ft. 1.5 in. (65 cm) tall. However, she suffers from osteogenesis imperfecta (characterized by brittle bones and other skeletal deformities) and is confined to a wheelchair. Her mother, Winnie, is just 2 ft. 2.5 in. (70 cm) tall.

The **shortest living man** is Taiwan's Lin Yih-Chih at 2 ft. 2.5 in. (67.5 cm). He, too, is confined to a wheelchair because of osteogenesis imperfecta.

The **shortest living mobile man** is He Pingping (China)—see the "Shortest Man" section on pages 444–449.

Shortest twins Matyus and Béla Matina (b. 1903–*ca.* 1935) of Budapest, Hungary—who later became American citizens—both measured 2 ft. 6 in. (76 cm) tall.

Greatest height difference between a married couple Fabien Pretou (France, b. June 15, 1968), who stood 6 ft. 2 in. (188.5 cm) tall, married Natalie Lucius (France, b. January 19, 1966), measuring 3 ft. 1 in. (94 cm) tall, at Seyssinet-Pariset, France, on April 14, 1990. Their height difference was 3 ft. 1 in. (94.5 cm).

Greatest weight difference between a married couple Jon Brower Minnoch (U.S.A.)—the **heaviest human being who ever lived** (see box on p. 78)—weighed 1,289 lb. (c, 585 kg), and his wife Jeannette (U.S.A.) just 110 lb. (50 kg) on the day of their wedding in March 1978. This is a record weight difference of 1,179 lb. (535 kg).

X-REF

How well do you know your own body? If you've ever been curious about your longest bone or largest organ, flip back to **Anatomy** on pp. 75–77. And remember; you're never too young (or old) to be a record breaker. Don't believe us? Then fast forward to **Youngest . . .** (p. 129) and **Oldest . . .** (p. 132).

BODY PARTS

Fewest toes Some members of the Wadomo tribe of the Zambezi Valley, Zimbabwe, and the Kalanga tribe of the eastern Kalahari Desert, Botswana, have two toes on each foot, owing to a single mutated, hereditary gene.

Largest hands Robert Wadlow (U.S.A.), the **tallest man ever** (see p. 78), had hands that measured 12.75 in. (32.3 cm) from the wrist to the tip of his middle finger. He wore a size-25 ring.

Hussain Bisad (UK, b. Somalia) has hands measuring 10.5 in. (26.9 cm) from wrist to tip of middle finger, the **largest hands on a living person.**

Largest feet Robert Wadlow (U.S.A.) wore U.S. size 37AA shoes (UK size 36; European size 75), equivalent to 18.5 in. (47 cm) in length.

The **tallest woman ever**, Zeng Jinlian (China, see also p. 78), had feet measuring 14 in. (35.5 cm) in length.

★**Most teeth** Meriano Luca (Italy) had 35 adult teeth as of January 15, 2004. (By way of comparison, it is normal to have up to 32 adult teeth.)

☆**Longest milk tooth** Ahmed Afrah Ismail (Maldives) had a milk tooth that measured 0.9 in. (2.3 cm), with a crown length of 0.39 in. (1 cm) and a root length of 0.5 in. (1.3 cm).

☆**Farthest eyeball pop** In Istanbul, Turkey, on November 2, 2007, Kim Goodman (U.S.A.) popped her eyeballs 0.47 in. (12 mm) beyond her eye sockets.

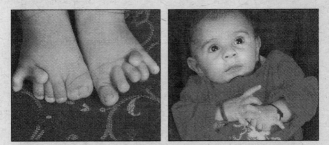

☆**MOST TOES AND FINGERS ON A LIVING PERSON** Two individuals possess 25 digits. Pranamya Menaria (India, above) has 12 fingers and 13 toes as a result of the conditions polydactyly and syndactyly. Devendra Harne (India) has also grown 12 fingers and 13 toes as a result of polydactyly.

A coroner's inquest held on a baby boy at Shoreditch in east London, UK, on September 16, 1921, confirmed that he had 14 fingers and 15 toes, the **most fingers and toes ever** recorded on a human being.

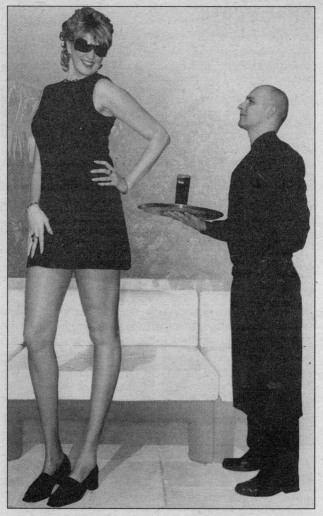

☆**LONGEST LEGS (FEMALE)** Svetlana Pankratova's (Russia) legs were measured at 51.9 in. (132 cm) long in Torremolinos, Spain, on July 8, 2003. Her unique gift presents certain challenges—she has to have some clothes specially made, ducks through most doorways, and needs lots of legroom in cars and airplanes. But that's a small price to pay if you're the "Queen of the Longest Legs"!

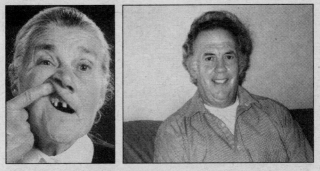

☆**OLDEST PERSON WITH A NEW TOOTH** In March 2007, Mária Magdolna Pozderka (b. Hungary, July 19, 1938, above left)—then 68—had an upper right canine tooth erupt.

The **oldest man to grow a new tooth** is Mark Tora (UK, above right), who was 61 years old when a lower right third molar (wisdom tooth) erupted in February 2002. (Wisdom teeth normally erupt between the ages of 15 and 25.)

★**Longest time to keep the eyeballs protruded** Keith Smith (U.S.A.) kept his eyes popped out of their sockets for 43 seconds on the set of *Lo Show dei Record*, in Madrid, Spain, on February 9, 2008.

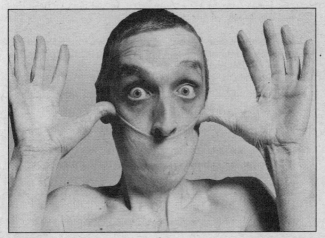

STRETCHIEST SKIN Owing to a rare condition called Ehlers-Danlos syndrome, Garry Turner (UK) has exceptionally malleable skin—so much so that he is able to perform the "human turtleneck" by pulling his neck skin up over his mouth!

LONGEST TONGUE Stephen Taylor's (UK) tongue measures 3.7 in. (9.5 cm) from the tip to the center of his closed top lip. The awesome organ was measured on the set of *Lo Show dei Record* in Milan, Italy, on January 5, 2006.

☆**Lowest heart rate** Martin Brady (UK) had a resting heartbeat of 27 beats per minute when he was tested at the Guernsey Chest and Heart Unit, Channel Islands, UK, on August 11, 2005.

★**Largest kidney stone** Vilas Ghuge (India) had a stone removed from his left kidney on February 18, 2004, by Dr. Hemendra Shah (India) at R. G. Stone Urological Research Institute, Mumbai, India. The stone was 5.1 in. (13 cm) at its widest point.

DID YOU KNOW?

On October 24, 2002, Matthew Adams (U.S.A.) had two wisdom teeth removed at the age of just 9 years 339 days, making him the **youngest person to have a wisdom tooth extracted.**

The **longest human tooth extracted** measured 0.99 in. (2.53 cm). It was removed from 12-year-old Philip Puszczalowski (Canada) in 1993.

THE FIVE SENSES

Hearing The intensity of noise or sound is measured in terms of pressure. The pressure of the **lowest pitch** that can be detected by a person of normal hearing at the most sensitive frequency of around 2,750 Hz is 2×10^{-5} pascal. One-tenth of the logarithm to this standard provides a unit termed a decibel (dB). A noise of 30 dB is negligible.

•The limit for the **highest detectable pitch** is accepted to be 20,000 Hz (cycles per sec), although it has been alleged that children with asthma can detect sounds of 30,000 Hz.

•According to a year-long online survey by Trevor Cox, Professor of Acoustic Engineering at Salford University, UK, the ★**most repellent sound to the human ear** is that of someone vomiting, which beat the jarring sounds of a baby's wailing, a dentist's drill, and microphone feedback (among many others) to reach the top spot.

Sight The **most distant object visible with the naked eye** is the Andromeda Galaxy in the constellation of Andromeda (mag. 3.47), known as Messier 31. It is a spiral galaxy situated about 2.2 million light-years away from Earth.

LOUDEST BURPS Paul Hunn (UK) delivered a burp measuring 104.9 dB on a certified and calibrated class 1 precision measuring noise level meter, from a distance of 8 ft. 2 in. (2.5 m) and 3 ft. 3 in. (1 m) high, at the offices of Guinness World Records, London, UK, on July 20, 2004.

The ★**loudest burp by a woman,** measured under the same conditions, read 104.75 dB and was achieved by Jodie Parks (U.S.A., above) on the set of *Lo Show dei Record,* in Madrid, Spain, on February 16, 2008.

LOUDEST SCREAM Classroom assistant Jill Drake (UK) had a scream that reached 129 dB when measured at the Halloween festivities held in the Millennium Dome, London, UK, in October 2000.

•The resolving power of the human eye is 0.0003 of a radian, or an arc of one minute (one-sixtieth of a degree), which corresponds to 100 microns from a distance of 10 in. (25 cm). A micron is a thousandth of a millimeter, so—at 100 microns—the **smallest visible object** would be less than four thousandths of an inch (0.01 cm) in size.

Smell Ethyl mercaptan ($C_2H_5\dot{S}H$) and butyl seleno-mercaptan (C_4H_9SeH) are the **smelliest molecules** in the world, with an odor reminiscent of a combination of rotting cabbage, garlic, onions, burned toast, and sewer gas.

•The **smelliest substances** are the man-made "Who-Me?" and "U.S. Government Standard Bathroom Malodor," which have five and eight chemical ingredients, respectively. Bathroom Malodor smells mainly of human feces

and becomes repellent to the human nose at just two parts per million. It was originally created to test the power of deodorizing products.

•Madeline Albrecht (U.S.A.) was employed at the Hill Top Research Laboratories in Cincinnati, Ohio, U.S.A., a testing lab for products by Dr. Scholl. She worked there for 15 years and had to smell thousands of feet and armpits. During her career, she sniffed

FASTEST TALKER Sean Shannon (Canada) recited Hamlet's soliloquy "To be or not to be" (260 words) in a time of 23.8 seconds (655 words per minute) in Edinburgh, UK, on August 30, 1995.

★ **SMELLIEST CHEESE** According to research conducted by Cranfield University, UK, in November 2004, the smelliest cheese is Vieux Boulogne. This soft cheese, matured for seven to nine weeks, is made from cow's milk by cheesemaker Philippe Olivier (France).

approximately 5,600 feet and an indeterminate number of armpits, giving her the record for **most feet and armpits sniffed.**

Taste The ☆ **sweetest substance** is Thaumatin, also known as Thalin®, obtained from arils (appendages found on certain seeds) of the katemfe plant (*Thaumatococcus daniellii*). It is 3,250 times sweeter than sugar (compared to a 7.5% sucrose solution).
•The **most bitter substances** contain the denatonium cation and have been produced commercially as benzoate and saccharide. Taste detection levels are as low as one part in 500 million.

Touch Our skin contains a variety of touch receptors with differing functions. Meissner's corpuscles react to light touch and are located in sensitive areas of the skin, such as our fingertips. Our fingers are so sensitive that they can detect a vibration with a movement of just 0.02 microns (0.000019 mm).

☆ **HOTTEST SPICE** The hottest of all spices is believed to be the chili pepper Bhut Jolokia, belonging to the species *Capsicum chinense,* which was measured at 1,001,304 Scoville Heat Units (SHU) at the New Mexico State University, Las Cruces, New Mexico, U.S.A. on September 9, 2006.

☆ **LONGEST FULL-BODY ICE-CONTACT ENDURANCE** On April 17, 2008, Wang Jintu (China) set a new world record when he spent 1 hour 30 minutes in direct, full-body contact with blocks of ice. The record was set at the Beijing Fu Li Cheng Building in Beijing, China.

HAIR

LONGEST . . .

Arm hair Robert Starrett (U.S.A.) has an arm hair that had grown to a length of 5.3 in. (13.5 cm) when measured in Mequon, Wisconsin, U.S.A., on December 7, 2006.

HAIR RAZORS

On September 11, 2004, Trevor Mitchell (UK) cut a full head of hair in a time of 1 min. 11 sec. at ITV London Studios, London, UK—☆ **the fastest haircut ever.**

The ☆ **highest hairstyle** measured 3 ft. (92.5 cm) and was achieved by Mirre Hammarling (Sweden) in Haningen, Sweden, on November 2, 2007.

LONGEST BEARD On August 18, 1997, the beard of Shamsher Singh (India) was measured in Punjab, India. From the end of his chin to the tip of the beard, it was an amazing 6 ft. (1.83 m) long.

Beard on a living woman Vivian Wheeler (U.S.A.), who first started to shave at the age of seven, finally grew a full beard in 1990. The longest strand of hair, from the follicle to the tip, measured 11 in. (27.9 cm) in 2000.

☆**Chest hair** The longest chest hair ever measured was 9 in. (22.8 cm) long and belonged to Richard Condo (U.S.A.). The length was verified on April 29, 2007.

Ear hair Radhakant Bajpai (India) has hair sprouting from the tragus—the skin covering a small cartilage flap just in front of the ear hole—that measures 5.19 in. (13.2 cm) at its longest point.

☆**Eyebrow hair** Toshie Kawakami (Japan) had an eyebrow hair 5.94 in. (15.1 cm) in length when measured at the Guinness World Records Museum in Tokyo, Japan, on January 22, 2008.

☆**Leg hair** Wesley Pemberton (U.S.A.) had a leg hair measuring 5 in. (12.7 cm) in Tyler, Texas, U.S.A., on August 10, 2007.

Mustache The mustache of Kalyan Ramji Sain (India) has been growing since 1976. By July 1993, it had a span of 11 ft. 1.5 in. (3.39 m)—the right side 5 ft. 7.75 in. (1.72 m) and the left side 5 ft. 5.75 in. (1.67 m).

☆**Nipple hair** A nipple hair belonging to Douglas Williams (U.S.A.) was 5.07 in. (12.9 cm) long on May 26, 2007, in New York City, U.S.A.

LONGEST HAIR Xie Qiuping (China) has been growing her hair from the age of 13 in 1973. When measured on May 8, 2004, her hair was 18 ft. 5.54 in. (5.627 m) long.

☆ **LARGEST BEARD AND MUSTACHE CHAMPIONSHIPS** The latest World Beard and Mustache Championships—held in Brighton, UK, on September 1, 2007—drew 250 entrants and 3,000 spectators. Overall winner Mr. Elmar Weisser of the Swabian Beard Club, Germany, sculpted his facial hair into the shape of London's Tower Bridge. Most competitors strive to complement their extravagant facial fuzz with suitably eye-catching costumes.

MOST...

☆ **Expensive haircut** A haircut by Stuart Phillips (UK) in Covent Garden, London, UK, on October 29, 2007, cost £8,000 ($16,420).

★ **Hair donated to charity in 24 hours** On May 21, 2007, 881 people donated hair in Clinton, Mississippi, U.S.A., in support of the Pantene Beautiful Lengths charity campaign. It weighed a whopping 107 lb. (48.72 kg).

★ **People shaving in one venue** On March 3, 2007, 1,580 people shaved simultaneously at the Gillette Fusion Shave for History and Charity event organized by P&G Singapore Private Ltd. at the Fountain of Wealth in Suntec City, Singapore.

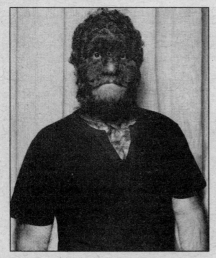

HAIRIEST FAMILY
Victor "Larry" Ramos Gomez (Mexico) is one of a family of 19, spanning five generations, and all suffering from the rare condition known as congenital generalized hypertrichosis, characterized by excessive facial and torso hair. The women of the family are covered with a light-to-medium coating of hair, while the men have thick hair on approximately 98% of their body, apart from their palms and soles.

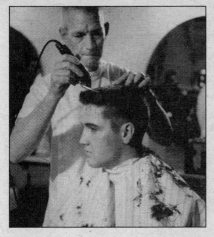

MOST EXPENSIVE HAIR SOLD A mass of hair cuttings from the head of Elvis Presley were sold by his personal barber, Homer Gilleland, for $115,120 (including buyer's premium) to an anonymous bidder during an online auction held by MastroNet Inc., Oak Brook, Illinois, U.S.A., on November 15, 2002. Here Presley is pictured with army barber James Peterson after his induction into the U.S. Army.

★**Shaved heads** A team of five hairstylists from Sears Hair Studio at Notre Dame College, Sudbury, Ontario, Canada, shaved 662 heads in four hours on April 8, 2006.

Splits to a single hair In 1976, Alfred West (UK) succeeded in splitting a human hair 17 times into 18 parts on eight occasions. All the divisions were made from the same point using a razor.

☆ **MOST SCISSORS USED TO CUT HAIR** Zedong Wang (China) used 10 pairs of scissors in one hand, controlling each pair independently, to style a head of hair on the set of *Zheng Da Zong Yi—Guinness World Records Special* in Beijing, China, on October 31, 2007.

HEALTH

☆**Most vaccinations in a working day** A total of 3,271 flu shots were administered by Florida Hospital Centra Care, working with Get Healthy Florida and Seminole County Health Department, at Florida Hospital Centra Care in Sanford, Florida, U.S.A., on November 9, 2006.

★**Largest body-mass index (BMI) check** On September 5, 2004, the body-mass indexes of 3,594 participants were recorded as part of the Singapore Ministry of Health's National Healthy Lifestyle Campaign Day, which took place on Sentosa Island, Singapore. The body-mass index (BMI) is a measure of your body's fat and muscle content. To calculate your BMI, divide your weight in kilograms by the square of your height in meters. A figure of 20–25 is considered acceptable; below this and you are underweight; above this, you are overweight (25–30), obese (30–35), or severely obese (35+).

Health budgets According to a World Health Organization (WHO) report for 2002 (the most recent data available), the U.S. government has the **highest health budget** per capita. In 2002, the equivalent allocation per person amounted to $5,274.

By contrast, North Koreans received the equivalent of just $0.30 per person on health care in 2002, the **lowest health budget** per capita, according to the WHO.

★**MOST BLOOD PRESSURE READINGS TAKEN IN 24 HOURS** The organization Novartis Pharma K.K. (Japan) took 2,109 blood pressure readings at the Chiba Marines Stadium in Chiba, Japan, on May 17, 2007.

"If appropriate action is not taken, by 2015 an estimated 20 million people will die from cardiovascular disease."

World Health Organization report

☆ **Life expectancy** As of 2007, Andorrans had the **highest life expectancy,** with an average of 83.52 years: 80.62 years for males and 86.62 years for females.

The **lowest life expectancy** is just 32.23 in Swaziland: 31.82 years for men and 32.62 years for women.

☆ **Happiest and unhappiest nations** According to the World Database of Happiness, the **happiest country** during 1995–2005 was Denmark,

HEALTH & DISEASE

Lowest rate of death

United Arab Emirates: 1.3 deaths per 1,000 (2005)

Highest rate of death

Swaziland: 31.2 deaths per 1,000 of the population (2005)

Lowest rate of infant mortality

Singapore: 3 deaths per 1,000 live births (2005)

Highest rate of infant mortality

Sierra Leone: 159.8 deaths per 1,000 live births (2005)

Most survivable cancer

Non-melanoma skin cancer: 97% survival rate

Most lethal cancer

Lung cancer: responsible for 17.8% of all cancer deaths in 2000. Followed by stomach cancer (10.4%) and liver cancer (8.8%)

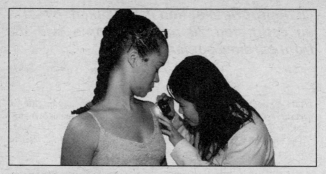

★ **LARGEST SKIN-CANCER SCREENING** The most extensive simultaneous skin-cancer screening involved 10,359 participants at 123 different locations across the U.S.A. for an event organized by the American Academy of Dermatology on May 6, 2006.

which scored an average of 8.2 out of 10 (where 10 was the highest level of contentment). By contrast, with an average score of 3.2, Tanzania ranked lowest, making it officially the **least happy country** in the world. The survey assessed how people in 95 different countries rated their enjoyment of life as a whole.

☆ **Most common cause of death** According to the latest WHO figures, the most common cause of death globally is cardiovascular disease, which

in 2005 caused the deaths of approximately 17.5 million people (equivalent to 30% of all deaths). Of this figure, 7.6 million were the result of heart attacks and 5.7 million were caused by strokes.

In 1998, the **most common cause of death among children** (defined by the WHO as aged between 0 and 4 years old) was infectious diseases, which accounted for 63% of all fatalities. The term "in-

☆ **HIGHEST CIGARETTE CONSUMPTION PER CAPITA** The Greeks smoke an average of 8.5 cigarettes per person per day, according to *The Economist*. In a similar study, the World Health Organization puts the annual total of cigarettes smoked in Greece at 3,230 per person.

★ MOST WIDESPREAD ZOONOSIS
Leptospirosis is the most widespread zoonosis—that is, a disease naturally transmitted from vertebrate animals such as rats, cattle, foxes, and other wild or domestic animals to humans through cuts or mucous membranes during contact with urine in contaminated soil or water. The disease can occur everywhere, but typical outbreaks are in tropical and subtropical areas, such as Nicaragua (pictured).

The World Health Organization (WHO) estimates the annual incidence of infection in these humid areas to be as high as 100 per 100,000.

fectious diseases" refers to all communicable diseases, including parasitic and zoonotic diseases, and some forms of respiratory and diarrheal diseases.

☆ **MOST PEOPLE MASSAGED** At Potters Fields Park in London, UK, on October 21, 2007, 154 people received a massage at the same time. All participants sat on inflatable chairs and were massaged for at least 15 minutes by qualified practitioners to celebrate the launch of a new range of offers from the Nectar (UK) customer loyalty card system.

DID YOU KNOW?

The world record for the ☆ **most bone marrow donors recruited in 24 hours** is 266 by Leben Spenden—KMT in Götzendorf, Austria, on September 2, 2007.

Most urgent health problem The WHO estimates that, by 2020, tobacco-related illnesses such as heart disease, cancer, and respiratory disorders will be the world's leading killer, responsible for more deaths than AIDS, tuberculosis, road accidents, murder, and suicide combined.

Deadliest disease Based on estimates from the United Nations Health Report 2004, 57 million people died of numerous causes in 2002. Of this total, the disease that killed the most people was ischemic heart disease, with an estimated 7.2 million deaths (12.6% of the total).

Among communicable diseases, HIV/AIDS caused the highest number of fatalities, with 2.8 million deaths (4.9% of the total).

FITNESS

MOST . . . IN ONE MINUTE

☆**Body skips** Brittany Boffo (Australia) was able to "skip" with her arms (stepping through her arms and bringing them up and over her head) a total of 68 times in a minute on the set of *Lo Show dei Record,* in Madrid, Spain, on February 9, 2008.

☆**Knee bends on an exercise ball** Stephen Buttler (UK) performed 54 knee bends in one minute while standing on an exercise ball in Shropshire, UK, on October 28, 2007.

★**Roundhouse kicks** Mark Scott (UK) performed a total of 148 roundhouse kicks in one minute at the Griphouse Gym, Glasgow, UK, on November 18, 2007.

☆**Sit-ups using an abdominal frame** On April 14, 2006,

★**MOST ROTATIONS ON A VERTICAL ROPE IN ONE MINUTE Brandon Pereyda (U.S.A.) completed 13 rotations on a vertical rope in one minute on the set of *Guinness World Records: Die Größten Weltrekorde* in Cologne, Germany, on November 23, 2007.**

at the New York Sports Club in Forest Hills, New York, U.S.A. Ashrita Furman (U.S.A.) completed a total of 177 sit-ups using an abdominal frame in one minute.

★**Side jumps** Alastair Galpin (New Zealand) made 90 side jumps (alternating each leg) in one minute at The Warehouse shop in Sylvia Park, Auckland, New Zealand, on October 27, 2007.

☆**Skips** Olga Berberich (Germany) completed 251 skips on the set of *Guinness World Records: Die Größten Weltrekorde,* in Cologne, Germany, on September 1, 2007.

☆**Squat thrusts** Craig De-Vulgt (UK) did 70 squat thrusts in one minute at the Wave for Wales event in Margam Country Park, UK, on June 24, 2007.

★**Jumping jacks** Ashrita Furman (U.S.A.) completed 51 jumping jacks in one minute in front of the Gateway Arch in St. Louis, Missouri, U.S.A., on January 28, 2008.

☆**Cartwheels** Ivan Koveshnikov (U.S.A.) completed 54 cartwheels in a minute at the Multnomah Athletic Club, Portland, Oregon, U.S.A., on August 13, 2007.

Push-ups (using backs of hands) John Morrow (U.S.A.) completed 123 push-ups using the backs of his hands in one minute at Saint Ambrose University in Davenport, Iowa, U.S.A., on May 5, 2006.

MOST . . . IN ONE HOUR

Bench presses Michael Williams (UK) achieved 1,438 repetitions of his bodyweight of 147.7 lb. (67 kg) in one hour by bench presses at Don Styler's Gymnasium, Gosport, UK, on April 17, 1989.

PADDY POWERS TO NEW HEIGHTS

Fitness and endurance champion Paddy Doyle (UK) had a record-breaking day at Stamina's Boxing Self Defence Gym at the Erin Go Bragh Sports Centre, Birmingham, UK, on November 8, 2007, when he powered his way to three new world records:

Paddy established a new mark for the ☆ **most full-contact kicks in one hour** when he completed 5,750 kicks.

He also completed the ☆ **most push-ups using the backs of the hands in one hour** with a record 1,940 repetitions.

Finally, the strongman pulled off the ☆ **most squats in one hour** with 4,708 squats in the 60-minute time limit.

"Sumo squats work every major muscle group in the body."

Dr. Thienna Ho, sumo-squat record holder

☆**Chin-ups** Stephen Hyland (UK) completed 812 chin-ups in one hour in Stoneleigh, Surrey, UK, on October 18, 2007.

★ **MOST FULL CONTACT PUNCH STRIKES IN ONE HOUR** Paddy Doyle (UK) made 29,850 full contact punch strikes in one hour at Stamina's Gym, Erin Go Bragh Sports Centre, Erdington, Birmingham, UK, on January 21, 2008.

MOST PARALLEL BAR DIPS IN ONE HOUR Simon Kent (UK) completed 3,989 parallel bar dips in one hour at Farrahs Health Centre, Lincoln, UK, on September 5, 1998.

FACT

Simon Kent (UK) (see above) also holds the record for the **most parallel bar dips in one minute**. Simon managed 173 dips within the 60-second time limit at Lincoln University, Lincoln, UK, on November 15, 2006.

Being Human

★ **MOST SUMO SQUATS IN ONE HOUR** Dr. Thienna Ho (Vietnam) performed 5,135 sumo squats in an hour at San Francisco State University, in San Francisco, California, U.S.A., on December 16, 2007. Thienna said the record was in honor of her father, a judo master, who had inspired her to practice sumo squats when she was in her twenties.

Push-ups The greatest number of push-ups in one hour is 3,416 by Canadian Roy Berger at the Central Canada Exhibition, Ottawa, Canada, on August 30, 1998.

☆ **Vaults** The 10-man Blue Falcons Gymnastic Display Team (all UK) carried out 5,685 vaults in Chelmsford, Essex, UK, on September 13, 2003.

ENDURANCE

★ **Treadmill—greatest distance covered in one week** Daniel Bocuze (France) ran 455.15 miles (732.5 km) on a treadmill in a week at the Casino Le Lion Blanc in St.-Galmier, Rhône-Alpes, France, between December 1 and 8, 2007.

☆ **Greatest average distance run daily over one year** Tirtha Kumar Phani (India) ran an average of 38.44 miles (61.87 km) every day from June 30, 2006, to June 29, 2007. He achieved this feat in Calcutta, India, running 14,031.15 miles (22,581.09 km) in total.

Most sit-ups in 24 hours Jack Zatorski (U.S.A.) did 130,200 sit-ups using an abdominal frame in 24 hours at Accelerated Physical Therapy, Fort Lauderdale, U.S.A. on September 24–25, 2005.

☆ GREATEST DISTANCE STATIC CYCLING IN 24 HOURS Brian O. Pedersen (Denmark) clocked up a distance of 856.11 miles (1,377.79 km) on a static cycle in 24 hours at Club La Santa, Lanzarote, Canary Islands, Spain, on June 10–11, 2004.

EXTREME BEAUTY

Longest fingernails (male) Melvin Boothe (U.S.A.) has a set of fingernails that had a combined length of 29 ft. 8.3 in. (9.05 m) when measured in Troy, Michigan, U.S.A. on June 2, 2007.

Longest toenails Louise Hollis (U.S.A.) hasn't cut her toenails since 1982. When measured at their longest in 1991, their combined length was 7 ft. 3 in. (2.2 m).

SMALLEST WAIST (LIVING PERSON) Cathie Jung (U.S.A., left) who stands 5 ft. 8 in. (1.72 m) tall, has a corseted waist measuring 15 in. (38.1 cm).

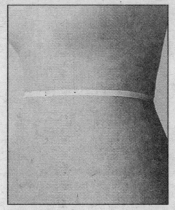

SMALLEST WAIST (EVER) The smallest waist on a person of normal stature was 13 in. (33 cm), and was recorded on Ethel Granger (UK, 1905–82). Ethel was 60 years old, 5 ft. 3 in. (160 cm) tall and weighed 119 lb. (54 kg) when her corseted waist measured 13 in. (33 cm). Her bust measurement was 34 in. (86.3 cm) and her hips 40 in. (101.6 cm). She did not commence waist reduction until she was 25, after the birth of her daughter. A measurement of 13 in. (33 cm) was also claimed for the actress Mlle. Polaire (b. Emile Marie Bouchand, France, 1881–1939).

☆ **LONGEST FINGERNAILS (FEMALE)** Lee Redmond (U.S.A.) hasn't cut her nails since 1979, and has grown and carefully manicured them to reach a total combined length of 28 ft. 4.5 in. (8.65 m).

PLASTIC SURGERY

☆ **Most plastic surgery procedures (country)** Nearly 11.5 million cosmetic surgical and nonsurgical procedures took place in the U.S.A. in 2006—92% on women. The American Society for Aesthetic Plastic Surgery (ASAPS) records 3,181,592 Botox injections for that year, making this the ☆ **most popular nonsurgical procedure.**

The ☆ **most popular surgical procedure for women** in 2006 was breast augmentation, with 383,885 operations performed. The ☆ **most popular**

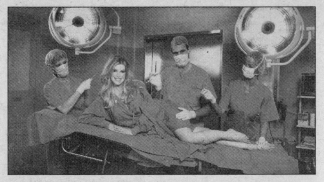

MOST COSMETIC SURGERY Cindy Jackson (U.S.A.) has spent over $100,000 on more than 50 cosmetic procedures, including nine full-scale surgical operations, since 1988. The Midwestern farmer's daughter is the pioneer of the "Extreme Makeover" and has been dubbed a "Living Barbie Doll" by the world's media. Her treatments have included facelifts, a nose job, breast implants, liposuction, chemical peels, oxygen facials, Botox, chin-bone reduction, cheek implants, filler injections, microdermabrasion, dermal vitamin injections, and tattooed lipstick and eyeliner! She is pictured here with cosmetic surgeon Dr. Jose Campo and assistants at the Xanit hospital near Malaga, Spain. You can visit Cindy online at www.cindyjackson.com.

surgical procedure for men in that year was liposuction, with a total of 53,263 operations performed.

Most breast augmentation procedures

The late Lolo Ferrari (b. Eve Valois, France, 1962–2000) had a bust measurement of 5 ft. 11 in. (180 cm) and a bra size of 54G—the result of at least 22 breast enlargement procedures over the course of five years from 1990.

☆**LARGEST AUGMENTED BREASTS** When measured on February 4, 2005, Maxi Mounds (U.S.A.) had an under-breast measurement of 36 in. (91.44 cm), an around-chest-over-nipple measurement of 60.5 in. (153.67 cm), and a U.S. bra size of 42M. She had her first implants (350 cc silicone) in 1991, which were replaced in 1993 with 700 cc saline. These were then inflated to 1,000 cc and, in 1998, replaced with 2,000 cc saline expander bags. In 1999, she had 1,100 cc of fluid and 2,000 cc of string implants added.

Longest penis extension A patient of Dr. Bayard Olle Fischer Santos (Brazil) has had his penis enhanced by 6.29 in. (16 cm) through surgery and physiotherapy. The first treatment was administered on February 20, 1995, and the patient's full distension of 10.62 in. (27 cm) was achieved by March 28, 2000.

PIERCINGS

Most piercings in one session In a single session lasting 7 hr. 55 min., Charlie Wilson (UK) pierced Kam Ma (UK) with 1,015 temporary metal rings at Sunderland Body Art, Tyne and Wear, UK, on March 4, 2006.

Most pierced man Luis Antonio Agüero, from Havana, Cuba, has 230 permanent piercings on his body and head. His face alone carries more than 175 rings.

☆ **MOST PIERCED WOMAN** Since having her first piercing in January 1997, Elaine Davidson (UK) has had 4,225 piercings all over her body as of June 8, 2006.

TATTOOS

Most tattooed person Lucky Diamond Rich (Australia, born New Zealand), has spent over 1,000 hours having his body modified by hundreds of tattoo artists. His "body suit" of colorful designs has been entirely blacked in—including eyelids, the delicate skin between the toes, down into the ears, and even his gums—and he is now being tattooed with white designs on top of the black, and colored designs on top of the white!

★ **MOST SURGICAL PROCEDURES TO LOOK LIKE AN ANIMAL** Dennis Avner (U.S.A.) a.k.a. Cat Man, has undergone 14 separate surgical procedures in order to give cat-like features to his face, ears, and teeth. His feline feat was verified on the set of *Lo Show dei Record*, in Madrid, Spain, on February 9, 2008.

> *"I'm just taking a very old tradition that, to my knowledge, is not practiced anymore."*
>
> *Dennis Avner, a.k.a. Cat Man*

Most tattooed woman The world's most decorated woman is strip artiste Krystyne Kolorful (Canada). Tattoos cover 95% of her body and took 10 years to complete.

Longest session The record for the longest tattoo session stands at 43 hr. 50 min. and was achieved by Stephen Grady and Melanie Grieveson (both Australia) at the Twin City Tattoo and Body Piercing, Wodonga, Victoria, Australia, from August 26 to 28, 2006.

DID YOU KNOW?

Dennis Avner's feline transformations (see p. 105) included three operations on the ears, five implants in the forehead, cheekbones, and chin, one modification of the upper lip, one modification of the nose, and four dental modifications.

GOLDEN OLDIES

☆**Oldest person baptised** Phyllis Nina Stewart (UK) was christened on April 14, 2002, aged 91 years 114 days, at Bishops Tawton Parish Church in Barnstaple, Devon, UK. She was born on December 21, 1910.

Oldest adoption Jo Anne Benedict Walker (U.S.A.) was aged 65 years 224 days when she was officially adopted by Frances Ensor Benedict (U.S.A.) on April 5, 2002, in Putnam County, Tennessee, U.S.A.

Frances (b. May 11, 1918) was 83 years 329 days old when she adopted Jo Anne, making Ms. Benedict the **oldest adoptive parent.**

☆ **OLDEST LIVING PERSON** On August 13, 2007, Edna Parker (U.S.A.) became the oldest living person, aged 114 years 115 days.

"It's hard to believe!"

Edna Parker's (U.S.A.) reaction at becoming the world's oldest living person

Oldest bride Minnie Munro (Australia) was 102 years old when she married Dudley Reid, aged 83, at Point Clare, New South Wales, Australia, on May 31, 1991.

The **oldest bridegroom** to date is Harry Stevens (U.S.A.), who was aged 103 when he married Thelma Lucas, aged 84, at the Caravilla Retirement Home in Wisconsin, U.S.A., on December 3, 1984.

Oldest person to get divorced On November 21, 1980, at the age of 101, Harry Bidwell of East Sussex, UK, divorced his 65-year-old wife.

Oldest divorced couple—aggregate age On February 2, 1984, a divorce was granted in Milwaukee, Wisconsin, U.S.A., to Ida Stern, aged 91, and her husband Simon, 97. Their combined age was 188.

Oldest male twins The oldest male twins authenticated were Glen and Dale Moyer (U.S.A.), both of whom reached the age of 105. Born on June 20, 1895, they became the oldest living twins on January 23, 2000.

The youngest of four children born to Mahlon and Anna Moyer, Dale was a retired farmer and was 20 minutes older than Glen, a retired teacher. Glen Moyer passed away on April 16, 2001, aged 105 years, 9 months, and 26 days.

OLDEST PERSON The greatest confirmed age to which any human has lived is 122 years 164 days by Jeanne Louise Calment (France). Born on February 21, 1875, to Nicolas and Marguerite (née Gilles), Jeanne died at a nursing home in Arles, France, on August 4, 1997.

OLDEST TWINS Kin Narita (left) and Gin Kanie (both Japan, b. August 1, 1892), whose names mean "gold" and "silver," were the **oldest female twins** recorded to date. Kin died of heart failure on January 23, 2000, at the age of 107 years 175 days.

Oldest mothers Maria del Carmen Bousada Lara (Spain, b. January 5, 1940) gave birth by cesarean section to twin boys—Christian and Pau—aged 66 years 358 days, at the Sant Pau Hospital, Barcelona, Spain, on December 29, 2006. This makes her both the **oldest mother** and the ☆ **oldest person to give birth to twins.**

The **oldest mother to have quadruplets** is Australia's Merryl Thelma Fudel (née Coward), who gave birth to three girls and one boy on April 18, 1998, aged 55 years 286 days.

OLDEST TRIPLETS The longest-lived triplets recorded to date were Faith, Hope, and Charity Cardwell, who were born on May 18, 1899, in Elm Mott, Texas, U.S.A. Faith died on October 2, 1994, aged 95 years 137 days.

DID YOU KNOW?

The Ottman quadruplets of Munich, Germany—Adolf, Anne-Marie, Emma, and Elisabeth—were born on May 5, 1912. All four quads lived to the age of 79, making them the **oldest quadruplets.**

Being Human

☆ **OLDEST BRIDESMAID** Edith Gulliford (UK, b. October 12, 1901) served as bridesmaid at the wedding of Kyra Harwood and James Lucas (both UK) on March 31, 2007, at Commissioner's House, Chatham, UK, at the age of 105 years 171 days.

THE TEN OLDEST OLDIES

1. **Jeanne Calment (France):** 122 years 164 days

2. **Shigechiyo Izumi (Japan):** 120 years 237 days*

3. **Sarah Knauss (U.S.A.):** 119 years 97 days

4. **Lucy Hannah (U.S.A.):** 117 years 248 days

5. **Marie-Louise Meilleur (Canada):** 117 years 230 days

6. **Maria Esther de Capovilla (Ecuador):** 116 years 347 days

7. **Tane Ikai (Japan):** 116 years 175 days

8. **Elizabeth Bolden (U.S.A.):** 116 years 118 days

9. **Carrie White (U.S.A.):** 116 years 88 days*

10. **Kamato Hongo (Japan):** 116 years 45 days*

*There is some doubt about the authenticity of these cases

☆ **OLDEST LIVING MAN** Tomoji Tanabe was born in Miyakonojo, Miyazaki Prefecture, Japan, on September 18, 1895, and became the world's oldest living man on January 24, 2007 (upon the death of Emiliano Mercado Del Toro of Puerto Rico), aged 111 years 128 days.

☆ **Oldest woman living with Down Syndrome** Joyce Greenman (UK, b. March 14, 1925) became the oldest living woman with Down Syndrome on December 12, 2007, aged 82 years 273 days.

Peter Davison (UK, b. October 20, 1939) is currently the ☆ **oldest living man with Down Syndrome.** He was 67 years 216 days old as of May 24, 2007.

☆ **Most siblings to reach retirement age** The 19 siblings (seven sons and 12 daughters) born to Canadians Eugene (1892–1962) and Alice Theriault (1896–1967) between 1920 and 1941 were all claiming a government pension in 2007. They ranged in age from 66 to 87.

GUINNESS WORLD RECORDS DAY

MOST KISSES IN ONE MINUTE Adrian Chiles (UK) received 78 kisses in one minute on BBC 1's *The One Show,* London, UK, on November 8, 2007, in celebration of GWR Day.

☆ **LONGEST WHEELIE ON A SKATEBOARD (FLAT SURFACE)** Stefan Akesson (Sweden) performed a one-wheel manual (wheelie) measuring 224 ft. 10 in. (68.54 m) on a flat surface at the Gallerian Shopping Center, Stockholm, Sweden, on November 2, 2007.

★ **FARTHEST-LEANING TOWER** The leaning tower of the Protestant church in Suurhusen, Germany, was unveiled as an official record to the world on GWR Day 2007. It leans at an angle of inclination of 5.1939 degrees.

☆ **MOST RATTLESNAKES (BATHTUB)** Jackie Bibby (U.S.A.), a.k.a. The Texas Snake Man, shared a bathtub with 87 snakes for 45 minutes on November 5, 2007, in Dublin, Texas, U.S.A., as part of GWR Day.

★ MOST CANS COLLECTED The most aluminum cans collected in one month is 1,971,026, weighing 135,458 lb. (61,443 kg). The event was organized by Collect-a-Can, MySchool, and Pan Macmillan in South Africa from October 1 to 31, 2007.

☆ LONGEST LINE OF RIVERDANCERS During the Guinness World Records Day 2007 celebrations on November 8, 216 dancers from CLRG Dance Schools, Leinster Province, Ireland, danced in a "Riverdance" line. The event was held at St. Stephen's Green, Dublin, Ireland.

.LARGEST & SMALLEST DOGS Gibson, the world's tallest living dog (measuring 42.2 in.; 107 cm tall), and Boo Boo, the smallest living dog (at 4 in.; 10.16 cm), met for a photo shoot in Sacramento, California, U.S.A., on GWR Day 2007. Read more about them on p. 210.

★ LARGEST DULCE DE LECHE A dulce de leche—a "caramelized milk candy" popular throughout Latin America—made by Rosario Olvera in Loreto, Zacatecas, Mexico, weighed a record 3,129 lb. 12 oz. (1,419.65 kg). And if you fancy making it yourself, here's the ingredients list:
• **milk:** 462 gallons (1,750 liters)
• **sugar:** 475 gallons (1,800 litres)
• **cinnamon:** 26 lb. (12 kg) cane and 22 lb. (10 kg) powder
• **baking powder:** 6 lb. 9 oz. (3 kg)
• **walnuts:** 220 lb. (100 kg)
• **almonds:** 220 lb. (100 kg)

The final dessert measured: 8 in. wide by 850 ft. long (20 cm by 259.08 m).

GET INVOLVED IN GWR DAY . . .

Want to set or break a record on the next Guinness World Records Day? Find out how to register at **www.guinnessworldrecords.com/gwrday.** Good luck!

★ **FASTEST 100 M BIKE SLED RACE (FOUR DOGS, ON SAND)** The record for the fastest 100 m on a dog sled pulled by four dogs on sand is 11.65 seconds by Suzannah Sorrell (UK) at Holkham National Nature Reserve in Holkham, Norfolk, UK, on November 6, 2007. On the same day, she also broke the record with six and eight dogs in times of 11.53 seconds and 10.65 seconds, respectively.

★ **MOST CONSECUTIVE ONE-GAME WINS OF WII SPORTS TENNIS** Staš Kostrzewski (France) had 21 consecutive one-game wins of Wii Sports Tennis at the Virgin Megastore, Paris, France, on November 7, 2007, as part of GWR Day. This is the most wins by an individual against multiple players.

★ **MOST LETTERS TO SANTA IN A XMAS SEASON** During Christmas 2006, Santa received 1.06 million letters and 44,166 e-mails (each one responded to with the help of Santa's very special Canada Post elves). More than 11,000 Canada Post volunteers helped respond to these letters in 11 languages, including Braille. They were presented with their certificate on GWR Day 2007.

BUS PULLING One of Britain's strongest men pulled a double-decker bus over a distance of 16 ft. 4.8 in. (5 m) using only his ears. Manjit Singh managed to get a giant 7.5-metric ton Routemaster moving, but unfortunately he failed in his bid to break a world record. He had hoped to pull the bus 33 ft. (10 m) to kick off the third annual Guinness World Records Day, but only succeeded in moving the vehicle half of the way.

★ **MOST BARS JUMPED ON A TRAIL BIKE** In celebration of GWR Day 2007, Vittorio Brumotti, a.k.a. "100%" (Italy), jumped 20 gapping bars on the back wheel of his trail bike in Milan, Italy (above).

Brumotti subsequently broke his own record by achieving 24 jumps on the set of *Lo Show Dei Record,* in Madrid, Spain, on February 9, 2008.

★ **LARGEST HANDHELD GAME CONSOLE PARTY** *K-Zone* magazine and Nintendo held a party involving 381 gamers playing their own Nintendo DS for 10 minutes in Parramatta, NSW, Australia.

MISSED OUT ON GWR DAY? THERE'S ALWAYS NEXT YEAR

If you didn't take part in the last GWR Day, you can always try again next year. We're always keen to hear about your ideas, but you need to get in touch with our Records Management Team in plenty of time—preferably a couple of months before. Find out more by visiting: **www.guinnessworldrecords.com/gwrday.**

PREHISTORIC LIFE

WIDEST DINOSAUR Anklyosaurs, distinguished by a large club at the end of the tail, were up to 16 ft. 4 in. (5 m) wide and included the most heavily armored dinosaurs of all—the "tanks" of the Cretaceous world. The entire back was covered with bony plates, studs, and spikes, and the head—right down to the eyelids—also were heavily armored.

LONGEST CLAWS The therizinosaurids ("scythe lizards") from the late Cretaceous period, found in the Nemegt Basin, Mongolia, had the largest claws of any known animal. In the case of *Therizinosaurus cheloniformis,* they measured up to 3 ft. (91 cm) along the outer curve. It has been suggested that these talons were designed for grasping and tearing apart large victims, but this creature had a feeble skull, partially or entirely lacking teeth, and probably lived on termites.

TALLEST DINOSAUR Dinosaur remains discovered in 1994 in Oklahoma, U.S.A., belong to what is believed to be the largest creature to have ever walked the earth. The Sauroposeidon stood at 60 ft. (18 m) tall and weighed 132,277 lb. (60 metric tons). The length of its neck is about a third more than that of the Brachiosaurus, its nearest competitor. It lived about 110 million years ago, during the mid-Cretaceous period.

LONGEST DINOSAUR The suborder of dinosaurs called the sauropoda were herbivorous land animals that first appeared in the late Triassic period, around 200 million years ago. They included the well-known Diplodocus and Brachiosaurus, but the longest of them all was Amphicoelias, estimated to have been around 197 ft. (60 m) long.

LARGEST LAND-BASED CARNIVOROUS DINOSAURS

The therapods ("beast-footed") included the fearsome *T. rex*, Allosaurus, and the even bigger Giganotosaurus (pictured), which could grow to an estimated 42 ft. (13 m) long with a weight of 13,227 lbs. (6 metric tons).

MOST SUCCESSFUL DINOSAUR GROUP

In terms of longevity and diversity, the most successful group of dinosaurs were the therapods. They were bipedal and mainly carnivorous and dominated the land from around 200 million years ago right up to the extinction of the dinosaurs some 65 million years ago. Allosaurus (pictured) grew up to around 33 ft. (10 m) long and was the largest land-based carnivore of the late Jurassic period (144–150 million years ago) and existed some 85 million years before *Tyrannosaurus rex*.

LARGEST DINOSAUR SKULLS The Ceratopsids were herbivorous dinosaurs characterized by their beaks, huge skull frills, and horns, and included Triceratops and Torosaurus (pictured). A Pentaceratops skull on display in the U.S.A. measures 10 ft. (3.2 m) in height.

LARGEST PREHISTORIC INSECT The dragonfly *Meganeura monyi*, which existed about 280 million years ago, was the largest insect that ever lived. Fossil remains (impressions of the creature's wings) discovered at Commentry, France, indicate a wingspan of up to 2 ft. 3.5 in. (70 cm).

MOON LANDINGS

MOST REMOTE GOLF SHOT In February 1971, astronaut Alan Shepard Jr. (U.S.A.) struck two golf balls in the Fra Mauro region on the surface of the Moon. He used a club made from a sampling tool with a six-iron attached. One of the balls traveled a distance of around 50 ft. (15 m).

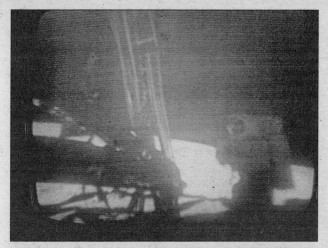

LARGEST TV AUDIENCE FOR A SPACE EVENT The first moonwalk by the *Apollo 11* astronauts was watched on TV by an estimated 600 million people, a fifth of the world's population at the time. The astronauts—Neil Armstrong, Edwin "Buzz" Aldrin, and Michael Collins (all U.S.A.)—were the stars of a parade through New York City, U.S.A., on August 14, 1969, to celebrate their historic achievement.

LARGEST ROCKET The *Saturn V* was the largest rocket launched. It stood 363 ft. (110.6 m) tall with the *Apollo* spacecraft on top and weighed around 6,613,000 lb. (3,000 metric tons) on the launchpad, depending upon the specific mission. The *Saturn V* had a liftoff thrust of 7,600,000 lb. (3,447 metric tons). The five main engines had a combined thrust equivalent to 40 jumbo jets, and burned 6,613 lb. (3 metric tons) of fuel per second. The first *Saturn V* launch, pictured left, took place on November 9, 1967 and the 13th (and last) on May 14, 1973.

CAPTAIN GENE CERNAN,
THE LAST MAN ON THE MOON

U.S. astronaut Captain Gene Cernan orbited the Moon in *Apollo 10* and, as commander of *Apollo 17*, was the last man to walk on its surface. He talked to Guinness World Records about his experience....

Can you describe the launch of the *Saturn V*? I'm one of three people who had the chance to ride the *Saturn V* twice. I called it my "mistress." It was an unbelievable experience. During liftoff, if the booster guidance failed I could flip a switch and manually control 7.6 million lb. (3,440 metric tons) of rocket thrust into Earth orbit and onto the Moon. I literally almost dared it to fail. I didn't want it to fail, but I thought, "If you fail, sweetheart, I can handle you!"

What was it like to fly the lunar module? People are going to look back in 50 or 100 years and say "how the hell did they get to the Moon in that thing?" Any movement you input, you had to take back out because it would continue until you stopped it as there were no aerodynamic effects in space to damp them out. When we were landing, if we didn't like what we saw, we could throttle up the descent engine or jettison it and use the ascent engine and get out of there. But once you're on the Moon, you have to put all your confidence in the ascent engine.

What impressed you most about the Moon? The thing that impressed me when I made my first steps was that for the first time I was stepping on something that wasn't the Earth. You could climb the highest mountain on this planet of ours or go to the depths of the deepest ocean but you're still on Earth! But all of a sudden I was on something else out there in the Universe, with magnificent mountains. People would love me on this Earth of ours if I could turn everything into 1/6th gravity. It's just wonderful and there were only 12 people who ever experienced it! After three days on the Moon, standing on the ladder looking down at my last footprint, looking over my shoulder at the Earth in all its splendor, I realized I was not coming this way again. I literally wanted to stop the clock and press the freeze button. I wanted that moment to last forever.

When will we return to the Moon? Some of my final words on the Moon were "May America's challenge of today lead to man's destiny of tomorrow." When I talk to 4th and 5th graders in school, I look them in the eye and say, "If I can go to the Moon before your mom and dad were born, you can tell me what you can do in your lifetime if you want to do it badly enough."

APOLLO 11 **Crew**: Neil Armstrong, commander; Edwin "Buzz" Aldrin Jr., lunar module pilot; Michael Collins, command module pilot; During landing, Armstrong took manual control of the lunar module to avoid a boulder field. The extra maneuvers meant that when *Apollo 11* finally touched down, less than 30 seconds of fuel remained in the descent engine's tank, the ★ least amount of fuel upon landing.

APOLLO 12 **Crew**: Charles Conrad, commander; Alan L. Bean, lunar module pilot; Richard F. Gordon, command module pilot; *Apollo 12* was to bring back samples of the robotic *Surveyor 3*, which landed on the Moon in April 1967. The *Apollo 12* lander, crewed by Charles Conrad and Alan Bean, touched down on November 19, 1969, less than 656 ft. (200 m) from *Surveyor 3*, the ★ nearest landing to an unmanned probe.

APOLLO 14 **Crew:** Alan B. Shepard Jr., commander; Edgar D. Mitchell, lunar module pilot; Stuart A. Roosa, command module pilot; Alan Shepard Jr. became the ★ **oldest person to land on the Moon,** aged 47 years old, when he touched down on February 4, 1971.

APOLLO 15 **Crew:** David R. Scott, commander; James B. Irwin, lunar module pilot; Alfred M. Worden, command module pilot; *Apollo 15,* as the first of the more extensive "J" missions, was the ★ **first lunar mission to include a lunar rover** when it landed on August 7, 1971.

APOLLO 16 **Crew**: John W. Young, commander; Charles M. Duke Jr., lunar module pilot; Thomas K. Mattingly II, command module pilot. The **highest lunar speed record** was set by the manned *Apollo 16* rover, driven by John Young, with 11.2 mph (18 km/h) achieved downhill.

APOLLO 17 **Crew**: Gene A. Cernan, commander (seated); Harrison H. Schmitt, lunar module pilot (left); Ronald E. Evans, command module pilot (standing, right); Cernan and Schmitt spent 74 hr. 59 min. 40 sec. on the lunar surface, the **longest time spent on the surface of any celestial body**. They also achieved the **longest moonwalk** in an extra-vehicular activity (EVA) that lasted 7 hr. 37 min.

FIRST MEN ON THE MOON Neil Alden Armstrong (U.S.A.), commander of the *Apollo 11* mission, became the first man to set foot on the Moon, at 02:56 GMT on July 21, 1969. He was followed out of the lunar module *Eagle* by Edwin Eugene "Buzz" Aldrin Jr. (U.S.A., pictured left).

LAUNCH ESCAPE TOWER Capable of yanking the command module off the top of the rocket if it malfunctioned, aborting the mission.

COMMAND MODULE Home to the crew during launch and splashdown, this is the only part of the spacecraft that returns to Earth.

SERVICE MODULE Remains connected to the command module until just before reentry and splashdown. Contains propulsion and life-support systems.

LUNAR EXCURSION MODULE Lunar lander for two of the three crew. It has one engine for the lunar landing and another for liftoff. Third crew member remains in the command module.

SATURN V ROCKET Everything below the lunar excursion module is the huge rocket itself.

THE SATURN V ROCKET The Saturn V was a multistage rocket whose sections can be seen to the above right. The bottom section, or "stage," had five main engines that propelled the rocket and spacecraft to an altitude of 37.9 miles (61 km) until the fuel in the tank above it ran out. Then this first stage was jettisoned, allowing the engines of the second stage to fire up, which accelerated the spacecraft to speeds approaching Earth orbital velocity. After the second stage was jettisoned, the third stage was used to boost the spacecraft to orbital velocity, and then again to break away from Earth orbit into a trajectory to the Moon.

HUMAN
ACHIEVEMENTS

CONTENTS

YOUNGEST ...

★**Alpine skier to win Olympic gold** Kjetil André Aamodt (Norway) won the first of his four career Olympic golds in Albertville, France, on February 16, 1992, aged 20 years 167 days.

F1 world champion Fernando Alonso (Spain) won his first Formula One World Championship title on September 25, 2005, at Interlagos, Brazil, aged 24 years 59 days.

★**Golfer to win a pro tournament** Ryo Ishikawa (Japan) was 15 years 245 days old when he won the Munsingwear Open KSB Cup at Tojigaoka Marine Hills Golf Club, Okayama, Japan, on May 20, 2007.

☆**Professor** Alia Sabur (U.S.A., b. February 22, 1989), was appointed as a full-time faculty professor in the Department of Advanced Technology Fusion at Konkuk University, Seoul, South Korea, in effect from February 19, 2008, aged 18 years 362 days.

★**Kitesurfing world champion (female)** Gisela Pulido (Spain) won her first Kiteboard Pro World Tour (KPWT) World Championship on November 4, 2004, aged 10 years 294 days. She won her first Professional Kiteboard Riders Association Championship on August 26, 2007, aged 13 years 224 days.

Nobel Peace Prize winner In 1992, Rigoberta Menchú Tum (Guatemala) was awarded the Nobel Peace Prize "in recognition of her work in social justice and ethnocultural reconciliation based on respect for the rights of indigenous people." At 33, she was the first indigenous person, and the youngest person ever, to receive this honor.

Pool world champion Chia-ching Wu (Taiwan) was 16 years 121 days old when he won the pool world championship title in Kaohsiung, Taiwan, on June 10, 2005.

Rodeo world champion After more than four decades, Anne Lewis's (U.S.A.) rodeo record still stands. She was 10 years old when she won the WPRA barrel racing title in 1968. In this event, the rider has to successfully maneuver their horse in a clover-leaf pattern around three barrels.

X-REF

Does golf suit you to a tee? Then putter across to p. 366 in the Sports section for more golf stats.

> ### *"Facebook has 52 million active users, and could have 200 million users by the end of 2008."*
>
> *www.portfolio.com, November 2007*

☆**Wearer of a full set of dentures** Daniel Sanchez-Ruiz (UK) was given a full set of dentures on February 25, 2005, at the age of 3 years and 301 days. He lost his teeth due to a condition called hypohidrotic ectodermal dysplasia.

☆**BILLIONAIRE The youngest U.S. dollar billionaire is Mark Zuckerberg (U.S.A., b. May 14, 1984) who had an estimated net worth of $1.5 billion (£756 million) when listed on Forbes.com on March 5, 2008, aged 23 years 296 days. Mr. Zuckerberg is the CEO of the social networking site Facebook, which he founded in February 2004.**

★**HEAD OF STATE At the age of 26 years, on April 30, 1992, Valentine Strasser (Sierra Leone) assumed control of his country following a military coup. Strasser became head of state on May 7, 1992, and ruled until he was ousted from power on January 16, 1996.**

Human Achievements

☆ **TRAVELER TO ALL SEVEN CONTINENTS** Thomas Lucian Staff (UK) was born on January 14, 2006. On January 4, 2007, aged 355 days, he visited Antarctica—the seventh continent since his birth. With his parents, Neil Staff and Susan Crawford, Thomas visited Asia (Apr. 14–19), North America (Jun. 8–13), Australia (Sep. 2–9), Europe (Oct. 20–22), Africa (Nov. 30–Dec. 12), South America (Dec. 29, 2006–Jan. 11, 2007), and Antarctica (Jan. 4–8).

★ YOUNGEST SPORTSPEOPLE ★

RECORD HOLDER	YOUNGEST...	AGE
Kim Yun-Mi (South Korea)	Team Olympic gold medalist	13 years 85 days
Marjorie Gestring (U.S.A.)	Individual Olympic gold medalist	13 years 268 days
Souleymane Mamam (Togo)	World Cup soccer player (qualifier)	13 years 310 days
Hasan Raza (Pakistan)	Cricket test player	14 years 227 days
Charlotte Dod (UK)	Wimbledon ladies' singles tennis champion	15 years 285 days
Martina Hingis (Switzerland)	Australian Open ladies' singles tennis champion	16 years 117 days
Monica Seles (U.S.A. b. Yugoslavia)	French Open ladies' singles tennis champion	16 years 169 days
Tracy Austin (U.S.A.)	U.S. Open ladies' singles tennis champion	16 years 271 days
Rodney W. Heath (Australia)	Australian Open men's singles tennis champion	17 years
Norman Whiteside (UK)	World Cup soccer player (finals)	17 years 41 days
Michael Chang (U.S.A.)	French Open men's singles tennis champion	17 years 109 days
Boris Becker (Germany)	Wimbledon men's singles tennis champion	17 years 227 days
Jermaine O'Neal (U.S.A.)	NBA player	18 years 53 days
Fred Lindstrom (U.S.A.)	World Series baseball player	18 years 339 days
Pete Sampras (U.S.A.)	U.S. Open men's singles tennis champion	19 years 28 days
Marco Andretti (U.S.A.)	Indycar race winner	19 years 167 days
Henri Cornet (France)	Tour de France winner	19 years 350 days

★ HOLE-IN-ONE GOLFER (FEMALE)
Soona Lee-Tolley (U.S.A.) was only
5 years 103 days old when she hit a
hole-in-one at the par 3 seventh at
Manhattan Woods Golf Club, West
Nyack, New York, U.S.A. on July 1,
2007.

☆ CLUB DJ DJ Jack Hill (UK, b. May 20, 2000) played at CK's Bar and
Club in Weston-super-Mare, UK, on August 26, 2007, aged 7 years and
98 days. Jack, who started DJing when he was only three, has his own
full-size decks, but has to stand on a box to reach the controls.

OLDEST...

Oldest hole-in-one golfer Otto Bucher (Switzerland, b. May 12, 1885)
achieved a hole-in-one on the 130-yd. (119-m) 12th hole at La Manga GC in
Spain on January 13, 1985. At the time, he was aged 99 years 244 days.

Human Achievements

★ **OLDEST PRIMARY SCHOOL STUDENT** Kimani Ng'ang'a Maruge (Kenya) enrolled at Kapkenduiyo Primary School, Eldoret, Kenya, on January 12, 2004, aged 84. On April 6, 2004, Ng'ang'a passed his first end-of-term exams with straight As in English, Kiswahili, and math.

★**Alpine skiing Olympic gold medalist** Kjetil André Aamodt (Norway, b. September 2, 1971) won his fourth alpine skiing Olympic gold medal in Turin, Italy, on February 18, 2006, aged 34 years 169 days.

Professional bull rider Adriano Moraes (Brazil, b. April 10, 1970) competed in the 2005 Professional Bull Riders World Finals aged 35.

Sports record breaker Gerhard Weidner (West Germany, b. March 15, 1933) set a record 20-mile-walk time of 2 hr. 30 min. 38.6 sec. on May 25, 1974, aged 41 years 71 days. He is the oldest sportsperson to set an official world record that is open to all ages and recognized by an international governing body.

★**Person to ski to both Poles** Norbert H. Kern (Germany, b. July 26, 1940 skied to the South Pole on January 18, 2007, and the North Pole on April 27, 2007, aged 66 years 275 days.

☆**Lifeguard** Edwin McCarthy (U.S.A., b. April 8, 1925) has worked as a lifeguard since 1992.

☆**Current monarch** Abdullah bin Abdulaziz Al-Saud, the King of Saudi Arabia, was born in August 1924 and became the oldest living monarch on May 11, 2007, aged 82 years 253 days.

☆ **OLDEST SHOWGIRL** Dorothy Kloss (U.S.A., b. October 27, 1923) regularly performs in the chorus line of The Fabulous Palm Springs Follies, Palm Springs, California, U.S.A.

Newly appointed chief of state
After the German invasion of France in 1940, Henri Philipe Pétain (1856–1951) was recalled to active military service as adviser to the minister of war. On June 16, 1940, aged 84, he succeeded Paul Reynaud as premier of France.

★ **Oldest ballet dancer (male)** The oldest male ballet dancer is Frank Russell Galey (U.S.A., b. September 7, 1932) who was aged 74 years and 101 days at this latest performance in *The Nutcracker* with Mendocino Ballet, Ukiah, California, U.S.A., on December 17, 2006.

Nobel laureate In 1966, Professor Francis Peyton Rous (U.S.A., 1879–1970) shared in the physiology or medicine prize, aged 87.

★ **College graduate** Allan Stewart (Australia, b. March 7, 1915) received a Bachelor of Laws degree aged 91 years and 214 days when he graduated from the University of New England, New South Wales, Australia, on October 7, 2006.

Bank robber J. L. Hunter Rountree (U.S.A., b. 1911) admitted stealing $1,999 from a bank in Texas, U.S.A., and was sentenced to 151 months in prison on January 3, 2004, aged 92.

Rountree, nicknamed Red, said he had robbed his first bank when he was around 80 years of age because he wanted revenge on banks for sending him into a financial crisis.

★ **OLDEST BAND** The Peace Old Jazz band comprises six veteran musicians whose average age is 76 (as of November 2007). They have performed every night for over 20 years in Shanghai, China.

"Dirty, badly dressed, and disagreeable!"

*Jeanne Louise Calment, the oldest person ever,
on the artist Vincent van Gogh, whom she knew*

☆**Best man** Gerald W. Pike (U.S.A., b. October 12, 1910) was best man at the marriage of Nancy Lee Joustra and Clifford Claire Hill (both U.S.A.), aged 93 years 166 days, on March 26, 2004, in Kent County, Michigan, U.S.A.

☆**Billionaire** The oldest living U.S. dollar billionaire is John Simplot (U.S.A., b. January 4, 1909), who had a net worth valued at $3.2 billion when listed by Forbes on March 8, 2007, aged 98 years 63 days. Mr. Simplot of Boise, Idaho, U.S.A., made his fortune in agriculture, notably in potato products.

★**Professional artist** Moses Aleksandrovich Feigin (Russia, b. October 23, 1904) held his last exhibition at the Central House of the Artist in

★ OLDEST SPORTSPEOPLE ★

NAME/NATIONALITY	OLDEST...	AGE
Firmin Lambot (Belgium)	Tour de France winner	36 years 4 months
Kenneth Robert Rosewall (Australia)	Australian Open men's singles tennis champion	37 years 62 days
William Larned (U.S.A.)	U.S. Open men's singles tennis champion	38 years 242 days
P. J. "Babe" McDonald (U.S.A.)	Olympic athletics gold medallist (25.4 kg weight throw)	42 years 26 days
Albert Roger Milla (Cameroon)	FIFA World Cup player and scorer	42 years 39 days
Robert Parish (U.S.A.)	NBA basketball player	43 years 231 days
W. H. "Billy" Meredith (UK)	International football player	45 years 229 days
Juan Manuel Fangio (Argentina)	F1 world champion	46 years 41 days
Martina Navratilova (U.S.A.)	Wimbledon tennis champion	46 years 261 days
Tebbs Lloyd Johnson (UK)	Olympic athletics medallist (50,000 m walk)	48 years 115 days
Wilfred Rhodes (UK)	Test cricket player	52 years 165 days
Louis Alexandre Chiron (Monaco)	F1 Grand Prix driver	55 years 292 days
Leroy "Satchel" Page (U.S.A.)	Baseball player	59 years 80 days
Oscar Swahn (Sweden)	Olympic gold medallist (Running Deer shooting team)	64 years 258 days
Julia Jones (UK)	Hockey player	71 years
Tércio Mariano de Rezende (Brazil)	Football player	b. December 31, 1921
Arthur Sweeney (UK)	Table tennis player	88 years
Dimitrion Yordanidis (Greece)	Marathon runner	98 years
José Guadalupe Leal Lemus (Mexico)	Tennis player	b. December 13, 1902

★ **OLDEST BARBER** Anthony Mancinelli (U.S.A., b. March 2, 1911) has been a practicing barber since 1924. Mr. Mancinelli continues to work today at the age of 97 years.

Moscow, Russia, from April 27 to May 10, 2007. At the time, he was 102 years 199 days old.

Prisoner Bill Wallace (Australia, 1881–1989) was the oldest prisoner on record, having spent the final 63 years of his life in Aradale Psychiatric Hospital in Ararat, Victoria, Australia, after killing a man in December 1925. He remained there until his death on July 17, 1989, shortly before his 108th birthday. Once asked why he was in prison, he replied: "There was a man ... Well, to tell you the truth, I don't know."

Actress Jeanne Louise Calment (France, 1875–1997) portrayed herself at the age of 114 in the movie *Vincent and Me* (Canada, 1990)—a modern-day fantasy about a young girl who travels back through time to the 19th century to meet the artist Vincent van Gogh. Calment, the **oldest person** whose age has been fully authenticated (see p. 107), is regarded as the last living person to have known van Gogh.

DON'T TRY THIS AT HOME

★ **Longest underwater submergence** Ronny Frimann (Norway) remained under water for 4 days and 4 hours (100 hours in total), from June 14 to 18, 2007, to raise cash for the World Wildlife Fund. During the sub-

★HIGHEST STACK OF CHAIRS
Luo Jun (China), from the Zun Yi Acrobatic Group, successfully balanced on 11 stacked chairs on the set of *Zheng Da Zong Yi— Guinness World Records Special* in Beijing, China, on September 15, 2007.

mergence in a water tank at the Central Station in Oslo, Norway, he wore a diving drysuit and helmet equipped with a catheter and tubes for nutritional fluids and air supply. During the feat, he lost 16 lb. 8 oz. (7.5 kg).

☆**Sharing a bathtub with the most rattlesnakes** Jackie Bibby (U.S.A.), a.k.a. The Texas Snake Man, sat in a bathtub with 87 snakes on November 5, 2007, in Dublin, Texas, U.S.A., for 45 minutes as part of GWR Day.

☆**Longest time to hold one's breath** On February 23, 2008, Tom Sietas (Germany) held his breath voluntarily for 16 min. 13 sec. in a swimming pool on the set of *Lo Show dei Record* in Madrid, Spain.

☆**Longest time spent on a bed of nails** The duration record for lying on a bed of nails—with sharp 6-in. (15.2-cm) nails placed 2 in. (5 cm) apart—is 300 hours by Ken Owen (UK) from May 3 to 14, 1986. The longest uninterrupted stretch of lying down lasted 132 hr. 30 min.!

★**Heaviest weight lifted with glue** A Ford pick-up truck weighing 9,127 lb. 2 oz. (4,140 kg) was lifted for one hour by a crane, suspended on a 2-in.-diameter (7-cm) steel cylinder, which had been glued together one hour earlier using nine drops of the commercially available household adhesive "UHU Alleskleber Super Strong & Safe" in Bühl, Germany, on October 11, 2007.

★**Heaviest train pulled by rice-bowl suction on the stomach** By pressing a rice bowl on to his abdominal muscles, Zhang Xingquan (China)

X-REF

Still got an appetite for eccentricity? Then seek out **Bizarre Behavior** (pp. 153–157). But if you're in search of truly heroic acts, our **Spirit of Adventure** chapter (pp. 167–190) boasts a host of admirable feats.

☆ **GREATEST WEIGHT TO BALANCE ON TEETH**
On May 17, 2007, Frank Simon (U.S.A.) balanced a refrigerator weighing 140 lb. (63.5 kg) on his teeth for a duration of 10 seconds on the set of the *Circo Massimo Show* in Rome, Italy.

created enough suction to pull a 79,700-lb. (36.15-ton) train for 131 ft. 2 in. (40 m) in Dehai City, Jilin Province, China, on August 3, 2007.

★**Most iron bars broken by the head**
Wang Xianfa (China) broke 26 iron bars on his head on the set of *Zheng Da Zong Yi—Guinness World Records Special* in Beijing, China, on September 18, 2007.

Strangest diet Michel Lotito (France, 1950–2006), a.k.a. Monsieur Mangetout, started eating metal and glass in 1959. Gastroenterologists X-rayed his stomach and described his ability to consume 2 lb. (900 g) of metal per day as unique. His diet since 1966 included 18 bicycles, 15 supermarket carts, seven TV sets, six chandeliers, two beds, a pair of skis, a computer and even a Cessna light aircraft! He is said to have provided the only example in history of a coffin (handles and all) ending up *inside* a man. Despite his strong stomach—the lining was twice as thick as normal—he couldn't bear to eat boiled eggs!

★**MOST TIMES HIT BY A CAR** Dietmar Löffler (Germany) was hit eight times by a car in two minutes on the set of *Guinness World Records: Die Größten Weltrekorde* in Cologne, Germany, on November 23, 2007.

"Over a period of 40 years, Michel Lotito literally ate about 9 tons of metal."

Craig Glenday, Editor-in-Chief, Guinness World Records

Deadliest magic trick At least 12 people have been killed during the bullet-catching trick, in which a gun loaded with a marked bullet is fired at the magician, who apparently catches the bullet in his teeth. Even though the feat involves illusionary elements, it is fraught with danger.

☆**Longest motorcycle ride through a tunnel of fire** Clint Ewing (U.S.A.) successfully rode a motorcycle through a tunnel of fire measuring 200 ft. (60.96 m) long at Universal City, Los Angeles, U.S.A., on January 27, 2008. The daredevil record was being staged for the NBC TV special *Guinness World Records Live—The Top 100*.

☆**Highest flame blown by a fire-breather** Tim Black (Australia) blew a flame 23 ft. 7 in. (7.2 m) high on the set of *Zheng Da Zong Yi—Guinness World Records Special* in Beijing, China, on September 15, 2007.

☆**Farthest fire-walk** Trever McGhee (Canada) walked 597 ft. (181.9 m) over embers with a temperature of between 1,214°F and 1,307°F (657.67°C–853.33°C) at Symons Valley Rodeo Grounds, Calgary, Alberta, Canada, on November 9, 2007.

☆**Longest wall of fire** On September 16, 2007, Rich's Incredible Pyro (U.S.A.) created a wall of fire 6,636 ft. (2,022 m) long during the Terre Haute Air Fair in Terre Haute, Indiana, U.S.A.

★**POWER DRILL ROTATIONS** The Guy Hiang (Germany) performed 141 rotations in one minute, while hanging from a power drill, on the set of *Guinness World Records: Die Größten Weltrekorde* in Cologne, Germany, on September 1, 2007.

☆ **MOST PEOPLE FIRE-BREATHING AT ONCE** At an event organized by TSV D'artagnan and De Rooie Sok, 115 people performed a simultaneous display of fire-breathing on the Heuvelplein in Tilburg, the Netherlands, on March 14, 2007.

☆ **GREATEST WEIGHT LIFTED BY BEARD** Antanas Kontrimas (Lithuania) lifted a 139-lb. 5-oz. (63.2-kg) woman about 3 feet off the ground on the set of *Zheng Da Zong Yi—Guinness World Records Special* in Beijing, China, on September 16, 2007.

DO TRY THIS AT HOME

FASTEST TIME TO . . .

☆ **Pop 1,000 balloons** OC&C Strategy Consultants (UK) popped 1,000 balloons in 8.78 seconds during its annual International Training Week in Barcelona, Spain, on September 8, 2007.

LONGEST TIME TO SPIN A FRYING PAN ON ONE FINGER Anders Björklund (Sweden) was able to spin a frying pan on his finger for 14 minutes on the set of *Guinness Rekord TV,* Stockholm, Sweden, on November 29, 2001.

★**Model five balloon sculptures** blindfolded On February 16, 2008, Daniele Bottalico, a.k.a. "Mago Ciccio" (Italy), created five balloon sculptures blindfolded in 1 min. 24 sec. on the set of the Guinness World Records program *Lo Show Dei Record,* in Madrid, Spain.

☆**Hop 100 m on one leg** Rommell Griffith (Barbados) hopped 100 m in 15.57 seconds at the Barbados World Record Festival at the Barbados National Stadium, St. Michael, on March 31, 2007.

☆**Complete a 100 m piggyback race** The record time for the fastest piggyback race over 100 m is 16.97 seconds. It was set by Rommell Griffith, carrying Ulinda Griffith (both Barbados), as part of the Barbados World Record Festival at the Barbados National Stadium on March 31, 2007.

MOST ...

☆**Apples bobbed in one minute** Ashrita Furman (U.S.A.) bobbed 32 apples in one minute in Jamaica, New York City, U.S.A., on June 11, 2007.

X-REF

The human body is a fantastic creation, whether it's performing crazy feats or not. For some absolutely amazing anatomical facts and statistics, check out the **Being Human** chapter (pp. 73–110).

MOST YO-YOS SPUN AT ONCE Eric Lindeen (Sweden) was able to keep a total of nine yo-yos spinning simultaneously on hooks at the Gallerian Shopping Center, Stockholm, Sweden, on November 4, 2006.

☆**Bananas peeled and eaten in one minute** Christopher "Big Black" Boykin (U.S.A.) successfully peeled and ate three bananas on MTV's *The Rob & Big Show* in Los Angeles, California, U.S.A., on September 17, 2007.

☆**MOST DECKS OF PLAYING CARDS MEMORIZED** Dave Farrow (Canada) memorized, on a single sighting, a random sequence of 59 separate card packs (3,068 cards in all) at CTV Studios, The Daily Planet, Toronto, Canada, on April 2, 2007.

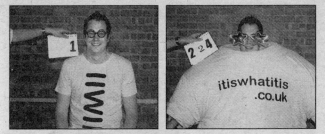

☆ **MOST T-SHIRTS WORN AT ONCE** Charlie Williams (UK) put on a combined total of 224 T-shirts in an attempt organized by itiswhatitis Ltd., at St. Antony's Catholic Primary School in Woodford Green, Essex, UK, on September 14, 2007.

PEERLESS PUZZLERS

RUBIK'S CUBE

Fastest time to solve: 9.55 seconds, by Ron van Bruchem (Netherlands), on November 24, 2007.

Fastest time to solve blindfolded: 41.16 seconds, by Chen Danyang (China), on October 28, 2007.

BEDLAM CUBE

★ **Fastest time to assemble**: 7.77 seconds, by Aleksander Iljasov (Norway), on September 28, 2007.

★ **Fastest time to assemble blindfolded**: 36.41 seconds, by Danny Bamping (UK), on November 8, 2007.

GWR HASBRO PUZZLE

Fastest completion: 14 min. 58 sec. by Elaine Lewis (UK), on June 11, 2007.

TETRIS

★ **Smallest game**: played (with a microscope) using tetraminoes made of tiny glass spheres, at Vrije University, Amsterdam, the Netherlands, in November 2002. Each block measured 1 micrometer (0.001 mm) across.

☆ **LARGEST RUBBER-BAND BALL** Bryce, Tanner, Austin, Nicole, and Steve Milton (U.S.A.) created a rubber-band ball that weighed 4,594 lb. (2,083.8 kg). The outsized orb was measured in Chicago, Illinois, U.S.A., on November 21, 2006.

★**Longest string of apple pips** The largest string of apple pips is 250 m (820 ft.) long and was completed by Zdzislawa Szydlowska (Poland) on May 28, 2001.

☆**Eggs held in one hand** On December 20, 2007, Zdenek Bradac (Czech Republic) managed to hold a total of 20 eggs in one hand at the same time at Sheffield Castle College, in South Yorkshire, UK.

☆**Balloon sculptures in an hour** John Cassidy (U.S.A.) made 747 balloon shapes in one hour at Buck County Community College in Newtown, Pennsylvania, U.S.A., on November 14, 2007.

★**Spoons twisted in one minute** On December 18, 2006, Kong Tai (China) twisted five spoons 180 degrees in one minute, bare-handed, in Beijing, China.

FEATS OF STRENGTH

☆**Greatest weight lifted with an ear** Zafar Gill (Pakistan) lifted gym weights totaling 136 lb. (61.7 kg), which were hanging from a clamp at-

★ **BUS PULLING WITH THE EARS** Manjit Singh (UK) pulled a single-decker bus a record 20 ft. (6.1 m) on cables attached to his ears, to raise money for the Manjit Fitness Academy at the Loughborough Tesco in Loughborough, UK, on March 31, 2008.

tached to his right ear, during the event Vienna Recordia, in Vienna, Austria, on September 30, 2007.

Greatest weight lifted with teeth Walter Arfeuille (Belgium) lifted weights totaling 620 lb. 10 oz. (281.5 kg) a distance of 6.75 in. (17 cm) off the ground with his teeth in Paris, France, on March 31, 1990.

★ **Greatest weight lifted by the neck** Frank Ciavattone (U.S.A.) lifted a weight of 808 lb. (366.5 kg), supported by his neck, at the New England Weightlifting Club in Walpole, Massachusetts, U.S.A., on November 15, 2005.

MANJIT'S MANY STRENGTHS

Manjit Singh (UK) holds several records, all of which involve great strength and stamina. He enjoys setting records not only for a sense of personal achievement but also to raise money for charity. This and the one pictured above are his latest achievements:

☆ **SQUAT LIFTING**

Manjit set the record for the **most weight squat lifted in one hour** by one person, achieving 66,998.48 lb. (30,390 kg) at Montee Hair and Beauty Salon in Leicester, UK, on December 20, 2007.

★**LONGEST TIME RESTRAINING A CAR AT FULL THROTTLE** Franz Müllner (Austria) restrained a Lamborghini Diablo—a car with an output of over 400 hp—driving away from him at full throttle, for seven seconds on the set of *Die Größten Weltrekorde* in Cologne, Germany, on September 1, 2007.

☆**Heaviest boat pulled** George Olesen (Denmark) pulled a 22.7-million lb. (10,300-metric ton) passenger ferry for 16 ft. 8.8 in. (5.1 m) at Gothenburg Ferry Terminal, Gothenburg, Sweden, in June 2000.

Heaviest elephant lifted In 1975, while performing with Gerry Cottle's Circus (UK), Khalil Oghaby (Iran) lifted an elephant that weighed approximately 4,409 lb. (2 metric tons) off the ground. He stood on a platform above the animal and raised it by means of a harness.

★**Heaviest deadlift** Andy Bolton (UK) deadlifted 1,003 lb. (455 kg) at the World Powerlifting Organization Semi-Finals in Lake George, New York, U.S.A., on November 4, 2006.

☆**Heaviest deadlift with the little finger** Using just his little finger, Kristian Holm (Norway) deadlifted 210 lb. 3 oz. (95.38 kg) in Herefoss, Norway, on March 24, 2007.

☆**Heaviest vehicle pulled over 100 ft.** Powerlifting pastor Rev. Kevin Fast (Canada) pulled a vehicle weighing 125,680 lb. (57,000 kg) over a level 100-ft. (30.48-m) course in Cobourg, Ontario, Canada, on May 12, 2007.

Heaviest weight dangled from a swallowed sword Matthew Henshaw (Australia) swallowed a non-retractable 1-ft. 3.9-in. (40.5-cm) long sword and then held a sack of potatoes weighing 44 lb. 5 oz. (20.1 kg) attached to the handle of the sword for five seconds at the studios of *Guinness World Records* in Sydney, New South Wales, Australia, on April 16, 2005.

★ Franz Müllner (Austria, pictured above) also holds the record for the **longest time restraining a truck at full throttle**. On November 3, 2007, Franz held back a 400 hp truck for 8.40 seconds on the set of *Zheng Da Zong Yi—Guinness World Records Special* in Beijing, China.

HIGHEST BEER-KEG TOSS Heini Koivuniemi (Finland, pictured) threw a 27-lb. 1-oz. (12.3-kg) beer keg over a bar set at a height of 11 ft. 4.2 in. (3.46 m) on the set of *Guinness World Records* in Helsinki, Finland, on August 9, 2001—the **highest beer-keg toss by a woman.** Juha Rasanen (Finland) threw a 27-lb. 1-oz. (12.3-kg) beer keg over a bar at a height of 23 ft. 3 in. (7.1 m) on August 26, 2005—the **highest beer-keg toss by a man.**

CONCRETE BLOCK-BUSTER The record for the ☆ **most concrete blocks broken in one minute** is 386, achieved by Eduardo Estrada (Mexico) at the University of Coahuila in Saltillo, Coahuila, Mexico, on November 22, 2007.

FASTEST 10-M DASH CARRYING A TABLE AND WEIGHT IN THE MOUTH
Letting only his teeth take the strain, Georges Christen (Luxembourg) successfully carried a woman sitting on a table over a distance of 10 m (32 ft. 9 in.) in 7.5 seconds on the set of *L'Été de Tous Les Records* in La Tranche Sur Mer, France, on July 28, 2004.

INSPIRATIONAL ACTS

CHARITY AUCTIONS: MOST EXPENSIVE . . .

Calendar "To Touch an Angel's Wings," a wall calendar designed for the Muir Maxwell Trust epilepsy charity, sold at a charity auction for £15,000 ($26,100) on December 10, 2005, to Stephen Winyard (UK) of Stobo Castle Health Spa, Peeblesshire, UK.

Telephone number An anonymous Qatari bidder paid 10 million QAR ($2.75 million) for the cell phone number 666-6666 during a charity auction hosted by Qatar Telecom in Doha, Qatar, on May 23, 2006.

Guitar A Fender Stratocaster guitar signed by a host of music legends including Mick Jagger, Eric Clapton, and Paul McCartney (all UK) sold for $2.7 million at a charity auction for Reach Out To Asia at the Ritz-Carlton Hotel, Doha, Qatar, on November 17, 2005. The Reach Out To Asia campaign seeks to support worthy causes around the world, with particular emphasis on the Asian continent.

> **"I ran my first marathon aged 71, and will keep going as long as my legs keep carrying me!"**
>
> *Jenny Wood-Allen, oldest female to complete a marathon (91!)*

CHARITY WORK

☆**Largest fund-raising event held annually** Held every year around the streets of London, UK, the Flora London Marathon is the largest annual charity fund-raiser. The 2007 race, held on April 22, generated the most money to date, with £46.5 million ($91.9 million) accumulated by 24,750 runners for numerous charities. In the 11 London Marathons held between 1996 and 2006, the average amount raised per event was £28,027,550 ($53,318,770).

★**Most breast milk donated** Erica Hines from Port Orange, Florida, U.S.A., has donated 4,581 fl. oz. (135.5 liters) of breast milk to WakeMed Mother's Milk Bank in Raleigh, North Carolina, U.S.A., as of June 8, 2007.

☆**Longest concert by a group** The Comaganin Raaga Priya Light Music Orchestra played continuously for 50 hours for the visually impaired in Chennai, India, on April 27–29, 2007.

Most lives saved by a parrot In December 1999, a gray parrot named Charlie woke his owner, Patricia Tunnicliffe (UK), when her home in Durham, UK, caught on fire. The bird began to squawk frantically as the flames in the front room took hold, which woke Ms. Tunnicliffe and gave her time to get her five children out of the house unharmed. Sadly, Charlie was not so lucky and died in the inferno.

☆**MOST MONEY RAISED BY A MARATHON RUNNER** Steve Chalke (UK) raised £1,841,138 ($3,669,325) for the Oasis UK charity by completing the Flora London Marathon, in London, UK, on April 22, 2007.

MOST MONEY RAISED BY A CHARITY RUN
The greatest amount of money raised by a charity run or walk is Can$24.7 million ($20.7 million) by Terry Fox (Canada, 1958–1981). Terry, who had an artificial leg, ran from St. John's, Newfoundland, to Thunder Bay, Ontario, Canada, in 143 days from April 12 to September 2, 1980. He covered 3,339 miles (5,373 km).

LARGEST FUND-RAISING CHARITY The Salvation Army, U.S.A., has raised more funds annually than any other charity for 10 consecutive years. In 2001 alone, the charity raised $1.39 billion, down from $1.44 billion in 2000. In the U.S.A., The Salvation Army has 1.6 million dedicated volunteers. Lay members who subscribe to the doctrines of The Salvation Army are called soldiers, and, along with officers, they are also known as Salvationists.

LARGEST SIMULTANEOUS ROCK CONCERT TV AUDIENCE Live Aid, the world's largest simultaneous charity rock concert in terms of viewers, was organized by Bob Geldof (Ireland). Held in London, UK, and Philadelphia, U.S.A., on July 13, 1985, over 60 of rock's biggest acts played for free to 1.5 billion TV viewers throughout the world in order to raise money for African famine relief.

RESCUERS

Most people rescued at sea (civilians) On January 23, 1946, the crew of the cargo ship USS *Brevard* (AK-164), commanded by Lt. John Elliott (U.S.A.), rescued 4,296 Japanese civilians whose ship, the *Enoshima Maru,* was sinking after hitting a mine off Shanghai, China.

Most celebrated canine rescuer The most famous canine rescuer of all time is a St. Bernard called Barry, who lived from 1800 to 1814. Barry rescued more than 40 people during a career on the Swiss Alps that spanned 12 years. One of the life-saving dog's more celebrated rescues was that of a boy who lay half frozen under an avalanche in which his mother had died. Barry spread himself across the boy's body to warm him, licked the young-ster's face until he woke up and then carried him to the nearest dwelling.

FACT

The **largest live audience for a simultaneous rock concert** is an estimated one million people for Live 8, held at venues in 10 cities around the world, including London, Philadelphia, Paris, Johannesburg, Berlin, Rome, and Moscow on July 2, 2005.

OLDEST LIFESAVING ORGANIZATION The Royal National Lifeboat Institution (RNLI), a British lifesaving group, was formed by royal edict in March 1824 and celebrated its 180th anniversary in 2004. In 2006, an average of 22 people were rescued each day.

MOST DECORATED WAR HERO Audie Murphy (U.S.A., 1924–71) was the most decorated soldier in American history, winning 24 medals from the Congressional Medal of Honor down. His exploits were the subject of the movie *To Hell and Back* (U.S.A., 1956), in which he starred as himself (above).

BIZARRE BEHAVIOR

★**Farthest distance traveled by "the worm" move** James Rubec (Canada) traveled 108 ft. 9 in. (33.14 m) using "the worm" at the Rogers Centre in Toronto, Canada, on November 9, 2007, as part of Guinness World Records Day 2007. To perform the worm, a breakdance move, you lie flat on the ground and propel yourself forward with a rippling motion of the body.

☆**Largest underwater press conference** At a press conference organized by Eric J. Pittman (Canada) to promote the release of his new book *Emails from a Nut!!!*, 61 journalists dived to a depth of 32 ft. 10 in. (10 m) at Crystal Pool in Victoria, British Columbia, Canada, on November 4, 2006.

☆**Largest custard pie fight** A total of 105 participants flung flan at a pie fight organized by Camp Toukley in New South Wales, Australia, on July 11, 2007.

☆**Fastest time to push an orange one mile with the nose** Ashrita Furman took 22 min. 41 sec. to push an orange one mile with his nose at the Green Acres Mall in Valley Stream, New York, U.S.A., on November 2, 2007.

★**Largest robot dance** On September 17, 2007, 276 students at the University of Kent (UK) dressed as robots and danced for a minimum of five minutes in Canterbury, Kent, UK.

LONGEST FULL-BODY BURN Ted A. Batchelor (U.S.A.), a professional stuntman with a lifelong love of fire, endured a full-body burn—without any oxygen supply—for 2 min. 38 sec. on an island at Ledges Quarry Park in Nelson, Ohio, U.S.A., on July 17, 2004.

☆ **FARTHEST DISTANCE TRAVELED UNDERWATER BY POGO STICK** Ashrita Furman (U.S.A.) jumped 1,680 ft. (512.06 m) underwater on a pogo stick at the Nassau County Aquatic Center in East Meadow, New York, U.S.A., on August 1, 2007.

☆**Longest human suction suspension by the stomach** By pressing a rice bowl to his abdominal muscles, Li Kangle (China) was able to create enough suction to suspend himself from a helicopter on a rope for 7 min. 6 sec. in Pingyi County, Shandong Province, China. The record was attempted for *Zheng Da Zong Yi—Guinness World Records Special* in Beijing, China, on September 6, 2007.

★ **FASTEST MALE PANTOMIME HORSE** Charles Astor and Tristan Williams (both UK) ran 100 m in a time of 13.51 seconds . . . remaining inside a pantomime horse costume! Charles (front) and Tristan (rear) competed in an event organized by the advertising agency Claydon Heeley Jones Mason at Harrow School in Harrow-on-the-Hill, Middlesex, UK, on August 18, 2005. On the same day, a record was set for the **fastest female pantomime horse**—18.13 seconds—by Samantha Kavanagh (front) and Melissa Archer (rear).

★ HEAVIEST OBJECT SWORD-SWALLOWED Thomas Blackthorne (UK) swallowed the 1-in.-thick (25-mm) drill bit of a Dewalt D25980 demolition hammer weighing 83 lb. 12 oz. (38 kg), then held the full weight of the hammer and bit for over three seconds, on the set of *Guinness World Records: Die Größten Weltrekorde* in Cologne, Germany, on November 23, 2007.

MOST...

★ MOST PEOPLE PERFORMING FULL-BODY BURNS Thomas Hangarter and his team (all Germany) performed 10 simultaneous full-body burns on the set of *Guinness World Records—Die Größten Weltrekorde* in Cologne, Germany, on September 1, 2007.

> *"I've set 183 Guinness World Records, 76 of which are still current and unbeaten. Bizarre? Maybe to you ... To me, it attests to the limitless capabilities of the human spirit."*
>
> **Ashrita Furman, holder of the most GWRs**

★**Clothespins clipped on a hand in one minute** Mohammed Ahmed Elkhouly (UAE) pinned 48 clothespins to one of his hands at Bab Al Shams Desert Resort & Spa in Dubai, UAE, on April 21, 2007.

☆**People wearing Groucho Marx glasses** A group of 3,459 people donned plastic Groucho Marx glasses (to resemble the famous American comedian) at an event organized by the United Way of the Columbia-Willamette in Hillsboro, Oregon, U.S.A., on August 4, 2007.

★**Kilts worn** While guest-hosting *The New Paul O'Grady Show* on November 7, 2007, Lorraine Kelly (UK) donned three kilts, one at a time, in a minute at the London Studios, UK.

☆ **MOST SNAILS ON THE FACE** Alastair Galpin (New Zealand) held eight snails on his face for 10 seconds at The Warehouse store in Sylvia Park, Auckland, New Zealand, on October 27, 2007. On the same occasion, he set the record for the ★ **most T-shirts torn in one minute** (nine).

Previously, Galpin had achieved the ★ **most gloves worn on one hand** (seven) at The Old Homestead Community House in Auckland on May 11, 2006; and, on April 28, 2007, at the same venue, he set the record for the ☆ **most rubber bands stretched over the face** (62).

★ **MOST TOILET SEAT LIDS BROKEN** Kevin Shelley (U.S.A.) broke 46 wooden toilet seat lids with his head on the set of the TV show *Guinness World Records: Die Größten Weltrekorde* in Cologne, Germany, on September 1, 2007.

★ **People dressed as sea animals** A total of 5,590 participants dressed as sea animals for an event held in Shenjiamen Fishing Harbor, Zhoushan City, Zhejiang Province, China, on August 10, 2007.

☆ **Underpants worn** Joel Nathan (Australia) was able to pull on 20 pairs of underpants in one minute at the Paramount Nightclub in Perth, Australia, on July 27, 2007.

★ **Eggs smashed with the head** Osi Anyanwu (UK) smashed 40 eggs against his head in one minute on *The New Paul O'Grady Show* in London, UK, on November 7, 2007.

SOLO PERFORMANCE

FASTEST . . .

☆ **Escape from a straitjacket** Matt the Knife (U.S.A.) took just 18.80 seconds to escape from a regulated straitjacket at the Media Center Hotel in Beijing, China, on September 17, 2007.

Matt also holds the record for the ☆ **fastest time to escape from a straitjacket while submerged underwater,** after completing the task in 15.41

★FASTEST 100 M ON A HOPPITY HOP (FEMALE) On September 26, 2004, Dee McDougall (UK) covered 100 m (328 ft.) in 39.88 seconds while bouncing on a "space hopper" at the University of St. Andrews, Fife, UK.

seconds for *Zheng Da Zong Yi—Guinness World Records Special* in Beijing, China, on September 13, 2007.

☆**Frog jump (10 m)** Ashrita Furman (U.S.A.) frog jumped (i.e., holding his toes) 33 ft. (10 m) in 8.22 seconds in Jamaica, New York, U.S.A., on November 7, 2007.

★FASTEST TIME TO SKIP 5 KM WITHOUT A ROPE Ashrita Furman (U.S.A.) skipped a distance of 5 km (3.1 miles) without using a rope in a time of 35 min. 19 sec. at Wat Pa Luangta Yannasampanno Forest Monastery in Kanchanaburi, Thailand, on February 5, 2007. Ashrita's performance wasn't entirely solo—for part of his trip, he was joined by a tiger!

☆**Text message** On November 12, 2006, Ang Chuang Yang (Singapore) typed a set 160-character text on his cell phone in 41.52 seconds at the Suntec Convention Centre, Singapore.

☆**Balloon modeling behind the back** With his arms behind his back, Daniele Bottalico (Italy), a.k.a. Mago Ciccio, made a balloon poodle in 4.54 seconds in Cassano delle Murge, Bari, Italy, on November 10, 2007.

MOST . . .

☆**Head spins** Aichi Ono (Japan) performed 101 head spins in one minute on the set of *Zheng Da Zong Yi—Guinness World Records Special* in Beijing, China, on September 18, 2007.

☆**Kisses received** Adrian Chiles (UK) received 78 kisses in one minute on BBC 1's *The One Show* in London, UK, on November 8, 2007, in celebration of GWR Day.

★**Mental calculations** Chen Ranran (China) solved eight mental arithmetic problems in one minute on the set of *Zheng Da Zong Yi—Guinness*

CHAINSAW JUGGLING: MOST CATCHES In a dazzling display of bravado (some would say recklessness!), Aaron Gregg (Canada) was able to juggle three running chainsaws, making a total of 86 successful catches, in Portland, Oregon, U.S.A., on September 23, 2005. To those eager to replicate this at home (please don't!), the model used was an Echo CS-301.

MOST APPLES CHOPPED IN THE AIR USING A SWORD Martial arts master Kenneth Lee (U.S.A.) cut 23 apples in the air in one minute, using a samurai sword, on the set of *Live With Regis & Kelly* in New York City, U.S.A., on September 14, 2006.

World Records Special in Beijing, China, on November 2, 2007. Each calculation consisted of 11 numbers with a total of 120 digits. The calculations were supplied in a sealed envelope by the Abacus and Mental Arithmetics Federation.

☆ **Ducks and Drakes** "Ducks and Drakes," a.k.a. stone-skimming, -skipping, or -skiffing, involves throwing a smooth stone across a body of water in order to make it bounce across the surface. The record for the most consecutive skips of a stone on water is an incredible 51, held by Russell Byars (U.S.A.). His cast was achieved at Riverfront Park, Franklin, Pennsylvania, U.S.A., on July 19, 2007.

X-REF

You'll find a whole universe of space records elsewhere in *GWR 2009*. Lift off with **Space Technology** (p. 21), gaze at **Stars** (p. 3) and **Galaxies & Nebulas** (p. 6), visit **Heavenly Bodies** (p. 9), and have a close encounter with **Asteroids, Comets, & Meteors** (p. 14).

★ **MOST WOOD BLOCKS CHOPPED IN HALF** On November 23, 2007, Robert Ebner (Germany) chopped 70 wood blocks in half in one minute on the set of *Guinness World Records—Die Größten Weltrekorde* in Cologne, Germany.

MARATHONS

☆ **Drumming:** 85 hr. 30 min., Gery Jallo (Belgium), Pakenhof, Heverlee, Belgium, February 22–25, 2007.

★ **Beatboxing:** 24 hr. Michael Krappel (Austria), Vienna, Austria, September 30, 2007.

☆ **Karaoke:** 38 hr. 30 min. Thomas Brian Jones (UK), Vienna, Austria, September 30, 2007.

☆ **Keyboard playing:** 70 hr. 57 min., Patricia Jones (U.S.A.), Teresa's Piano Gallery, Jacksonville, Florida, U.S.A., November 12–15, 2007.

☆ **Singing:** 75 hr. Marcus LaPratt (U.S.A.), Heartland Health Care Center, Allen Park, Michigan, U.S.A., August 28–31, 2007.

☆ **Upside-down juggling (three objects):** 2 min. 11 sec., Ashrita Furman (U.S.A.), Jamaica, New York, U.S.A., December 24, 2007.

★ **Harp:** 24 hr. 30 min., Laurita Pacheco (Peru), Bolivar Hotel, Lima, Peru, May 20–21, 2004.

Dance: 100 hr., Suresh Joachim (Australia), Mississauga, Ontario, Canada, February 16–20, 2005.

★ **FARTHEST INVERTED POLE CLIMB** Nele Bruckmann (Germany) climbed 31 ft. 11 in. (9.73 m) up a pole, while inverted, in one minute on the set of *Guinness World Records—Die Größten Weltrekorde* in Cologne, Germany, on September 1, 2007.

☆ **Lecture:** 120 hr., Jayasimha Ravirala (India), FAPCCI Hall, Hyderabad, India, March 24–29, 2007.

TEAM EFFORTS

LONGEST . . .

☆ **Concert (multiple artists)** From November 4–12, 2006, a 200-hour-long concert by multiple artists took place at Manhattan's Pizza Bistro and Music Club in Gelph, Ontario, Canada.

★ **Conga on ice** The record for the longest conga on ice involved 107 participants and was achieved at an event organized by Leeds Metropolitan University (UK) at the "Ice Cube" temporary outdoor ice rink in Millennium Square, Leeds, UK, on February 1, 2008.

★ **Graffiti scroll** A 2,000-ft.-long (609.6-m) scroll of paper was covered in graffiti by students and teachers at Bergen County Technical High School (U.S.A.) in Paramus, New Jersey, U.S.A., on November 2, 2007.

MOST . . .

☆ **MOST PEOPLE BRUSHING TEETH (MULTIPLE VENUES)** A total of 177,003 people brushed their teeth at 380 locations across India during an event organized by Colgate-Palmolive Ltd., (India) on October 9, 2007.

★ MOST ICE-CREAM SCOOPS THROWN AND CAUGHT IN ONE MINUTE BY A TEAM OF TWO Thrower Gabriele Soravia (left) and catcher Lorenzo Soravia (both Germany) threw and caught 25 ice-cream scoops in a minute on the set of *Guinness World Records—Die Größten Weltrekorde* in Cologne, Germany, on September 1, 2007.

☆ MOST PEOPLE KISSING SIMULTANEOUSLY The largest kiss took place in Weston-super-Mare, UK, on July 22, 2007, when 32,648 people puckered up for a minimum of 20 seconds for the *T4 On The Beach* TV show.

☆ **LARGEST GUITAR ENSEMBLE** Led by the band Party Blues in Bb, a guitar ensemble comprising 1,802 participants played "Smoke on the Water," by Deep Purple, simultaneously in Leinfelden-Echterdingen, Germany, on June 26, 2007.

★ **Dancers en pointe** A total of 190 ballet dancers gathered at an event organized by Reach for a Dream Foundation and South African Ballet Theatre (both South Africa) in Pretoria, South Africa, to stand *en pointe*—that is, on the tips of their toes—for a minute on February 25, 2006.

★ LARGEST . . . ★

EVENT	PARTICIPANTS	LOCATION	DATE
★ Ballet class (barres)	551	Pretoria, South Africa	Feb. 25, 2006
★ Bodhran ensemble	980	Sydney, Australia	Mar. 17, 2006
☆ Bunny hop	3,841	Delta, Utah, U.S.A.	Jul. 4, 2007
☆ Dance by couples	540	Hong Kong, China	Jul. 7, 2007
☆ Full drum-kit ensemble	533	Seattle, Washington, U.S.A.	May 13, 2006
★ Gathering of pirates	1,140	Soltau, Germany	Jun. 2, 2007
★ Gathering of soft toys	2,304	Washington, D.C., U.S.A.	Dec. 6, 2006
★ Halloween gathering	63	Somerville, Mass., U.S.A.	Oct. 27, 2007
☆ Harmonica ensemble	3,898	Trossingen, Germany	Sep. 9, 2007
☆ Kazoo ensemble	2,600	Rochester, New York, U.S.A.	Dec. 31, 2006
☆ Mascot gathering	119	Edmonton, Alberta, Canada	Aug. 30, 2004
★ Matouqin ensemble	1,199	Jilin Province, China	Sep. 1, 2006
☆ Music lesson	1,577	Chicago, Illinois, U.S.A.	Aug. 7, 2007
★ Ocarina ensemble	103	Les-Ponts-de-Martel, Switzerland	Jun. 24, 2006
☆ School reunion	3,299	Tacoma, Washington, U.S.A.	Sep. 16, 2006
★ Sirtaki dance	268	Agia Napa, Cyprus	Sep. 16, 2007
★ Speed-dating event	120	Vienna, Austria	Sep. 30, 2007
★ Spoons ensemble	481	Saskatchewan, Canada	Jun. 2, 2007
★ Trumpet ensemble	1,166	Oruro, Bolivia	Feb. 19, 2006

☆**LARGEST DALEK GATHERING** Visitors to the Museum of Science and Industry (MOSI) in Manchester, UK, on August 26, 2007, could have been forgiven for thinking that planet Earth was under attack from an alien race when 70 Daleks—well, people dressed as Daleks from the TV show *Doctor Who*—descended upon the museum.

☆**Litter collectors** On August 7, 2005, a litter-collection project in Oita City, Japan, attracted 146,679 volunteers.

☆**Smurfs in one venue** A total of 451 participants dressed as Smurfs for an event organized by the University of Warwick Students Union in Coventry, UK, on June 20, 2007.

☆**People inside a soap bubble** Fan Yang (Canada) enclosed 42 people in a bubble on the set of *Live with Regis and Kelly* in New York City, U.S.A., on August 7, 2007.

☆**Basketballs dribbled** On May 17, 2007, at the BAA Edinburgh Youth Games at Meadowbank Sports Centre in Edinburgh, UK, 1,289 people dribbled basketballs simultaneously.

★**People whistling** WhiStle Radio's "Whistle Off" at the Strawberry Festival in Whitchurch-Stouffville, Ontario, Canada, attracted 199 people on June 30, 2007.

★**Scarecrows** On October 12, 2003, 3,311 scarecrows were displayed at the Cincinnati Horticultural Society's Flower and Farm Fest in Coney Island, Ohio, U.S.A.

★**People rain dancing** The Rotary Club of Brisbane Planetarium held a 113-strong aboriginal rain dance at the Royal National Association showground in Brisbane, Australia, on November 11, 2007.

SPIRIT OF ADVENTURE

CONTENTS

AROUND THE WORLD

FIRST . . .

Circumnavigation On September 20, 1519, the Spanish ship *Vittoria* set out from Sanlùcar de Barrameda, Andalucía, Spain, as part of a five-vessel expedition led by the Portuguese explorer Ferdinand Magellan.

Under the command of the Spanish navigator Juan Sebastian de Elcano, *Vittoria* rounded Cape Horn, crossed the Pacific via the Philippines and returned to Europe, arriving in Seville, Spain, on September 8, 1522.

The aim of the voyage was to plunder the riches of the Spice Islands and

---

PIONEERING FIRSTS

First circumnavigation by aircraft

Two U.S. Army Douglas DWC seaplanes circled the world in 57 "hops" between April 6, and September 28, 1924, beginning and ending in Seattle, Washington, U.S.A. The *Chicago* was piloted by Lieutenant Lowell H. Smith and Lieutenant Leslie P. Arnold, and the *New Orleans* by Lieutenant Erik H. Nelson and Lieutenant John Harding (all U.S.A.). The flight time for the 26,345-mile (42,398-km) trip was 371 hr. 11 min.

First circumnavigation by aircraft without refueling

Richard G. "Dick" Rutan and Jeana Yeager (both U.S.A.) circumnavigated westward from Edwards Air Force Base, California, U.S.A., in nine days from December 14 to 23, 1986, without refueling.

First circumnavigation via both poles by aircraft

Captain Elgen M. Long (U.S.A.) achieved the first circumpolar flight in a twin-engined Piper PA-31 Navajo from November 5 to December 3, 1971, covering 38,896 miles (62,597 km) in 215 flying hours.

First woman to sail around the world (solo, nonstop)

Kay Cottee (Australia) left Sydney, Australia, on November 29, 1987, in her 36-ft. long (11-m) yacht, *First Lady,* returning there 189 days later on June 5, 1989.

★FIRST CIRCUMNAVIGATION VIA BOTH POLES BY HELICOPTER The first (and **fastest**) circumnavigation via both poles by helicopter was achieved by Jennifer Murray and Colin Bodill (both UK), from December 5, 2006, to May 23, 2007, in a Bell 407 helicopter. The journey started and finished in Fort Worth, Texas, U.S.A.

return the spoils to the Spanish king Charles V. As the journey progressed, the fleet suffered huge losses and Magellan himself was killed in a tribal battle in the Phillippines on April 27, 1521.

By the time the expedition left the Spice Islands, two ships remained, but only de Elcano's *Vittoria* made it back to Spain, with just 18 of the original 270-man crew returning home.

Solo circumnavigation by aircraft Wiley Post (U.S.A.) made the first solo flight around the world from July 15 to 22, 1933, in a Lockheed Vega called *Winnie Mae*. Post took off from New York, U.S.A., and landed in Berlin, Germany, 26 hours later (a record at the time). He flew on to Moscow, Russia, where he was forced to stop for repairs, then on to Alaska, where he crash-landed. Finally, 7 days 19 hr.—and a total of 11 stops—later, Post landed in New York.

Surface circumnavigation via both poles Sir Ranulph Fiennes and Charles Burton (both UK) of the British Trans-Globe Expedition traveled south from Greenwich, London, UK, on September 2, 1979, crossed the South Pole on December 15, 1980, the North Pole on April 10, 1982, and returned to Greenwich on August 29, 1982. Their trip covered 35,000 miles (56,000 km).

FASTEST . . .

Circumnavigation by powered boat *Cable & Wireless Adventurer* circled the world in 74 days 20 hr. 58 min. 30 sec. between April 19 and July 3, 1998. The 115-ft.-long (35.05-m) vessel was captained by Ian Bosworth (UK) and traveled more than 26,000 miles (41,841 km).

Circumnavigation sailing solo (female) Ellen MacArthur (UK) sailed solo and nonstop around the world in 71 days 14 hr. 18 min. 33 sec. from November 28, 2004, to February 7, 2005, in the trimaran *B&Q*. She started off Ushant, France, rounded the Cape of Good Hope (South Africa), sailed south of Australia and rounded Cape Horn (Argentina) before heading up the Atlantic to Ushant.

Circumnavigation by car The record for the first and fastest man and woman to have circumnavigated the Earth by car, covering six continents under the rules applicable in 1989 and 1991 and embracing more than an equator's length of driving (24,901 road miles; 40,075 km), is held by Saloo Choudhury and his wife Neena Choudhury (both India). The journey took 69 days 19 hr. 5 min. from September 9 to November 17, 1989. The couple drove a 1989 Hindustan "Contessa Classic," starting and finishing in Delhi, India.

Circumnavigation via both poles by airplane A Boeing 747 SP piloted by Captain Walter H. Mullikin (U.S.A.) completed an aerial circumnavigation of the Earth via both geographical poles in 54 hr. 7 min. 12 sec. (including refueling stops) between October 28 and 31, 1977. The journey began and ended in San Francisco, U.S.A., with stops in Cape Town (South Africa) and Auckland (New Zealand).

★ **FARTHEST DRIVE BY CAR USING ALTERNATIVE FUEL** Rainer Zietlow, Florian Hilpert, Falk Gunold, and Franz Janusiewicz (all Germany) traveled 23,697 miles (38,137 km) in a Volkswagen Caddy EcoFuel using natural gas. Their journey started in Cologne, Germany, on October 15, 2006, and finished in Leipzig, Germany, on April 13, 2007.

☆ **FASTEST ROUND-THE-WORLD CYCLE** Mark Beaumont (UK) cycled the world in 194 days 17 hr. covering a distance of 18,296.74 miles (29,445.81 km). The journey started and finished in Paris, France, from August 5, 2007, to February 15, 2008, and took in Europe, Pakistan, Malaysia, Australia, New Zealand, and the U.S.A.

☆ **FASTEST CIRCUMNAVIGATION SAILING SOLO** Francis Joyon (France) sailed solo and nonstop around the world in 57 days 13 hr. 34 min. 6 sec. from November 23, 2007, to January 20, 2008, in the 97-ft. (29.5-m) maxi-trimaran *IDEC II*. Joyon began and ended his 24,170-mile (38,900-km) journey in Brest, France, beating the previous record set by Ellen MacArthur (UK) by 14 days.

EPIC JOURNEYS

Water baby As part of the four-woman crew of *Silver Cloud,* Rachel Flanders (UK, b. September 3, 1990) became the **youngest person to row across an ocean.** She crossed the Atlantic (east to west), leaving La Gomera, the Canary Islands on December 2, 2007, and reaching Antigua on February 14, 2008. Rachel was 17 years 91 days old at the start of the trip.

Channel champions The **youngest person to swim the English Channel** is Thomas Gregory (UK, b. October 6, 1976), who was aged 11 years 336 days when he achieved the feat in 11 hr. 54 min. on September 6, 1988.

The **youngest female to swim the English Channel** is Samantha Druce (UK, b. April 22, 1971), who completed the crossing in 15 hr. 27 min., aged 12 years 118 days on August 18, 1983.

(*NB: current rules state that all Channel swimmers must be at least 16 years old.*)

The **oldest person to swim the English Channel** was George Brunstad (U.S.A., b. August 25, 1934), who was aged 70 years 4 days when he swam from Dover, UK, to Sangatte, France, in 15 hr. 59 min. on August 29, 2004.

Linda Ashmore (UK, b. October 21, 1946) is the ☆**oldest female to swim the English Channel.** She crossed from England to France in 15 hr. 11 min., aged 60 years 302 days, on August 19, 2007.

The ★**most crossings of the English Channel completed by a male swimmer** is 34 by Kevin Murphy (UK) between 1968 and 2006.

★**FASTEST DOUBLE-CHANNEL SWIM IN RELAY (FEMALE)** The fastest two-way swim of the English Channel by a female team is 18 hr. 59 min. by the six-woman Altamar 66K (all Mexico) on August 10, 2007.

FASTEST TIMES TO SWIM THE ENGLISH CHANNEL The ☆fastest
swim of the English Channel, and the ☆ fastest swim of the
England-France route, is 6 hr. 57 min. 50 sec. by Petar Stoychev
(Bulgaria), who crossed from Shakespeare Beach, UK, to Cap Gris Nez,
France, on August 24, 2007.

  The ☆ fastest one-way swim of the English Channel by a
woman is 7 hr. 25 min., achieved by Yvetta Hlavacova (Czech Republic)
from England to France on August 5, 2006.

THE WEBB WONDER

The **first person to swim the English Channel** from shore to shore
(without a life jacket) was Merchant Navy captain Matthew Webb (UK),
who swam an estimated 38 miles (61 km) to make the 21-mile (33-km)
crossing from Dover, UK, to Calais Sands, France, in 21 hr. 45 min. from
12:56 p.m. to 10:41 a.m. on August 24–25, 1875. Strong currents off
Cap Gris Nez delayed Webb's arrival in France for five hours.

FIRST CHANNEL CROSSING (FEMALE)
The first woman to successfully swim the English Channel was Gertrude Caroline Ederle (U.S.A., b. October 23, 1906), who swam from Cap Gris Nez, France, to Deal, UK, on August 6, 1926, in a time of 14 hr. 39 min.

The Queen of the English Channel—that is, the ★**female swimmer who has swum the English Channel the most times**—is Alison Streeter (UK) with 43 crossings from 1982 until July 24, 2004. She also holds the record for the ★**most crossings of the English Channel by any swimmer.**

★**Oldest person to row across any ocean** Pavel Rezvoy (Ukraine, b. November 28, 1938) rowed the Indian Ocean in his boat *Ukraine,* leaving the Cocos (Keeling) Islands, Australia, on September 13, 2005, aged 66 years 289 days, and arriving on Mahe Island, the Seychelles, on November 9, 2005.

Solar-powered ocean crossings The ★**fastest transatlantic crossing made by solar power** is 29 days by *sun21* (Switzerland) and its crew of five from Las Palmas, Gran Canaria, Spain, to Le Marin, Martinique, from January 4 to February 2, 2007.

Kenichi Horie (Japan) made the **fastest crossing of the Pacific Ocean by solar power** when he traveled 10,000 miles (16,092 km) from Salinas, Ecuador, to Tokyo, Japan, in 148 days between March 20 and August 5, 1996.

☆**FASTEST ROW ACROSS THE ATLANTIC** Led by Leven Brown (UK), the crew of *La Mondiale* crossed the Atlantic in 33 days 7 hr. 30 min. The team rowed east to west, leaving Gran Canaria, Spain, on December 15, 2007 and arriving at Barbados on January 17, 2008.

★ **SMALLEST ROWBOAT TO CROSS AN OCEAN** Graham Walters (UK) rowed his boat *Puffin*—15 ft. 6 in. (4.65 m) in length and 5 ft. 6 in. (1.65 m) in beam—across the Atlantic, east to west, from La Gomera, Canary Islands to St.-Barthélemy between February 3 and May 13, 2007.

Longest row across an ocean The longest solo ocean row of 312 days 2 hours was completed by Erden Eruç (Turkey) who rowed the Pacific east to west in *Around-n-Over,* leaving Bodega Bay, California, U.S.A. on July 10, 2007 and finishing at Papua New Guinea on May 17, 2008. The row was part of Erden's project to travel "around the world by human power."

★ **Fastest time to sail from San Francisco to Tokyo solo (male)** Peter Hogg (New Zealand) single-handedly sailed from San Francisco, U.S.A., to Tokyo, Japan, in a time of 34 days 6 hr. 26 min. between April 13, 1992, and May 19, 1992.

★ **Longest journey nonstop in a flats boat** The longest nonstop ocean voyage in a flats boat (a flat-bottomed craft with square ends) was 774 miles (1,245.63 km) and was set by Ralph and Robert Brown (both U.S.A.), who traveled from St. George's, Bermuda, to New York Harbor, U.S.A., from May 9 to 11, 2007.

☆ **Longest ongoing pilgrimage** The greatest distance claimed for an around-the-world pilgrimage is 37,502 miles (60,353 km) by Arthur Blessitt (U.S.A.) since December 25, 1969. He has visited all seven continents, having crossed 310 "nations, island groups, and territories" carrying a 12-ft.-tall (3.7 m) wooden cross and preaching from the Bible throughout.

Longest journey by taxi The longest taxi journey on record covered 21,691 miles (34,908 km) at a cost of £40,210 ($64,645). Jeremy Levine, Mark Aylett (both UK), and Carlos Arrese (Spain) traveled from London, UK, to Cape Town, South Africa—and back—via taxi from June 3 to October 17, 1994.

Longest motorcycle ride (distance) Emilio Scotto of Buenos Aires, Argentina, completed the world's longest journey by a motorcycle, covering over 457,000 miles (735,000 km) and 214 countries and territories, from January 17, 1985, to April 2, 1995.

★ **First overland crossing of the Darien Gap** Richard E. Bevir (UK) and Terence John Whitfield (Australia) made the first overland crossing of

☆ **HIGHEST SLACKLINE WALK** Christian Schou (Norway) walked 39 ft. (12 m) on a 1-in.-wide (2.5-cm) line suspended 3,280 ft. (1,000 m) above the ground, at Kjerag Lysefjorden, Norway, on August 3, 2006.
   On October 7, 2007, Aleksandar Mork (Norway, inset) achieved the same feat.

the Darien Gap in their Land Rover *La Cucaracha* during the Trans Darien Expedition. The gap, which consists of dense jungle and numerous rivers, is famous for being the "missing" portion of the Pan-American Highway that links North and South America. They departed from Chepo, Panama, on June 3 and reached Quibdo, Colombia, on June 17, 1960.

Farthest distance flown in a balloon The official Fédération Aéronautique Internationale (FAI) distance record for a manned balloon is 25,361 miles (40,814 km). It was set by Bertrand Piccard (Switzerland) and Brian Jones (UK), who piloted the *Breitling Orbiter 3* from March 1 to 21, 1999.

ON THE WING

The **longest nonstop flight by any manned aircraft** was achieved by Steve Fossett (U.S.A.), who flew 26,389.3 miles (42,469.4 km) in the *Virgin Atlantic GlobalFlyer* airplane. Fossett left the Kennedy Space Center, Florida, U.S.A., on February 8, 2006, and landed 76 hr. 45 min. later in Bournemouth, Dorset, UK, on February 11, 2006. He beat the previous record, held by the *Breitling Orbiter 3* balloon, by 102.8 miles (165.4 km).

SIR RICHARD BRANSON
REMEMBERS STEVE FOSSETT

Multiple world record-holder Steve Fossett (U.S.A.) was lost on September 3, 2007, while on a flight over north-western Nevada, U.S.A. His remains and the ruins of his aircraft were found in eastern California in October 2008. Friend and fellow record-breaker Sir Richard Branson (UK, pictured below left) shares some of his memories of Steve:

I first met Steve Fossett on a freezing January evening at the Busch stadium in St. Louis. He was about to attempt a solo circumnavigation of the world by balloon and, although we were rivals, I decided to see him off in the spirit of sportsmanship that still

inhabits the world of record-breaking. As I neared his balloon, a TV crew approached and I found my-self being filmed chatting with a man I thought was one of his crew. I said one had to be a bit crazy to test oneself in this way. The quiet American in front of me looked at me sympathetically and said, "I am Steve Fossett."

That was the beginning of a long and close friend-ship with one of the most generous, good-natured, and kind people I have ever met, but also one of the bravest and most determined adventurers and explorers of all time. Steve held more adventuring world records than any other human being. He began in a modest way, swimming the English Channel in 1985. Over the next 22 years, he amassed over 115 records in aviation, gliding, ballooning, sailing, power boating, mountaineering, skiing, triathlon, even dog sledding. He truly was the adventurer's adventurer.

In no project Steve undertook did he demonstrate greater skill than during his circumnavigation of the globe in the *Virgin Atlantic GlobalFlyer.* He later described this in his autobiography, *Chasing the Wind,* as one of his proudest achievements. The aircraft, now displayed in the Smithsonian Institute, was a unique carbon composite jet that led the way in new, energy-efficient technology now being developed by Boeing and Airbus. Steve proved it was possible to safely fly an ultralight high-altitude jet burning lean fuel. He did so by sitting in one alone for three days and four nights without rest (apart from a few of his legendary power naps) in difficult weather conditions at altitudes of over 50,000 ft. (15,240 m); outside his tiny Plexiglas canopy, it was 80 degrees below zero (-112°F).

Steve was a true record breaker, a man who tested not only him-

self, but through his record attempts, new green technologies and materials to the limit.

He will be truly missed, not only by all of us who knew him and loved him but by the millions of people around the world who watched in awe a man who believed world records were there to be broken, and break them he did.

☆ **LONGEST AUTORIKSHAW JOURNEY** Susi Bemsel and Daniel Snaider (both Germany) covered 23,245 miles (37,410 km) between Bangkok, Thailand, and Eichstätt, Germany, from February 8 to December 17, 2005. They visited Thailand, Laos, Cambodia, Japan, Russia, Mongolia, Kazakhstan, Kyrgistan, Uzbekistan, Turkmenistan, Iran, Turkey, Syria, Jordan, Egypt, Libya, Tunisia, Italy, France, Spain, and Germany.

★ **GREATEST DISTANCE WITH A HUMAN-POWERED VEHICLE (24 HOURS)** The farthest distance covered with a human-powered vehicle in a 24-hour period is 647 miles (1,041.24 km), achieved by Greg Kolodziejzyk (Canada) at Redwood Acres Raceway in Eureka, Alberta, Canada, on July 18, 2006.

☆ **FASTEST JOURNEY ON FOOT ACROSS AUSTRALIA (PERTH TO SYDNEY)** Donnie Maclurcan (Australia) completed the fastest journey on foot across Australia when he ran across the continental mainland from Cottesloe Beach, Perth, Western Australia, to Bondi Beach, Sydney, New South Wales, in 67 days 2 hr. 57 min., from January 5 to March 13, 2002.

☆ **LONGEST DRIVEN JOURNEY** Emil and Liliana Schmid (both Switzerland) have covered 383,609 miles (617,359 km) in their Toyota Land Cruiser since October 16, 1984, crossing 156 countries and territories in the process.

★ **Farthest distance traveled on a skateboard in 24 hours** Skateboarder James Peters (U.S.A.) covered 184 miles (296.12 km) in 24 hours in Seattle, Washington, U.S.A., on May 11, 2007.

DID YOU KNOW?

Donnie Maclurcan's epic 2,471-mile (3,978-km) run (see top photo) raised in excess of AUS$30,000 (U.S.$15,660) for the international sight-restoring work of The Fred Hollows Foundation.

★Greatest distance on a motorcycle in 24 hours (individual)
Eduardo Vergara Schaffner (Uruguay) covered 937.58 miles (1,508.89 km) by motorcycle in 24 hours on November 2–3, 2002, in Colonia, Uruguay. He traveled at an average speed of 39 mph (63 km/h) on a 125 cc Vince Lifan motorcycle.

Longest camper van journey Harry B. Coleman and Peggy Larson traveled 143,716 miles (231,288 km) in a Volkswagen Camper between August 20, 1976, and April 20, 1978. Their journey took them through 113 countries.

POLAR PIONEERS

★Oldest person to visit the North Pole Dorothy Davenhill Hirsch (U.S.A., b. May 11, 1915) reached the North Pole aboard the Russian nuclear icebreaker *Yamal* on August 28, 2004, aged 89 years and 109 days.

Fastest solo unsupported trek to the North Pole Børge Ousland (Norway) skied his way to the North Pole from the Severnaya Zemlya archipelago in Russia, without any external assistance, in 52 days from March 2 to April 23, 1994. He was also the **first person to make a solo and unsupported journey to the North Pole from land.**

Fastest surface journey to the North Pole An expedition consisting of Hugh Dale-Harris, Matty McNair (both Canada), Andrew Gerber (South Africa), Tom Avery and George Wells (both UK), along with a team of 16 husky dogs, reached the North Pole on April 26, 2005, having traveled for 36 days 22 hr. 11 min. The team, which left from Cape Columbia on Ellesmere Island in Arctic Canada, were attempting to re-create as closely as possible the disputed 1909 expedition of American explorer Robert Peary. Just like Peary, the expedition team had four resupplies along the way.

FASTEST SOLO KITE-ASSISTED JOURNEY TO THE SOUTH POLE Børge Ousland (Norway) traveled to the South Pole on skis, with assistance from a parafoil kite, in 34 days from November 15 to December 19, 1996. The journey was solo and unsupported—in other words, he received no outside assistance.

★**FASTEST TO THE "THREE POLES"** The shortest time taken to reach the three extreme points of the Earth—Mt. Everest, the North Pole, and the South Pole (also known as the Three Poles)—is 1 year 217 days by Adrian Hayes (UK). Mr. Hayes summitted Mt. Everest on May 25, 2006, reached the North Pole on April 25, 2007 (from Ward Hunt Island, Canada), and finally claimed the South Pole, journeying from the Hercules Inlet, on December 28, 2007.

THE POLES

Unless specified, the records on these pages refer to the geographic North and South poles; but did you realize there are, in fact, eight poles?

The **North Pole,** or **Geographic North Pole,** is the northernmost point, a.k.a. "true north." This pole floats on sea ice, so explorers use a GPS (global positioning system) to pinpoint its location. The **South Pole,** or **Geographic South Pole,** is the southernmost point of the Earth's surface.

The Earth has its own magnetic field, created by its iron core and its spinning motion. The northern and southern points of this field are the **Magnetic North Pole** and the **Magnetic South Pole,** respectively. These are not fixed, and move continually.

The Earth, which rotates on an axis tilted at 11 degrees, has a geomagnetic field that behaves as if it had a bar magnet inside its core. The **Geomagnetic North Pole** and **Geomagnetic South Pole** are the northernmost and southernmost points of this field, respectively.

The **North Pole of Inaccessibility** is the farthest point from any northern coastline; it is purely a geographical reference, not a physical spot. The **South Pole of Inaccessibility** marks the farthest point from any coast on the Antarctic continent.

"Many times I have thanked God for a bite of raw dog."

Polar explorer Robert Peary (U.S.A., 1856–1920)

First person to visit both poles Dr. Albert Paddock Crary (U.S.A., 1911–87), a polar geophysicist and glaciologist, reached the North Pole by Dakota aircraft on May 3, 1952. On February 12, 1961, he arrived at the South Pole by Sno Cat with a scientific traverse party that had set out from McMurdo Station on December 10, 1960.

First flight in an airplane over Antarctica The first heavier-than-air flight over the Antarctic continent was made on November 16, 1928, by Sir Hubert Wilkins (Australia) and Carl Ben Eielson (U.S.A.) in a Lockheed Vega aircraft.

First flight over the South Pole Pioneering aviator Richard Byrd (U.S.A.) made the first flight over the South Pole on November 29, 1929. The round trip to and from the expedition's base on the Ross Ice Shelf took 19 hours.

First person to reach the South Pole Leading a Norwegian party of five men, Captain Roald Amundsen (Norway, 1872–1928) reached the South Pole at 11:00 a.m. on December 14, 1911, after a 53-day march with dog sleds from the Bay of Whales.

FIRST TO REACH THE NORTH POLE The title "first person to reach the North Pole" has long been a matter of debate, with two American explorers staking a claim early in the 20th century. Robert Peary led an expedition (illustrated above) that he claimed reached the North Pole on April 6, 1909; however, Frederick Cook claimed he had done so a year earlier, on April 21, 1908.

FIRST SOLO EXPEDITION TO THE NORTH POLE Naomi Uemura
(1941–84), a Japanese explorer and mountaineer, became the first
person to reach the North Pole in a solo trek across the Arctic sea ice at
4:45 a.m. GMT on May 1, 1978. He had traveled 450 miles (725 km),
setting out on March 7, 1978, from Cape Edward on Ellesmere Island in
northern Canada.

FIRST SOLO EXPEDITION TO THE SOUTH POLE Erling Kagge (Norway)
became the first person to reach the South Pole after a solo and
unsupported surface trek on January 7, 1993, aged 29. His 870-mile
(1,400-km) journey from Berkner Island took 50 days.

PEAK PERFORMANCE

★ **Youngest person to climb the Seven Summits** Samantha Larson (U.S.A., b. October 7, 1988) became the youngest climber of the Seven Summits (Kosciuszko list) when she reached the seventh peak—Mt. Everest—on May 17, 2007, aged 18 years 222 days. Samantha then went on to climb Carstensz Pyramid on August 4, 2007, aged 18 years 301 days, making her the ★ **youngest person to summit the Carstensz version** of the seven summits challenge.

★ **Fastest climb of the Seven Summits (Kosciuszko list)** Mastan Babu Malli (India) climbed the highest peak on each continent in 172 days between January 19, 2006, when he summited Vinson Massif (Antarctica), and July 10, 2006, when he topped Mt. Denali (U.S.A.).

★ **Busiest year for Everest ascents** There were a record 526 ascents of Everest in the calendar year 2007.

Fastest ascent of Mt. Everest (north side) Hans Kammerlander (Italy) completed the fastest ascent of Mt. Everest on the northern side, making the climb from base camp to the summit in 16 hr. 45 min. on May 23–24, 1996.

Fastest ascent of Mt. Everest (south side) Pemba Dorje Sherpa (Nepal) climbed from base camp to the summit of Mt. Everest in a time of 8 hr. 10 min. on May 21, 2004. This is the fastest ever ascent of the world's tallest mountain.

Most ascents of Mt. Everest by a woman Lakpa Sherpa (Nepal) successfully reached the summit of Mt. Everest for the fifth time on June 2, 2005. She made the climb with her husband, George Demarescu (U.S.A.), who was himself completing his seventh ascent of the world's tallest mountain.

★ **First ascent of K2 (west face)** Russia's Andrew Mariev and Vadim Popovich completed the first successful ascent of the notoriously vicious west face of K2. The expedition—led by Viktor Kozlov (Russia)—reached the 28,251-ft.-high (8,500-m) peak on August 21, 2007, after a grueling 10-week climb.

FACT

The "Death Zone" in climbing refers to the altitude above 26,245 ft. (8,000 m) at which the human body can no longer adapt to the climatic conditions. In other words, you start to die!

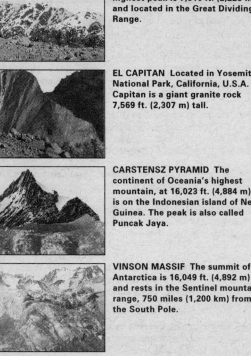

KOSCIUSZKO Named after a Polish military general, Australia's highest peak is 7,310 ft. (2,228 m) and located in the Great Dividing Range.

EL CAPITAN Located in Yosemite National Park, California, U.S.A. El Capitan is a giant granite rock 7,569 ft. (2,307 m) tall.

CARSTENSZ PYRAMID The continent of Oceania's highest mountain, at 16,023 ft. (4,884 m), is on the Indonesian island of New Guinea. The peak is also called Puncak Jaya.

VINSON MASSIF The summit of Antarctica is 16,049 ft. (4,892 m) and rests in the Sentinel mountain range, 750 miles (1,200 km) from the South Pole.

ELBRUS Europe's tallest mountain has a peak height of 18,510 ft. (5,642 m) and sits in the Caucasus range of Russia.

KILIMANJARO Reaching high above the African plains of Tanzania, "Kili" stands 19,340 ft. (5,895 m) tall. Classified as an inactive stratovolcano, Kili has never recorded an eruption.

DENALI North America's highest peak is also known as Mt. McKinley. This Alaskan mountain is 20,321 ft. (6,194 m) tall.

ACONCAGUA The highest point of South America is in the Andes mountain range of Argentina, and measures 22,841 ft. (6,962 m). It was first summited on January 14, 1897.

K2 At 28,251 ft. (8,611 m), K2—in the Karakoram range on the Pakistan–China border—is the world's second highest mountain. It was first climbed on July 31, 1954.

EVEREST The highest mountain in the world, at 29,029 ft. (8,848 m), is in Asia's Himalayan region. Its other names are Sagarmatha and Chomolungma.

☆ **OLDEST PERSON TO CLIMB MT. EVEREST** Katsusuke Yanagisawa (Japan, b. March 20, 1936), a former schoolteacher, reached the summit from the north side with team Himex on May 22, 2007, aged 71 years 63 days

☆ **Highest unclimbed peak** At 24,835 ft. (7,570 m), Gangkar Punsum in Bhutan is the world's 40th highest peak, and the highest mountain yet to be climbed. Unsuccessful attempts were made to summit the peak in the 1980s, then in 1994 a partial of ban of mountaineering in the country was declared. Since 2003, all climbing in Bhutan has been outlawed—for religious reasons—so it could remain unclimbed for many years to come.

The **highest unclimbed peak where climbing is not prohibited** is the demanding east face of Saser Kangri II in Indian Kashmir, which reaches 24,665 ft. (7,518 m).

THE SUMMITS

The mountaineering challenge of the "Seven Summits" entails climbing to the very top of the highest mountains on the Earth's seven continents: Africa, Antarctica, Asia, North America, South America, Europe, and Oceania. So why are there eight mountains and two lists?

Depending upon how a continent is defined geographically, there are two possible contenders for the highest mountain in continental Australia.

Carstensz Pyramid (a.k.a. Puncak Jaya) is the tallest mountain in Oceania, a region that includes Australia, New Zealand, and New Guinea.

If Australia is considered to be the only continental country in the region (with no land borders to other countries), then Mt. Kosciuszko, near Sydney, is the tallest.

It is a great achievement for climbers to summit either list, but often they choose to do both to avoid any doubt!

☆ **HIGHEST ALTITUDE CONCERT ON LAND** A concert was performed at a height of 19,911 ft. (6,069 m) by Musikkapelle Roggenzell—10 musicians from Germany and Bolivia—on Mt. Acotango, Bolivia, on August 6, 2007.

☆ **OLDEST FEMALE TO CLIMB THE SEVEN SUMMITS (KOSCIUSZKO LIST)** Jeanne Stawiecki (U.S.A., b. June 24, 1950) became the oldest woman to climb the Seven Summits, including Mt. Kosciuszko, when she completed her last climb (Mt. Everest, Nepal) on May 22, 2007, aged 57 years 36 days.

☆**FASTEST CLIMB OF THE SEVEN SUMMITS (CARSTENSZ LIST)** Daniel Griffith (Canada) climbed the highest peak on each continent in 187 days between May 24, 2006—when he ascended Mt. Everest in Nepal—and November 27, 2006—when he conquered Vinson Massif in Antarctica.

☆**HIGHEST ALTITUDE REACHED BY CAR** Gonzalo Bravo and Eduardo Canales (both Chile) drove to an altitude of 21,942 ft. (6,688 m) in their modified 1986 Suzuki Samurai, on the slopes of the Ojos Del Salado volcano, near the Atacama Desert, Chile, on April 21, 2007.

MODERN LIFE

CONTENTS

COLLECTIONS

★**Bells** Myrtle B. Eldridge (U.S.A.) has 9,638 bells that she has collected since the 1980s.

☆**Board games** As of February 21, 2007, Brian Arnett (U.S.A.) had collected 1,345 different board games. Brian started his collection in 1996.

★**Candles** Kathrin Koch (Germany) had amassed 1,820 different candles by May 3, 2007. She began her collection in 1993.

☆**Four-leafed clovers** Edward Martin Sr. (U.S.A.) has been collecting four-leafed clovers since 1999 and had amassed 111,060 of them by May 2007.

★**Ladybugs** Sheri Gartner (U.S.A.) had put together a collection of 2,050 ladybug-related items as of November 2007.

☆**Model cars** Michael Zarnock (U.S.A.) had collected 8,128 different Hot Wheels model cars as of February 14, 2007. He began his collection in 1968.

☆**Model buses** By December 4, 2007, Geoff Price (UK) had collected 10,017 model buses, having begun in 1959.

★**Licence plates** Mohammed Yahya Al-Aseeri (Saudi Arabia) had a collection of 80 different car licence plates as of August 31, 2007.

★**Paper dolls** Malin Fritzell (Sweden) has been collecting paper dolls since the 1960s. As of March 23, 2006, his collection numbered 4,720.

☆**LARGEST MASK COLLECTION Gerold Weschenmoser (Germany) had acquired 5,121 different masks by January 22, 2008. He even has one of his own face! He began collecting in 1957.**

☆ **MOST ROSARIES** Mohammed Yahya Al-Aseeri (Saudi Arabia) had collected 3,220 rosaries as of August 31, 2007. Closely associated with Roman Catholicism, rosaries—strings of beads used in prayer—are also common to other faiths.

★ **Pencil sharpeners** Demetra Koutsouridou (Greece) has collected 8,514 different pencil sharpeners since 1997.

★ **Santa Claus memorabilia** Since 1988, Jean-Guy Laquerre (Canada) has built up a collection of 13,014 items of Santa Claus memorabilia.

★ **Simpsons memorabilia** Cameron Gibbs (Australia) had a collection of 951 different Simpsons items as of April 23, 2007. He has been collecting for five years.

★ **Snowmen** As of March 23, 2007, Kathleen G. Sauk (U.S.A.) had collected 1,693 different snowmen-related items. Her collection is nine years old.

★ **Sports mascots** Soeren Christian Hesse (Germany) presented his record-breaking collection of 161 sports mascots in the AOL Arena, Hamburg, Germany, on March 28, 2007.

X-REF

In January 2001, teachers and students at St. Joseph School in Cairo, Illinois, U.S.A., made the **largest rosary**, which measured 173 ft. 9 in. (52.9 m) long. For more oversized records, turn to **Big Stuff** on p. 250.

"We wanted to share the angels with more people than we could accommodate at home..."

Joyce Berg (U.S.A.), co-owner of the largest collection of angels and cofounder of the Angel Museum, Beloit, Wisconsin, U.S.A.

BACK SCRATCHERS Manfred S. Rothstein (U.S.A.) has 518 back scratchers housed in his dermatology clinic in Fayetteville, North Carolina, U.S.A. He started his collection in the 1970s.

☆**Teapots** The largest collection of teapots belongs to Tang Yu (China), who has amassed 30,000 different teapots dating from the Song Dynasty to modern times. He began his collection in 1955.

★ TOP 20 MOST UNUSUAL GWR COLLECTIONS ★

COLLECTION	NUMBER	NAME (NAT.)
★ Angels	13,165	Joyce & Lowell Berg (U.S.A.)
★ Artificial apples	2,300	Erika & Kurt Werth (Italy)
☆ Armored vehicles	229	Jacques Littlefield (U.S.A.)
★ Bus tickets	21,000	G. Vasanthakumar (India)
★ Casino chips	374	Bruce & Sue Wunder (U.S.A.)
★ Commemorative church plates	1,206	Tom & Barbara Southwell (U.S.A.)
☆ "Do Not Disturb" signs	7,806	Jean-François Vernetti (Switzerland)
Hair from historical figures	115	John Reznikoff (U.S.A.)
Lipstick prints	39,537	Breakthrough Breast Cancer and Avon Cosmetics (UK)
Matchbox labels	743,512	Teiichi Yoshizawa (Japan)
Nail clippers	505	Andrè Ludwick (South Africa)
★ Nativity sets	874	Sue Koenig (U.S.A.)
★ Parking meters	292	Lotta Sjölin (Sweden)
★ "Robin" Christmas cards	11,010	Joan Gordon (UK)
☆ Motion sickness bags	5,180	Niek Vermeulen (Netherlands)
Spoon-rests	635	Frank Cassa (U.S.A.)
★ Stamps featuring ships	6,459	Celso Fernandes (Canada)
★ Tea bag labels	8,661	Felix Rotter (Germany)
★ Trolls	490	Sophie Marie Cross (UK)
Vintage lawn mowers	790	Andrew Hall & Michael Duck (UK)

★**PHONES** As of April 20, 2007, Zhang Dafang (China) had collected 600 telephones from all eras and from all over the world, including a phone in the shape of a whisky bottle. He found his oldest piece, dating from 1900, in a Russian flea market.

EXTREME CUISINE

AGAINST THE CLOCK

Most apples picked in eight hours The greatest recorded weight of apples collected in eight hours is 15,830 lb. (7,180.3 kg), picked by George Adrian of Indianapolis, Indiana, U.S.A., on September 23, 1980.

☆**Fastest time to eat a raw onion** Samuel Grazette (Barbados) ate a raw onion in 48 seconds at the 2007 Barbados World Records Festival held at the National Stadium, Barbados, on March 31, 2007.

★**Fastest time to open 2,000 beer bottles** Krunoslav Budiselic (Croatia) opened 2,000 beer bottles in 37 min. 39 sec. The record was achieved in Karlovac, Croatia, on August 25, 2007.

☆**Most pancakes made in eight hours (team)** Members of the Fargo Kiwanis Club in Fargo, North Dakota, U.S.A., made 34,818 pancakes in eight hours at the 50th Annual Pancake Karnival at the Fargo Civic Auditorium on February 9, 2008. All the pancakes counted were served to and eaten by visitors to the Karnival.

☆**Fastest time to peel and eat a lemon** Serial record-breaker Ashrita Furman (U.S.A.) peeled and ate a lemon in just 10.97 seconds at the Panorama Cafe in Jamaica, New York, U.S.A., on August 24, 2007.

☆ **MOST RICE GRAINS EATEN IN THREE MINUTES** Rob Beaton (U.S.A.) ate 78 grains of rice, one by one, using only a pair of chopsticks, in three minutes in Ocean Gate, New Jersey, U.S.A., on November 9, 2007.

☆ **Most coconuts smashed in one minute** Using just one hand, Muhamed Kahrimanovic (Germany) successfully smashed a total of 81 coconuts in one minute in Hamburg, Germany, on December 6, 2007.

☆ **Most ice-cream cones prepared in one minute** The greatest number of ice-cream cones prepared in one minute is 19, achieved by Mitch Cohen (U.S.A.) of Baskin-Robbins. He broke the record on the Food Network TV show *Paula's Party* on June 28, 2007.

TALLEST . . .

★**Cookie tower** Members of the Girl Scouts—Seal of Ohio Council, Inc., managed to construct a tower of cookies 5 ft. 2 in. (1.57 m) tall in Columbus, Ohio, U.S.A., on September 15, 2007.

★**Stack of doughnuts** Members of Twentieth Century Fox and Capital Radio (both UK) created a stack of doughnuts measuring 43.5 in. (110.5 cm) tall to celebrate the premiere of *The Simpsons Movie* (U.S.A., 2007) in London, UK, on July 25, 2007.

☆**Champagne fountain** Luuk Broos (Netherlands) and his team made a Champagne pyramid fountain consisting of 41,664 glasses, forming 62 storys, in Zeelandhallen, Goes, the Netherlands, on September 12, 2007.

★ **MOST MENTOS-AND-SODA FOUNTAINS** A total of 973 Mentos-and-soda fountains were made by residents of southeast Missouri at Arena Park, Cape Girardeau, Missouri, U.S.A., on October 3, 2007. Each eruption had an average height of 13 ft. 1 in. (4 m).

MISC.

★**Fastest time to open 100 mussels** Kannha Keo (New Zealand) managed to open 100 mussels in a record-breaking time of 2 min. 11 sec. at the Havelock Mussel Festival, Havelock, New Zealand, on March 17, 2007.

★**Most people tossing eggs** The Wrangell Chamber of Commerce (U.S.A.) managed to amass 338 people to toss eggs in Wrangell, Alaska, U.S.A., on July 3, 2007.

★ **MALTESER CATCHING** The record for the most Maltesers (chocolate-covered honeycomb malt balls) thrown 6 ft. 6 in. (2 m) and then caught in the mouth in a minute is 19, by thrower Ranald Mackechnie (pictured left) and catcher Stuart Hendry (both UK) at the Guinness World Record Offices in London, UK, on September 28, 2007.

★ **MOST WINE GLASSES HELD IN ONE HAND** The most wine glasses held in one hand (without using equipment of any kind) is 39 by Reymond Adina (Philippines) at the Quatre-Cats restaurant in Barcelona, Spain, on October 24, 2007. There is strong competition between waiters in Barcelona to hold this "smashing" record.

★ **MOST CHICKENS SPIT-ROASTED SIMULTANEOUSLY** Using a 65-ft. 7-in.-long (20-m), 16-ft. 5-in.-high (5-m) rotisserie wall, chef Jiang Bing (China) managed to spit-roast 2,008 chickens at the same time in Nanning, Guangxi, China, on October 24, 2007.

☆ **MOST EXPENSIVE COCKTAIL** The Skyview Bar in the Burj Al Arab Hotel in Dubai, UAE, offers a cocktail named "27321" that costs 27,321 Dirham ($7,439). The cocktail, an ultra-luxurious version of a traditional Old Fashioned, consists of 55-year-old Macallan whisky from Scotland, ice made from the water used at their distillery, a drop or so of exclusive dried fruit bitters, and passionfruit-scented sugar. It is stirred using a rod made from a Macallan cask, and served in a glass produced in the French town of Baccarat.

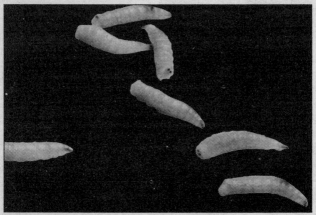

★ **MOST DANGEROUS CHEESE** The most dangerous cheese to human health is casu marzu ("rotten cheese"), made from sheep's milk and considered a delicacy in Sardinia, Italy—even though it is illegal to buy there. Casu marzu is essentially a Pecorino cheese left to rot. Flies can then lay their eggs in it, resulting in thousands of maggots. The enzymes produced by these maggots assist the fermentation process of the cheese, which supposedly adds to the desired taste. If the maggots survive the digestive juices in the human stomach, however, they can provoke vomiting, abdominal pain, and bloody diarrhea.

INCREDIBLE EDIBLES

★**Most layers in a layer cake** Jayn Parenti (U.S.A.) baked a layer cake containing 230 layers on July 4, 2006. Jayn's patriotic red, white, and blue creation was prepared and displayed at the Springdale Country Club, Springdale, Arkansas, U.S.A.

Highest pancake toss Bill Weir (U.S.A.), one of the hosts of the television show *Good Morning America!* (ABC, U.S.A.), tossed a pancake 14 ft. (4.2 m) outside the ABC television studios in Times Square, New York City, U.S.A. on August 7, 2006.

★**Longest nougat** A nougat measuring 1,340 ft. 6 in. (408.61 m) in length was made by chef Paolo Attili (Italy) in collaboration with the Associazione Turistica Pro Camerino to celebrate the Day of Torrone (nougat) in Camerino, Italy, on January 7, 2007.

★**Longest onion string** The longest string of onions measured 2.8 miles (4.518 km) and was made by 48 people from Pericei, Salaj County, Romania, as part of the Pericei Onion Fest on September 8, 2007.

★**Longest ice-cream dessert** To celebrate the 25th birthday of its much-loved Viennetta ice-cream dessert, producer Unilever–Wall's prepared a Viennetta measuring 74 ft. 7 in. (22.75 m) in length at the company's Barnwood Factory in Gloucester, UK, on July 11, 2007.

☆ **MOST EXPENSIVE SANDWICH Comprising 24-hour fermented sourdough bread, Iberico ham, poulet de Bresse, white truffles, quail eggs, and semi-dried Italian tomatoes, the most expensive commercially available sandwich is the von Essen Platinum Club Sandwich, created by Daniel Galmiche (UK) for the menu at Cliveden, Buckinghamshire, UK. Costing £100 ($200), the sandwich was added to the menu in March 2007.**

★LARGEST BOWL OF CEREAL The world's largest bowl of cereal contained 2,204 lb. 10 oz. (1,000 kg) of Kellogg's cornflakes and was made by Kellogg's South Africa, Sync Communications, and Automatic in Johannesburg, South Africa, on July 2, 2007. The bowl itself measured 8 ft. 6 in. (2.6 m) in diameter and 4 ft. 11 in. (1.5 m) in height.

☆LARGEST BURGER A hamburger tipping the scales in at 134 lb. (60.78 kg) is commercially available on the menu at Mallie's Sports Grill & Bar in Southgate, Michigan, U.S.A., for $350. It takes three people to flip the "Absolutely Ridiculous Burger," which takes 12 hours to prepare. It is topped with cheese, bacon, tomatoes, onions, and lettuce, and weighs the same as an average adult male!

☆**Longest garlic string** A string of garlic measuring 836 ft. 7 in. (255 m) was made for the annual Garlic Festival in Mako, Hungary, on September 8, 2006.

☆**Longest salami** A salami with a length of 2,358 ft. 7 in. (718.9 m) was created in San Donà di Piave, Venice, Italy, on December 4, 2005. The successful record attempt was organized by Giuseppe Vidotto (Italy).

★ **BIG FOOD** ★

FOOD	SIZE	NAME (NAT.)	YEAR
☆Chocolate bar	7,892 lb. 8 oz. (3,580 kg)	Elah Dufour—Novi (Italy)	2007
☆Cup of coffee	795 gal. (3,613 liters)	Vinacafe Bien Hoa (Vietnam)	2007
☆Dulce de leche	3,129 lb. 12.6 oz. (1,419.65 kg)	Rosario Olvera (Mexico)	2007
★Fishcake	235 lb. (106.59 kg)	Dover Downs Hotel & Casino and Handy International (U.S.A.)	2006
☆Fudge (slab)	5,050 lb. (2.29 metric tons)	Chantelle Gorham of Northwest Fudge Factory (Canada)	2007
☆Gingerbread man	1,308 lb. 8 oz. (593.53 kg)	Smithville Chamber of Commerce (U.S.A.)	2006
★Goulash soup (bowl)	1,583.78 gal. (7,200 liters)	Orizont TV (Romania)	2007
☆Guacamole serving	4,011 lb. 12 oz. (1,819.7 kg)	APEAM, A. C. (Mexican Avocado Industry) and the FECADEMI (Michoacan Community Federation in California)	2007
★Hotpot	460 lb. 8 oz. (208.904 kg)	Garstang and District Partnership (UK)	2007
★Nougat	2,866 lb. (1,300 kg)	Jerome Guigon and Bernard Morin (both France)	2005
★Okonomiyaki	3,527 lb. (1.6 metric tons)	Kamigata Okonomiyaki Takoyaki Cooperative Association (Japan)	2002
★Pupusa	10 ft. 2 in. (3.09 m)	Chamber of Commerce El Salvador-California and Liborio Markets, Inc. (both U.S.A.)	2007
★Ravioli	35 lb. 4 oz. (16 kg)	16 cooks in Saas-Fee (Switzerland)	2007
★Salad	22,619 lb. 6 oz. (10,260 kg)	Sde Warburg Agricultural Association (Israel)	2007
★Scotch egg	11 lb. 15 oz. (5.435 kg)	*Loaded* magazine (UK)	2007
☆Soup (bowl)	3,962 gal. (15,000 liters)	Ministerio del Poder Popular para la Alimentación (Venezuela)	2007
★Tiramisu	674 lb. 8 oz. (305.95 kg)	Alpini Group of Caronno Pertusella and Bariola (Italy)	2007

★ **TALLEST POPPADOM STACK** Richard Bradbury, Kristopher Growcott, Marley Bradbury, and Millie Bradbury (all UK) created a stack of poppadoms 4 ft. 7.9 in. (1.42 m) tall in aid of the Indian Flood Relief charity at La Porte Des Indes Restaurant, London, UK, on November 8, 2007.

★**Most expensive pizza** The most expensive commercially available pizza is a thin-crust, wood fire-baked pizza topped with onion puree, white truffle paste, fontina cheese, baby mozzarella, pancetta, cep mushrooms, and freshly picked wild mizuna lettuce, and garnished with fresh shavings of a rare Italian white truffle, itself worth $2,800 per kilogram (2 lb. 3 oz.). Depending upon the amount of truffles available each season, the pizza is regularly sold at £100 ($200) each to customers at Gordon Ramsay's Maze restaurant, London, UK.

★**Longest tamale** Measuring 51 ft. 9 in. (15.78 m), the longest tamale was made at the El Chico in Jackson, Tennessee, U.S.A., on May 5, 2006.

★ **LARGEST SALAD** The record for the largest salad is 22,619 lb. 6 oz. (10,260 kg), achieved by the Sde Warburg Agricultural Association in Sde Warburg, Israel, on November 10, 2007. It contained 19,841 lb. (9,000 kg) of lettuce, 3,307 lb. (1,500 kg) of carrots, 1,102 lb. (500 kg) of cherry tomatoes, and 211 gal. (800 liters) of salad dressing!

☆ **MOST EXPENSIVE ICE-CREAM SUNDAE** The Frrrozen Haute Chocolate, costing $25,000, was added to the menu of the Serendipity 3 restaurant, New York City, U.S.A., on November 7, 2007. Made in partnership with luxury jeweler Euphoria of New York, the sundae uses a fine blend of 28 cocoas, including 14 of the world's most expensive. It is decorated with 0.17 oz. (5 g) of edible 23-carat gold and is served in a goblet lined with edible gold. The base of the goblet is an 18-carat gold bracelet with 1 carat of white diamonds. The dessert is eaten with a gold and diamond spoon, which can also be taken home.

☆ **Longest strand of pasta** Gewerbe-Verein Siblingen (Siblingen trade association, Switzerland) created a strand of pasta measuring 10,935 ft. (3,333 m) in length in Siblingen, Switzerland, on September 12, 2004.

GARDEN GREATS

★ **Largest cucumber plant** Covering an area of 610 ft.² (56.7 m²), the largest cucumber plant can be found at the Epcot Science project at Walt Disney World Resort in Lake Buena Vista, Florida, U.S.A. The plant was measured in July 2006.

The Epcot Science project is home to the world's ★ **largest tomato plant** too, which also covered an area of 610 ft.² (56.7 m²) when measured on

☆ **HEAVIEST KALE** Scott Robb (U.S.A.) exhibited a kale weighing a record 105 lb. 14.5 oz. (48.04 kg) at the Alaska State Fair, Palmer, Alaska, U.S.A., on August 29, 2007.

March 27, 2007. Both the tomato plant and the cucumber plant are grown on a rectangular trellis measuring 20 ft. × 30 ft. 6 in. (6.1 × 9.3 m).

★ **Most cucumbers harvested from one plant in one year** The cucumber plant at the Epcot Science project (see previous record) produced a crop weighing 2,078 lb. (943 kg). The harvest started on March 24, 2006, and ended on July 5, 2006.

★ HEAVIEST FRUIT & VEGETABLES ★

FRUIT/VEG	WEIGHT	NAME/NATIONALITY	YEAR
Apple	4 lb. 1 oz. (1.84 kg)	Chisato Iwasaki (Japan)	2005
Avocado	4 lb. 6 oz. (1.99 kg)	Anthony Llanos (Australia)	1992
Beet	156 lb. 10 oz. (71.05 kg)	Piet de Goede (Netherlands)	2005
Blueberry	0.24 oz. (7 g)	Brian Carlick (UK)	2005
Broccoli	35 lb. (15.87 kg)	John & Mary Evans (both U.S.A.)	1993
Brussels sprout	18 lb. 3 oz. (8.3 kg)	Bernard Lavery (UK)	1992
Cabbage	124 lb. (56.24 kg)	Bernard Lavery (UK)	1989
Cabbage (red)	42 lb. (19.05 kg)	R. Straw (UK)	1925
Cantaloupe	64 lb. 13 oz. (29.4 kg)	Scott & Mardie Robb (both U.S.A.)	2004
Carrot	18 lb. 13 oz. (8.61 kg)	John Evans (U.S.A.)	1998
Cauliflower	54 lb. 3 oz. (24.6 kg)	Alan Hattersley (UK)	1999
Celery	63 lb. 4 oz. (28.7 kg)	Scott & Mardie Robb (both U.S.A.)	2003
Cherry	0.76 oz. (21.69 g)	Gerardo Maggipinto (Italy)	2003
Cucumber	27 lb. 5 oz. (12.4 kg)	Alfred J. Cobb (UK)	2003
Garlic head	2 lb. 10 oz. (1.19 kg)	Robert Kirkpatrick (U.S.A.)	1985
Gooseberry	2 oz. (61.04 g)	Kelvin Archer (UK)	1993
Gourd	94 lb. 5 oz. (42.8 kg)	Robert Weber (Australia)	2001
☆ Grapefruit	7 lb. 12 oz. (3.21 kg)	Cloy Dias Dutra (Brazil)	2006
Jackfruit	76 lb. 4 oz. (34.6 kg)	George & Margaret Schattauer (both U.S.A.)	2003
☆ Kale	105 lb. 14.5 oz. (48.04 kg)	Scott Robb (U.S.A.)	2007
Kohlrabi	96 lb. 15 oz. (43.98 kg)	Scott Robb (U.S.A.)	2006
Leek	17 lb. 13 oz. (8.1 kg)	Fred Charlton (UK)	2002
Lemon	11 lb. 9 oz. (5.26 kg)	Aharon Shemoel (Israel)	2003
Mango	6 lb. 13 oz. (3.1 kg)	Tai Mok Lim (Malaysia)	2006
Marrow	136 lb. 9 oz. (62 kg)	Mark Baggs (UK)	2005
Nectarine	12 oz. (360 g)	Tony Slattery (New Zealand)	1998
Onion	16 lb. 8 oz. (7.49 kg)*	John Sifford (UK)	2005
☆ Parsnip	10 lb. 14 oz. (4.95 kg)	Joe Atherton (UK)	2007
Peach	25 oz. (725 g)	Paul Friday (U.S.A.)	2002
Pear	4 lb. 8 oz. (2.1 kg)	Warren Yeoman (Australia)	1999
Pineapple	17 lb. 12 oz. (8.06 kg)	E. Kamuk (Papua New Guinea)	1994
Pomegranate	2 lb. 3 oz. (1.04 kg)	Katherine Murphy (U.S.A.)	2001
Potato	7 lb. 11 oz. (3.5 kg)	K. Sloane (UK)	1994
Potato (sweet)	81 lb. 9 oz. (37 kg)	Manuel Pérez Pérez (Spain)	2004
Pummelo	10 lb. 10 oz. (4.86 kg)	Seiji Sonoda (Japan)	2005
☆ Pumpkin	1,689 lb. (766.12 kg)	Joseph Jutras (U.S.A.)	2007
Quince	5 lb. 2 oz. (2.34 kg)	Edward Harold McKinney (U.S.A.)	2002
Radish	68 lb. 9 oz. (31.1 kg)	Manabu Oono (Japan)	2003
Zucchini (Courgette)	64 lb. 8 oz. (29.25 kg)	Bernard Lavery (UK)	1990

☆HEAVIEST PUMPKIN Weighing in at a whopping 1,689 lb. (766.12 kg), the heaviest pumpkin was presented by Joseph Jutras (U.S.A.), at the New England Giant Pumpkin Weigh-off at Topsfield Fair in Topsfield, Massachusetts, U.S.A., on September 29, 2007. Joseph's gigantic vegetable beat the previous record for the heaviest pumpkin by a massive 186.9 lb. (84.8 kg).

☆**Longest carrot** A carrot grown by Joe Atherton (UK) measured 19 ft. 1.96 in. (5.841 m) at the UK National Giant Vegetable Championship in Somerset, UK, on September 2, 2007. Joe grew his champion carrot in a special tube tilted at 45 degrees.

☆**Longest gourd** A gourd grown at the Beidaihe Jifa Agriculture Sightseeing Garden, in Beidaihe, China, measured 13 ft. 3 in. (4.05 m) in length on October 12, 2006.

★**Most blooms on a hellebore plant** On May 4, 2006, Anna Maclean (UK) counted a record 66 blooms on a hellebore (*Helleborus*) plant growing in her garden in Richmond, Surrey, UK.

★**Most plant species grafted onto the same plant** A single host chrysanthemum plant had a record 513 varieties of chrysanthemum grafted onto it as part of the celebrations for the 9th China (Xiaolan, Zhongshan) Chrysanthemum Exhibition in Xiaolan Town, China, on November 23, 2007.

Largest ginseng root A ginseng root weighing 2 lb. 0.5 oz. (0.92 kg) on July 1, 1999, was grown by Don and Joy Hoogesteger (both U.S.A.) of Ridgefield, Washington, U.S.A.

☆**Tallest collard** A collard plant (a green-leafed member of the cabbage family) was found to be 13 ft. 4 in. (4.06 m) tall when it was measured on May 24, 2007, in Leesburg, Florida, U.S.A. It was grown by Woodrow Wilson Granger (U.S.A.).

☆**Largest seed collection** The Millennium Seed Bank Project, housed at the Wellcome Trust Millennium Building, Wakehurst Place, West Sussex, UK, had 20,495 species collected as of January 10, 2008. The seeds are

★ TALLEST PLANTS ★

PLANT	HEIGHT	NAME/NATIONALITY	YEAR
☆ Amaranthus	23 ft. 2 in. (7.06 m)	Brian Moore (U.S.A.)	2007
Bean plant	46 ft. 3 in. (14.1 m)	Staton Rorie (U.S.A.)	2003
Brussels sprout	9 ft. 3 in. (2.8 m)	Patrice & Steve Allison (both U.S.A.)	2001
Cactus (homegrown)	70 ft. (21.3 m)	Pandit S. Munji (India)	2004
Celery	9 ft. (2.74 m)	Joan Priednieks (UK)	1998
Chrysanthemum	14 ft. 3 in. (4.34 m)	Bernard Lavery (UK)	1995
Coleus	8 ft. 4 in. (2.5 m)	Nancy Lee Spilove (U.S.A.)	2004
☆ Collard	13 ft. 4 in. (4.06 m)	Woodrow Wilson Granger (U.S.A.)	2007
Cosmos	12 ft. 3 in. (3.75 m)	Cosmos Executive Committee, Okayama, Japan	2003
☆ Cotton	29 ft. 8 in. (9.04 m)	D. M. Williams (U.S.A.)	2007
Daffodil	5 ft. 1 in. (1.55 m)	M. Lowe (UK)	1979
☆ Dandelion	4 ft. 2.4 in. (1.28 m)	Jeppe, Elise & Simon Hvelplund (all Denmark)	1991
Eggplant (Aubergine)	18 ft. (5.5 m)	Abdul Masfoor (India)	1998
Fuchsia (climbing)	37 ft. 5 in. (11.40 m)	Reinhard Biehler (Germany)	2005
Herba cistanches	6 ft. 4 in. (1.95 m)	Yongmao Chen (China)	2006
Papaya tree	44 ft. (13.4 m)	Prasanta Mal (India)	2003
☆ Parsley	6 ft. (1.82 m)	Herbert Jonas (Germany)	2007
Pepper	16 ft. (4.87 m)	Laura Liang (U.S.A.)	1999
Periwinkle	7 ft. 2 in. (2.19 m)	Avind, Rekha, Ashish & Rashmi Nema (all India)	2003
Petunia	19 ft. 1 in. (5.8 m)	Bernard Lavery (UK)	1994
Rosebush (self-supported)	13 ft. 3 in. (4.03 m)	Paul & Sharon Palumbo (both U.S.A.)	2005
Rose (climbing)	91 ft. (27.7 m)	Anne & Charles Grant (both U.S.A.)	2004
Sugarcane	31 ft. (9.5 m)	M. Venkatesh Gowda (India)	2005
Sunflower	25 ft. 5 in. (7.76 m)	Martien Heijms (Netherlands)	1986
Sweetcorn (maize)	31 ft. (9.4 m)	D. Radda (U.S.A.)	1946
Texas Bluebonnet	5 ft. 5 in. (1.64 m)	Margaret Lipscomb & Arthur Cash (both U.S.A.).	2005
Tomato	65 ft. (19.8 m)	Nutriculture Ltd., Lancashire, UK	2000
Umbrella	27 ft. (8.22 m)	Konstantinos Xytakis & Sara Guterbock (both U.S.A.)	2002
Zinnia	12 ft. 6 in. (3.81 m)	Everett Wallace Jr. & Melody Wagner (both U.S.A.)	2004

TALLEST TOPIARY Since 1983, Moirangthem Okendra Kumbi of Manipur, India, has been shaping the shoots of a Sky Flower bush (*Duranta repens variegata*) in his "Hedge to Heaven" garden, which has grown to a height of 60 ft. 11.9 in. (18.59 m). Overall, with the help of a specially constructed ladder, he has cut 41 structural shapes repeating a design of a rounded umbrella followed by two discs. Moirangthem was originally informed that his plant would be unlikely to grow higher than 20 ft. (6 m), but with his twice-daily pruning, it's now a record holder!

stored in underground frozen vaults and are part of an international conservation project, managed by the Royal Botanical Gardens of Kew (UK), with the aim of insuring thousands of species against possible extinction. The project banked its billionth seed, a type of African bamboo called *Oxytenanthera abyssinica,* in April 2007.

Heaviest edible fungi An edible "chicken of the woods" mushroom (*Laetiporus sulphureus*) weighing 100 lb. (45.35 kg) was found in the New Forest, Hampshire, UK, by Giovanni Paba of Broadstone, Dorset, UK, on October 15, 1990.

☆ **CLOVER WITH THE MOST LEAVES** An 18-leaf clover was discovered by Shigeo Obara of Hanamaki City, Iwate, Japan, on May 25, 2002. This luckiest of clovers beat the previous record holder by four leaves.

PETS

☆**Most skips by a dog in one minute** Sweet Pea, an Australian shepherd/border collie cross, completed 75 jump-rope skips in one minute, aided by her owner Alex Rothaker (U.S.A.), on the set of *Live with Regis and Kelly* in New York, U.S.A. on August 8, 2007.

TALLEST AND SHORTEST DOGS The **tallest living dog** is Gibson, a harlequin Great Dane, who measured 42.2 in. (107 cm) tall on August 31, 2004, and is owned by Sandy Hall of California, U.S.A.

The ☆**shortest living dog** is a long-haired Chihuahua called Boo Boo, who measured 4 in. (10.16 cm) tall on May 12, 2007 and is owned by Lana Elswick of Kentucky, U.S.A.

★ **LONGEST RABBIT** Amy, a Flemish giant rabbit belonging to Annette Edwards (UK), measured 2 ft. 8 in. (81.5 cm)—from the tip of her nose to the tip of her tail—when measured on March 23, 2008. The Flemish giant is the **largest rabbit breed**, weighing up to 17 lb. 10 oz. (8 kg). *NB: Animal weight records are not monitored by GWR.*

★ **Most keys removed from a keyring by a parrot in two minutes** Smudge, a parrot owned by Mark Steiger (Switzerland), removed 20 keys from a keyring in two minutes on the set of the *Circo Massimo Show,* in Rome, Italy, on May 23, 2007.

★ **Most quarantined domestic animal** Smarty, a ginger cat, was quarantined for the 40th time in Larnaca, Cyprus, after her 79th flight from Cairo, Egypt, on June 28, 2005. Smarty—owned by Peter and Carole Godfrey (UK), who live in Cairo, Egypt—also holds the record for the **most flights by a cat.**

★ **Oldest horse twins** Taff and Griff, identical male twins of the Cremello breed, were born in 1982. They measure 11.2 hands (3 ft. 10 in.; 1.16 m) and are owned by the Veteran Horse Society in Wales, UK. They have spent their entire lives together, giving rides to children at London Zoo before retiring to Wales.

☆ **Oldest documented caged parrot** Sandra LaFollette of Chariton, Iowa, U.S.A., bought her pet parrot Fred in 1968 when he was six months old. Fred was still going strong in 2007, aged 39 years.

Oldest caged canary A caged canary named Joey lived to the venerable age of 34 years under the care of his owner, Mrs. K. Ross of Hull, UK. Joey was purchased in Calabar, Nigeria, in 1941 and died on April 8, 1975.

FACT

Both the Netherland and Polish dwarf rabbits have a weight range of just 2–2 lb. 7 oz. (0.9–1.13 kg). The two breeds tie for the record of the **smallest breed of rabbit.**

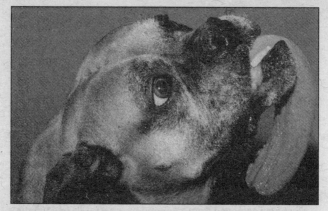

LONGEST TONGUE ON A DOG The longest canine tongue belonged to a boxer dog named Brandy and measured 17 in. (43 cm). She lived with her owner, John Scheid, in St. Clair Shores, Michigan, U.S.A., until her death in September 2002.

Heaviest dog breed The Old English mastiff and the St. Bernard share the record for the heaviest breed of domestic dog (*Canis familiaris*), with males of both species regularly weighing 170 lb. (78 kg).

LONGEST DOG LIVING With a nose-to-tail length of 91.3 in. (232 cm), Mon Ami von der Oelmühle is the longest dog alive today. The Irish Wolfhound was bred by Jürgen Rösner (pictured) and is owned by Joachim and Elke Müller of Wegberg-Arsbeck, Germany.

☆**LARGEST PET SPIDER** Rosi, a 12-year-old female Goliath bird-eating spider (*Theraphosa blondi*), weighed 6.17 oz. (175 g), had a body length of 4.7 in. (12 cm), a leg-span of 10.2 in. (26 cm), and a mandible measuring 0.9 in. (2.5 cm) on July 27, 2007. She belongs to Walter Baumgartner of Andorf, Austria.

Longest tail on a domestic cat Furball, a domestic cat who lives with her owner, Jan Acker (U.S.A.), in Battle Creek, Michigan, U.S.A., had a tail length of 16 in. (40.6 cm) when measured on March 21, 2001.

SMALLEST DOMESTIC HAMSTER BREED The domesticated Roborovski hamster (*Phodopus roborovskii*) typically grows to a length of 1.52 in. (4.5 cm). Roborovski hamsters originate from Mongolia and northern China.

Largest pigeon A Canadian Giant Runt Cock pigeon called Doc Yeck, owned by Leonard Yeck of Brantford, Ontario, Canada, weighed an unprecedented 4 lb. (1.8 kg) and had a chest width of 5 in. (12.7 cm) when measured on March 6, 1999.

LONG-LIVED PETS . . .

★**Chicken** As of 2007, the oldest living chicken was Blacky, a black bantam, who was born in 1986 and belongs to Veronika and Ladislav Seljak of Geelong, Australia.

Domestic bird Excluding the ostrich, which has been known to live up to 68 years, the longest-lived domesticated bird is the goose (*Anser a. domesticus*), which has an average lifespan of about 25 years. On December 16, 1976, a gander named George, owned by Florence Hull of Thornton, Lancashire, UK, died aged 49 years 8 months. He was hatched in April 1927.

★**Pig** A pig named Cedric was born in 1988 and lived with his owner, Faye Fyfe, in Nimbin, Australia, until he died on October 5, 2006, aged 18 years.

FASHION

☆**Largest dress** Created by the Association de la Femme Artisane Agadir and displayed at the Kaftan show in Agadir, Morocco, from July 7–11, 2006, the largest dress measured 36 ft. 8.9 in. (11.2 m) in length.

☆**Largest T-shirt** OMO Safe Detergent created a T-shirt that measured 187 ft. 7 in. (57.19 m) long and 134 ft. 1 in. (40.88 m) wide in Ho Chi Minh City, Vietnam. It was displayed on March 9, 2006.

First designer label Charles Frederick Worth, who died in 1895, was the first designer to sign his work with a label and to show garments on live models. Born in Lincolnshire, UK, he moved to Paris, France, in 1845, where his designs were worn by the ladies of the court of Napoleon III. He started his own business and by 1871 was making $80,000 (£14,981) a year.

As the first designer who employed real models to wear his designs for clients, he is also seen as the **first haute couturier.**

Youngest haute couturier Yves (-Mathieu) Saint-Laurent (France, b. 1936), who became Christian Dior's assistant at age 17, was named head of the House of Dior on Dior's death in 1957. In 1962, he opened his own fashion house, and in the 1970s created ready-to-wear lines, household linens, and fragrances.

"I've never been to the gym. I do nothing."

Adriana Lima (Brazil), the youngest model on the
Forbes Celebrity 100 List, discussing her fitness regime

Longest catwalk A group of 111 fashion models walked the entire length of a 3,645-ft. (1.111-km) catwalk built in the parking lot of Seacon Square shopping center, Sri Nakarin Road, Thailand, between May 27 and 30, 1998.

Longest catwalk marathon A 10-hour catwalk marathon took place as part of the *More* magazine fashion awards 2005 (UK) at the Commonwealth Club, London, UK, on February 4, 2005. The show included exhibits from 24 popular retailers with over 530 summer outfits, shoes, and accessories.

★Oldest model on the *Forbes* Celebrity 100 list Heidi Klum (Germany, b. June 1, 1973) was aged 34 years 13 days when *Forbes'* Celebrity 100 list was published on forbes.com on June 14, 2007. Klum was ranked number 84 on the list, with a wealth estimated at $8 million.

Highest annual earnings by a model Brazilian beauty Gisele Bündchen earned $35 million in 2007, according to *Forbes*. The model, famously discovered at the age of 14 while eating in a McDonald's restaurant, has worked for famous brands such as Ralph Lauren, Dolce & Gabbana, Versace, Valentino, Celine, and Gianfranco Ferré.

★YOUNGEST MODEL ON THE *FORBES* CELEBRITY 100 LIST Adriana Lima (Brazil, b. June 12, 1981) was aged 26 years 2 days when she first featured in *Forbes'* Celebrity 100 list, on forbes.com, on June 14, 2007. Best known for her modeling contracts with Maybelline and Victoria's Secret (both U.S.A.), Lima was listed at number 99, with a wealth estimated at $4 million.

☆ **MOST EXPENSIVE PERFUME** A 1-fl.-oz. (30-ml) bottle of "Clive Christian No.1 for Men" or "No.1 for Women" typically costs $2,355. In November 2005, Clive Christian created "No.1 Imperial Majesty," a 10-bottle, limited edition of the Clive Christian No.1 Collection, priced at $205,000 per 17 fl. oz. (500 ml). The price included delivery in a Bentley.

☆ **LARGEST UNDERPANTS** On November 15, 2007, swimwear and underwear company aussieBum made a pair of underpants 52 ft. 1 in. (15.9 m) across the waist and 34 ft. 7 in. (10.5 m) from crotch to waistband. It was displayed in Sydney's Royal Botanic Gardens, New South Wales, Australia.

DID YOU KNOW?

The world's **most expensive bra** is the $10-million "Millennium Bra" produced by Victoria's Secret and first unveiled on *The Tonight Show* by model Heidi Klum on November 11, 1999. The bra has 3,024 stones—including diamonds and 1,988 sapphires.

★MOST EXPENSIVE SARI The most costly sari was sold for 3,931,627 rupees ($100,021) on January 5, 2008. Made of silk, it was manufactured by Chennai Silks, India, and features reproductions of 11 paintings by the celebrated Indian artist Raja Ravi Varma.

Richest woman Liliane Bettencourt (France), the 85-year-old heiress to the L'Oréal cosmetics fortune (and daughter of founder Eugene Schueller), is estimated to be worth $22.9 billion.

LARGEST KIMONO On March 23, 2001, the largest kimono in the world was created as part of the National Kimono Festival in Cho Kagoshima City, Japan. The giant kimono was 35 ft. 4 in. (11.72 m) wide, 41 ft. 10 in. (12.8 m) high, and weighed 220 lb. 6 oz. (100 kg).

★ LARGEST PHOTO SHOOT OF PEOPLE WEARING BIKINIS A total of 1,010 participants took part in a bikini photo shoot organized by *Cosmopolitan* magazine and Venus Breeze (both Australia) on Bondi Beach in Sydney, Australia, on September 26, 2007.

WEALTH & POVERTY

HIGHS & LOWS

Highest The **highest-value notes in circulation** are those for $10,000 released by the U.S. Federal Reserve between 1865 and 1945. High-denomination bills were discontinued in the U.S.A. in 1969, but the 200 $10,000 bills that remain in circulation are still legal tender.

HIGHEST AND LOWEST EDUCATION BUDGETS The country with the ☆ highest percentage of Gross Domestic Product (GDP) spent on education is Cuba (left) with 9.8%, according to the latest annual figures available for 2000–05. Meanwhile, Equatorial Guinea (above) has the ☆ lowest percentage of Gross Domestic Product (GDP) spent on education, with just 0.6% over the same period.

HIGHEST AND LOWEST INFLATION RATES The country with the world's ☆highest annual rate of consumer price inflation is Zimbabwe (top, left) with a rate of 349.8% between 2001 and 2006.

Between 2001 and 2005, the country with the world's ☆lowest annual rate of consumer price inflation was Libya (bottom left) with a rate of -3.1%.

Lowest The one-sen (or 1/100th of a rupiah) Indonesian note had an exchange value of 358,624 to the UK£ in July 1996, making it the **lowest-value legal tender note ever.**

☆**Highest budget expenditure** It has been estimated that the U.S. government spent $2.731 trillion—including capital expenditures—in 2007, the greatest governmental expenditure of any country.

☆**Highest GNI per capita** According to the World Bank figures for September 2007, the country with the highest Gross National Income (GNI) per capita for 2006 was Luxembourg, with $76,040. Gross National Income is the total value of goods and services produced by a country in one year, divided by its population. GNI per capita shows how much of a country's GNI each person would have if GNI were divided equally.

☆**Lowest GNI per capita** According to the World Bank figures from September 2007, the country with the lowest Gross National Income (GNI) per capita in 2006 was Burundi, with $100.

★**Lowest budget expenditure** The Pitcairn Islands in the Pacific Ocean had a budget expenditure of $878,119—including capital expenditures—as of December 2003.

☆ **HIGHEST COST OF LIVING** According to the Economist Intelligence Unit's Worldwide Cost of Living Survey, the world's most expensive city is Oslo, Norway, as of March 2007.

★Lowest budget revenue As of December 2003, Tokelau in the south Pacific had a budget revenue of $430,830.

☆Largest national debt By April 22, 2008, the U.S. national debt stood at $9,372,485,723,263.83, making America the largest debtor nation in history. You can watch the progress of the debt live online at the U.S. Treasury Office website: www.treasurydirect.gov/NP/BPDLogin?application=np.

☆Highest rate of unemployment Macedonia is the country with the highest rate of unemployment—37.2% of the labor force is without a job, despite being available for work.

★Highest percentage of GDP taxed (country) When viewed as a percentage of a country's Gross Domestic Product (GDP), the country that taxed the highest amount (of national income) in 2006 was Sweden, with 50%.

★Most expensive city to eat in restaurants According to Zagat restaurant guides, London, UK, is the world's most expensive city for dining out. In 2007, the average cost of a three-course meal plus one glass of wine

★ MOST SUCCESSFUL CHIMPANZEE ON WALL STREET Raven, a six-year-old chimpanzee, became the 22nd most successful money manager in the U.S.A. after choosing her stocks by throwing darts at a list of 133 internet companies. The chimp created her own index, dubbed MonkeyDex, and in 1999 delivered a 213% gain—outperforming more than 6,000 professional brokers on Wall Street. "She quadrupled the performance of the Dow and doubled the performance of the Nasdaq composite," said Roland Perry, editor of the *Internet Stock Review*.

★ **FASTEST TIME TO EARN A BIG MAC** The banking giant UBS (Switzerland) has created the Big Mac Index to estimate how long the average person from 70 countries worldwide would have to work to earn enough money to buy a Big Mac. The worldwide average is 35 minutes, but in Japan the average time required is just 10 minutes. The index measures purchasing power by eliminating variables such as exchange rates. In Bogota, Colombia, people must work an average of 97 minutes in order to buy a Big Mac, illustrating that the purchasing power in Central and South America is one-third of that in a typical North American city.

was £39.09 ($79.66)—practically double that of New York City, U.S.A., where the equivalent meal cost $39.33.

☆ **Richest soccer team** According to Deloitte's annual Football Money League for the 2006/07 season, Real Madrid (Spain) is the world's richest soccer team. The Spanish champions had a total income of €318.2 million ($465.1 million) for the year.

Largest animal legacy A standard poodle called Toby was the beneficiary of the largest legacy ever devoted to an animal. On her death in 1931, Ella Wendel of New York City, U.S.A., bequeathed $15 million to her favorite pet. Using the Retail Price Index as an indicator, Toby's inheritance would be worth $220 million today.

CRIME & PUNISHMENT

★ **First hijacking of a commercial airliner** The first hijacking of a commercial airliner occurred on July 17, 1948, when terrorists attempted to gain control of a Cathay Pacific Airways seaplane en route from Macau to Hong Kong, ultimately causing it to crash into the sea off the coast of Macau. One person out of 26 passengers and crew survived.

★ **FIRST HIJACKING OF AN AIRCRAFT** The first recorded aircraft hijacking took place on February 21, 1931, in Peru, when Byron Rickards (U.S.A.) was flying a Ford Tri-motor from Lima to Arequipa. Once he had landed the plane, he was surrounded by soldiers and told he had become the prisoner of a revolutionary organization. He was released on March 2, of the same year.

★ **Greatest payout for sexual abuse** The largest amount of compensation awarded to victims of sexual abuse is $660 million. On July 15, 2007, the Roman Catholic Archdiocese of Los Angeles, U.S.A., agreed to share this amount out to 508 people who had suffered from abuse by members of the clergy over a period of 50 years.

★ **LARGEST FRAUD BY A ROGUE TRADER** On January 24, 2008, major French bank Société Générale declared that it had uncovered a fraud that had generated losses totaling €4.9 billion ($7.16 billion), following rogue trading by a member of its staff. On January 26, 2008, bank trader Jerome Kerviel (France) was taken into police custody and was later said to have admitted hiding his activities from his superiors.

★ **LARGEST OPIUM PRODUCER** Afghanistan is the world's leading producer of opium, having cultivated 476,910 acres (193,000 ha) of opium poppies in 2007—a 17% increase over 2006. The war-torn country produced an extraordinary 18 million lb. (8,200 metric tons) of opium in 2007, which amounts to 93% of the global opiates market.

★ **Longest career as a police officer** Detective Lieutenant Andrew F. Anewenter (U.S.A., b. January 12, 1916) worked continuously as a police officer for 61 years for the Milwaukee (Wisconsin) Police Department from June 1, 1942, until his retirement on May 15, 2003.

★ **First use of "forensic gait analysis" evidence in court** Forensic gait analysis is the study of a person's style of walking (gait) as a method of identification. The first time that this form of evidence became admissible in criminal law occurred in the case R. versus Saunders at The Old Bailey, London, UK, on July 12, 2000. Consultant podiatrist Haydn Kelly (UK) was able to identify jewelry thief John Saunders (UK) as the person attempting to rob a store from earlier police surveillance footage. Despite Saunders wearing two pairs of trousers, a mask, and gloves, Mr. Kelly was able to confirm that less than 5% of the UK population had walking mechanics that were similar to those of the suspected thief, evidence that helped end Saunders' lucrative criminal career.

★ **Highest murder rate per capita (country)** According to the 9th United Nations Survey of Crime Trends and Operations of Criminal Justice Systems, the country with the highest murder rate—as of 2004—is Ecuador, with 18.87 per 100,000 people.

DID YOU KNOW?

Helmand Province, in southern Afghanistan, where much of the current fighting between NATO forces and the Taliban is taking place, provides 50% of the country's opium crop.

★ HIGHEST POPULATION OF PRISONERS (FEMALE) According to the World Female Imprisonment List of the International Centre for Prison Studies at King's College, London, UK, the country with the largest population of female prisoners is the U.S.A., with 183,400 as of April 2006. This figure represents 8.6% of the total U.S. prison population.

☆ MOST MURDERS PER YEAR (COUNTRY) According to the United Nations, the country with the highest number of murders for the latest year available is the Philippines, with 3,515 homicides in 2004.

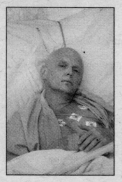

★ FIRST RECORDED MURDER BY RADIATION On November 23, 2006, Alexander Litvinenko (Russia) died from radiation poisoning in London, UK, becoming the first known victim of Polonium 210-induced acute radiation syndrome. The case is unsolved.

★ **HIGHEST INCIDENCE OF SHIP PIRACY (REGION)** The area that experiences the highest incidence of ship piracy is that around Southeast Asia, particularly in Indonesian waters. There were 43 attacks here in 2007 out of an annual worldwide total of 263.

☆ **Highest population of prisoners documented** According to figures released by the U.S. Bureau of Justice Statistics, the U.S.A. incarcerates more people than any other country. At the end of 2006, a total of 2,258,983 people were inmates in U.S. Federal or State prisons or in local jails, a rate of 751 per 100,000 U.S. residents.

WORLD AT WAR

★ **Youngest age to join the armed forces** In the east Asian country of Laos, the minimum age for military service is 15 years.

★ **Largest exporter of arms** According to the Stockholm International Peace Research Institute (SIPIRI) Arms Transfers Database, the U.S.A.

☆ **LARGEST LANDLOCKED NAVY** In 2007, Bolivia's landlocked navy had 4,800 personnel, of which marines comprise 1,700 (including 1,000 naval military police) to patrol the country's river systems and Lake Titicaca. The navy's headquarters is at Puerto Guayaramerín.

★ **LARGEST ALL-FEMALE PEACEKEEPING UNIT** For the first time ever, the United Nations has deployed an all-female police peacekeeping unit—to help rebuild the Liberian police force, which had acquired a bad reputation for corruption. The force of 103 women has been provided by the Indian government.

exported an annual average of $7,964,100,000 worth of arms—that is to say, major conventional weapons or systems—in the 10 years between 1998 and 2007.

★ **Largest importer of arms** From 1998 to 2007, China topped the list of the world's largest arms importers, averaging an annual spend of $2,318,200,000.

☆ **LARGEST PEACEKEEPING OPERATION** On July 31, 2007, the United Nations (UN) authorized the deployment of a hybrid UN/African Union force to support the Darfur Peace Agreement in Sudan, Africa. At full strength, it will be the largest peacekeeping mission in the world deployed on one operation, with nearly 26,000 personnel involved.

"Women police are seen to be much less threatening, although they can be just as tough as men."

Seema Dhundiya, commander of the United Nations' first women-only unit

★**Largest arms manufacturer** Excluding Chinese companies, for which data are limited, the top manufacturer of arms (not just the manufacture but also the research and development, maintenance, servicing, and repair of equipment used by the military) is Boeing (U.S.A.). In 2005, it sold $54,845,000,000 worth of primarily aircraft, electronics, missiles and space hardware.

★**Most dangerous country for the media** According to Reporters Without Borders, 210 journalists and media assistants have been killed in Iraq since the start of fighting in March 2003. This is more than in the 1955–75 Vietnam War.

★**Richest insurgency group** The Revolutionary Armed Forces of Colombia (FARC) is considered to be the richest insurgent group in the world, thanks mostly to profits made from drug trafficking topped up with extortion and kidnap ransoms.

Estimates place the FARC's funds at anywhere up to $1 billion, with annual profits from the drugs trade bringing in between $200 million and $300 million according to the U.S. Council on Foreign Relations.

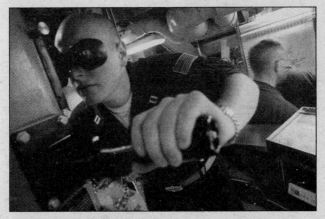

☆ **LARGEST NAVY BY ARMED SUBMARINES** The U.S. Navy has 71 armed submarines (14 strategic ballistic missile craft and 57 tactical craft). The U.S.A.'s entire submarine fleet is nuclear powered.

☆ **HIGHEST PERCENTAGE OF MILITARY PERSONNEL (COUNTRY) In 2007, 4.75% of North Korea's total population of 23,301,725 was actively engaged in military duty.**

★ **Largest militarized territorial dispute** According to the *CIA World Factbook,* the dispute between China, India, and Pakistan for the Kashmir region is the largest and most militarized territorial dispute currently on the planet, despite the massive earthquake that devastated the area in 2005, killing 80,000 people.

The former Indian state has been fought over since the end of British rule

MOST WANTED TERRORIST Osama bin Laden (Saudi Arabia), figurehead of the terrorist organization Al-Qaeda, is the only terrorist on the U.S. Federal Bureau of Investigation (FBI) "Ten Most Wanted" list, and is sought by many nations for his alleged terrorist activites

X-REF

If you're a real military buff, shoot forward to our **Weapons** section on p. 269. Plane crazy? Spot record-breaking **Aircraft** on p. 265.

of India and partition in 1947. India also refuses to recognize Pakistan's ceding of Kashmir lands to China in 1964, and recently claimed that China transferred nuclear weapons to Pakistan.

At any one time, up to 1 million troops confront each other across the Line of Control that separates Indian- and Pakistani-controlled Kashmir.

★**Country with most troops deployed overseas** As of May 2005, the country with the highest number of military personnel serving their country, but overseas, is the U.S.A. with approximately 350,000 personnel on active duty. This figure includes those forces normally present in Germany, Italy, the United Kingdom, and Japan, unless bases at those locations are actively supporting a combat operation.

SCIENCE &
ENGINEERING

CONTENTS

SCIENCE FRONTIERS

☆ **Darkest substance** The darkest man-made substance is a low-density carbon nanotube array created by researchers from U.S. colleges Rensselaer Polytechnic Institute (Zu-Po Yang, James A. Bur, Prof. Shawn-Yu Lin) and Rice University (Dr. Lijie Ci, Prof. P. M. Ajayan). Regular black paint reflects between 5% and 10% of light (it absorbs the rest), but this new coating is so dark that it reflected only 0.045% of light when tested at Rensselaer Polytechnic Institute on August 24, 2007.

★ **Longest document scanned** A document measuring 3,875 ft. (1,181 m) was scanned on a Trüper 3600 scanner by Böwe Bell + Howell (U.S.A.) at the Healthcare Information and Management Systems Society's Annual Conference, Orlando, Florida, U.S.A., on February 25, 2008.

☆ **Largest known prime number** The largest known prime number is $2^{32,582,657}$ -1. It was discovered by a team at Central Missouri State University in September 2006. With a staggering 9,808,358 digits, this latest "Mersenne Prime" is close to claiming a $100,000 reward for discovering the first 10-million-digit prime number.

☆ **Most powerful pulsed spallation neutron source** The Spallation Neutron Source at the Oak Ridge National Laboratory (U.S.A.) is the most powerful of its kind in the world. By using a proton beam to pound a target with more than 300 kW of energy, it is able to produce 4.8×10^{16} neutrons per second. Eventually, these neutrons will be focused into beams that will allow the molecular analysis of advanced materials.

★ **Smallest object filmed in motion** In February 2008, Swedish scientists announced they had footage of an electron riding a wave of light just after being pulled away from an atom.

★ **LONGEST-LASTING AA BATTERY CELLS** Panasonic's EVOLTA alkaline battery cells—produced by Matsushita Battery Industrial Co., Ltd., and Matsushita Electric Industrial Co., Ltd. (both Japan)—are the longest-lasting AA battery cells available, keeping gadgets running 20% longer than current batteries. To assess the cells, discharge tests were conducted in accordance with guidelines set by the International Electrotechnical Commission (IEC).

★ **LARGEST PARTICLE DETECTOR** The ATLAS Detector, part of the Large Hadron Collider (LHC) at CERN—located on the border between France and Switzerland—measures 150 ft. (46 m) long and 82 ft. (25 m) wide and high. It weighs 15.4 million lb. (7,000 metric tons) and contains 100 million sensors that measure particles produced in proton-proton collisions in the Compact Muon Solenoid, seen above. The last piece of ATLAS was installed in March 2008.

★ **Quantum communication distance record** In March 2008, scientists announced they had detected and identified single photons of light bounced off an orbiting satellite some 922 miles (1,485 km) above the Earth. This achievement is a critical step toward establishing a space-based quantum communications channel—the holy grail of secure and uninterceptable digital communications researchers.

★ **Most powerful laser (output)** In terms of output in wattage, the Texas Petawatt Laser at the University of Texas, U.S.A., is the most powerful laser in the world. On March 31, 2008, it achieved an output of 1 petawatt, or 1,000,000,000,000,000 watts, when it was fired for a tenth of a trillionth of a second (0.0000000000001 second).

DID YOU KNOW?

Built at a cost of over $6 billion and with a 16-mile (27-km) circumference, the LHC (see photo above) is designed to smash particles together at close the speed of light. Scientists hope that by studying the results of these collisions they will be able to discover more about the way that matter works.

234   Science & Engineering

★ **MOST POWERFUL TESLA COIL** The Tesla coil at the Mid-America Science Museum in Hot Springs, Arkansas, U.S.A., can produce 1,500,000 volts of electricity. (By comparison, a bug zapper operates at 1,500 volts.) It is enclosed in a steel Faraday cage to protect visitors from the "lightning" (corona discharges).

☆ **MOST POWERFUL HANDHELD LASER** Tested three times for five-minute durations using two separate photon-measuring devices, the Hercules 500 outputted a 1 W peak and 940 mW (+/- 20 mW) average of brilliant-green (532nm) laser light. Made by Laserglow Technologies of Ontario, Canada, the Class IV handheld battery-powered device features five independent safety devices to make it legal to use around the world. Its long-range applications include construction and antenna alignment, but at close range it is capable of starting fires.

★ **LARGEST MAN-MADE AIR VORTEX** The Mercedes-Benz museum in Stuttgart, Germany, boasts a unique smoke-elimination system. On detecting a fire, air is injected into the interior courtyard of the museum in such a way that it generates a 112-ft.-high (34.4-m) artificial tornado; this collects smoke, which is then discharged outside via a smoke-elimination ventilator located in the upper part of the building.

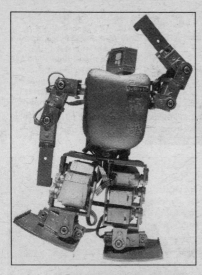

☆ **SMALLEST ROBOT HUMANOID** Be-Robot, measuring just 6 in. (153 mm) high, is able to walk, kick, and perform push-ups. The robot was manufactured by GeStream (Taiwan) and demonstrated at the Global SMEs Convention 2007 on September 6, 2007, in Kuala Lumpur, Malaysia.

★ **MOST POWERFUL ELECTRO-ACOUSTIC SPEAKER** The Hyperspike HS-60, invented by Curt Graber of Wattre Corporation, U.S.A., is an Acoustic Hailing Device (AHD) capable of producing a coherent beam of sound—like a laser beam in the human voice range. In certified field tests conducted in March 2007, its beam remained coherent for 866 ft. (264 m), and output was measured at 140.2 decibels (dB) at a 420-ft. (128-m) range using less than 3 kW of electricity. Its output is equivalent to 182 dB from a distance of 3 ft. (1 m) and, under optimal conditions, it can transmit audible voice communications to a target across a distance of over 2 miles (3 km).

GENETICS

Largest cat hybrid The largest hybrid of the cat family (Felidae) is the liger (no scientific name), which is the offspring of a male lion and a tigress. Ligers typically grow larger than either parent, reaching lengths of 10–12 ft. (3-3.6 m). The size and appearance of the liger can vary, depending upon which subspecies of lion or tiger is involved. Although these hybrids could occur in the wild, wherever lions and tigers inhabit the same territory—for example, the Gir forest in India, such crossbreeding usually happens in zoos or private menageries.

First cloned dog The first cloned dog to survive birth is Snuppy, an Afghan hound puppy created by Hwang Woo-Suk (South Korea) and his team at Seoul National University (SNU) in South Korea, after which the dog was named. Snuppy's growth was stimulated when a donor egg cell fused with deoxyribonucleic acid (DNA) from the ear of a three-year-old male Afghan hound named Tie, before being transferred to a surrogate female for 60 days of pregnancy. Snuppy was born on April 25, 2005.

First gene therapy recipient The first attempt to fix a genetic disorder in a human being was made in September 1990. Four-year-old Ashanthi De-Silva (U.S.A.) suffered from a deficiency of adenosine deaminase (ADA). As a result of her weak immune system caused by the condition, she had been chronically ill for her whole life. Her pioneering doctors gave her healthy copies of the gene that produces ADA by placing the gene in a modified virus, which was then allowed to infect her blood cells. She now lives a healthy life.

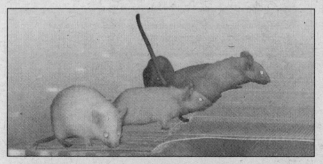

★ **STRONGEST GENETICALLY MODIFIED MOUSE** In November 2007, U.S. scientists announced the creation of a genetically modified mouse with extraordinary physical abilities. In tests, the mouse astonished scientists by running nonstop at 65 ft. (20 m) per minute for five hours. It also lives longer than normal mice and is described as being 10 times more active.

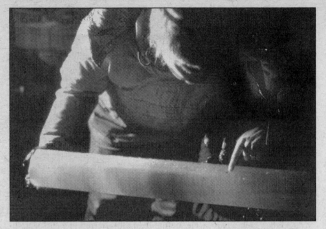

☆ **OLDEST DNA** In July 2007, scientists announced they had discovered DNA dating back as far as 800,000 years from ice cores taken from Greenland's ice sheet. The DNA reveals that moths and butterflies were abundant in the spruce and pine forests that existed in Greenland during this much warmer period of its history.

KEY DATES

1859—Charles Darwin (UK) publishes *The Origin of Species*

1882—Walter Fleming (Germany) discovers and names "chromosomes"

1906—the word "genetics" is used for the first time

1952—Martha Chase and Alfred Hershey (both U.S.A.) prove that inherited traits are passed down by DNA

1953—James Watson (U.S.A.) and Francis Crick (UK) discover the double-helix shape of DNA

1977—Fred Sanger (UK) develops a breakthrough method of sequencing DNA

1984—Alec Jeffreys (UK) introduces DNA fingerprinting

1990—The Human Genome Project is launched

1997—Ian Wilmut (UK) creates Dolly the sheep, the first cloned mammal

2001—Advanced Cell Technologies clones human embryos for the first time

2003—The Human Genome Project is completed and published

MOST GENETICALLY DIVERSE PEOPLE Pygmies and the bushmen of Africa are the most genetically diverse people on Earth. For some genetic traits, they have as many as 17 variations, whereas most people have only two or three. A possible explanation is that our oldest ancestors came from these regions, perhaps 200,000 years ago, and that not all of them left to spread around the world.

First use of DNA profiling to overturn a conviction The first person to have a conviction overturned due to DNA profiling was Gary Dotson (U.S.A.), who was wrongly accused of raping Cathleen Crowell (UK). In

★**FASTEST-EVOLVING ANIMAL** *Sphenodon punctatus,* a type of reptile known as a tuatara, is evolving almost 10 times faster than the average for all animals. In March 2008, a report revealed that the species is making about 1.37 substitutions per base pair every million years, compared to the average of just 0.2.

★FIRST PUBLICATION OF A HUMAN GENOME In September 2007, scientist and entrepreneur Dr. Craig Venter (U.S.A.) published his own genome (genetic code) in its entirety. This complete record of his genetic makeup contained some 6 billion letters and was retrieved at an estimated cost of $35 million.

July 1979, he was sentenced to 25–50 years for the rape and the same again for aggravated kidnapping. In 1988, DNA tests (not available earlier) were conducted proving that Dotson was innocent. This led to Dotson being exonerated on August 14, 1989, having served eight years of his sentence.

First use of DNA profiling in a conviction The first person to be convicted of a crime using DNA evidence was Robert Melias (UK), who was found guilty of rape and convicted by a British court on November 13, 1988. Soon after in the U.S.A., Tommy Lee Andres (U.S.A.) became the first American to be convicted based on DNA evidence.

First use of DNA profiling to clear a suspect The world's first DNA-based manhunt took place between 1986 and 1988 in Enderby, Leicestershire, UK, during the investigation of a double rape-murder. The prime suspect, a local boy named Richard Buckland (UK), confessed to the second killing, but DNA profiling of the victims revealed that his DNA did not match that of the killer. Buckland thus became the first suspect cleared using DNA profiling. The actual killer, Colin Pitchfork (UK), who sent another man's blood sample during the testing of 5,000 local men, was finally caught after the deception was discovered. Pitchfork's DNA matched that of the killer and he was sentenced to life imprisonment in 1988.

Farthest traced descendant by DNA Adrian Targett, a teacher from Cheddar, Somerset, UK, can trace his family tree back some 300 generations. He is a direct descendant, on his mother's side, of Cheddar Man, a 9,000-year-old skeleton and one of the oldest complete skeletons found in the UK.

FACT

Dr. Venter's genome (see photo above) confirms the blue color of his eyes and reveals he has a genetic degree of protection against tobacco addiction. Some of the sequences in his genome are associated with increased risk of antisocial behavior, Alzheimer's, and cardiovascular diseases.

★ **LARGEST PRODUCER OF GENETICALLY MODIFIED SEEDS** Food biotechnology giant Monsanto (U.S.A.) currently dominates the global market for genetically modified seeds. In 2006, the company saw a global revenue of $7.344 billion.

INTERNET

★**Most popular MMORPG game** In terms of the number of online subscribers, *World of Warcraft* is the most popular Massively Multiplayer Online Role-Playing Game (MMORPG), with 10 million subscribers as of January 2008. According to its developers, Blizzard Entertainment, *World of Warcraft* hosts over 2 million subscribers in Europe, more than 2.5 million in North America, and around 5.5 million in Asia.

★**Largest source of spam** Research by spam and virus experts Sophos reveals that during the third quarter of 2007, 28.4% of all unsolicited e-mails worldwide originated in the U.S.A. South Korea was second with 5.2% of global spam.

★**Largest data warehouse** Sybase, Inc. and Sun Microsystems (both U.S.A.) operate a data warehouse containing 1 petabyte (1,000 terabytes) of raw data. Its data capacity is such that it could track every credit and debit card transaction that has taken place worldwide in the past seven years.

★**Fastest residential internet connection** Sigbritt Lothberg (Sweden) has a home broadband connection of 40 Gbps—thousands of times greater than the average for domestic broadband. Her connection is a

★ HIGHEST PERCENTAGE OF ILLEGALLY DOWNLOADED MUSIC (COUNTRY) According to a report in January 2008 by the International Federation of the Phonographic Industry (IFPI), 99% of all digital music files distributed in China had been pirated from the internet. Described as "potentially the largest online music-buying population," the Chinese spent only $76 million in 2007 on legal online music downloads.

☆ MOST SEARCHED-FOR PERSON ON THE INTERNET In 2007, the most searched-for person on the internet was Britney Spears (U.S.A.). The record-breaking singer spent the year in and out of drug and alcohol rehabilitation centers, fought and lost a custody battle for her children, shaved her hair off with electric clippers, was charged with a hit-and-run incident and driving without a licence, and made a critically panned (but commercially successful) comeback at the MTV Video Music Awards performing "Gimme More."

★ **FIRST ROYAL CHRISTMAS PODCAST** In December 2006, the Christmas message delivered by Her Majesty Queen Elizabeth II (UK) was made available as a podcast for the first time. The Queen owns a 6 GB silver iPod mini; she also has her own channel on YouTube, launched 50 years after her first televised Christmas message in 1957. A Buckingham Palace spokesperson said that the Queen "always keeps abreast with new ways of communicating with people."

demonstration arranged by her son, the Swedish internet guru Peter Lothberg, and it allows Sigbritt to download a full high-definition DVD in around two seconds.

★ **Most people to deliberately download a computer virus** In an experiment by Belgian IT expert Didier Stevens in 2007, 409 people willingly and deliberately downloaded a virus onto their computer. Stevens had been running a Google Adwords campaign for six months that offered users a free virus via the slogan "Is your PC virus-free? Get it infected here!"

★ **FIRST TRUE VIRTUAL EMBASSY** On May 30, 2007, Sweden opened a virtual copy of its Washington D.C., U.S.A., embassy in *Second Life*. The avatar of Minister for Foreign Affairs Carl Bildt (Sweden) performed the "cutting of the ribbon" for the virtual embassy, which is intended to provide information to *Second Life* players about Sweden.

★ **MOST DOWNLOADED MOVIE** In 2007, the movie downloaded most often using the BitTorrent peer-to-peer (P2P) protocol was *Transformers* (U.S.A., 2007), which was accessed 569,259 times on Mininova alone. Globally, considering the vast number of P2P websites, the actual figure will be much higher.

★ **First speedcabling competition** The world's first speedcabling competition was held in Los Angeles, California, U.S.A., in January 2008. The aim of this new "sport," invented by IT developer Steven Schkolne (U.S.A.), is to untangle a mass of cables and wires in the fastest time and in such a way that the wires can still carry a network signal. The winner of the final—in which contestants were required to unknot 12 ethernet cords up to 25 ft. (7.5 m) long, then hold them above their heads—was web designer Matthew Howell (U.S.A.).

★ **Worst internet blackout** In just one week during January 2008, four undersea internet cables were severed, causing loss of connection for millions of users in Asia, the Middle East, and North Africa. Some experts have blamed ships dragging their anchors across the seafloor, while others suspect sabotage by unknown agents.

★ **First Google bomb** Google bombing is a technique where internet users manipulate Google search results by using specific terms to link to an-

★ 2007 TOP 10 MOVIE DOWNLOADS ★

MOVIE (NAT., YEAR)	DIRECTOR	NUMBER
1. *Transformers* (U.S.A., 2007)	Michael Bay	569,259
2. *Knocked Up* (U.S.A., 2007)	Judd Apatow	509,314
3. *Shooter* (U.S.A., 2007)	Antoine Fuqua	399,960
4. *Pirates of the Caribbean: At World's End* (U.S.A., 2007)	Gore Verbinski	379,749
5. *Ratatouille* (U.S.A., 2006)	Brad Bird & Jan Pinkava	359,904
6. *300* (U.S.A., 2006)	Zack Snyder	358,226
7. *Next* (U.S.A., 2007)	Lee Tamahori	354,044
8. *Hot Fuzz* (UK, 2007)	Edgar Wright	352,905
9. *The Bourne Ultimatum* (U.S.A., 2007)	Paul Greengrass	336,326
10. *Zodiac* (U.S.A., 2007)	David Fincher	334,699

Source: www.mininova.org

other page. The first significant Google bomb occurred in 1999 when search results for the term "more evil than satan himself" brought up the home page for Microsoft. In 2005, Google bombing forced searches for "miserable failure" to bring up the official biography of U.S. President George W. Bush.

MOBILE TECHNOLOGY

MOBILE PHONES

★**Fastest national mobile broadband network** Next G, announced by Telstra (Australia) in February 2007, can achieve peak network download speeds of 14.4 Mbps—in other words, up to 250 times faster than a standard dial-up connection.

☆**Largest mobile phone** A functioning, scaled-up version of Sony Ericsson's W810i measured 8 ft. 2.4 in. × 3 ft. 8.8 in. × 1 ft. 7.2 in. (2.5 × 1.14 × 0.49 m) when examined at the MTN ScienCenter in Cape Town, South Africa, on September 20, 2007. The phone is fully functional and made from the same materials as the normal-sized version.

☆**Thinnest mobile phone** As of February 2008, the world's thinnest mobile phone is the Samsung Ultra Edition II, at just 0.2 in. (5.9 mm) thick. The handset has a 3-megapixel camera and 11 hours of music play time.

FAMOUS FIRST WORDS

•The telephone was invented by Alexander Graham Bell (UK), who filed his patent on February 14, 1876. The **first intelligible phone call** occurred in March 1876 in Boston, Massachusetts, U.S.A., when Bell phoned his assistant in a nearby room and said: "Mr. Watson—come here—I need you."

•The concept of a portable telephone first appeared in 1947 at Lucent Technologies' Bell Labs in New Jersey, U.S.A., but the **first portable telephone handset** was invented by Martin Cooper (U.S.A.) of Motorola. He made the **first mobile phone call** on April 3, 1973, to his rival, Joel Engel, head of research at Bell Labs. The **first commercial mobile phone network** was launched in Japan in 1979.

•On April 28, 1999, at 10:30 a.m. (GMT), the **first pole-to-pole phone call** was made between NASA employees Mike Comberiate and Andre Fortin (both U.S.A.).

★ **LARGEST SCREEN ON A MOBILE PHONE** The Readius, by Dutch company Polymer Vision, is due to go on sale in late 2008. As well as being a mobile phone, it can browse the internet and read e-books. Its revolutionary flexible screen measures 5.1 in. (13 cm) diagonally and can fold up into the body of the Readius when not in use.

Samsung's Ultra Edition 8.4 is the **world's thinnest 3G mobile phone,** with a 2-megapixel camera in a body just 0.3 in. (8.4 mm) thick.

Highest resolution mobile phone camera In March 2006, Samsung unveiled the SCH-B600, a mobile phone with the world's highest-resolution

★ **LIGHTEST MOBILE PHONE** Made by modu Ltd. (Israel) and launched on February 11, 2008, the modu weighs just 1.41 oz. (40.1 g) and measures 2.8 × 1.4 × 0.3 in. (72.1 × 37.6 × 7.8 mm). It has a full-color screen and 1 Gb of internal memory.

★ **BEST-SELLING SMARTPHONE**
According to research firm iSuppli, Apple's iPhone outsold all other smartphones in the U.S.A. in July 2007, its first full month on sale. In the last four months of 2007, the company sold 2,315,000 iPhones, helping to push its net quarterly profits to $1.58 billion—Apple's most profitable quarter ever—and making the iPhone the fastest-selling smartphone ever.

camera at 10 megapixels—higher than many digital cameras. The LCD can reproduce 16 million colors, and users can also watch live TV through a satellite DMB (digital multimedia broadcasting) function.

☆ **Most enduring mobile phone number** David Contorno of Lemont, Illinois, U.S.A., has owned and used the same mobile telephone number since August 2, 1985. His first mobile phone was an Ameritech AC140 and his carrier has been Ameritech Mobile Communications, the first company in the United States to provide a cellular mobile phone service to the general public, ever since.

Most expensive mobile phone A mobile phone designed by GoldVish of Geneva, Switzerland, was sold for €1 million ($1,287,200) at the Millionaire Fair in Cannes, France, on September 2, 2006.

★ **Smallest GPS chip** In February 2008, NXP Semiconductors (Netherlands) announced the launch of its GNS7560 GPS receiver chip. Designed to be incorporated into mobile phones and PDAs, it measures just $0.1 \times 0.09 \times 0.02$ in. ($3.6 \times 2.4 \times 0.6$ mm) and consumes less than 15 mW of power.

PORTABLE MEDIA

★ **Most versatile wire-free gadget charger** The WildCharger, by U.S.A. company, WildCharge, is a pad that allows portable gadgets to recharge without wires. Any gadget that is fitted with a special adapter can be recharged by resting it on the conductive WildCharger pad. Up to five gadgets can recharge on the pad at any one time. So far adapters are available for Motorola RAZR V3, iPod nano 2G, iPhone, Blackberry Pearl, Blackberry 8800 and iPod.

★ **MOST EXPENSIVE PSP COVER** A PlayStation Portable jacket made from 14-carat gold with 8-carat black and yellow diamonds on the front can be purchased for $35,000. It is made by Simmons Jewelry Co. (U.S.A.) and made its debut at the Pacific Design Center, West Hollywood, California, U.S.A., on March 14, 2005.

★ **Cheapest laptop** Founded by Nicholas Negroponte (U.S.A.), the One Laptop Per Child Program is a project to deliver very cheap laptops for educational use in the developing world. As of February 2008, the program had an annual production rate of 110,000 laptops, each priced at just $187.

Highest definition screen on a TV wristwatch The sharpest picture achieved by a wearable television screen is on the NHJ TV Wristwatch, with 130,338 pixels. The 1.5-in. (3.8-cm) color TV screen relies on TFT (Thin Film Transistor) technology to deliver high-resolution images.

★ **Most popular format for music** The compact disc (CD) remains the most popular format for listening to music, with a global sales revenue of over $17 billion in 2005—although this represents a drop of 6% on the previous year.

FACT

The PSP case (see photo above), backed with real alligator skin, was designed by Kimora Lee Simmons as part of a gamer-chic catwalk event thrown for a variety of designers and celebrities, including Marc Jacobs, Nicole Richie, and Jennifer Lopez.

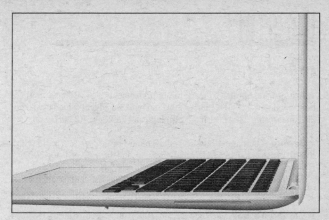

★ THINNEST MAC The MacBook Air, which was launched by Apple Inc. (U.S.A.) in January 2008, is the thinnest Mac currently in production. At its thickest point, the laptop measures 0.76 in. (1.94 cm), and at its thinnest 0.16 in. (0.4 cm). The MacBook Air's screen measures 13.3 in. (33.7 cm), and it weighs 3 lb. (1.63 kg). Apple say the thinness of the MacBook Air is the result of numerous innovations, including a slimmer hard drive and a lower-profile battery than other laptops.

☆ FASTEST RADIO-CONTROLLED MODEL CAR The highest speed ever reached by a battery-powered radio-controlled model car is 134.4 mph (216.29 km/h), set by the 1:10 scale Associated Nitro TC3 car, built and driven by Nic Case (U.S.A.) at the Auto Club Dragway, Fontana, California, U.S.A., on July 20, 2007.

BIG STUFF

LARGEST . . .

☆**Advent calendar** To mark the refurbishment of St. Pancras train station, London, UK, in December 2007, an outsized advent calendar was created, measuring 232 ft. 11 in. (71 m) high and 75 ft. 5 in. (23 m) wide.

☆**Bonfire** The largest bonfire had a volume of 60,589 ft.³ (1,715.7 m³). It was constructed by ŠKD mladi Boštanj and lit on April 30, 2007, in Boštanj, Slovenia, to celebrate Labor Day.
    Its 142-ft. 6.2-in. (43.44-m) height also qualifies the conflagration as the ★**tallest bonfire.**

☆**Cardboard box** On October 30, 2007, students of Aarhus Business College in Aarhus, Denmark, designed and manufactured a cardboard box measuring 37 ft. 10 in. × 15 ft. 1.5 in. × 7 ft. 7 in. (11.53 × 4.61 × 2.31 m).

☆**Disco ball** Raf Frateur (Belgium) of Frateur Events created a mirrored disco ball with a 24-ft. 1.3-in. (7.35-m) diameter. It was displayed at a party in the nightclub Studio 54 in Antwerp, Belgium, on July 20, 2007.

☆**LARGEST SKATEBOARD On August 17, 2007, students in Jerry Havill's team problem solving course at Bay de Noc Community College (all U.S.A.) designed and produced a skateboard 31 ft. 0.5 in. (9.4 m) long, 8 ft. (2.4 m) wide, and 47 in. (1.19 m) high. It was made in Escanaba, Michigan, U.S.A.**

★LARGEST PLASTIC DUCK As part of the Loire Estuary Project 2007, which involved a series of art installations along the riverbank from June to September 2007, the port of Saint-Nazaire, France, hosted an 82-ft.-tall (25-m) plastic duck.

☆**Soccer ball** MTN Sudan made a soccer ball measuring 34 ft. 7 in. (10.54 m) in diameter in Khartoum, Sudan, on August 23, 2007.

☆**Gingerbread house** Roger A. Pelcher (U.S.A.) built a gingerbread house with an internal volume of 36,600 ft.³ (1,036 m³) at Mall of America in Bloomington, Minnesota, U.S.A., on November 22, 2006. The house was 45 ft. 6 in. (13.86 m) long, 35 ft. 6 in. (10.81 m) wide, and around 60 ft. (18.28 m) tall at its highest point.

★Gold coin The largest gold coin weighs 220 lb. 7 oz. (100 kg), measures 19.6 in. (50 cm) in diameter, 1.1 in. (3 cm) in thickness, and is made from bullion with a purity of 99.999 percent.

The legal-tender coin was introduced on May 3, 2007, by the Royal Canadian Mint with a face value of CAN$1 million ($900,375).

★Paperclip On July 12, 2007, a solid steel paperclip measuring 15 ft. 2-in. (4.62 m) in height—and created by the town of Kipling, Saskatchewan, Canada—was unveiled.

★Photo album Dodge Brand (U.S.A.) created a photo album measuring 12 × 9 ft. (3.6 × 2.7 m) in Orlando, Florida, U.S.A., on September 6, 2007. It held 21 double-sided pages; all photos were to scale.

★Pom-pom A pom-pom measuring 2-ft. 11.43 in. (90 cm) in diameter and 8 ft. 4.8 in. (2.56 m) in circumference was manufactured and displayed by the children, parents, and staff of the Ribby with Wrea Endowed Church of England Primary School in Preston, UK, on March 16, 2007.

DID YOU KNOW?

The **largest collection of rubber ducks** belongs to Charlotte Lee (U.S.A.). Charoltte started her collection in 1996 when she bought a pack of rubber ducks for her bathroom. Friends soon began to give her ducks as gifts. As of April 3, 2006, Charoltte has amassed 2,583 ducks, all displayed in glass showcases throughout her home.

"We made him like a parade float."

Maria Reidelbach (U.S.A.), on creating the largest garden gnome

★**Printed map** In December 2006, Stiefel Eurocart (Germany) produced a printed map that measured 14 ft. 3 in. × 10 ft. 1 in. (4.35 × 3.09 m) in Lenting, Germany.

☆**Puppet** A 49-ft. 11-in. (15.21-m) marionette named Zozobra was presented by the Kiwanis Club in Santa Fe, New Mexico, U.S.A., at the Fiestas de Santa Fe, on September 7, 2007.

★**Special stamp** Measuring 1 ft. 11 in. × 1 ft. 7 in. (600 mm × 493 mm), the largest special stamp was made by Koninklijke Joh. Enschedé and issued by TNT Post for Team Nationaal Schoolontbijt (Team National School Breakfast) in the Netherlands on November 6, 2007. The stamp was used to send a giant Thank You card to Dutch Bakeries for delivering breakfasts to schools.

☆**Sweater** Dalang Woollen Trade Center (China) created a sweater with a chest measurement of 28 ft. 2 in. (8.6 m), body length of 16 ft. 4 in. (5 m), and sleeve length of 14 ft. 1 in. (4.3 m) in Dongguan City, Guangdong Province, China, on October 18, 2007.

★**Trousers** On December 27, 2006, Value Planning Co., Ltd., created a pair of trousers 35 ft. 6.4 in. (10.83 m) long with a 21-ft. 3.2-in. (6.48-m) waist. They were displayed at Kobe City Central Gymnasium in Kobe City, Japan.

LARGEST GARDEN GNOME
Created by Maria Reidelbach, with the help of Ken Brown and John Hutchison (all U.S.A.), the largest garden gnome is 13 ft. 6 in. (4.11 m) tall. It resides at the Gnome on the Grange Mini Golf Range at Kedler's Farm, Kerhonkson, New York, U.S.A.

★ **LARGEST PAIR OF SCISSORS** A pair of functional scissors 5 ft. 10.25 in. (1.78 m) from tip to handle, made by Michael Fish (Canada) and his team from Keir Surgical Ltd., was displayed at the Operating Room Nurses Association of Canada's (ORNAC) 20th national conference in Victoria, Canada, on April 24, 2007.

★ **TALLEST SANDCASTLE** Camp Sunshine created a sandcastle 31 ft. 6 in. (9.6 m) tall at the Point Sebago Resort in Casco, Maine, U.S.A., on September 1, 2007.

COLOSSAL CHRISTMAS

• The ☆ **largest Christmas stocking** measured 106 ft. 9 in. (32.56 m) long and 49 ft. 1 in. (14.97 m) wide (heel to toe). It was made by the Children's Society (UK) in London, UK, on December 14, 2007.

• The ☆ **largest floating Christmas tree** was 278 ft. 10 in. (85 m) tall. Erected in Rio de Janeiro, Brazil, for Christmas 2007, it was sponsored by Bradesco Seguros e Previdência.

★ **LONGEST BALLPOINT PEN** The largest ballpoint pen measures 10 ft. 11 in. (3.33 m) long and weighs 17 lb. 10 oz. (8 kg). The prodigious pen was manufactured by Olaf Fügner (Germany) in Sachsen, Germany, during 2005.

EPIC ENGINEERING

Card castle On December 12, 2004, Bryan Berg (U.S.A.) constructed a replica of the Walt Disney castle using only playing cards. Measuring 13 ft. 10.5 in. (4.22 m) tall, 11 ft. 10 in. (3.6 m) wide, and 8 ft. 7.25 in. (2.61 m) deep, the castle, built at Walt Disney World in Orlando, Florida, U.S.A. needed 1.62,000 cards to complete.

★ **Longest dike** The Saemangeum Seawall is located on the southwest coast of South Korea. Measuring 20.5 miles (33 km) in length, it links two headlands near the industrial port of Gunsan and has created 154 miles^2 (400 km^2) of new farmland, as well as a freshwater reservoir in the former Saemangeum Estuary. It was completed in April 2006.

Most extensive underground rail system The New York City subway system in the U.S.A. has a total track extent of 842 miles (1,355 km), including 186 miles (299 km) of track in yards, shops, and storage.

Largest manmade archipelago The World Islands, 2.5 miles (4 km) off the coast of Dubai, is an enormous project to construct more than 300 small islands that collectively resemble the shape of Earth's continents. When complete, it will cover an area of 5.5×3.7 miles (9×6 km), with each island measuring between 247,570–925,696 ft.² (23,000–86,000 m²). As of December 2006, more than 90% of the land reclamation on which each is-land will be developed was complete.

Longest plastic bridge The longest span reinforced-plastic bridge is at the Aberfeldy Golf Club in Aberfeldy, Perth and Kinross, UK. The main span is 206 ft. 8 in. (63 m) and the overall bridge length 370 ft. 9 in. (113 m).

Longest road tunnel The two-lane Lærdal tunnel on the main road be-tween Bergen and Oslo, Norway, measures 15.2 miles (24.5 km) in length. The tunnel was opened to the public in 2001, having cost a reported $113.1 million to build.

☆**Largest wind generator** The largest wind turbine is the Enercon E-126, which has a hub height of 443 ft. (135 m) and a rotor diameter of 416 ft. (127 m). Its capacity is rated at 6 MW (or 20 million kilowatt hours each year)—enough to fuel 5,000 four-person households! The wind generator was manufactured by Enercon GmbH (Germany), installed on the Rysumer Nacken in Emden, Germany, and began operation in November 2007.

Largest irrigation project The Great Manmade River Project was be-gun in 1984. Its aim is to transport water from vast underground natural aquifers to the coastal cities of Libya. As of 2007, over 3,100 miles (5,000 km) of pipelines had been completed, capable of carrying 229.5 million ft.³ (6.5 million m³) of water per day from around 1,000 wells in Libya's desert.

Largest high-speed rail network According to the Interna-tional Union of Railways (UIC), Japan has the largest high-speed rail network in the world, with 1,678 miles (2,700 km) of high-speed lines in operation or under con-struction. The country opened the world's first dedicated high-speed line between Tokyo and Osaka in 1964.

★**Longest powerline** The Inga-Shaba Electrical Transmission Proj-ect is a powerline that stretches from

☆**TALLEST HOUSE OF CARDS**
Bryan Berg (U.S.A.) constructed a freestanding house of cards that measured 25 ft. 9.44 in. (7.86 m) tall. It was completed on October 15, 2007, as part of the state fair of Texas, in Dallas, Texas, U.S.A.

the Inga hydroelectric dam at the mouth of the Congo River to distant copper mining regions in the Democratic Republic of the Congo, 1,056 miles (1,700 km) away. It took 10 years to construct and was completed in 1982.

★ **Most powerful water pump** The most powerful water pump operates at a rate of 60,000 liters (15,850 gal.) per second and was made by Nijhuis Pumps in Winterswijk, the Netherlands, in 2004.

THE NEW 7 WONDERS OF THE WORLD

A little more than 2,200 years after the Seven Wonders of the Ancient World were declared in 200 B.C., the New 7 Wonders campaign was launched in 2000 by filmmaker and aviator Bernard Weber (Canada). Its aim was to select seven new wonders of the world as a celebration of human achievement in the last two millennia.

The selection process was billed as "the world's first global election campaign" and was open to anyone who had access to the internet or a cell phone.

After seven years of campaigning and 100 million votes received, the results of the global ballot were announced on July 7, 2007, in Lisbon, Portugal. During a spectacular gala show in the "Estadio da Luz," in the presence of 50,000 spectators and watched by millions of TV viewers worldwide, the New 7 Wonders were revealed: The Pyramid at Chichén Itzá (pre-A.D. 800), Yucatan Peninsula, Mexico; Cristo Rendentor (1931), Rio de Janeiro, Brazil; The Colosseum (A.D. 70–82), Rome, Italy; The Great Wall of China (220 B.C. and A.D. 1368–1644), China; Machu Picchu (1460–70), Peru; Petra (9 B.C.–A.D. 40), Jordan; and The Taj Mahal (A.D. 1630), Agra, India.

Of these incredible monuments, three are officially acknowledged as Guinness World Record holders. The Great Wall of China is the **longest wall in the world** and has a main length of 2,150 miles (3,460 km) plus 2,195 miles (3,530 km) of branches and spurs; Machu Picchu is recognized as the **largest Inca discovery,** having been "found" in 1911 by a Yale University expedition led by U.S. historian Hiram Bingham; finally, GWR lists Cristo Redentor, in Brazil, as the **largest statue of Jesus** (see p. 257).

LARGEST RAILROAD NETWORK The U.S.A. is the country with the largest railroad network, with 141,198 miles (227,236 km) of rail lines.

WIDEST BRIDGE The widest long-span bridge is the 1,650 ft. (503 m) Sydney Harbour Bridge, Australia, which is 160 ft. (48.8 m) wide. It carries two electric overhead railroad tracks, eight lanes of roadway, and a cycle track and footway. It was officially opened on March 19, 1932.

Longest rail tunnel The Seikan rail tunnel is 33.46 miles (53.85 km) long and links Tappi Saki on the main Japanese island of Honshu with Fukushima on the northern island of Hokkaido. The first test run through the tunnel took place on March 13, 1988.

Longest rubber dam The Xiaobudong rubber dam is situated on the Yihe River, Shandong Province, China. Completed on July 1, 1997, it measures 3,723 ft. (1,135 m) long and consists of 16 sections, each of which is 229 ft. (70 m) long.

Longest cantilever bridge The Quebec Bridge (Pont de Quebec) over the St. Lawrence River in Canada has a cantilever truss span measuring 1,800 ft. (549 m) between the piers and 3,239 ft. (987 m) overall. The bridge carries a railroad and two carriageways. Work started in 1899 and it was finally opened to traffic on December 3, 1917.

★**LARGEST STATUE OF CHRIST** The concrete statue Cristo Redentor (Christ the Redeemer), on the Corcovado mountain in Rio de Janeiro, Brazil, stands 130 ft. (39.6 m) tall and weighs over 700 metric tons.

HOTELS

★**Largest group** InterContinental Hotels is the world's largest hotel operator by number of bedrooms, with 537,500 rooms divided between 3,606 hotels. In the year to December 31, 2005, the group reported a turnover of $2.425 billion from nearly 100 countries.

Largest The First World Hotel has 6,118 rooms. It is part of the Genting Highlands Resort in Pahang Darul Makmur, Malaysia, and was completed in 2005.

Highest altitude The Hotel Everest View above Namche, Nepal—the village closest to Everest base camp—is at a record height of 13,000 ft. (3,962 m).

Heaviest relocated The three-story brick Hotel Fairmount (built 1906) in San Antonio, Texas, U.S.A., which weighed 3,198,907 lb. (1,451 metric tons), was moved on 36 dollies with pneumatic tires over city streets approximately five blocks and over a bridge, which had to be reinforced. The move took six days, from March 30 to April 4, 1985.

☆**Most expensive room** As of July 2006, the most expensive hotel room was the presidential suite at the Hotel Martinez, Cannes, France,

TALLEST The all-suite Burj Al Arab (The Arabian Tower), situated 9 miles (15 km) south of Dubai, United Arab Emirates, is the tallest hotel in the world, standing at 1,052 ft. (320.94 m) high from ground level to the top of its mast, when measured on October 26, 1999. Built on a man-made island, the hotel, shaped like a sail, has 202 suites, 28 "double-height" stories, and covers a total floor area of 1.2 million ft.^{2} (111,480 m^2).

LARGEST HOTEL ROLLS-ROYCE FLEET The Peninsula Group has purchased a total of 50 Rolls-Royces since its first order of seven Brewster Green Silver Shadows in 1970.

which cost $37,200 (€29,600) for one night's stay. This soundproofed suite on the seventh floor has four bedrooms and a private terrace with a jacuzzi.

★**Most restaurants** The Venetian Resort Hotel Casino, opened in May 1999 in Las Vegas, Nevada, U.S.A., has 17 different restaurants.

★**Highest library** The library on the 60th floor of the J. W. Marriott Hotel at Tomorrow Square in Shanghai, China, is situated 757 ft. 6 in. (230.9 m) above street level. Membership is available to the public, and the 103 shelves in the library contain an ever-expanding collection of Chinese and English books.

Most fountains The Bellagio hotel in Las Vegas, U.S.A., features an artificial lake covering 12 acres (4.8 ha)—equivalent to the area of nearly 70 tennis courts—containing more than 1,000 fountains.

☆**Largest casino** The largest casino is the 550,000-ft.^{2} (51,100-m^2) gambling area in the Venetian Macau, a casino-hotel resort owned by the Las Vegas Sands Corporation, U.S.A., which opened in Macau, China, on August 27, 2007. Guests can play on 3,400 slot machines or at 870 gaming tables, while staying in one of 3,000 suites.

FACT

The Peninsula Group (see photo above) operates eight hotels in Hong Kong, New York, Chicago, Beverly Hills, Tokyo, Bangkok, Beijing, and Manila. The Peninsula Shanghai (China) opens in 2009.

LARGEST FLOOR AREA OF POLISHED MARBLE TILES The Venetian Resort Hotel Casino in Las Vegas, U.S.A., which opened on May 3, 1999, has a total floor area of 1.5 million ft.^{2} (139,354 m^2) covered in cream, brown, and black marble tiles imported from Italy and Spain. This space is equivalent to the area of 535 tennis courts.

★**Tallest revolving door** The tallest revolving door measures 15 ft. 9 in. (4.8 m) and is located in the Novotel Citygate Hong Kong hotel in Tung Chung, Hong Kong. The door was measured during the hotel's official opening on June 12, 2006.

Largest presidential suite The largest hotel presidential suite is the Villa Salaambo attached to the Hasdrubal Thalassa Hotel in Yasmine Hammamet, Tunisia. It covers a total area of 16,597 ft.^{2} (1,542 m^2).

Largest ice hotel The Ice Hotel in Jukkasjärvi, Sweden, has a total floor area of between 43,000 ft.^{2} and 54,000 ft.^{2} (4,000 m^2–5,000 m^2), and in the winter of 2004–05 featured 85 rooms, as well as an ice bar and an ice church. Lying 120 miles (200 km) north of the Arctic Circle, the hotel has been re-created (and enlarged) every December since 1990.

Most northerly The most northerly full-service hotel is the Radisson SAS Polar Hotel in Longyearbyen, Svalbard, Norway. Svalbard consists of several islands from Bjornoya in the south to Rossoya in the north, Europe's northernmost point. About 60% of the archipelago is covered by ice.

Most remote concierge Anna Morris (U.S.A.) works 80 miles (130 km) from the hotel where she is employed as a concierge. Guests at the Westin

OLDEST The Hoshi Ryokan in the village of Awazu in Japan is the world's oldest hotel, dating back to A.D. 717, when Taicho Daishi built an inn near a hot-water spring that was said to have miraculous healing powers. The waters are still celebrated for their recuperative effects, and the Ryokan now has 100 bedrooms.

Hotel in Santa Clara, California, U.S.A., can talk to her via an interactive webcam, while Anna can see the guests via a camera in the hotel.

Largest demolition On May 26, 1972, the 21-story Traymore Hotel, Atlantic City, New Jersey, U.S.A., was demolished. This 600-room hotel had a cubic capacity of 6,403,926 ft.^{3} (181,340 m^3).

Highest density of hotel rooms Las Vegas, Nevada, U.S.A., boasts an incredible 120,000 hotel and motel rooms—that's nearly one for every four of its 456,000 inhabitants. The city single-handedly accounts for roughly one-thirtieth of all hotel rooms in the U.S.

MEGA MOTORS

Fastest jet-powered fire truck The world's fastest fire truck is the jet-powered *Hawaiian Eagle,* owned by Shannen Seydel of Navarre, Florida, U.S.A., which attained a speed of 407 mph (655 km/h) in Ontario, Canada, on July 11, 1998.

The truck is a red 1940 Ford, powered by two Rolls-Royce Bristol Viper engines boasting 6,000 hp (4,470 kW) per engine, which generate 12,000 lb. (5.443 kg) of thrust.

☆**Fastest production pickup truck** A standard VZ HSV Maloo R8 pickup truck ("ute"), driven by 39-year-old HSV racecar driver Mark Skaife (Australia), reached 168.7 mph (271.44 km/h) on a road in the Woomera Prohibited Area, Australia, on May 25, 2006.

★ **FIRST FULLY SUBMERSIBLE SPORTS CAR** The Rinspeed sQuba car, manufactured by Rinspeed (Switzerland), can be driven on land, float on the surface of water, and can also be steered to underwater depths of 33 ft. (10 m) by a driver wearing breathing apparatus.

LARGEST LAND VEHICLE The largest machine capable of moving on land under its own power is the RB293 bucket wheel excavator, an earth-moving machine manufactured by TAKRAF GmbH of Leipzig, Germany. It is currently employed in an open-cast mine owned by RWE Rheinbraun in Hambach, Germany.

The vehicle's 18 bucket scoops are attached to the outside of a giant wheel at the front of the machine. As the wheel revolves, the buckets scoop up earth and then dump it onto a conveyor belt to be carried away.
- **WEIGHT**: 31.3 million lb. (14,196 metric tons)—three times heavier than the space shuttle
- **LENGTH**: 722 ft. (220 m)—as long as two football fields
- **HEIGHT**: 310 ft. (94.5 m)—just taller than the Statue of Liberty and her pedestal
- **BUCKET-WHEEL HEIGHT**: 71 ft. (21.6 m)—as tall as a four-story building!
- **BUCKET VOLUME**: 1,452 gal. (6,600 liters)—each bucket can hold the same as 80 bathtubs
- **EARTH MOVED PER DAY**: 8.475 million ft.³ (240,000 m³)—enough to fill the *Hindenburg,* the largest airship ever built!

★**Largest production car engine** The largest standard engine installed in any car currently in series production is the 8.275-liter (505 cu. in.) V10 engine of the Dodge Viper SRT-10. It produces 500 hp (373 kW) of power and 525 lb.-ft. (712 Nm) of torque, enough to power the Viper to 60 mph (96.5 km/h) in under four seconds.

★**Vehicle engine with the most cylinders** Simon Whitelock (UK) has built a motorcycle with a two-stroke engine that has 48 cylinders and a capacity of 256 cu. in. (4,200 cc). It consists of 16 Kawasaki KH250 three-cylinder engines arranged in six banks of eight, and is road-legal.

★ **HEAVIEST MOTORCYCLE** The heaviest motorcycle is the Harzer Bike Schmiede, created by Tilo Niebel of Zilly, Germany, which weighed 10,470 lb. (4.749 metric tons) on November 23, 2007. The massive machine, which is 17 ft. 4 in. (5.28 m) long, 7 ft. 6 in. (2.29 m) tall and powered by a Russian tank engine, took a team of welders and mechanics nearly a year to build.

Most powerful motorcycle The $185,000 MTT Turbine Superbike's Rolls-Royce Allison gas turbine engine is claimed by its manufacturer to supply 286 hp (213 kW) of power at the rear wheel, with 425 lb.-ft. (577 Nm) of torque at 2,000 rpm, making the Superbike the most powerful motorcycle ever to enter into series production.

CAR CLASSICS

• The **largest car produced for private use** is the Bugatti "Royale" Type 41, known in the UK as the "Golden Bugatti." First built in 1927, it measures over 22 ft. (6.7 m) in length.

• The **greatest confirmed price paid for a car** is $15 million for the 1931 Bugatti Type 41 "Royale" Sports Coupe by Kellner, sold by Nicholas Harley (UK) to the Meitec Corp. (Japan) on April 12, 1990.

• The world's **most expensive production car** is the Mercedes Benz CLK/LM, which cost $1,547,620 when launched in 1997. It has a top speed of 200 mph (320 km/h) and can travel from 0 to 100 km/h (62 mph) in 3.8 seconds.

• The MTT Turbine Superbike, powered by a Rolls-Royce Allison gas turbine engine, cost $185,000 in 2004, making it the **most expensive production motorcycle.** The bike's turbine engine produces 286 hp (213 kW) of power at the rear wheel.

• The **fastest car speed**—and the **official land-speed record holder**—(measured over one mile) is 763.035 mph (1,227.985 km/h, or Mach 1.020), set by Andy Green (UK) on October 15, 1997, in the Black Rock Desert, Nevada, U.S.A., driving *Thrust SSC.*

☆**FASTEST CAR IN PRODUCTION** The Ultimate Aero TT SuperCar, built by Shelby SuperCars (U.S.A.), is the fastest car currently in production. It achieved two-way timed speeds in excess of 256 mph (412 km/h) on Highway 221 in Washington State, U.S.A., on September 13, 2007.

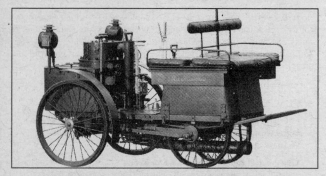

★**OLDEST CAR** La Marquise, a steam-powered, four-wheeled, four-seater vehicle, was manufactured by De Dion, Bouton et Trépardoux (France) in 1884; three years later it won the world's first automobile race, powering along the 19-mile (30.5-km) track at an average speed of 26 mph (42 km/h) from Paris to Neuilly, France. It was sold at auction for $3,520,000 on August 19, 2007.

FACT

The SSC Ultimate Aero TT (see top photo) retails at around $585,000 (£290,075) and was originally planned to have a limited-edition production of around 25 vehicles. It houses a 1,183 bhp twin-turbo Chevrolet V8 engine, can go from 0–60 mph in just 2.78 seconds and in tests covered 0.25 miles (0.4 km) in 9.9 seconds, at a speed of 144 mph (89.4 km/h).

★**FASTEST CAR POWERED BY DRY CELL BATTERIES** The Oxyride Racer is the fastest car to be powered by dry cell batteries. It achieved an average speed of 65.83 mph (105.95 km/h) on August 4, 2007, using a power pack of 194 "AA" batteries. It was set by the Oxyride Speed Challenge Team consisting of Matsushita Electric Industrial Co., Ltd., and Osaka Sangyo University (both Japan) in Ibaraki, Japan. The frame of the lightweight Oxyride Racer is made of carbon-fiber-reinforced plastic and weighs just 84 lb. (38 kg).

★**Largest convoy of trucks** A total of 416 trucks, all driven by women, took part in a convoy in Dronten, Netherlands, on November 6, 2004, at an event organized by VTL.

AIRCRAFT

TRANSATLANTIC FLIGHTS

First Lt. Cdr. Albert Cushing Read (1887–1967) and his crew flew the U.S. Navy/Curtiss flying boat NC-4 from Newfoundland, (now Canada), via the Azores, to Lisbon, Portugal, from May 16 to 27, 1919.

First nonstop John William Alcock and Arthur Whitten Brown (both UK) flew a Vickers Vimy biplane from St. John's, Newfoundland (now Canada) to Clifden, Ireland, on June 14, 1919.

Fastest On September 1, 1974, USAF Major James V. Sullivan and Major Noel F. Widdifield flew a Lockheed SR-71A Blackbird eastward across the Atlantic in 1 hr. 54 min. 56.4 sec.

★**First monoplane flight** The first monoplane to achieve successful flight was *Trajan Vuia 1,* built by Trajan Vuia, a Romanian inventor who lived in Paris, France. Vuia flew his monoplane at an altitude of 3 ft. (1 m) for 40 ft. (12 m) in Montesson, Paris, France, on March 18, 1906.

★ **LARGEST CONTRACT TO PRODUCE MILITARY ENGINES** The Eurojet EJ200 production program is contracted to produce more than 1,400 engines for the Eurofighter Typhoon fighter aircraft—the world's ★ **most advanced multi-swing-role aircraft**—making it the ★ **largest military engine production program** under contract. Each engine provides 20,000 lb.-force (90 kilonewtons) of power with afterburner and 13,500 lbf (60kN) without.

★ **Fastest-selling airliner** The new Boeing 787 Dreamliner is the fastest-selling airliner in history, with a total of 857 orders from 56 customers worldwide, following an initial order for 16 Boeing 787s from Gulf Air at the beginning of 2008.

The company launched the aircraft in April 2004, and it was originally scheduled to enter service in May 2008. The Dreamliner will seat between 210 and 250 passengers (although later models will carry more) and fly at speeds of Mach 0.85.

★ **Largest private jet** In November 2007, it was announced that HRH Prince Waleed Bin Talai of Saudi Arabia had ordered the first private Airbus A-380 for around $300 million (£150 million). With a wing-span of 261 ft.

★ **SMALLEST AUTOPILOT** Weighing only 0.58 oz. (16.65 g) and measuring 2 × 1.37 × 0.47 in. (5 × 3.4 × 1.2 cm), the Kestrel Autopilot is the smallest and lightest full-featured autopilot currently on the market. Manufactured by Procerus Technologies (U.S.A.), the Kestrel Autopilot is designed for use in Unmanned Aerial Vehicles (UAVs) with surveillance and reconnaissance applications.

☆ **LARGEST CAPACITY FOR A JET AIRLINER** The double-decker Airbus 380 (manufactured by EADS [Airbus S.A.S.]), which had its maiden flight in Toulouse, France, on April 27, 2005, has a nominal capacity of 555 seats but has a potential maximum seating capacity of 853, depending on the interior configuration.

8 in. (79.8 m) and a maximum designed take-off weight of 1,235,000 lb. (560 tons), it is the largest private jet in the world.

★ **Fastest business jet** On June 13, 2005, the Bombardier Global 5000 set a new transcontinental speed record for a business jet. It flew 3,510 nautical miles (4,040 miles; 6,500 km) from Chicago (Palwaukee Airport), U.S.A., to Paris (Le Bourget), France, in 7 hr. 15 min., flying at Mach 0.88. The aircraft first entered service on April 18, 2005.

★ **Farthest flight by an unmanned aircraft (non-FAI approved)** During trials at the U.S. military White Sands Missile Range in New Mexico on September 10, 2007, the Zephyr High Altitude Long Endurance UAV (Unmanned Aerial Vehicle) from the British defense technology company QinetiQ, powered by new solar array technology, achieved a flight time of 54 hours to an altitude of 58,355 ft. (17,786 m). However, as no Fédération Aéronautique Internationale (FAI) official was present during the trial, this is not currently the official FAI-approved world record.

The **longest FAI-approved flight ever completed by a full-scale unmanned conventional aircraft** is 8,600 miles (13,840 km), by the USAF Northrop Grumman Global Hawk *Southern Cross II,* which took off from Edwards Air Force Base in California, U.S.A., on April 22, 2001, and landed at RAAF Base Edinburgh, South Australia, 23 hr. 23 min. later on April 23, 2001.

X-REF

The Airbus 380 (see photos above) has a wingspan of 261 ft. 8 in. (79.8 m), a range of 8,000 nautical miles (9,320 miles; 15,000 km), and a cruising speed of Mach 0.85 (652 mph; 1,049 km/h). Find out about more incredible feats of construction on **Epic Engineering** on pp. 254–257.

★**LONGEST CARGO LOADER** In order to transport large components of the Boeing 787 Dreamliner aircraft from production centers around the world for assembly at the company's facility in Everett, Washington, U.S.A., Boeing unveiled the world's longest cargo loader on June 12, 2006. Designed by TLD of Quebec, Canada, it measures 118 ft. 1 in. (35.96 m) long and will be used with the modified Boeing 747-400 "Dreamlifter" freighters.

★**Longest flight for a micro unmanned aerial vehicle** The "Pterosoar," a joint micro Unmanned Aerial Vehicle (UAV) project between Oklahoma State University and California State University (both U.S.A.), flew 74.5 miles (120 km) in Lancaster, California, U.S.A., consuming only 0.5 oz. of the 2.5 oz. (16 g of the 64 g) of hydrogen carried on board in a pressurized hydrogen tank. The distance achieved was itself a record—however, the UAV could potentially increase it significantly to nearly 310 miles (500 km) based on fuel capacity.

Farthest flight by a commercial aircraft A Boeing 777-200LR Worldliner flew 11,664 nautical miles (13,422.7 miles; 21,601.7 km) non-stop and without refueling from Hong Kong, China, to London, UK, from November 9 to 10, 2005, in 22 hr. 42 min.—the longest flight ever by an un-modified commercial aircraft. The 777-200LR is powered by two massive General Electric GE90-115Bs, the world's **most powerful jet engine.** The first aircraft were delivered in early 2006.

ECO FUEL FIRSTS: ELECTRICITY On December 23, 2006, a wood and fabric single-seat aircraft (the Electra F-WMDJ, above) powered by an electric, 25-hp (18-kW) British-made motor (often used to power golf carts), flew for 48 minutes over 30 miles (50 km) around the southern Alps in France, making it the ★**first electric-powered aircraft.**

BIODIESEL On October 2, 2007, a Czech Delfin L-29 Albatross (above) achieved the ★**first flight of a jet fighter powered only by 100% biodiesel fuel** in Reno, Nevada, U.S.A.

Natural gas On February 1, 2008, an Airbus A-380 MSN004 completed the ★**first flight by a commercial aircraft using a liquid fuel processed from gas** (gas to liquid [GTL] fuel). The flight from Filton, UK, to Toulouse, France, took three hours.

WEAPONS

★**Newest class of nuclear submarine** The newest class of Sub Surface Nuclear Submarine was introduced with the launch of HMS *Astute* by the British Royal Navy on June 8, 2007. With four on order, this new class will be armed with Spearfish torpedoes and Tomahawk cruise missiles and will represent the largest and most powerful attack submarines operated by the Royal Navy.

★**First nuclear-powered aircraft carrier** The USS *Enterprise*, which was launched in 1960 and commissioned by the U.S. Navy in 1961, was the first nuclear-powered aircraft carrier. The ship has taken part in numerous missions, including the Cuban missile crisis of 1962 and operations during the war in Vietnam (1959–75); it was the first nuclear ship to transit the Suez Canal and has supported operations in Afghanistan and Iraq. It is currently due to remain in commission until 2015.

★**Fastest anti-tank missile** Lockheed Martin's LOSAT (Line of Sight Anti-Tank) missile can achieve speeds of over 500 ft./s. (154 m/s). With a

★ **MOST MAIN BATTLE TANKS IN ONE ARMY** In 2006, the Russian Federation was credited with at least 22,831 Main Battle Tanks (MBT), making it the army with the most tanks in the world. It is estimated that the U.S.A. possesses approximately 7,620 MBTs while China has about 7,580.

range of 5 miles (8 km), it does not require explosives, but instead relies on the power of its kinetic energy to drive a penetrator rod into an enemy tank. Its guided missile test flight occurred at the White Sands Missile Range, New Mexico, U.S.A., in June 2003.

First nuclear submarine The U.S. Navy's USS *Nautilus,* the world's first nuclear-powered submarine, was launched at Groton, Connecticut, U.S.A., on January 21, 1954. Built by General Dynamics Electric Boat, *Nautilus* was 324 ft. (98.7 m) long with a beam of 88 ft. (26.8 m). *Nautilus* was also the ★ **first submarine to travel under the ice cap to the North Pole,** arriving there at 11:15 a.m. on August 3, 1958.

★**Most powerful electromagnetic railgun** Electromagnetic (EM) railguns use an extremely high current flow to create an electromagnetic force that can propel projectiles at speeds greater than Mach 7.0 and destroy targets through sheer force of impact (i.e., without explosives being used) at ranges in excess of 200 nautical miles (230 miles; 370 km).

On January 16, 2007, a test shot was fired at the U.S. Naval Warfare Center Dahlgren Division, with a muzzle energy of 7.4 megajoules and an achieved velocity of 7,040 ft./s. (2,146 m/s).

FACT

The 17,200,000-lb. (7,800-metric ton) HMS *Astute* (see p. 269) uses a Rolls-Royce PWR 2 (pressurized water reactor) for propulsion and will be capable of speeds of over 20 knots (23 mph; 37 km/h). The craft is designed to complete a service-life of over 25 years without refueling.

★ First laser gunship The first laser gunship was built at Kirkland Air Force Base, New Mexico, U.S.A., on December 4, 2007, when the Boeing Company installed a high-energy chemical laser on a Hercules C-130H aircraft. It is seen as a further step in the development of the Advanced Tactical Laser, which will be able to destroy ground targets more accurately and with less collateral damage than conventional guns or missiles.

Largest crew on a warship The U.S. Navy Nimitz-class nuclear-powered aircraft carriers each carry at least 5,680 personnel when battle-ready, of which around 3,200 are ship's company and at least 2,280 belong to the Air Wing. Five Nimitz-class aircraft carriers, including the USS *Ronald Reagan*, have a displacement of 224.8 million lb. (102,000 tons) fully loaded, a length of 1,040 ft. (317 m) and beam of 133 ft. 10 in. (40.8 m), making them the **largest warships** afloat.

★ First successful test of UAVs in cooperative flight The first successful demonstration of Unmanned Aerial Vehicles (UAVs) flying fully autonomously in cooperative flight was achieved by the United States Air Force (USAF), under the operational control of the USAF UAV Battle Lab, at Creech Air Force Base, Nevada, U.S.A., between July 1 and 11, 2007. SkyWatcher and SkyRaider UAVs were flown in these cooperative test flights, each guided by its own onboard virtual pilot but controlled by Sky-Force Distributed Management System (DMS), which enabled one operator to manage four aircraft.

★ MOST ADVANCED WARSHIP Due to enter service in 2009, the Royal Navy's HMS *Daring* is the world's most capable air defense ship. It is equipped with the Principal Anti-Air Missile System (PAAMS)—a surface-to-air missile system that enables the ship to defend itself (and others) from enemy aircraft or missiles approaching at subsonic or supersonic speed.

☆ **LARGEST NONNUCLEAR CONVENTIONAL WEAPON** The largest
nonnuclear conventional weapon was reportedly successfully tested by
Russia on September 11, 2007. With destruction achieved by an
ultrasonic shockwave and extremely high temperatures, this weapon is
said to be four times more powerful than the previous record holder,
the U.S. Massive Ordnance Air Blast Bomb (MOAB)—or more commonly
the "Mother Of All Bombs" (a precision-guided weapon weighing 21,500
lb. or 9,752 kg).

WEAPONRY FIRSTS

Cannon The **oldest dated cannon** in existence is the Dardanelles Gun,
cast in 1464 for Sultan Mehmet II in Turkey. It is made from bronze, weighs
37,037 lb. (16.8 metric tons), and measures 17 ft. (5.2 m) long.

Tank The No. 1 Lincoln was built by William Foster Co., Ltd., of Lincoln,
Lincolnshire, UK, and, after modification, became known as "Little Willie."
It first ran on September 6, 1915, and although it never saw active service, it
is recognized as the **first real tank.**

Rockets The **first use of true rockets** was reported in 1232 when the Chinese and Mongols were at war with each other. During the battle of Kai-
Keng, the Chinese repelled the Mongol invaders by a barrage of "arrows of
flying fire."

Gun Documentary evidence of guns dates from 1326. However, the **first
known example of a gun** was found in the ruins of the castle of Monte
Varino in Italy. The castle was destroyed in 1341.

ENTERTAINMENT

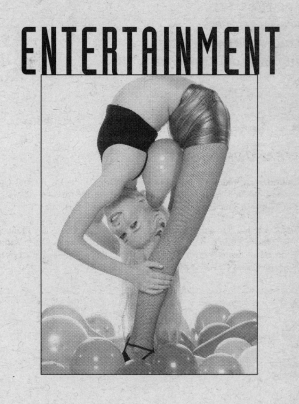

CONTENTS

ART & SCULPTURE

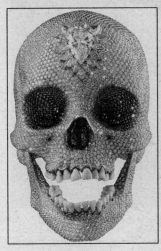

★ **MOST EXPENSIVE RAW MATERIALS USED IN AN ARTWORK** *For the Love of God* by Damien Hirst (UK) was created in 2007 from materials worth $23.7 million. The human skull (of a European male living between 1720 and 1810) was cast in 76 oz. (2,156 g) of platinum and set with 8,601 ethically sourced flawless diamonds (weighing 1,106.18 carats), including a 52.4-carat, pear-shaped pink diamond surrounded by 14 white brilliant-cut pear-shaped diamonds (weighing 37.81 carats) on the forehead. The skull's original teeth were also set in the jaws of the skull. The work was unveiled at The White Cube gallery, London, UK, on June 1, 2007.

LARGEST . . .

★ **Sculpture of an animal** Milka (Germany) created the sculpture of a cow that measured a height of 46 ft. 6 in. (14.18 m), a width of 38 ft. 7 in. (11.77 m) and a total length of 69 ft. 8 in. (21.24 m) when measured in Berlin, Germany, on November 11, 2007.

★ **Mural by one artist** Pontus Andersson (Sweden) painted a mural measuring 7,494 ft.² (696.3 m²) on a concrete wall in Gothenburg, Sweden. It depicts Gothenburg's harbor and coast, and took 250 working days (stretched across a period of six years) to complete.

☆ **Popcorn sculpture** Using popcorn, 50 members of the Sri Chinmoy Center in Jamaica, New York, U.S.A., created a sculpture of a five-tiered cake measuring 20 ft. 10 in. (6.35 m) tall, 12 ft. 9 in. (3.88 m) wide, and weighing 11,688 lb. (5,301.59 kg) on August 27, 2006.

★ **Picture made of Lite-Brite pegs** Mark Beekman (U.S.A.) used 124,418 Lite-Brite pegs to depict Leonardo da Vinci's *The Last Supper.* It was unveiled in Malvern, Pennsylvania, U.S.A., on November 6, 2006.

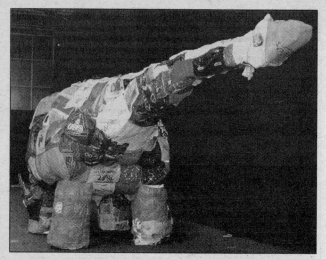

★ LARGEST PLASTIC BAG SCULPTURE On February 16, 2007, a dinosaur sculpture—13.1 ft. (4 m) tall and 49.2 ft. (15 m) long, and made of 16,651 recycled plastic shopping bags—was exhibited at Thinktank in Millennium Point, Birmingham, UK.

★ LARGEST BLU-TACK SCULPTURE *Spiderus Biggus* is a giant model of a common house spider made by Elizabeth Thompson (UK, seen here posing next to her creation). It went on display as part of the BUGS! exhibition at London Zoo, UK, in October 2007 to launch a *Spider-Man 3* competition. The artist used 4,000 packs of Blu-Tack adhesive to make the sculpture, also known as "Blu-ey." It weighs 440 lb. (200 kg) and has a span of 4 ft. (1.2 m).

> *"Liz showed what a terrific medium Blu-Tack can be for modelling anything you can imagine."*
>
> **Bostik, Blu-Tack creators**

LONGEST . . .

☆**Drawing** A drawing titled *The Longest Train* was created by 3,573 people from Kinokawa City and Iwade City, Japan. The work of art was begun on May 6 and finished on August 5, 2007, when it measured 15,297 ft. 2 in. (4,662.6 m).

★**Painting by numbers** On July 17, 2007, Knights Templar School in Baldock, UK, finished a 472-ft. 5-in.-long (144-m) painting by numbers.

☆**Painting** Círculo Artístico e Cultural Artur Bual and the City of Amadora in Portugal produced a 13,129-ft.-long (4,001.8-m) painting on September 15, 2007.

★**Photo negative** Using a handmade panoramic camera, Shinichi Yamamoto (Japan) printed a photograph 475 ft. 8 in. (145 m) long and 14 in. (35.6 cm) wide, after producing a single photographic negative 100 ft. (30.5 m) long and 2 in. (7 cm) wide on December 18, 2000.

☆ **LARGEST SNOW SCULPTURE** A team of 600 sculptors from 40 countries used 120,000 ft.³ (3,398 m³) of snow to create a French-themed landscape, including a cathedral and an ice maiden, entitled *Romantic Feelings.* It measured 115 ft. (35 m) tall and 656 ft. (200 m) long, and was part of the annual Harbin International Ice and Snow Sculpture Festival, which opened in Heilongjiang Province, China, on December 20, 2007.

★ **LARGEST COAT HANGER INSTALLATION** *Silver Back* is an installation by David Mach (UK) made entirely from coat hangers. David created a 7-ft.-tall (2.1-m), 9-ft.-long (2.7-m), 5-ft.-wide (1.5-m) sculpture of a male gorilla using 7,500 metal coat hangers. *Silver Back* took 2,705 working-hours to create and first went on display at the FIAC art fair in Paris, France, in October 2007.

MOSAIC MASTERPIECES

PICTURES

The world's ★ **largest picture mosaic** was created as part of a competition by Liberty Life financial services that asked children to draw pictures of their dreams. The resulting 8,064 colorful drawings were organized into a mosaic measuring 10,817 ft.² (1,005 m²), depicting the South African flag. It was unveiled at Sharonlea Primary School, Johannesburg, South Africa, on March 12, 2007.

FRUIT

On September 25–26, 2007, 341,969 apples were used to make the ★ **largest fruit mosaic,** measuring 16,145 ft.² (1,500 m²). It was created for an event organized by the People's Government of Zhaoyang, Zhaotong City, Yunnan Province, China.

TOOTHPICKS

The ★ **largest toothpick mosaic** was made by Saimir Strati (Albania) and measured 86 ft.² (8 m²). It was displayed in Tirana, Albania, on September 4, 2007.

★**Woodblock print** Christopher Brady (U.S.A.) exhibited a 281-ft. 9-in.-long (85.87-m) woodblock print at Vaught-Hemingway Stadium in Mississippi, U.S.A., on March 29, 2007. The work of art formed part of Brady's master's thesis project and took about four months to complete.

☆**Largest nude photo shoot** On May 6, 2007, a total of 18,000 naked people volunteered to pose together in Zócalo Square, Mexico City, Mexico. Photographer Spencer Tunick (U.S.A.) wanted the world to see how the naked body could be treated as art, not pornography.

DID YOU KNOW?

To support the weight of the Blu-Tack (roughly equivalent to the weight of three grown men) Liz (see bottom photo p. 276) first had to make a thin steel frame. She then used a pasta maker to form strips of Blu-Tack that she wrapped around the frame.

MOVIE MILESTONES

★**2007: FIRST PIRATED HD DOWNLOAD** The sci-fi action movie *Serenity* (U.S.A., 2005) was the first full-resolution rip of an HD DVD movie. The 19.6 GB file was made available on BitTorrent as an .evo file, confirming the suspicion that the copyright protection on HD DVDs had been bypassed.

GUINNESS WORLD RECORDS AGAINST MOVIE PIRACY

Manufacturing, selling, or distributing motion pictures or television programs without the consent of the copyright owner is illegal. If you want to download movies, please use sites that offer legal downloads. Report piracy at **http://www.mpaa.org/**.

1893: FIRST MOVIE STUDIO
Thomas Edison's (U.S.A.) "Black Maria," a frame building covered in black roofing material, was built at the Edison Laboratories in West Orange, New Jersey, U.S.A., and completed at a cost of $637.67 on February 1, 1893.

1925: FIRST IN-FLIGHT MOVIE
The first movie shown on an aircraft was First National's *The Lost World* (U.S.A., 1925), screened during an Imperial Airways flight in a converted Handley-Page bomber traveling from London to Paris in April 1925.

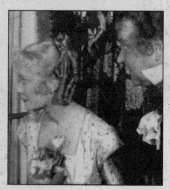

1935: FIRST USE OF TECHNICOLOR
Rouben Mamoulian's (Russia) *Becky Sharp* (U.S.A., 1935), an adaptation of William Thackeray's 1847 novel *Vanity Fair,* starring Cedric Hardwicke and Miriam Hopkins, is historically important as being the first full-length feature filmed in Technicolor—a color film process that gave movies of the time a distinctive "saturated" look.

1895: FIRST CINEMA

The Cinématographe Lumière at the Salon Indien—a former pool hall in the Grand Café, 14 Boulevard de Capucines, Paris, France—first admitted the public on December 28, 1895. The opening performance, to an audience of 35, included *L'Arrivée d'un train en gare* (France, 1895) by the Lumière brothers.

1954: FIRST MOVIE BASED ON A TV SHOW *Dragnet* (U.S.A., 1954) starred Jack Webb (U.S.A.) as Sergeant Joe Friday, a role he had created in the NBC TV series (1951–59) of the same name.

1971: FIRST MOVIE WITH DOLBY SOUND Dolby—a noise reduction system that removes hiss from recorded sound—was first used on the masters of Stanley Kubrick's *A Clockwork Orange* (UK, 1971).

1975: FIRST BLOCKBUSTER Steven Spielberg's (U.S.A.) *Jaws* (U.S.A., 1975) is considered the first summer blockbuster. People lined up around the block to see the movie, which also became the first movie to earn $100 million at the box office.

1985: FIRST CG CHARACTER A stained-glass knight that comes alive in *Young Sherlock Holmes* (U.S.A./UK, 1985) was the first character to be entirely computer-generated in a full-length feature. It was designed by *Toy Story* (U.S.A., 1995) creator John Lassiter (U.S.A.).

1994: FIRST MOVIE BUDGET TO EXCEED $100 MILLION *True Lies* (U.S.A., 1994), starring Arnold Schwarzenegger (Austria) and Jamie Lee Curtis (U.S.A.), was the first movie that cost over $100 million to make. It ended up grossing $365 million.

1997: HIGHEST GROSSING MOVIE OF ALL TIME Love it or hate it, the movie with the highest earnings is *Titanic* (U.S.A., 1997), which took $1,834,165,466 at the international box office. It also became the **first movie to gross $1 billion.**

2003: FASTEST TIME TO GROSS $1 BILLION *The Lord of the Rings: The Return of the King* (U.S.A./NZ, 2003) grossed $1 billion in just 9 weeks 4 days! It went on to win a record-equaling 11 American Academy Awards (Oscars)—see p. 283.

2004: FIRST MOVIE PRODUCED WITH ENTIRELY COMPUTER-GENERATED SETS The first publicly released movie in which the background footage was wholly created using computer-generated imagery (CGI) was *Able Edwards* (U.S.A., 2004). The movie combined real actors shot against a green screen.

2006: HIGHEST GROSSING MOVIE SERIES The 21 Bond movies, from *Dr. No* (UK, 1962) to *Casino Royale* (UK/U.S.A., 2006), have grossed over $4.49 billion worldwide. The 22nd movie, *Quantum of Solace* (2008, pictured left), was released in November 2008.

OSCAR TIMELINE

1929: First Oscar ceremony The first Academy Awards were held at the Hollywood Roosevelt on May 16, 1929.

1936: First person to refuse an Oscar Dudley Nichols (U.S.A.), screenwriter of *The Informer* (U.S.A., 1935), refused his award because of a union boycott of the ceremony that year.

1949: First person to direct himself to a best actor win The first actor to direct himself in an Oscar-winning performance was Laurence Olivier (UK), who directed himself in the lead role of *Hamlet* (UK, 1948) and went on to win best actor and best picture (making it the **first non-American director to win best picture**).

1953: Most Oscars won in a single year Walter (Walt) Elias Disney (U.S.A.) won four Academy Awards in 1953.

1959: Most Oscars won *Ben-Hur* (U.S.A., 1959) won 11 of its 12 nominations; the only other movies to win 11 statues are *Titanic* (U.S.A., 1997), from 14 nominations, and *The Lord of the Rings: The Return of the King* (U.S.A./NZ, 2003), from 11 nominations.

1977: First posthumous best actor winner Peter Finch (UK) died on January 14, 1977, while promoting the movie *Network* (U.S.A., 1976). His performance in the movie later won him the best actor Oscar.

1999: Longest Oscar ceremony The 71st Academy Awards, hosted by Whoopie Goldberg (U.S.A.) on March 21, 1999, and broadcast by ABC, lasted 4 hr. 2 min.

2003: First anime to win an Oscar *Sen to Chihiro no kamikakushi,* a.k.a. *Spirited Away* (Japan, 2001), won the Oscar for best animated feature on March 23, 2003.

2007: HIGHEST GROSSING MOVIE (OPENING DAY) *Spider-Man 3* (U.S.A., 2007), starring Tobey Maguire (U.S.A.), took a record $59.8 million on its opening day in the U.S.A. on May 4, 2007.

★ **2007: LARGEST 3D OPENING** Robert Zemeckis' *Beowulf* (U.S.A., 2007) opened on November 16, 2007, in 1,000 3D-equipped theaters, beating Zemeckis' previous record-holder, *The Polar Express* (U.S.A., 2004). Between the release of the two movies, the number of 3D-ready theaters had increased greatly to over 1,100, not including the 120 IMAX screens and 80 Dolby 3D Digital theaters.

POP DIVAS

☆ **Slowest climber on the Hot 100** On June 2, 2007, "Before He Cheats," by *American Idol* winner Carrie Underwood (U.S.A.), finally reached the U.S. Top 10 in its 38th week on the Hot 100 chart.

★ **Youngest person to enter the UK album chart** Connie Talbot (UK, b. November 20, 2000), who was runner-up in the first *Britain's Got Talent* (ITV, UK) TV series, became the youngest artist to reach the UK album chart when her debut record *Over The Rainbow* entered at No. 35 on December 8, 2007, just 18 days after her seventh birthday.

★ **Best start on the U.S. Dance Club Play chart** On December 8, 2007, vocalist Rihanna (Barbados, born Robyn Rihanna Fenty) topped the U.S. Dance Club Play chart with her seventh release, "Shut Up And Drive." It was a feat also accomplished by all of her previous six singles across her first two albums.

★ **Best-selling debut album on the UK chart by a female artist** Dido (UK) had sold 3 million copies of her debut album *No Angel* (2000) in the UK by November 2006.

★ **BEST START TO AN ALBUM CAREER (U.S.)** New York recording star Alicia Keys (U.S.A., born Alicia Cook) has released four albums since 2001 and every one has topped the Billboard 200—the best start on the U.S. Album chart by a female artist.

★ **Most weeks on the U.S. adult contemporary chart** UK singer Natasha Bedingfield's recording of "Unwritten"—from her 2004 debut album of the same name—topped the U.S. Adult Contemporary chart on March 3, 2007—its 51st week on that chart.

★ **Most hits on the U.S. country songs chart by a female artist** On September 29, 2007, veteran country star Dolly Parton (U.S.A.) had her record 105th U.S. Country Songs chart entry with "Better Get to Livin',"

AN ALBUM WITH THE X FACTOR Leona Lewis (UK) won the talent show *The X Factor* (ITV, UK) in 2006 and has been breaking records ever since. Leona's debut album, *Spirit,* sold 375,872 copies in its first week on sale in November 2007, making it the ★ best-selling debut album in the UK in one week by a female. The album continued to sell in huge numbers, with sales reaching 1 million copies in the UK in just 29 days, becoming the ★ fastest-selling album to reach 1 million copies in the UK by a female artist.

★ **FIRST U.S. FEMALE TO WRITE A MILLION-SELLING DEBUT ALBUM** In 2007, 17-year-old Pennsylvania-born country music singer/songwriter Taylor Swift (U.S.A.) became the first U.S. female to write or co-write every track on a million-selling debut album (*Taylor Swift*).

taken from her *Backwoods Barbie* album. Two dozen of her 105 hits have reached No. 1 on the Country Songs chart.

★ **Most consecutive top 10 hits by a female group (UK)** Girls Aloud (UK), the winners of the 2002 TV show *Popstars: The Rivals* (ITV, UK) became the first female group to achieve 17 successive UK Top 10 singles when "Call The Shots" achieved that feat on December 1, 2007.

★ **Highest-grossing movie of a music tour** The most commercially successful film of a music tour is *Hannah Montana/Miley Cyrus: Best of Both Worlds Concert Tour* starring Miley Cyrus (U.S.A., a.k.a. Hannah Montana), which grossed an unprecedented $53.4 million (£26.9 million) in just two weeks in February 2008.

★ **Oldest artist to reach no. 1 on the U.S. Dance Club Play chart** At the age of 73 years 321 days, Yoko Ono (Japan), the wife of late Beatle

---

DID YOU KNOW?

In 1978, Kate Bush (UK) released her entirely self-penned debut album *The Kick Inside,* which sold over 1 million copies in the UK alone, making her the **first female in pop history to write a million-selling debut album.**

★ FIRST DOWNLOAD-ONLY NO. 1 UK SINGLE BY A UK ACT On October 6, 2007, the Sugababes' (UK) single "About You Now" became the first track by a British pop act to top the singles chart solely on the strength of download sales. The song was also the ☆ **biggest chart mover to the No. 1 position in the UK,** leaping from No. 35 to the top spot.

John Lennon (UK), became the oldest person to top the U.S. Dance Club Play chart when "No, No, No" reached the peak on January 12, 2007.

★ Best-selling download album in the UK As of January 2008, Amy Winehouse's (UK) album *Back to Black* was the most downloaded album in the UK, with sales of over 80,000.

GRAMMY WINEHOUSE The ★ **most Grammy Awards won by a British female act in a single year** is five by Amy Winehouse (UK) at the 50th Annual Grammy Awards in Los Angeles, California, U.S.A., on February 10, 2008. She took home the prizes for: Record of the Year, Best New Artist, Song of the Year, Best Pop Vocal Album, and Best Female Pop Vocal Performance.

★LONGEST SPAN ON THE UK SINGLES CHART BY A FEMALE ARTIST
Shirley Bassey (UK) reached the Top 50 on August 4, 2007, with "Get
The Party Started" aged 70 years 208 days, more than 50 years after her
first hit in February 1957, with "The Banana Boat Song."

ROCK JOCKS

DOWNLOADS

☆ **Most download sales in one week in the U.S.A.** During the week
ending December 29, 2007, almost 43 million tracks were legally downloaded in the U.S.A.—a figure 42.5% higher than the record set on the same
week in the previous year. In total, a record 844.1 million tracks were downloaded in 2007 (45% up on the previous, record-breaking year) and this figure included an unprecedented 50 million complete album downloads,
beating 2006's total by 53.5%.

★ **Best-selling download album in the U.S.A.** Singer/songwriter
Jack Johnson's (U.S.A.) fifth album *Sleep Through The Static* debuted at
No. 1 on the U.S. album chart on February 23, 2008 with 139,000 down-
loads.

☆ **BEST-SELLING DOWNLOAD SINGLE IN THE U.S.A. IN ONE WEEK**
U.S. rapper Flo Rida (born Tramar Dillard) sold 467,000 downloads of
the track "Low" during the week ending December 29, 2007. In the same
week, a record 27 tracks sold over 100,000 downloads.

★ **BEST-SELLING DOWNLOAD SINGLE IN THE U.S.A. IN ONE YEAR**
"Crank That (Soulja Boy)" by 17-year-old Chicago, U.S.A., rapper Soulja
Boy Tellem (born DeAndre Cortez Way) sold an unprecedented 2.7
million downloads in 2007.

★HIGHEST DEMAND FOR TICKETS FOR ONE MUSIC CONCERT There were over 20 million requests for tickets to rock band Led Zeppelin's (UK) one-time reunion show at the 02 Arena, London, UK, on December 10, 2007. Such was the demand that tickets were selling at a record £914 ($1,783)—over seven times their original price of £125 ($244)—in the secondary market.

CHART LONGEVITY

★**Most successful songwriter** In terms of the number of songs that have reached the UK singles chart since its launch in November 1952, the most successful songwriter is Sir Paul McCartney (UK), who has written/cowritten 188 charted records, of which 129 are different songs. Of these records, 91 reached the Top 10 and 33 made it to No. 1. In total, the songs have spent 1,662 weeks on the chart (up to the end of 2007).

★**Most UK chart entries in one year by the same artist** In 2006, Michael Jackson (U.S.A.) notched up 19 UK chart hits, more than any other act in one year. The singles, reissued as part of Jackson's *Visionary—The Video Singles* box set, were released from February 25 to July 1, 2006. All 19 tracks made the Top 40.

FACT

The White Stripes (Jack and Meg White, both U.S.A.) performed the ★ **shortest music concert ever** when, on July 16, 2007, they played just one note at St. John's in Newfoundland, Canada. This short gig was the culmination of a tour that took the duo to every province and territory in Canada.

THE DARK SIDE OF THE MOON On April 12, 2008, Pink Floyd's (UK) album *The Dark Side Of The Moon* spent its 1,600th week on the U.S. best-sellers charts—over 35 years after making its debut at No. 95 on March 17, 1973, making it the album with the **longest stay on the U.S. album charts**. *The Dark Side Of The Moon*'s chart run straddles two charts: The Billboard 200 and the Top Pop Catalog chart, to which albums move when they are more than 18 months old and have fallen below position 100 on The Billboard 200. It is estimated that the album has sold over 40 million copies worldwide.

☆ **Longest time-span between UK No. 1 singles** A reissue of Elvis Presley's (U.S.A.) "It's Now Or Never" hit No. 1 in the UK singles chart in 2005, 48 years after "All Shook Up" took the top spot in 1957.

★ **MOST WEEKS AT NO. 1 ON THE U.S. MODERN ROCK CHART** On December 29, 2007, Seattle, U.S.A., rock group the Foo Fighters' track "The Pretender" completed a record 18 weeks at the top of the U.S. Modern Rock chart.

BIGGEST-SELLING BOY BAND ALBUM The Backstreet Boys' (U.S.A.) *Millennium* album, released in 1999, had sales of 13 million by March 2001. The record entered the U.S. Billboard 200 album chart at No. 1 in June 1999. It sold 1,134,000 copies in its first week, shattering Garth Brooks's one-week sales world record.

BEST-SELLERS

Best-selling album The year 2007 marked the 25th anniversary of the first release of Michael Jackson's (U.S.A.) 1982 album *Thriller.* At that time, estimations from Sony and the Recording Industry Association of America (RIAA) put sales at over 55 million copies, although Jackson's management claim that international sales have pushed the total worldwide figure to over 100 million. While it is impossible to verify the final global sales, there is no doubt that it remains the biggest-selling album of all time.

Best-selling single since charts began Elton John's (UK) "Candle In The Wind 1997/Something About The Way You Look Tonight" is the biggest-selling single since UK and U.S. singles charts began in the 1950s, having accumulated worldwide sales of 33 million copies. As of October 20, 1997, the single had also reached No. 1 in 22 countries. (The **best-selling single of all time** was released before the first pop charts—see p. xxx.)

THE PRINTED WORD

☆ **Largest magazine** Bayard Revistas S.A. (Spain) published a 36-page, scaled-up issue of *Caracola* measuring 2 ft. 11.6 in. × 3 ft. 4.2 in. (90.5 × 102.1 cm). It was unveiled in the Palacio de Congresos in Madrid, Spain, on May 19, 2007.

☆ **Largest published book** Eidouro Publicacoes S.A. (Brazil) have created a 128-page edition of Antoine de Saint Exupéry's (France) *The Little Prince* measuring 6 ft. 7 in. (2.01 m) high and 10 ft. 1 in. (3.08 m) wide when open. It was created presented at the XIII Biannual Book Fair of Rio de Janeiro, Brazil, on September 13, 2007.

Smallest published book Measuring just 0.9 × 0.9 mm, the smallest printed book is an edition of *Chameleon* by the Russian author Anton Chekhov. This tiny version was made and published by Anatoliy Konenko of Omsk, Siberia, Russia, in 1996. Each book consists of 30 pages.

☆ **Largest online bookstore** Amazon.com, founded in 1994 by Jeff Bezos (U.S.A.), opened its virtual doors in July 1995. Twelve years on, it has over 69 million active customer accounts.

In 2006, the company shipped products to more than 200 countries. Its catalog of more than 40 million items also makes it the **largest online store.**

☆ **Highest daily newspaper circulation** Founded in 1874 and published in Tokyo, Japan, the *Yomiuri Shimbun* had a combined morning and evening circulation of 14,532,694 in 2005.

★ **Most comics published by one author** Shotaro Ishinomori (Japan) created 770 published comic titles and is today known as "The King of Manga."

☆ **SMALLEST NEWSPAPER** The most diminutive newspaper measured just 1.25 × 0.86 in. (32 × 22 mm). It was created by First News newspapers in West Horsley, Surrey, UK, and published on November 8, 2007, in celebration of Guinness World Records Day.

☆ **LARGEST PHOTO ALBUM** The record for the largest photo album measures 9 ft. 10 in. × 13 ft. 1 in. (4 m × 3 m). It is entitled "Women of Vietnam" and was created by Canon Singapore displaying photographs by Hitomi Toyama (Japan). It was presented in Hanoi, Vietnam, on April 7, 2008.

★ **LONGEST-RUNNING MONTHLY COMIC** Since Issue #1 in March 1937, *Detective Comics* has been printed every month by DC Comics in the U.S.A. The comic introduced the character of Batman in Issue #27, which was published in May 1939.

DID YOU KNOW?

The **youngest commercially published author** is Dorothy Straight (U.S.A., b. May 25, 1958), who wrote *How the World Began* in 1962, aged four. It was published in August 1964 by Pantheon Books.

MOST LETTERS PUBLISHED Subhash Chandra Agrawal (India) has had 3,699 letters published by editors of various national newspapers in India, the ★ **most letters published in newspapers in a lifetime.**

His wife, Madhu Agrawal (India), also pictured here, had a total of 447 letters published during 2004 in 30 prominent Indian papers, with circulations of over 50,000—the ☆ **most letters published in newspapers in one year.**

PAULO COELHO

The Alchemist, by Paulo Coelho (Brazil), had been translated into 67 different languages as of March 2008, giving Coelho the record for the ★ **most translated living author.** The success of *The Alchemist* took the author himself by surprise. He told GWR that he had no idea why this book in particular—which he sees as "my own journey"—became so popular.

Coelho admires a number of writers, from visionary English poet William Blake ("because he privileges inspiration, not memories") to controversial 20th-century U.S. author Henry Miller ("because there is blood, sweat, and tears in his words") and fellow Brazilian Jorge Amado ("because he understands the Brazilian soul").

And how does this best-selling author feel about having a Guinness World Record? "It is a benchmark—the most respected one—for everyone who wants to exceed his or her limits."

☆**MOST TRANSLATED AUTHOR** William Shakespeare's (England, 1564–1616) works had been translated into at least 116 languages as of October 2005.

OLDEST . . .

Mechanically printed book It is widely accepted that the first mechanically printed, full-length book was the Gutenberg Bible, printed in Mainz, Germany, *ca.* 1455 by Johann Henne zum Gensfleisch zur Laden, who was known as zu Gutehberg.

Novel The Greek author Chariton's *Chaireas & Callirhoe,* subtitled "Love Story in Syracuse," was written in the first century A.D. Apuleius' *The Golden Ass,* or *Metamorphoses,* reportedly written in A.D. 123, is the only Latin novel that survives whole.

Daily newspaper *Wiener Zeitung,* the Austrian government's official gazette, was first published in 1703.

Male author In February 2003, Constantine Kallias (Greece, b. June 26, 1901) published a first-edition, 169-page paperback titled *A Glance of My Life.*

Female author Louise Delany's (U.S.A.) second book, *The Delany Sisters' Book of Everyday Wisdom*—co-written with her sister A. Elizabeth Delany—was published by Kodansha America in October 1994, when she was 105.

Best-selling copyright book Excluding non-copyright works such as the Bible—the **best-selling non-fiction book of all time** (with an estimated 6 billion copies sold)—and the Koran, the world's best-selling book is *Guinness World Records* (formerly *The Guinness Book of Records*). First published in October 1955, global sales, in some 37 languages, exceeded 100 million copies as of October 2003.

MOST BOOKS TYPED BACKWARD Using a computer and four blank keyboards, and without looking at the screen, Michele Santelia (Italy, pictured below) has typed 64 books (3,361,851 words—19,549,382 characters) backward in their original languages, including *The Odyssey* and *Macbeth.* He completed reverse-typing the volumes of the Dead Sea Scrolls in ancient Hebrew on July 26, 2007.

TOWERING TOMES Michele assembled a 12-ft. 4-in.-high (3.78-m) tower of the books he has typed with the largest, a copy of the *Egyptian Book of the Dead,* at the bottom of the stack. That book weighed 173.7 lb. (78.8 kg) and had 610 huge pages 41.14 × 25.98 in. (104.5 × 66 cm).

TV HEAVEN

GREATEST TV AUDIENCES

Comedy The final episode of *M*A*S*H* (CBS, U.S.A.)—*Goodbye, Farewell, and Amen*—had an estimated audience of 125 million people when it was shown on February 28, 1983.

Live broadcast An estimated 2.5 billion people watched the funeral of Diana, Princess of Wales (UK, 1961–97), broadcast live from Westminster Abbey, London, UK, on September 6, 1997.

Series At its peak of popularity, *Baywatch* (NBC, then syndicated, U.S.A.) had an estimated weekly audience of more than 1.1 billion people in 142 countries in 1996.

Soccer An estimated 300 million viewers watched Italy beat France in the 2006 FIFA World Cup soccer final in Germany on July 9th.

Football 138.5 million viewers watched the NBC transmission of Super Bowl XXX on January 28, 1996.

Highest annual earnings by a TV actor Jerry Seinfeld earned an estimated $267 million in 1998, according to the 1999 *Forbes* Celebrity 100 list, the highest annual earnings ever by a television or movie actor.

★ MOST WATCHED CURRENT TV SHOW (U.S.A.) The Wednesday night episodes of *American Idol* broadcast in 2007 were watched by 17.3% of homes in the U.S.A. This made the program the most popular regularly scheduled TV show in the United States up to that time (as opposed to the most popular show voted for by the public).

"You can have it all. You just can't have it all at once."

<blockquote>Oprah Winfrey, highest paid TV personality</blockquote>

Highest annual earnings for a television actress Helen Hunt, the star of *Mad About You* (1992–99), became the world's wealthiest TV actress with annual earnings estimated at $31 million in 1999, according to the *Forbes* 2000 list.

Highest paid TV producer *Ally McBeal* creator David E. Kelley (U.S.A.) became the highest paid TV producer ever after a $300 million, six-year deal with Twentieth Century Fox Television (U.S.A.) in January 2000.

Highest paid television cast According to *Forbes'* Celebrity 100, the cast of *The Sopranos* (HBO, U.S.A.) earned a combined salary of $52 million for the seventh series of the New Jersey-based Mob drama. James Gandolfini (U.S.A.), who plays Mob boss Tony Soprano, reportedly secured himself a $1 million fee for each of the last eight episodes.

Highest annual earnings by a TV talk show host Oprah Winfrey (U.S.A.) continually tops the list of the world's top-earning television talk show hosts; according to *Forbes*, Oprah earned $225 million in 2005.

★**MOST DOWNLOADED TELEVISION SHOW** According to data from the peer-to-peer (P2P) media site Mininova, the TV show most frequently downloaded in 2007 using BitTorrent protocol is *Heroes* (NBC, U.S.A.), which was downloaded 2,439,154 times. Considering that Mininova is just one of many P2P sites, the actual number of downloads will be much higher.

MOST HOURS LIVE ON TV IN ONE WEEK
Mino Monta (Japan) regularly hosts 11 live-broadcast programs each week. He appears on TV for a total of 21 hours and 42 minutes weekly, which has earned him the sobriquet "host among hosts."

Most expensive TV pilot The production budget for the two-hour pilot of *Lost* (ABC, U.S.A.), which first aired on September 22, 2004, was $12 million—far greater than the cost of most television shows. This led to Disney firing ABC Entertainment Chairman Lloyd Braun (U.S.A.) for green-lighting the show, which went on to become one of the channel's most successful ever.

Longest-running show U.S. news program *Meet the Press* (NBC, U.S.A.) was first transmitted on November 6, 1947, and subsequently each week since September 12, 1948.

Longest TV commercial A television commercial for Lipton Ice Tea Green (Unilver Bestfoods, Netherlands) lasted for 24 minutes and was broadcast by the Yorin television channel, the Netherlands, on March 27, 2005.

Most characters voiced by one artist in a TV cartoon series Kara Tritton (UK) voiced 198 different cartoon characters for the same TV show, the most by a single artist. The characters appeared in *Blues Clues* (Nick Jr.), which ran for 75 episodes over six series, with episode 75 first broadcast on the Nickelodeon Channel on March 15, 2003.

Most successful TV soap *Dallas* (CBS, U.S.A.) began in 1978 as a mini-series and went on to become the most successful soap opera of all time. By 1980, it was watched by an estimated 83 million people in the

---

DID YOU KNOW?

The **largest TV telephone vote** was for the season six finale of *American Idol*, when 74,030,147 votes were cast by telephone and text messaging from viewers selecting the winner of the singing contest. The results were announced on May 22, 2007, with Jordin Sparks (U.S.A.) declared the winner.

★ **MOST WINS OF THE WACKY RACES**
Four of the regular entrants to the Wacky Races—as seen in Hannah-Barbera's eponymous cartoon TV series, broadcast from 1968 to 1970—share the record for the most wins, with four first-place victories each: Penelope Pitstop (driving the *Compact Pussycat*), the Ant Hill Mob (*Bullet Proof Bomb*), Lazy Luke and Blubber Bear (*Arkansas Chug-a-bug*), and Peter Perfect (*Turbo Terrific*). The fewest wins, of course, was zero by Dick Dastardly and Mutley (*Mean Machine*), who always came to a sticky end at the conclusion of each race.

U.S.A.—giving it a record 76% share of the TV audience—and was seen in more than 90 countries. The last episode aired in the U.S. on May 3, 1991.

☆ **Longest TV talk show marathon** Kristijan Petrovic (Croatia) interviewed and hosted on live television continuously for 36 hr. 15 min. on August 27–28, 2007. The marathon talk show took place on VTV Television in Varazdin, Croatia.

☆ **MOST POPULAR CURRENT TV SHOW** According to TV.com, a CNET Networks Entertainment website, the most popular TV show as of February 2008—with a review score of 9.4 out of 10—is the hospital drama *House* (Fox, U.S.A.), starring Hugh Laurie (UK) as the unconventional, maverick doctor Gregory House.

★ **MOST WATCHED TV SHOW ONLINE** Market research analyst Hitwise names *Deal or No Deal* (NBC, pictured above) as the TV show most commonly watched online, taking 15.46% of the total online TV viewership.

CIRCUS SKILLS

MOST . . .

★ **Candles extinguished by a whip in one minute** Jai Wancong (China) extinguished 22 candles by cracking a whip, without touching the wax, in one minute on the set of *Zheng Da Zong Yi—Guinness World Records Special* in Beijing, China, on November 2, 2007.

★ **Diabolo catches in one minute** Wang Yueqiu (China) threw and caught a diabolo a minimum of 19 ft. 8 in. (6 m) high 16 times in one minute in Beijing, China, on September 20, 2007.

★ **Hula hoops caught and spun in one minute** The greatest number of hula hoops caught and spun in one minute is 236, achieved by Liu Rongrong (China) on the set of *Zheng Da Zong Yi—Guinness World Records Special* in Beijing, China, on September 17, 2007.

☆ **Knives thrown in one minute** The record for the most knives thrown around a human target in one minute is 102 and was achieved by David Adamovich (U.S.A.) in Freeport, New York, U.S.A., on December 26, 2007.

☆**HIGHEST SHALLOW DIVE** The loftiest shallow dive took place from a height of 35 ft. 2 in. (10.7 m) and was achieved by Darren Taylor (U.S.A.) on the set of the TV show *Kiteretsu Superman Award 2007* in Tokyo, Japan, on July 25, 2007.

Adamovich, who uses the name the Great Throwdini, threw his knives at Dick Haines during the attempt.

☆**People on unicycles** On June 12, 2005, 1,142 people rode unicycles simultaneously at an event organized by Andrea Hardy (Germany) at the Dultplatz in Regensburg, Germany.

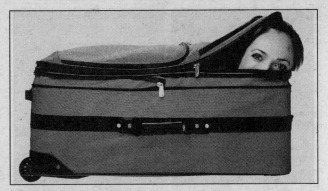

★ **FASTEST ESCAPE FROM A SUITCASE** Leslie Tipton (U.S.A.) escaped from a zipped suitcase in 13.31 seconds at the offices of Guinness World Records, London, UK, on September 27, 2007.

★ **Spears caught from a speargun underwater in one minute** Anthony Kelly (Australia) successfully caught five spears fired from a gun underwater in the swimming pool of the University of New England (UNE) at Armidale, New South Wales, Australia, on September 16, 2007.

★ **Swords swallowed simultaneously** Nine members of the Sword Swallowers Association International (eight men and one woman, all from the U.S.A.) simultaneously swallowed 52 swords at Wilkes-Barre, Pennsylvania, U.S.A., on September 2, 2005. Matt Henshaw (U.S.A.) holds the solo record, with 14 swords swallowed on April 6, 2000, at Fremantle, Perth, Australia.

★ **Tightrope walking—steepest gradient** Abulaiti Maijun (China) completed a 191-ft. 0.9-in. (58.24-m) tightrope walk, with an average slope of 34.15 degrees, in Xinjiang, China, on August 24, 2007. The record attempt took place for *Zheng Da Zong Yi—Guinness World Records Special* in Beijing, China.

DID YOU KNOW?

Contortionists Daniel Smith, Bonnie Morgan, and Leslie Tipton (all U.S.A.) together climbed into a box with an interior measuring 26 × 27 × 22 in. (66.04 × 68.58 × 55.88 cm) and were able to stay inside for 2 min. 55 sec. in Madrid, Spain, on December 5, 2001.

"Mostly what contortionists do is . . . we sit on our own heads!"

Leslie Tipton (U.S.A.), professional contortionist and circus performer

FIRST . . .

Double-back somersault Eddie Silbon (UK) achieved the first double-back somersault on the flying-return trapeze at the Paris Hippodrome, Paris, France, in 1879.

Human arrow Tony Zedoras (U.S.A.), billed as "Alar," performed the first human arrow trick at the Barnum & Bailey Circus in the U.S.A. in 1896.

Human cannonball The first human cannonball was "Zazel," who was shot a distance of 20 ft. (6.1 m) at Westminster Aquarium, London, UK, in 1877.

Flying-return trapeze act The first flying-return trapeze act was performed by Jules Léotard (France) at Cirque Napoleon, Paris, France, on November 12, 1859.

The **highest trapeze act** was carried out by Mike Howard (UK), hanging from a hot-air balloon above Glastonbury and Street, Somerset, UK, between altitudes of 19,600 ft. and 20,300 ft. (6,000 m and 6,200 m), on August 10, 1995.

Triple somersault on the trapeze The first public performance of this trick took place at the Chicago Coliseum, U.S.A., in 1920.

Three-ring circus The world's first three-ring circus was presented by "Lord" George Sanger (UK) in 1860.

★**FASTEST TIME TO BURST THREE BALLOONS WITH THE BACK** Julia Gunthel, a.k.a. "Zlata" (Germany), burst three balloons in 12 seconds, using just her back, for *Guinness World Records—Die Größten Weltrekorde* in Cologne, Germany, on November 23, 2007.

★ YOUNGEST LION TAMER Jorge Elich (Spain), the world's youngest lion tamer, has been learning his trade since the age of five. He most recently performed in this capacity for the Circus Paris in El Ejido, near Almeria, Spain, in January 2008, aged eight.

★ LONGEST TIME TO MAINTAIN A HUMAN FLAG Dominic Lacasse (Canada) maintained the pose of a human flag for 39 seconds on the set of *Guinness World Records—Die Größten Weltrekorde* in Cologne, Germany, on November 23, 2007.

☆ **MOST SUCCESSFUL ENTERTAINMENT LAUNCH** On April 29, 2008, the release of Rockstar's controversial *Grand Theft Auto IV* generated $310 million worth of first-day sales worldwide. This is more than five times the $60 million revenue generated by the most successful 24 hours for a movie, held by *Spider-Man 3* (U.S.A., 2007). The "Midnight Madness" launch at thousands of stores worldwide made *GTA IV* the **most successful entertainment product launch in history.**

★ BEST-SELLING VIDEO GAMES 2007 ★

RANK	GAME	SALES
01	*Call of Duty 4* (*All*)	7.13 million
02	*Wii play with Remote* (*Wii*)	6.90 million
03	*Halo 3* (*Xbox 360*)	6.79 million
04	*More Brain Training* (*DS*)	5.29 million
05	*World of Warcraft: Burning Crusade* (PC/Mac)	4.81 million
06	*Super Mario Galaxy* (*Wii*)	4.66 million
07	*Pokemon Diamond/Pearl* (*DS*)	4.27 million
08	*Wii Sports* (*Wii*)	3.2 million
09	*Assassin's Creed* (*PS3*)	2.83 million
10	*Guitar Hero 3* (*All*)	2.82 million

Charts compiled using data sourced from The NPD group, Famitsu, Chart Track, The GFK Group and VG Chartz.

SPORTS

CONTENTS

ACTION SPORTS

★**Fastest 15-m speed climbs** The fastest International Federation of Sport Climbing 15-m climb by a man is 8.76 seconds by Qixin Zhong (China) in Aviles, Spain, on September 21, 2007.

The **fastest 15-m climb by a woman** is 12.90 seconds by Li Chun-Ha (China) in Macau, China, on October 30, 2007.

★**Fastest speed in a microlight over a straight 15/25 km course by a team of two** On October 19, 2005, Jiri Unzeitag and Vera Vavrinova (both Czech Republic) achieved an average speed of 170.74 mph (274.78 km/h) in a microlight over a straight 15/25 km course in Horovice, Czech Republic.

★**Fastest parachuting freefall style** The fastest men's parachuting freefall style is 5.18 seconds by Marco Pflueger (Germany) over Eisenach,

MOST PARACHUTE DESCENTS By 2007, Cheryl Stearns (U.S.A.) had made the ☆**most parachute descents by a woman**, with a total of 16,000.

Between 1961 and 2003, Don Kellner (U.S.A.) did 34,000 freefall skydives—the **most descents by a man.**

YOUNGEST KITE-SURFING CHAMPION Gisela Pulido (Spain, above and left) won her first Kiteboard Pro World Tour (KPWT) World Championship on November 4, 2004, at the age of 10 years 294 days. She won her first professional championship on August 26, 2007, at 13 years 224 days.

Germany, on September 15, 2007. In the freefall style discipline, skydivers must complete a predetermined set of maneuvers in the quickest possible time.

The **fastest women's parachuting freefall style** is 6.10 seconds by Tatiana Osipova (Russia) over Bekescsaba, Hungary, on September 19, 1996.

★LONGEST INDOOR FREEFALL The longest indoor freefall is 1 hr. 18 min. 22 sec. and it was achieved by Andy Scott (UK) at the Airkix Windtunnel, Xscape Centre, Milton Keynes, UK, on March 8, 2007.

☆ **FASTEST GLIDER** The highest speed achieved in a glider while setting an official FAI (Fédération Aéronautique Internationale) record is 190.6 mph (306.8 km/h) over an out-and-return course of 310 miles (500 km) by Klaus Ohlmann (Germany) on December 22, 2006, at Zapala, Argentina. He flew a Schempp-Hirth Nimbus 4 DM.

☆ **Farthest flight by a paraglider** Three pilots—Frank Brown, Marcelo Prieto and Rafael Monteiro Saladini (all Brazil)—each flew a distance of 286.8 miles (461.6 km) in a paraglider between Quixada and Duque, Brazil, on November 14, 2007.

★ **Highest skateboard ramp into water** On September 17, 2007, in Los Angeles, California, U.S.A., pro-skateboarder Rob Dyrdek (U.S.A.) achieved a skateboard ramp jump measuring 10 ft. 8 in. (3.29 m) high. It was broadcast on MTV's *The Rob & Big Show.*

★ **Longest ramp jump on a snowmobile** The world record for the longest ramp jump on a snowmobile is 263 ft. 6 in. (80.31 m) and was set by

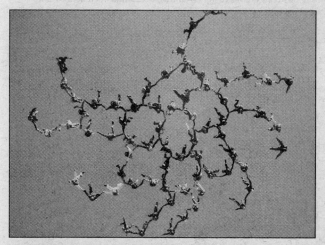

☆ **LARGEST PARACHUTE HEAD-DOWN FORMATION** On August 3, 2007, 69 skydivers from across the globe jumped in a free-flying head-down formation over Chicago, Illinois, U.S.A.

☆**FASTEST STREET LUGE** Streetluger Joel "Gravity" King (UK) reached a speed of 112.7 mph (181.37 km/h) on his jet engine-powered street luge at Bentwaters Airfield, UK, on August 28, 2007. King shattered the previous record of 98 mph (157 km/h), which had been held by Billy Copeland (U.S.A.) since May 2001.

Ross Mercer (Canada) in Steamboat Springs, Colorado, U.S.A., on March 10, 2007.

★**Most wins of the Class 1 World Powerboat Championship by a team** Bjorn Rune Gjelsten (Norway) and Steve Curtis (UK) won the Class 1 World Powerboat Championship five times (in 1998, 2002–04, and 2006).

★**Most wins of the Class 1 World Powerboat Championship by an individual** Steve Curtis (UK) won the Class 1 World Powerboat Championship six times, in 1998 and 2002–06. Curtis competed with Bjorn Rune Gjelsten (Norway) in 1998, 2002–04, and 2006; and with Bard Eker (Norway) in 2005.

FOOTBALL

☆**Most consecutive NFL game wins** The New England Patriots (U.S.A.) won 19 consecutive games from December 17, 2006, to December 29, 2007. This included a 16–0 record in 2007, which saw them become the

☆ **MOST FIELD GOALS BY AN INDIVIDUAL IN AN NFL GAME** Rob Bironas (U.S.A.) kicked eight field goals for the Tennessee Titans in an NFL game against the Houston Texans (both U.S.A.) on October 21, 2007.

SUPER BOWL STATS

ATTENDANCE

The **largest attendance at a Super Bowl** is 103,985 for Super Bowl XIV between the Pittsburgh Steelers and the L.A. Rams (U.S.A.) at the Rose Bowl, Pasadena, California, U.S.A., on January 20, 1980.

WINS

The **most Super Bowl wins by a player** is five by Charles Hayley (U.S.A.), who played for the San Francisco 49ers in 1989–90 and the Dallas Cowboys in 1993–94 and 1996.

MVP AWARDS

The **person with the most Most Valuable Player (MVP) awards** is San Francisco 49ers quarterback Joe Montana (U.S.A.), who was voted MVP in three Super Bowls: 1982, 1985, and 1990.

BRETT FAVRE Despite an inauspicious debut season in the National Football League (NFL) with the Atlanta Falcons (U.S.A.) in 1991, Brett Favre (U.S.A.) established himself as one of the most celebrated football players of all time. That first season saw Favre attempt just four passes in regular play, none of which was completed. However, Favre was traded to the Green Bay Packers (U.S.A.) in 1992 and, following an injury to the regular quarterback, started the fourth game of the season on September 27, 1992. From that game until he announced his retirement on March 4, 2008, Favre started 275 consecutive games (including playoffs), the ★ most by an NFL quarterback. During his career with the Packers, Favre amassed a host of records, among them: the ★ most touchdown passes (442); the ★ most pass attempts (8,758); the ★ most completed passes (5,377); the ★ most passing yards (61,655 yd.); and the ★ most victories as a starting quarterback (160). In July 2008 Favre announced that he had retired from football too early and was interested in rejoining the NFL. He became a member of the New York Jets that August.

★ **first team in the National Football League (NFL) to achieve an undefeated regular season** since the league went to a 16-game schedule in 1978.

★ **Fastest NFL player to reach 400 receptions** Anquan Boldin (U.S.A.) needed just 67 games to reach 400 catches in his career, which he achieved on December 24, 2007.

☆ **Most consecutive NFL games played** Punter Jeff Feagles (U.S.A.) has played a record 320 consecutive NFL games. His long career has taken in stints at the New England Patriots (1988–89), Philadelphia Eagles (1990–93), Arizona Cardinals (1994–97), Seattle Seahawks (1998–2002), and New York Giants (2002–07; all U.S.A.).

When Feagles appeared for the New York Giants in Super Bowl XLII, on February 3, 2008, aged 41 years 333 days, he became the ☆ **oldest player in Super Bowl history.**

★ **MOST YARDS PASSING IN AN NFL GAME BY A ROOKIE QUARTERBACK** Playing for the Arizona Cardinals, (U.S.A.) rookie quarterback Matt Leinart (U.S.A.) passed for 405 yd. (370 m) against the Minnesota Vikings (U.S.A.) at the Metrodome in Minneapolis, Minnesota, U.S.A., on November 26, 2006.

☆ **Most NFL games played by an individual** Morten Andersen (Denmark) has played in 382 games during his NFL career as a place kicker with the New Orleans Saints, Atlanta Falcons, New York Giants, Kansas City Chiefs, and Minnesota Vikings (U.S.A.) since 1982.

★ **MOST TOUCHDOWN CATCHES IN AN NFL SEASON** Randy Moss (U.S.A.) made 23 touchdown catches for the New England Patriots during the 2007 NFL season. The previous record of 22 was established by Jerry Rice (U.S.A.) of the San Francisco 49ers in 1987.

> ## "If your team is going to win, you need to play better than the other quarterback."
>
> *Peyton Manning, record-breaking quarterback*

★**Highest net punting average (season)** Shane Lechler (U.S.A.) had a net punting average of 41 yd. 3 in. (37.58 m) playing for the Oakland Raiders (U.S.A.) in 2007.

★**Most times sacked in an NFL career** John Elway (U.S.A.) was sacked 516 times during his career with the Denver Broncos (U.S.A.) from 1983 to 1998.

☆**Most touchdown passes in an NFL career** Brett Favre (U.S.A.) completed 442 touchdown passes from 1992 to 2008.

☆**Most yards gained rushing in an NFL season** Eric Dickerson (U.S.A.) recorded the most yards gained rushing in an NFL season with 2,105 yd. (1,924 m) when playing for the Los Angeles Rams (U.S.A.) in the 1984 season.

☆**Most seasons passing 4,000 yards in an NFL career** Peyton Manning (U.S.A.) of the Indianapolis Colts (U.S.A.) set an NFL record in 2007 by reaching 4,000 passing yards in a season for the eighth time in his illustrious career.

☆**HIGHEST SCORE IN AN NFL EUROPA WORLD BOWL** When the Hamburg Sea Devils defeated the Frankfurt Galaxy (both Germany) 37–28 in World Bowl XV at the Commerzbank-Arena in Frankfurt, Germany, on June 23, 2007, their combined score of 65 made the game the highest scoring in World Bowl history.

★ **OLDEST PAIR OF STARTING QUARTERBACKS** The oldest starting quarterback match-up in NFL history was formed by 44-year-old Vinny Testaverde (above right) of the Carolina Panthers and 38-year-old Brett Favre of the Green Bay Packers (all U.S.A.) on November 18, 2007.

★ **Most consecutive extra points by an individual in the NFL** Jeff Wilkins (U.S.A.) has kicked 371 consecutive extra points since 1999, equaling the record set by Jason Elam (U.S.A.) from 1993 to 2002.

☆ **Most touchdown passes in an NFL season** Tom Brady (U.S.A.) threw 50 touchdown passes playing for the New England Patriots during the 2007 season, surpassing the previous score of 49 by Peyton Manning (U.S.A.) in 2004.

★ **First NFL regular-season game played in Europe** On October 28, 2007, the Miami Dolphins (U.S.A.) played the New York Giants at Wembley Stadium in London, UK, in what was the first NFL regular-season game to be played in Europe. The New York Giants were 13–10 winners of a game played in front of 81,176 fans.

FACT

Aged 44 years 19 days, Vinny Testaverde (U.S.A.) became the **oldest starting quarterback to win a game** when he led the Carolina Panthers to a 31–14 win over the San Francisco 49ers (U.S.A.) at the Bank of America Stadium, Charlotte, North Carolina, U.S.A., on December 2, 2007.

TRACK & FIELD

Sprint speed When Usain Bolt (Jamaica) ran 100 m in 9.72 seconds in 2008 (see below), his average speed was 23.01 mph (37.03 km/h). When Michael Johnson (U.S.A.) ran 200 m in 19.32 seconds in 1996, his average speed was 23.15 mph (37.26 km/h). This makes Johnson—in theory, at least—the **fastest man in history**.

TRACK & FIELD

Fastest indoor 4 × 800 m relay (women) Moskovskaya Region (Anna Balakshina, Natalya Pantelyeva, Anna Emashova, Olesya Chumakova; all Russia) ran the 4 × 800 m relay in 8 min. 18.54 sec. at an indoor event in Volgograd, Russia, on February 11, 2007.

☆**Fastest indoor 1,500 m (female)** Yelena Soboleva (Russia) ran 1,500 m in 3 min. 57.71 sec. at an indoor event held in Valencia, Spain, on March 9, 2008, cutting over one quarter of a second off the previous record of 3 min. 58.05 sec., which she had set just 28 days earlier.

☆**Fastest indoor 3,000 m (female)** Meseret Defar (Ethiopia) ran 3,000 m on an indoor track in 8 min. 23.72 sec. at the Sparkassen Cup in Stuttgart, Germany, on February 3, 2007.

☆**Fastest 5,000 m (female)** Meseret Defar (Ethiopia) ran 5,000 m in 14 min. 16.63 sec. in Oslo, Norway, on June 15, 2007, knocking nearly eight

☆**FASTEST 100 M (MALE)** Jamaica's Usain Bolt ran the 100 m in 9.72 seconds at the Reebok Grand Prix in Icahn Stadium, New York City, U.S.A., on May 31, 2008. He broke the previous record, held by fellow Jamaican Asafa Powell, by 0.02 seconds, to become the "world's fastest man."

LONGEST HAMMER THROW (FEMALE)
Tatyana Lysenko (Russia) recorded a
hammer throw of 255 ft. 3 in. (77.8 m) at an
event in Tallinn, Estonia, on August 15, 2006.

seconds off the previous record, which she had
set a year earlier.

☆**Farthest distance run in one hour
(male)** Haile Gebrselassie (Ethiopia) ran
21,285 m in one hour in Ostrava, Czech Republic, on June 27, 2007. On his way to the one-
hour record, Gebrselassie broke the record for
the ☆**fastest 20,000 m,** which he achieved in a
time of 56 min. 26 sec.

☆**Highest indoor pole vault (female)** Yelena Isinbayeva (Russia) completed a 4.95-m
pole vault at an indoor event in Donetsk,
Ukraine, on February 16, 2008.

☆**FASTEST INDOOR 5,000 M (FEMALE)** Tirunesh Dibaba (Ethiopia) ran
the fastest indoor 5,000 m when she recorded a time of 14 min. 27.42
sec. at the Boston Indoor Games in Boston, U.S.A., on January 27, 2007.

☆**FASTEST INDOOR 60 M HURDLES (FEMALE)** Susanna Kallur (Sweden) ran the 60 m hurdles, indoors, in 7.68 sec. in Karlsruhe, Germany, on February 10, 2008.

ROAD

☆**Fastest 20 km road walk (male)** Vladimir Kanaykin (Russia) walked 20 km in 1 hr. 17 min. 16 sec. in the final of the IAAF Race Walking Challenge in Saransk, Russia, on September 29, 2007.

Fastest 20 km road walk (female) Olimpiada Ivanova (Russia) completed a 20 km road walk in 1 hr. 25 min. 41 sec. in Helsinki, Finland, on August 7, 2005.

★**Most 50 km World Race Walking Cup wins (male)** Since the inaugural competition was held in 1961, two male walkers have each won the 50 km event at the World Race Walking Cup on three occasions: Christoph Hohne (East Germany) was victorious in 1965, 1967, and 1970; and Raul Gonzalez (Mexico) was champion in 1977, 1981, and 1983.

☆**Fastest 20 km road run (female)** Lornah Kiplagat (Netherlands) ran 20 km in 1 hr. 2 min. 57 sec. in Udine, Italy, on October 14, 2007.

★**Most Half Marathon World Championships team wins (women)** Romania has won the women's IAAF Half Marathon World Championships team event on seven occasions: in 1993–97, 2000, and 2005.

★**Most wins of the World Road Running Championships by a team** Kenya won both the men's and women's team events at the World Road Running Championships in 2006 and 2007.

☆ **MOST WORLD CROSS COUNTRY CHAMPIONSHIP WINS (MALE)** Kenenisa Bekele (Ethiopia) has won the World Cross Country Championship, long course, on six occasions: in 2002–06 and 2008. Bekele has also won the short course title a record five times: 2002–06.

CROSS COUNTRY

Most World Cross Country Championship wins (female) Grete Waitz (Norway) has won the World Cross Country Championship, long course, on five occasions: in 1978–81 and 1983.

☆ **MOST EUROPEAN CUP WINS (WOMEN)** Russia has won the women's European Cup on 13 occasions: in 1993, 1995, and each year from 1997 to 2007.

X-REF

Are you inspired by the commitment and dedication it takes to become a world-record-breaking athlete? If so, check out **pp. 148–152** for a host of very different **Inspirational Acts.**

☆**MOST EUROPEAN CUP WINS (MEN)** Germany has won the men's European Cup on seven occasions: in 1994–96, 1999, 2002, and 2004–05.

OUTDOOR HURDLES

Women Yordanka Donkova (Bulgaria) ran the 100 m hurdles in 12.21 seconds on August 20, 1988.

Men Xiang Liu (China) ran the 110 m hurdles in 12.88 seconds on July 11, 2006.

MARATHONS

★**Fastest time to complete a marathon in orbit** NASA astronaut Sunita Williams (U.S.A.) achieved the fastest time to complete a marathon in orbit above Earth on board the *International Space Station*. Ms. Williams, who ran the 26.2 miles (42 km) strapped to a treadmill with bungy cord, competed as an official entrant of the 111th Boston Marathon (U.S.A.) on April 16, 2007, finishing in a time of 4 hr. 24 min.

★**Most triathlons completed** The most triathlons completed by one athlete is 250 by James "Flip" Lyle (U.S.A.) up to March 18, 2006.

☆**FASTEST HALF MARATHONS** Lornah Kiplagat (Netherlands) ran the women's half marathon in 1 hr. 6 min. 25 sec. in Udine, Italy, on October 14, 2007.

The men's half marathon record is held by Samuel Wanjiru Kamau (Kenya), who ran a time of 58 min. 35 sec. in The Hague, the Netherlands, on March 17, 2007.

★ **DRESSED AS A CLOWN** Jason Westmoreland (UK) ran the Flora London Marathon 2008 in London, UK, on April 13, 2008. He did so dressed as a clown and finished in 3 hr. 24 min. 4 sec.

☆ **FASTEST MARATHON** Haile Gebrselassie and Gete Wami (both Ethiopia) celebrate their victories as winners of the 34th Berlin Marathon on September 30, 2007, in Berlin, Germany. Gebrselassie became the world's **fastest male marathon runner** when he finished in a time of 2 hr. 4 min. 26 sec. at this event. Inaugurated in 2006, the **World Marathon Majors** is a competition encompassing the five annual marathon races in Berlin (Germany), London (UK), New York City, Boston, and Chicago (all U.S.A.), with athletes scoring points for top five finishes over two calendar years. The World Championship and Olympic marathons are also included in the years that they are run. The winner of the first women's championship in 2006–07 was Gete Wami, with 80 points.

☆ **KNITTING A SCARF** The longest scarf knitted by a runner while completing a marathon was 5 ft. 2 in. (1.62 m) by Susie Hewer (UK) at the Flora London Marathon on April 13, 2008.

★ **IN MILITARY UNIFORM** The record for the fastest marathon in a military uniform is 5 hr. 11 min. 42 sec. and was achieved by Myles Morson (UK) at the Flora London Marathon 2008, in London, UK.

★ FASTEST MARATHON ON STILTS
Michelle Frost (UK) ran the entire Flora London Marathon 2008 on stilts. She finished in a time of 8 hr. 25 min. on April 13, 2008, in London, UK.

Fastest marathon by a woman Paula Radcliffe (UK) ran the London Marathon in 2 hr. 15 min. 25 sec. on April 13, 2003, in London, UK.

Marathons on each of the seven continents The ☆ shortest time to finish a marathon on each of the seven continents by a man is 29 days 16 hr. 17 min. by Richard Takata (Canada), between February 4 and March 6, 2007.

The ☆ shortest time to finish a marathon on each continent by a woman is 48 days 15 hr. 49 min. 38 sec. by Dawn Hamlin (U.S.A.) between January 18, 2008, and March 5, 2008.

The fastest aggregate time for a man to run a marathon on each continent is 34 hr. 23 min. 8 sec. by Tim Rogers (UK) from February 13 to May 23, 1999.

The ☆ fastest aggregate time for a woman is 28 hr. 41 min. 24 sec. by Jeanne Stawiecki (U.S.A.), between October 8, 2006, and February 26, 2007.

Flora London marathon Other Guinness World Records broken:

Fastest marathon... ★ by a linked team: Oliver Holland, James Kennedy, James Wrighton, Eoghan Murray, and Nathan Jones: 3 hr. 38 min. 24 sec.

★ as a movie character: James McComish (Darth Maul): 3 hr. 55 min. 22 sec.

★ dressed as Santa: Ian Sharman: 3 hr. 12 min. 27 sec.

☆ dressed as a superheroine: Christina Tomlinson (Supergirl): 3 hr. 13 min. 33 sec.

★ in a fireman's uniform: Mark Rogers and Paul Bartlett: 5 hr. 36 min. 12 sec.

★ by a group of Masai warriors: 5 hr. 24 min. 47 sec.

★ DRIBBLING A BASKETBALL Jean-Yves Kanyamibwa (UK) ran the Flora London Marathon 2008 dribbling a basketball in 4 hr. 30 min. 29 sec.

★ TALLEST COSTUME WORN The tallest costume worn while running a marathon measured 14 ft. (4.27 m) high and was worn by Tim Rogers (UK) in aid of WellChild at the Flora London Marathon, London, UK, on April 22, 2007.

☆ MOST LINKED RUNNERS A group of 24 Metropolitan Police officers ran the Flora London Marathon 2008 while being linked with plastic chains that had been taped in place. They remained linked for the entire race in London, UK, on April 13, 2008.

AUTOSPORTS

NASCAR

☆**Highest career earnings** The highest career earnings in NASCAR is $89,397,060 by Jeff Gordon (U.S.A.) up to and including the 2007 season.

★**Most restrictor plate victories (career)** The most career victories at restrictor plate tracks is 12 by Jeff Gordon (U.S.A.) through the 2007 season. Gordon surpassed the previous mark held by Dale Earnhardt (U.S.A.) of 11 plate victories by winning at the Talladega Superspeedway in Talladega, Alabama, U.S.A., on October 7, 2007. Restrictor plates are devices installed on cars at certain tracks to increase safety by reducing engine power.

☆ **LEWIS HAMILTON** The 2007 season saw rookie driver Lewis Hamilton (UK) take Formula One by storm.
  Although he missed winning the title, Hamilton still set a number of F1 records.
  By securing six pole positions, Hamilton set a new mark for ★ **most pole positions in a rookie season**; and in winning four races, he claimed a share of the F1 record for ☆ **most wins in a season by a rookie**, also held by Jacques Villeneuve (Canada), who achieved the feat in 1996.

"Who would have thought I'd be ranked number two in my first year of Formula One?"

Lewis Hamilton

★**Most top ten finishes in one year** The NASCAR record for most top ten finishes in one year in the modern era (1972 to present) is 30 by Jeff Gordon (U.S.A.) in 2007. The all-time record is 43 by Richard Petty (U.S.A.) in 1964.

☆**Highest career earnings (Truck Series)** Jack Sprague (U.S.A.) holds the NASCAR Truck Series record for most career earnings with $6,762,094 up to and including the 2007 season.

☆**Most poles won in a career (Truck Series)** Mike Skinner (U.S.A.) has had more NASCAR Truck Series pole positions in his career than any other driver, with 43 up to and including the 2007 season.

☆**Most wins in a career (Truck Series)** Ron Hornaday Jr. (U.S.A.) has had 33 wins in his NASCAR Truck Series career up to and including the 2007 season.

☆ **MOST CONSECUTIVE SEASONS WINNING MULTIPLE RACES TO START A NASCAR CAREER** Tony Stewart (U.S.A.) has won multiple races in nine consecutive seasons from 1999 to 2007, the longest such streak at the start of a driver's career in National Association for Stock Car Auto Racing (NASCAR).

☆ MOST CONSECUTIVE NASCAR WINS Eight drivers have recorded four consecutive victories in the modern NASCAR era (since 1972); the most recent of these is Jimmie Johnson (U.S.A., left) in 2007. Richard Petty (U.S.A.) holds the all-time record for consecutive wins, with 10 victories in a row in 1967.

INDYCAR

★**Most race starts** Scott Sharp (U.S.A.) started 146 IndyCar Series races in a career stretching from 1996 to 2007.

★**Most poles won in a career** The IndyCar Series record for most poles won in a career is 23 by Helio Castroneves (Brazil) from 2001 to 2007.

MOST CONSECUTIVE INDYCAR SERIES WINS Three drivers have won three consecutive IndyCar Series races: Scott Dixon (New Zealand, above) in 2007, Dan Wheldon (UK) in 2005, and Kenny Brack (Sweden) in 1998.

★ **MOST RACES WON IN AN INDYCAR SERIES CAREER** Sam Hornish Jr. (U.S.A.) has had 19 IndyCar Series wins in a career that began in 2000.

★ **Most laps led in a single race by the race winner** The most laps led in a single race by the race winner is 242 by Dario Franchitti (Scotland) at Richmond International Raceway in Richmond, Virginia, U.S.A., on June 30, 2007.

DRAG RACING

☆ **Most wins in a National Hot Rod Association (NHRA) drag racing career** John Force (U.S.A.) has had more career wins than any other drag racer, with 125 victories up to and including 2007.

★ **Fastest speed in Pro Stock (car), NHRA drag racing** For a gas-driven, piston-engined car (Pro Stock), the highest velocity is 211.69 mph (340.61 km/h) by Jason Line (U.S.A.) in Gainesville, Florida, U.S.A., on March 18, 2007.

★ **Fastest speed in funny car, NHRA drag racing** Mike Ashley (U.S.A.) reached a velocity of 334.32 mph (537.02 km/h) in a Dodge Charger in Las Vegas, Nevada, U.S.A., on April 13, 2007.

FACT

The **largest margin of victory by a Busch Series champion** is 824 points by Kevin Harvick (U.S.A.) in 2006. That season, Harvick clinched the title with four races remaining, setting a record for **earliest clinch of the championship** on October 13, 2006.

BALL SPORTS

☆**Most matches played in international field hockey (male)**
Jeroen Delmee (Netherlands) made a record 373 international appearances
for the Netherlands from 1994 to 2008.

☆**Most men's Champions Trophy wins** The Champions Trophy was
first held in 1978, and since 1980 has been contested annually by the top six
men's field hockey teams in the world. The most wins is eight by Australia in
1983–85, 1989–90, 1993, 1999, and 2007.

★**Largest street hockey tournament** A total of 2,010 players in 192
teams took part in a street hockey tournament in Ladysmith, British Columbia, Canada, on June 3, 2007.

☆**Most pass completions by a quarterback in Canadian football**
Quarterback Damon Allen (U.S.A.) set a new professional football record
for the most career pass completions with 5,158 through the 2007 season.
Allen has played for seven teams during a 23-year Canadian Football
League career that began in 1985.

★**Most goals in the Korfball World Championships** The Netherlands has scored the most with 1,109 goals in the eight Korfball World
Championships held to 2007. In the same period, Australia conceded the
greatest number of goals with 615 goals against.

★**MOST SULTAN AZLAN SHAH CUPS** The Sultan Azlan Shah Cup is an
annual international field hockey tournament held in Malaysia.
Australia has lifted the cup more times than any other nation, winning
in 1983, 1998, 2004, 2005, and 2007.

☆ **MOST WOMEN'S HANDBALL WORLD CHAMPIONSHIPS** Three women's titles have been won by three teams: the GDR in 1971, 1975, and 1978; the USSR in 1982, 1986, and 1990; and Russia in 2001, 2005, and 2007. Pictured is Russia's Irina Bliznova.

☆ **Greatest prize money for a beach volleyball world tour** A record $7.37 million prize money fund was available for the Federation Internationale de Volleyball beach volleyball world tour in 2007.

☆ **Highest career earnings, AVP Tour, beach volleyball** Holly McPeak (U.S.A.) has won $1,466,396 in official AVP Tour earnings through to the end of the 2007 season, the **highest career earnings by an AVP Tour female player.**

Karch Kiraly (U.S.A.) has won $3,198,748 in official AVP Tour earnings through to the end of the 2007 season, the **highest career earnings by an AVP Tour male player.**

Most Brownlow Medal wins The most wins of the Brownlow Medal in the Australian Football League is three, held jointly by Haydn Bunton in 1931, 1932, and 1935; Dick Reynolds in 1934, 1937, and 1938; Bob Skilton in 1959, 1963, and 1968; and Ian Stewart in 1965, 1966, and 1971 (all Australia).

HANDBALL CHAMPIONS

The ★ **most African Handball Championships won by a men's team** is seven, by Tunisia.

The ★ **most Asian Handball Championships won by a men's team** is also seven, by South Korea.

☆ **MOST TOUCHDOWNS IN A CANADIAN FOOTBALL CAREER** By 2007, Milt Stegall (U.S.A.) had scored 144 touchdowns for Canadian Football League team the Winnipeg Blue Bombers. His career began in 1995.

☆ **Most Gaelic football All-Ireland final wins** The greatest number of All-Ireland Championships won by one team is 35, by Kerry between 1903 and 2007.

☆ **Most wins of All-Ireland hurling finals** Two teams have won 30 All-Ireland Hurling Championships: Cork between 1890 and 2005; and Kilkenny between 1904 and 2007.

★ **Oldest netball team** Poly Netball Club, London, UK, is the oldest netball team in continuous existence. The team was founded in 1907 and celebrated its centennial in 2007.

☆ **MOST NETBALL WORLD TITLES** Australia has won the Netball World Championships a record nine times: 1963, 1971, 1975, 1979 (shared), 1983, 1991, 1995, 1999, and 2007. The only other teams to have won are New Zealand in 1967, 1979 (shared), 1987, and 2003; and Trinidad & Tobago, who shared the title in 1979. Pictured is Australia's Mo'onia Gerrard.

★ MOST CONSECUTIVE MATCHES PLAYED IN THE AFL FROM DEBUT
Jared Crouch (Australia) played 194 consecutive Australian Football
League (AFL) matches for the Sydney Swans from his debut on May 10,
1998, until he was forced from play through injury in July 2006.

☆ MOST AVP BEST DEFENSIVE PLAYER AWARDS Two players have
won the Association of Volleyball Professionals (AVP) Pro Beach Tour
defensive player of the year award for a male athlete on four occasions:
Mike Dodd (U.S.A.) in 1994–97; and Todd Rogers (U.S.A., pictured) in
2004–2007.

☆ **Most National Bank Cup wins** The National Bank Cup is the elite
national tournament in New Zealand netball. Melbourne Southern Sting
(New Zealand) has won the cup on seven occasions: every season from
1999 to 2004 and again in 2007.

X-REF

If you are interested in all things Australian, take a look at the **Australia**
page in our **Gazetteer** section on **p. 451**. If it's more ball sports that
you're looking for, then check out our four pages of **Soccer**, which
begin on **p. 357**.

BASEBALL

★**Most valuable baseball franchise** The New York Yankees are valued at $1.026 billion, according to a *Forbes* magazine report in 2007, making them the first U.S. Major League Baseball (MLB) team—and the first baseball franchise—to pass the $1 billion mark.

★**First professional franchise to lose 10,000 games** The Philadelphia Phillies became the first professional sports franchise ever to lose 10,000 games, dropping a 10–2 loss to the St. Louis Cardinals on July 15, 2007. The franchise has a long history of losing, having played—and lost— its first game in May 1883. The Phillies have won only two World Series (1980 and 2008) in 125 years.

☆**Most strikeouts in a game by a batter** The MLB record for the most times struck out in a game is five—by many players, most recently Craig Monroe (U.S.A.) of the Detroit Tigers on June 14, 2007.

☆**Most saves in a career** The MLB record for most career saves is 524, recorded by Trevor Hoffman (U.S.A.) playing for the Florida Marlins and San Diego Padres from 1993 to 2007.

★**Most Gold Glove awards in a career** The Gold Glove is an MLB award for fielding excellence. The most Gold Gloves won in a career is 17 by Greg Maddux (U.S.A.) between 1990 and 2007, while playing for the Chicago Cubs, Atlanta Braves, Los Angeles Dodgers, and San Diego Padres.

★**FIRST RELIEF PITCHER TO RECORD 500 SAVES IN A CAREER** The first relief pitcher in MLB history to record 500 saves in a career is Trevor Hoffman (U.S.A.), playing for the Florida Marlins and San Diego Padres from 1993 to 2007.

★ **Most ejections in a career** Bobby Cox (U.S.A.) has been ejected 132 times from games while managing the Toronto Blue Jays and Atlanta Braves from 1978 to 2007.

★ **Highest slugging percentage by a rookie** Ryan Braun (U.S.A.) hit an average of .634 while playing for the Milwaukee Brewers in 2007.

★ **Most plate appearances in a season** Jimmy Rollins (U.S.A.) made 778 plate appearances for the Philadelphia Phillies in 2007.

★ **Youngest person to hit 50 home runs in a season** At 23 years 139 days, Prince Fielder (U.S.A., b. May 9, 1984) became the youngest major league player ever to hit 50 home runs in a season when he homered while playing for the Milwaukee Brewers against the St. Louis Cardinals at Miller Park in Milwaukee, Wisconsin, U.S.A., on September 25, 2007.

☆ **Oldest player to hit a home run** At the age of 48 years 254 days, Julio Franco (Dominican Republic, b. August 23, 1958) became the oldest player in MLB history to hit a home run when he connected off Randy Johnson (U.S.A.) to help the New York Mets to a 5–3 win over the Arizona Diamondbacks at Chase Field in Phoenix, Arizona, U.S.A., on May 4, 2007.

★ **Most batters consecutively retired by a pitcher** The MLB record for most consecutive batters retired is 41 by Bobby Jenks (U.S.A.) while pitching for the Chicago White Sox in several games from July 17, 2007, to August 12, 2007. He shares this record with Jim Barr (U.S.A.), who pitched two straight shutouts for the San Francisco Giants against the Pittsburgh Pirates on August 23, 1972, and against the St. Louis Cardinals on August 29, 1972. Barr retired the last 21 Pirates he faced and the first 20 Cardinals.

☆ **Most times hit by a pitch in a career** Craig Biggio (U.S.A.) was hit 285 times playing for the Houston Astros from 1988 to 2007—the most times in a career.

☆ **LONGEST BASEBALL MARATHON** A baseball marathon lasting 32 hr. 29 min. 25 sec. was played by the St. Louis chapter of the Men's Senior Baseball League at T. R. Hughes Ballpark, home to the River City Rascals, in O'Fallon, Missouri, U.S.A., on October 13–14, 2007. After a grueling 92 innings, the St. Louis Browns beat the St. Louis Stars 119–81.

★ **YOUNGEST PERSON TO HIT 500 HOME RUNS (CAREER)** At 32 years 8 days old, Alex Rodriguez (U.S.A., b. July 27, 1975) became the youngest player in baseball history to reach 500 career home runs. He homered off Kyle Davies (U.S.A.), pitching for the Kansas City Royals, at Yankee Stadium in the Bronx, New York, U.S.A., on August 4, 2007.

MOST HOME RUNS . . .

☆ IN A CAREER

Barry Bonds (U.S.A.) clocked up 762 home runs playing for the Pittsburgh Pirates and San Francisco Giants from 1986 to 2007.

IN A GAME BY ONE PLAYER

Robert Lincoln "Bobby" Lowe (U.S.A.) hit four home runs for Boston against Cincinnati on May 30, 1894. The same feat has been achieved many times since then.

★ BY A DESIGNATED HITTER

Frank Thomas (U.S.A.) hit 261 homers playing for the Chicago White Sox, Oakland Athletics, and Toronto Blue Jays (Canada) from 1990 to 2007.

★ IN A POSTSEASON CAREER

Manny Ramirez (Dominican Republic) has slugged 24 home runs playing for the Cleveland Indians and Boston Red Sox since 1995.

☆ FROM START OF CAREER UNDER ONE MANAGER

Chipper Jones (U.S.A.) hit 386 playing for manager Bobby Cox (U.S.A.) of the Atlanta Braves from 1993 to 2007.

★ **MOST STOLEN BASES IN A POSTSEASON CAREER** The record for most career stolen bases in the postseason is 34 by Kenny Lofton (U.S.A.), playing for several teams. Lofton surpassed the previous mark of 33 by Rickey Henderson (U.S.A.). See the awards panel below for more of Lofton's incredible achievements.

☆ **Most bases on balls in a major league baseball career** The record for most bases on balls in a career is 2,558 by Barry Bonds (U.S.A.), playing for the Pittsburgh Pirates and San Francisco Giants from 1986 to 2007.

☆ **Most expensive baseball card sold** A baseball card known as T206 Honus Wagner issued by the American Tobacco Company in 1909 was sold in a deal brokered by SCP Auctions (U.S.A.) to an anonymous collector for $2.8 million in September 2007.

★ **Oldest field** The oldest baseball diamond is Labatt Park in London, Ontario, Canada, which was established in 1877 and hosts baseball games to the present day.

KENNY LOFTON'S AWARDS

Kenny (pictured above) is a free agent MLB outfielder who has won recognition numerous times for his baseball talents:

• Six-time All-Star (1994–99)

• Four-time Gold Glove Award (1993–96)

• Five-time stolen bases league leader (1992–96)

BASKETBALL

NBA

★ **Oldest player ever** The oldest player in National Basketball Association (NBA) league history is Nat Hickey (U.S.A.), who as coach of the Providence Steamrollers (U.S.A.) activated himself for one game in 1948. He was aged 45 years 363 days at the time.

★ **Most consecutive games scoring 50 or more points** Wilt Chamberlain (U.S.A.) scored at least 50 points in seven consecutive games while playing for the Philadelphia Warriors (U.S.A.) in December 1961.

☆ **Most NBA playoff games won by a coach** Phil Jackson (U.S.A.) achieved the greatest number of playoff game victories by a coach in an NBA career. He won 179 playoff games as coach of the Chicago Bulls (U.S.A., 1989–97) and Los Angeles Lakers (U.S.A., 1999–2003 and 2005–07).

★ **YOUNGEST PLAYER TO SCORE 9,000 POINTS** At 22 years 252 days, LeBron James (U.S.A., b. December 30, 1984) is the youngest player in NBA history to score 9,000 career points. He reached the mark while playing for the Cleveland Cavaliers (U.S.A.) on December 18, 2007.

★ **YOUNGEST PLAYER TO REACH 20,000 POINTS (CAREER)** While
playing for the Los Angeles Lakers on December 23, 2007, Kobe Bryant
(U.S.A., b. August 23, 1978) reached 20,000 career points, aged 29 years
122 days.

☆ **Most three-point field goals scored in a game (team)** The NBA
record for the greatest number of three-point shots made in a game by a
team is 21 by the Toronto Raptors (Canada) on March 13, 2005.

★ **First European player named NBA finals' most valuable player**
Tony Parker (France) was named most valuable player of the NBA Finals
playing for the San Antonio Spurs (U.S.A.) in 2007.

The ★ **first European player to be named the most valuable player in
the NBA regular season** was Dirk Nowitzki (Germany). Nowitzki achieved
this accolade while playing for the Dallas Mavericks (U.S.A.) during the
2006/07 season.

DID YOU KNOW?

Christopher Eddy (U.S.A.) scored a field goal measured at 90 ft. 2.25 in.
(27.49 m)—the **longest shot in a basketball game**—for Fairview High
School vs. Iroquois High School in Erie, Pennsylvania, U.S.A., on
February 25, 1989. Eddy made the shot as time expired in overtime,
thereby winning the game for Fairview, 51–50.

★ YOUNGEST PLAYER TO RECORD 3,000 REBOUNDS At 21 years 343 days, Dwight Howard (U.S.A., b. December 8, 1985) is the youngest player in NBA history to record 3,000 career rebounds. He reached the mark while playing for the Orlando Magic (U.S.A.) on November 16, 2007.

★ MOST FORWARD FLIP SLAM DUNKS IN 30 SECONDS Using a trampoline, a team of five people (Willy Martinon, Lilian Martinon, Jimmy Gougaud, Mickael Richard, and Florian Januel, all France)—a.k.a. "The Crazy Dunkers"—completed 17 forward flips with a slam dunk into a net in 30 seconds on the set of *L'Ete De Tous Les Records*, La Tranche Sur Mer, France, on July 28, 2005.

WNBA

★ **Biggest comeback** The greatest comeback in Women's National Basketball Association (WNBA) playoff history is 22 points by the Indiana Fever (U.S.A.). They overcame a 39–17 second-quarter deficit to defeat the Connecticut Sun (U.S.A.) 93–88 in overtime in an Eastern Conference playoff game on August 27, 2007.

Most...

• ☆ **Games played (career).** Vickie Johnson (U.S.A.) has played in 346 games during her career with the New York Liberty (U.S.A.) between 1997 and 2005 and the San Antonio Silver Stars (U.S.A.) in 2006 and 2007.

• ☆ **Minutes played (career).** Johnson has also played a record 10,805 minutes in her WNBA career.

• ★ **Minutes played per game (career).** Katie Smith (U.S.A.) averaged 34.9

★ **FIRST COACH TO WIN TITLES IN NBA AND WNBA** Paul Westhead (U.S.A.) is the first and, to date, only coach to win championships in both the NBA and WNBA. Westhead guided the Los Angeles Lakers to the NBA title in 1980 and the Phoenix Mercury (U.S.A.) to the WNBA title in 2007.

minutes per game over the course of her career for the Minnesota Lynx (U.S.A.) from 1995 to 2005 and the Detroit Shock (U.S.A.) from 2005 to 2007.

•**Points scored (career).** Lisa Leslie (U.S.A.) scored 5,412 points for the Los Angeles Sparks (U.S.A.), 1997 to 2006.

•**Field goals scored (career).** During her career with the Los Angeles Sparks, Leslie scored 2,000 field goals.

•☆ **Three-point field goals.** Katie Smith scored 598 three-point field goals playing for the Minnesota Lynx from 1995 to 2005 and the Detroit Shock from 2005 to 2007.

•☆ **Rebounds.** Lisa Leslie recorded 2,863 rebounds while playing for the Los Angeles Sparks.

•☆ **Assists.** Ticha Penicheiro (Portugal) provided 1,851 assists in 306 games for the Sacramento Monarchs (U.S.A.) between 1998 and 2007.

•☆ **Steals (career).** The greatest number of steals in a WNBA career is 589 in 262 games by Sheryl Swoopes (U.S.A.) playing for the Houston Comets (U.S.A.) between 1998 and 2007.

•☆ **Blocks (career).** Margo Dydek (Poland) achieved 877 blocks in 321 games playing for the Utah Starzz (1998–2002), the San Antonio Silver Stars (2003–04), and the Connecticut Sun (2005–07).

NBA ALL-STAR JAM SESSION

★**Highest forward flip trampoline slam dunk** High Impact Squad member Jerry Burrell (U.S.A.) achieved the highest forward flip trampoline slam dunk when he reached 10 ft. 9 in. (3.22 m) at the NBA All-Star Jam Session, New Orleans, Louisiana, U.S.A., on February 17, 2008.

★**Longest time spinning a basketball on one finger (using one hand)** Joseph Odhiambo (U.S.A.) spun a basketball on one finger using one hand for 37.46 seconds at the NBA All-Star Jam Session, New Orleans, Louisiana, U.S.A., on February 13, 2008.

★**Longest time spinning a basketball on one toe** Jack Ryan (U.S.A.) spun a basketball on his toe for 9.53 seconds at the NBA All-Star Jam Session, New Orleans, Louisiana, U.S.A., on February 13, 2008.

★**Longest time spinning a basketball on the nose** Jack Ryan (U.S.A.) spun a basketball on his nose for 4 seconds at the NBA All-Star Jam Session, New Orleans, Louisiana, U.S.A., on February 13, 2008.

★**Most backward free throws made in one minute** Two people have made three backward free throws in one minute: Melvin Banks, wearing the NBA mascot costume Harry the Hawk, and Nicole Joseph Dumas, an NBA Jam Session spectator (both U.S.A.). Both achieved the feat at the NBA All-Star Jam Session, New Orleans, Louisiana, U.S.A., on February 17, 2008.

★**MOST BOUNCES OF A BASKETBALL IN ONE MINUTE** Jordan Farmar (U.S.A.) of the Los Angeles Lakers (U.S.A.) dribbled his way to a record by bouncing a basketball 228 times in one minute at the NBA All-Star Jam Session, New Orleans, Louisiana, U.S.A., on February 16, 2008.

★ **Most underhanded half-court shots made in one minute** Jason Kidd (U.S.A.) of the Dallas Mavericks (U.S.A.) made two underhanded half-court shots in one minute at the NBA All-Star Jam Session, New Orleans, Louisiana, U.S.A., on February 16, 2008.

★ **Most underhanded free throws made in one minute** NBA Hall of Famer Rick Barry (U.S.A.) made 24 underhanded free throws in one minute at the NBA All-Star Jam Session, New Orleans, Louisiana, U.S.A., on February 13, 2008.

☆ **Most free throws made in one minute (female)** Becky Hammon (U.S.A.) of the San Antonio Silver Stars (U.S.A.) made 38 free throws in one minute at the NBA All-Star Jam Session, New Orleans, Louisiana, U.S.A., on February 16, 2008.

★ **Most three-pointers made in two minutes** Jason Kapono (U.S.A.) of the Toronto Raptors (Canada) scored 43 three-pointers in two minutes at the NBA All-Star Jam Session, New Orleans, Louisiana, U.S.A., on February 17, 2008.

★ **Most blindfolded free throws made in one minute** Jack Ryan (U.S.A.) made five blindfolded free throws in one minute at the NBA All-Star Jam Session, New Orleans, Louisiana, U.S.A., on February 17, 2008.

★ **MOST HALF-COURT SHOTS MADE IN ONE MINUTE** Chris Paul (U.S.A.) of the New Orleans Hornets (U.S.A.) made four half-court shots in one minute at the NBA All-Star Jam Session in New Orleans, Louisiana, U.S.A. on February 16, 2008.

★ **MOST FREE THROWS IN ONE MINUTE FROM A WHEELCHAIR** National Wheelchair Basketball Association (NWBA) players Trooper Johnson of the Golden State Warriors and Jeff Griffin of the Utah Wheelin' Jazz (both U.S.A.) each made 25 free throws in one minute at the NBA All-Star Jam Session on February 14, 2008.

★ **MOST SLAM DUNK BOUNCE PASSES IN 30 SECONDS** The Milwaukee Bucks Rim Rockers' (U.S.A.) Kevin Vanderkolk, John Schwartz, Torie Gamez, Marcus Tyler, and Matt Marzo (all U.S.A.) completed 21 slam dunk bounce passes in 30 sec. at the NBA All-Star Jam Session, New Orleans, Louisiana, U.S.A., on February 14, 2008. Each player bounces off the trampoline and passes the ball back to the next person, who repeats the move, ending the cycle with a slam dunk.

☆ **FARTHEST FORWARD FLIP TRAMPOLINE SLAM DUNK** Milwaukee Bucks Rim Rockers member Kevin Vanderkolk (U.S.A.) made a forward flip trampoline slam dunk over a distance of 19 ft. 2 in. (5.84 m) at the NBA All-Star Jam Session, New Orleans, Louisiana, U.S.A., on February 14, 2008.

NBA All-Star Jam Session provides fans with the once-in-a-lifetime experience of participating in the NBA All-Star excitement, where the chance to meet, and collect free autographs from, NBA players and legends is just the beginning. Jam Sessions are nonstop basketball action, as fans can shoot, slam, dribble, and drive all day, compete against their friends in skills challenges, or get tips from NBA players and legends. NBA All-Star Jam Sessions allow fans to gain access to the NBA like never before!

CRICKET

TEST MATCHES

☆**Most wickets taken in Tests** Muttiah Muralitharan (Sri Lanka) is the leading Test match wicket taker, with 723 wickets (average 21.77 runs per wicket) in 118 matches from August 1992 to December 22, 2007.

☆**Most Test centuries** Sachin Tendulkar (India) has scored 39 Test match centuries between 1989 and January 2008.

Highest batting average in Tests Sir Donald Bradman (Australia) scored an average of 99.94 runs per innings playing for Australia in 52 Tests between 1928 and 1948. (Bradman scored a total of 6,996 runs in 80 Test innings.)

★**Most consecutive Test innings without scoring a duck** David Gower (UK) batted for 119 consecutive Test match innings without being dismissed for a duck (zero runs) between 1982 and 1990.

☆**Most catches by a wicket keeper in Tests** Mark Boucher (South Africa) has taken 394 catches in 109 Tests playing for South Africa as wicket keeper between 1997 and 2008.

★ **MOST SIXES IN A TEST MATCH CAREER** Australian wicket-keeper/batsman Adam Gilchrist hit 100 sixes in a Test cricket career encompassing 96 matches between 1999 and 2008, the most scored by an individual batsman.

"I was never told how to hold a bat."

Sir Donald Bradman, the world's greatest Test batsman

☆ **Most times to umpire in Tests** Steve Bucknor (Jamaica) has officiated at a total of 122 Test matches between 1989 and February 2008.

★ **Most man of the match awards in Tests** Jacques Kallis (South Africa) has won 20 man of the match awards in Test cricket between 1995 and 2008.

☆ **Most extras in a Test innings** India conceded 76 extras in Pakistan's 1st innings in Bangalore, India, from December 8 to 12, 2007. The figure consisted of 35 byes, 26 leg byes, and 15 no balls.

LIMITED OVERS

☆ **Lowest World Cup innings by a team** The lowest score (that is, the fewest runs) by a team in a World Cup match is 36 by Canada against Sri Lanka at Boland Park in Paarl, South Africa, on February 19, 2003.

☆ **Highest limited overs innings by a team** Surrey County Cricket Club (UK) scored 496–4 from 50 overs in their match against Gloucestershire County Cricket Club (UK) at the Brit Oval, London, UK, on April 29, 2007.

☆ **Fastest World Cup Century** Matthew Hayden (Australia) hit 101 runs from 68 balls during his team's World Cup 2007 match against South Africa at Warner Park, Basseterre, St. Kitts, on March 24, 2007.

★ **MOST CATCHES BY A FIELDER IN TWENTY20 INTERNATIONALS** The most catches taken in a Twenty20 International cricket career is 11 by Ross Taylor (New Zealand) for New Zealand in 12 matches between 2006 and 2008.

★ **MOST WICKETS IN TWENTY20 INTERNATIONALS** The most wickets taken in a Twenty20 International cricket career is 15 by three players: Nathan Bracken (Australia) for Australia in 12 matches between 2006 and 2008; Shahid Afridi (Pakistan) for Pakistan between 2005 and 2008; and Shaun Pollock (South Africa) for South Africa, also between 2005 and 2008.

HIT FOR SIX

INTERNATIONAL

Herschelle Gibbs (South Africa) became the **first person to score six sixes in one over in an international match** against the Netherlands in Basseterre, St. Kitts, on March 16, 2007.

YOUNGEST

Anthony McMahon (UK) became the **youngest player to hit six sixes in an over** playing for Chester-le-Street against Eppleton at Eppleton Cricket Club, Durham, UK, on May 24, 2003, when aged 13 years and 261 days.

★ **MOST RUNS IN TWENTY20 INTERNATIONALS** Graeme Smith (South Africa) has scored more runs in a Twenty20 International cricket career than any other player. He has totaled 364 for South Africa in 12 matches between 2005 and 2008.

★ **MOST RUNS SCORED IN WORLD CUP MATCHES (FEMALE)** Debbie Hockley (New Zealand) scored 1,501 runs across 45 games between 1982 and 2000—the most runs scored by an individual in women's cricket World Cup matches.

DID YOU KNOW?

Deborah Hockley also holds the world record for the **most international appearances in women's cricket:** 126 (19 Tests and 107 one-day internationals) between 1979 and 2000.

☆ **MOST CRICKET WORLD CUP WINS (WOMEN)** The greatest number of women's cricket World Cup wins by a national team is five, by Australia: 1978, 1982, 1988, 1997, and 2005.

CYCLING

ROAD CYCLING

☆**Most Tour of Spain wins** Two riders have won the Tour of Spain on three occasions: Tony Rominger (Switzerland), who won from 1992 to 1994; and Roberto Heras Hernandez (Spain), who won in 2000, 2003, and 2004. Hernandez also won the race in 2005, but he tested positive for the banned substance erythropoietin (EPO) and his win was handed to Denis Menchov (Russia).

★**Most Tour of Spain stage wins** Delio Rodriguez (Spain) won 39 stages of the Tour of Spain in races between 1941 and 1947.

★**Longest time between victories in the Tour de France** Gino Bartali (Italy) won his first Tour de France in 1938, aged 24 years old, and his second in 1948. The gap of 10 years between wins is the longest time between victories in the history of the race, which began in 1903.

Fastest average speed in the Tour de France Lance Armstrong (U.S.A.) finished first in the 2005 Tour de France—his last ever Tour—with

★ **MOST TOUR OF ITALY STAGE WINS**
Between 1989 and 2003, Mario Cipollini (Italy) won 42 stages of the Giro d'Italia (Tour of Italy), the most stage wins by an individual rider.

an average speed of 25.882 mph (41.654 km/h). He finished the 2,241-mile-long (3,607-km) Tour in 86 hr. 15 min. 2 sec.

★ **Most Tour of Britain wins** Malcolm Elliot (UK) has won the Tour of Britain on three occasions: in 1987 (pro-am), 1988, and 1990.

FASTEST WOMEN'S 500 M UNPACED STANDING START Anna Meares (Australia) cycled 500 m from a standing start and without a pacemaker in 33.588 seconds at the Palma Arena, Palma de Mallorca, Spain, on March 31, 2007.

X-REF

The **oldest winner of the Tour de France** was Firmin Lambot (Belgium), aged 36 years 4 months in 1922. For more records by golden oldies, check out our **Oldest** ... pages in the Human Achievements section on pp. 132–136.

☆ **MOST CYCLO-CROSS WORLD TITLES (FEMALE)** Instituted in 2000, the women's cyclo-cross World Championships have been won on four occasions by Hanka Kupfernagel (Germany), in 2000, 2001, 2005, and 2008.

★ **FASTEST MEN'S 500 M UNPACED FLYING START** Chris Hoy (UK) set a record time of 24.758 seconds for the men's 500 m cycle, riding unpaced and from a flying start, in La Paz, Bolivia, on May 13, 2007.

☆ MOST MOUNTAIN-BIKE DOWNHILL WORLD TITLES (WOMEN) Anne-Caroline Chausson (France) has won 12 mountain-bike downhill world titles—three in the junior championship from 1993 to 1995, and nine in the senior class from 1996 to 2005.

MOUNTAIN-BIKING

★ **Most four-cross World Cups (male)** Brian Lopes (U.S.A.) has won three four-cross mountain-biking World Cups: in 2002, 2005, and 2007.

★ **Most team relay World Titles** Spain has won three team relay mountain-biking World Championships: in 1999, 2000, and 2005.

☆ **Most Cross-Country World Titles (female)** Gunn-Rita Dahle Flesjaa (Norway) has won the Cross-Country World Championships on four occasions: in 2002, and from 2004 to 2006.

☆ MOST MOUNTAIN-BIKE CROSS-COUNTRY WORLD CUPS (MALE) Two men have each won the cross-country World Cup title on three occasions: Thomas Frischknecht (Switzerland) in 1992, 1993, and 1995; and Julien Absalon (France, left) in 2003, 2006, and 2007.

BMX

☆**Most World Championships (female)** Two female riders have each won the Union Cycliste Internationale BMX World Championships on two occasions: Gabriela Diaz (Argentina) in 2001 and 2002; and Willy Kanis (Netherlands) in 2005 and 2006.

☆**Most World Championships (male)** Kyle Bennett (U.S.A.) has won the Union Cycliste Internationale BMX World Championships on three occasions: in 2002, 2003, and 2007.

Most competitors in the BMX World Championships The 2005 UCI BMX World Championships in Paris, France, drew 2,560 competitors from 39 countries between July 29 and 31 of that year.

☆**MOST TRIALS CYCLING WORLD TITLES (MALE)** Benito Ros Charral (Spain) has won the elite men's trials cycling World Championships in the 20-in. (50.8-cm) wheel category four times: from 2003 to 2005 and in 2007.

SOCCER

Most goals in Europe The ★**most goals scored in European club competitions** is 63 by Filippo Inzaghi (Italy), playing for AC Milan to December 4, 2007.

INTERNATIONAL WINNERS

☆ **Most wins of the Africa Cup of Nations** Egypt has won the Africa Cup of Nations six times—in 1957, 1959, 1986, 1998, 2006, and 2008.

☆ **Most Women's World Cup wins** The German national team won its second Fédération Internationale de Football Association (FIFA) Women's World Cup in Shanghai, China, in 2007, having also won in 2003. This feat equaled the record held by the U.S.A., which won the tournament in 1991 and 1999.

★ **Most wins of the CONCACAF championships (female)** The most wins of the women's CONCACAF (the Confederation of North, Central American, and Caribbean Association Football) Championship is six by the U.S.A. in 1991, 1993, 1994, 2000, 2002, and 2006.

☆ **Most wins of the CONCACAF Gold Cup (male)** Two teams have won the CONCACAF Gold Cup a record four times: Mexico in 1993, 1996, 1998, and 2003; and U.S.A. in 1991, 2002, 2005, and 2007.

TOP SCORERS

★ **Africa Cup of Nations** The greatest number of goals scored in Africa Cup of Nations tournaments is 16, by Samuel Eto'o (Cameroon) playing for Cameroon between 1996 and 2008.

★ **FASTEST GOAL BY A SUBSTITUTE IN THE ENGLISH PREMIER LEAGUE** Playing for Arsenal, Nicklas Bendtner (Denmark) scored six seconds after coming on as a substitute against Tottenham Hotspur in an English Premier League match at the Emirates Stadium, London, UK, on December 22, 2007.

★ **MOST CLEAN SHEETS BY A PREMIER LEAGUE GOALKEEPER** David James (UK) has kept 159 clean sheets (conceding no goals in a game) playing for Liverpool, Aston Villa, West Ham, Manchester City, and Portsmouth (all UK) between 1992 and April 20, 2008—more than any keeper in the English Premier League.

★**Copa America** The highest goal tally in Copa America tournaments is 17, by two players: Zizinho (Brazil) between 1941 and 1953; and Norberto Mendez (Argentina) between 1945 and 1956.

★**FIFA Women's World Cup** Brigit Prinz (Germany) has scored 14 goals during the course of Fédération Internationale de Football Association (FIFA) Women's World Cup matches. This total includes her goal in the FIFA Women's World Cup final at the Hongkou Stadium in Shanghai, China, on September 30, 2007.

★**Major League Soccer** The Major League Soccer (MLS) record for most career goals is 115 by Jaime Moreno (Bolivia), up to May 2008.

MISC.

Highest transfer fee Zinedine Zidane (France) moved from Juventus to Real Madrid for a reported 13,033,000,000 Spanish pesetas ($66.36 million) on July 9, 2001.

Most capped player Kristine Lilly (U.S.A.) has played 340 international matches for the U.S. women's national team.

★**HIGHEST PAID MANAGER** English national team manager Fabio Capello (Italy) signed a four-and-a-half-year deal with the English Football Association reportedly worth £6 million ($12 million) a year. Capello began the role on January 7, 2008.

★ **MOST EXPENSIVE PLAYER (CAREER)** The highest combined transfer fees for a player is $169 million for Nicolas Anelka (France). Anelka has played for Paris St. Germain (France) twice, Arsenal (UK), Real Madrid (Spain), Liverpool, Manchester City (both UK), Fenerbahçe (Turkey), Bolton Wanderers, and Chelsea (both UK) between 1997 and 2008.

UEFA CHAMPIONS LEAGUE MOST . . .

☆ **Victories** The **most UEFA Champions League matches won by a team** is 73 by Real Madrid (Spain) between 1992 and December 11, 2007, scoring a record 263 goals.

★ **Clean sheets** The **most consecutive clean sheets by a team in Champions League matches** is 10, by Arsenal (UK) in 2006.

☆ **Games managed** Sir Alex Ferguson (UK) has **managed the most Champions League games.** He took charge of his 140th game as manager of Manchester United in the 2008 final in Moscow on May 21.

☆ **LARGEST SOCCER TOURNAMENT** The Copa Telmex, held in Mexico between February and October 2007, was contested by 8,600 teams totaling 148,714 players. The tournament was organized with the aim of improving the quality of life of Mexican youth.

★ **MOST TEAMS SCORED FOR IN THE UEFA CHAMPIONS LEAGUE**
Hernan Crespo (Argentina, pictured above left) scored goals in UEFA
Champions League matches for a record five different teams between
1997 and 2008. They were: Parma, Lazio, Inter Milan (all Italy), Chelsea
(UK), and AC Milan (Italy).

☆ **MOST CHAMPIONS LEAGUE APPEARANCES** Raúl González Blanco
(Spain) has made 118 Champions League appearances, from his
competition debut in 1994 to March 5, 2008, playing for Real Madrid.
Raúl also holds the record for the ☆ **most goals in Union of
European Football Associations (UEFA) Champions League
matches**, with 61.

Longest time to control a football Martinho Eduardo Orige (Brazil) juggled a regulation soccer ball for a period of 19 hr. 30 min. non-stop with feet, legs, and head without the ball ever touching the ground at Padre Ezio Julli Gym in Araranguá, Brazil, on August 2–3, 2003.

Most goals scored from corners (direct) The greatest number of goals scored directly from corner kicks in one match by an individual is three by Steve Cromey (UK) for Ashgreen United against Dunlop FC on February 24, 2002, at Bedworth, Warwickshire, UK, and by Daniel White (UK) for Street and Glastonbury under-11s against Westfield Boys on April 7, 2002.

Largest soccer complex (fields) The National Sports Center in Blaine, Minnesota, U.S.A., has 57 fields.

Longest FA Cup tie The FA Cup tie between Alvechurch and Oxford City (both UK) in the fourth qualifying round in November 1971 lasted for six games and 11 hours. The match results sequence was 2–2, 1–1, 1–1, 0–0, 0–0, with Alvechurch eventually winning 1–0.

Most territories visited on a football tour Lenton Griffins FC (UK) visited a total of 12 territories from July 3 to August 3, 2004: Wales, Belgium, Luxembourg, Germany, Austria, Liechtenstein, Italy, Switzerland, France, Andorra, Spain, and Morocco.

☆ **Longest five-a-side marathon** The Rossendale Mavericks and the Fearns Community Sports College (both UK) played five-a-side soccer for 24 hr. 30 min. at Fearns Community Sports College Hall in Waterfoot Rossendale, Lancashire, UK, on November 23–24, 2007.

Most penalty "bookings" in one match In the local cup match between Tongham Youth Club, Surrey, and Hawley, Hants (both UK), on November 3, 1969, the referee booked all 22 players, including one who went to hospital, and one of the linesmen. The match, which was won by Tongham 2–0, was described by one player as "a good, hard game."

It was reported on June 1, 1993, that in a league match between Sportivo Ameliano and General Caballero in Paraguay, referee William Weiler ejected 20 players. Trouble flared after two Sportivo players were sent off; a 10-minute fight ensued and Weiler then dismissed a further 18 players, including the rest of the Sportivo team. Not surprisingly, the match was abandoned.

SILKY SKILLS

☆ **Most people doing "keepie uppies" (single venue)** The greatest number of people to keep a soccer ball in the air at the same time is 627. The record, organized by the Stadt Wien, was set during the event Vienna Recordia in Vienna, Austria, on September 30, 2007.

> **"I knew I could do it. It was just a matter of not being too nervous."**
>
> *Chloe Hegland, record-breaking player*

☆**Most touches of a ball with the head in a minute** The most touches of a soccer ball in a minute, using only the head to keep the ball in the air, is 341 by Gao Chong (China) in Beijing, China, on November 3, 2007.

Longest throw-in Michael Lochner (U.S.A.) performed the longest throw-in of a soccer ball when projecting a ball a distance of 158 ft. 0.5 in. (48.17 m) at Bexley High School, Ohio, U.S.A., on June 4, 1998.

Longest time controlling a soccer ball with the head while seated The longest time to keep a ball in the air by using just the head while seated on the floor is 4 hr. 9 min. 26 sec., and was achieved by Tomas Lundman (Sweden) in Märsta, Stockholm, Sweden, on April 20, 2007.

MOST TOUCHES OF A BALL The ☆**most touches of a soccer ball in 30 seconds, while keeping the ball in the air, by a female is 163, by Chloe Hegland (Canada)** on the set of *Lo Show dei Record* in Madrid, Spain, on February 23, 2008. She also holds the record for the **most touches of a ball in one minute**, having recorded 339 touches without the ball hitting the ground on the set of *Zheng Da Zong Yi— Guinness World Records Special* in Beijing, China, on November 3, 2007.

★ **MOST "AROUND THE WORLD" BALL-CONTROL TRICKS IN ONE MINUTE** John Farnworth (UK) achieved 83 "Around the World" soccer ball tricks in one minute on the set of *Zheng Da Zong Yi—Guinness World Records Special* in Beijing, China, on November 2, 2007.

MOST SOCCER BALLS JUGGLED Victor Rubilar (Argentina) juggled five regulation soccer balls for 10 seconds at the Gallerian Shopping Center, Stockholm, Sweden, on November 4, 2006.

SKILLS FROM HEAD TO TOE

The **most soccer ball rolls across the forehead** is 50, and it was achieved by Victor Rubilar (Argentina) as part of the Guinness World Records Tour 2007, at the ICA Maxi, in Haninge, Sweden, on November 2, 2007.

The record for the **longest time controlling a soccer ball with the soles** is 6 min. 1 sec., and was achieved by Tomas Lundman (Sweden) at the Nordstan Shopping Mall in Gothenburg, Sweden, on November 24, 2007.

★ MOST "KEEPIE UPPIES" (MULTIPLE VENUES) The greatest number of people to keep a ball airborne without using their hands—simultaneously, at multiple locations—is 634 and was achieved by The Likeaballs and students from 21 UK schools in support of Sport Relief 2008 on March 4, 2008.

☆ LONGEST TIME CONTROLLING A SOCCER BALL LYING DOWN Tomas Lundman (Sweden) controlled a soccer ball without using his hands while lying down for 10 min. 4 sec. at the Nordstan Shopping Mall in Gothenburg, Sweden, on November 24, 2007.

GOLF

YOUNGEST . . .

Scorer of a hole-in-one Christian Carpenter (U.S.A.), aged 4 years 195 days, at the Mountain View Golf Club, Hickory, North Carolina, U.S.A., on December 18, 1999.

★Curtis Cup player Michelle Wie (U.S.A.), aged 14 years 244 days, at the Formby Golf Club, Merseyside, UK, on June 11, 2004.

EXTREME GOLF

☆**Fastest time to play a round of golf on six continents** Heinrich du Preez (South Africa) played an 18-hole round of golf on six of the seven continents (excluding Antarctica) in 119 hr. 48 min. between May 22 and 27, 2007.

Largest golf facility Mission Hills Golf Club, China, had 12 18-hole courses fully operational in December 2006.

Highest golf course The golf course situated at the highest altitude is the Yak golf course at 13,025 ft. (3,970 m) above sea level in Kupup, East Sikkim, India. It was measured on October 10, 2006.

Most holes played in a year Leo Fritz of Youngstown, Ohio, U.S.A., played 10,550 holes of golf in 1998, averaging 28.9 holes per day.

Fastest round of golf by an individual The fastest 18-hole round played (allowing the golf ball to come to rest before each new stroke) is 27 min. 9 sec. by James Carvill (UK) at Warrenpoint Golf Course (18 holes; 6,154 yd.; 5,628 m) in County Down, Ireland, on June 18, 1987.

☆**LARGEST UNDERWATER GOLF TOURNAMENT** Five players, all following regular golf rules, took part in a golf tournament in a 50-ft.-deep (15-m) water tank at Zuohai Aquarium in Fuzhou, Fujian Province, China, on May 28, 2007.

★ MOST 18-HOLE GOLF COURSES PLAYED IN ONE YEAR Glenn Turner (UK) played 381 different 18-hole golf courses in one year between April 1, 2006, and March 31, 2007. All of the courses he played were in the UK and Spain.

PRO GOLF

Largest margin of victory in a major Tiger Woods (U.S.A.) won the 2000 U.S. Open by 15 shots. He finished with a round of 67 to add to rounds of 65, 69, and 71 for a 12 under par total of 272, the biggest margin of victory in any of the four major golf tournaments (Masters, Open Championship, U.S. Open, and U.S. PGA).

LARGEST DRIVING RANGE The SKY72 Golf Club Dream Golf Range has 300 individual bays, making it the largest driving range in the world. The facility opened in Joong-Ku, Incheon, Korea, on September 9, 2005.

★ **LARGEST ONE-DAY GOLF TOURNAMENT** A record 614 golfers took part in the largest one-day golf tournament at the La Cala Resort in Mijas, Malaga, Spain, on July 22, 2007.

☆ **Most World Match Play Championships** Ernie Els (South Africa) has won more World Match Play Championships than any other golfer, triumphing in 1994–96, 2002–04, and 2007 to win seven titles.

The Masters Nick Price (Zimbabwe), in 1986, and Greg Norman (Australia), in 1996, both shot 63, the **lowest single-round score at the Masters,** at the Augusta National Golf Course, Georgia, U.S.A.

The **lowest aggregate score for the four rounds at the Masters** is 270 (70, 66, 65, 69) by Tiger Woods (U.S.A.) in 1997.

Most major tournament titles by a man Jack Nicklaus (U.S.A.) triumphed in 18 major tournaments between 1962 and 1986. Nicklaus won the Masters six times, the Open Championship three times, the U.S. Open four times, and the U.S. PGA championship five times.

Most women's British Open wins Karrie Webb (Australia), in 1995, 1997, and 2002, and Sherri Steinhauer (U.S.A.), in 1998, 1999, and 2006, have both won the British Open golf tournament on three occasions. The British Open only became an LPGA major in 2006.

HIGHEST EARNINGS . . .

☆ **Career—PGA European Tour** Colin Montgomerie (UK) won €22,912,717 ($34,455,227) on the PGA European Tour between 1986 and 2008.

☆ **Career—U.S. LPGA Tour** Annika Sorenstam (Sweden) amassed total winnings of $21,069,392 on the U.S. LPGA Tour between 1993 and 2008.

☆ **Season—PGA European Tour** Ernie Els (South Africa) won €4,061,905 ($6,011,002) on the PGA European Tour in 2004.

☆HIGHEST-EARNING GOLFER Tiger Woods (U.S.A.) amassed a total of $78,865,376 in prize money on the U.S. PGA Tour between 1996 and 2008, the ☆highest career earnings of any golfer.

In the year to June 2007, Woods earned an estimated $100 million, according to *Forbes,* the ☆highest earnings, including endorsements, by a golfer in one year.

☆**Season—Ladies European Tour** Laura Davies (UK) won €471,727 ($698,084) on the Ladies European Tour in 2006.

☆HIGHEST SEASON'S EARNINGS (U.S. PGA) Vijay Singh (Fiji) won $10,905,166 in prize money on the U.S. PGA tour in 2004.

ICE HOCKEY

Fastest goals scored in ice hockey Per Olsen (Denmark) scored two seconds after the start of the game for Rungsted vs. Odense in the Danish First Division on January 14, 1990.

Jorgen Palmgren Erichsen (Norway) scored three goals in 10 seconds for Frisk vs. Holmen in a Norway junior league match on March 17, 1991.

Fastest NHL hat trick Bill Mosienko (Canada) scored a hat trick in 21 seconds playing for the Chicago Blackhawks against the New York Rangers (both U.S.A.) on March 23, 1952.

★**Best start in an NHL season** The best start by a team in National Hockey League (NHL) history is 26 points in the first 14 games of the 2007–08 season by the Ottawa Senators (Canada). The Senators started the season with a 13–1 win–loss record.

★**Largest attendance at an NHL match** The largest crowd to attend an NHL game is 71,217 people for a game between the Pittsburgh Penguins and Buffalo Sabres (both U.S.A.) at Ralph Wilson Stadium in Orchard Park, New York, U.S.A., on January 1, 2008.

★**OLDEST NHL PLAYER** Gordie Howe (Canada, b. March 31, 1928) was the oldest player in NHL history when he retired in 1980, aged 52 years. In 1997, Howe was signed to a one-game contract by the Detroit Vipers (U.S.A.) of the International Hockey League, aged nearly 70.

> *"All hockey players are bilingual. They know English and profanity."*
>
> *Gordie Howe, NHL legend*

☆ **Longest suspension for an infraction during a game** The National Hockey League record for longest suspension is 30 games, given to Chris Simon (Canada) of the New York Islanders (U.S.A.) as punishment for stepping on the leg of Pittsburgh's Jarkko Ruutu (Finland) with his skate on December 15, 2007.

★ **Highest save percentage in Stanley Cup finals** Terry Sawchuk (Canada), playing for the Detroit Red Wings (U.S.A.) in 1952, achieved the best save percentage in a Stanley Cup final series. Sawchuk recorded a percentage of .981, saving 104 of the 106 shots he faced.

★ **Oldest person to lead an NHL season in goals scored** Bill Cook (Canada, b. October 9, 1896) was 37 years old when he was the league's top goal scorer, while playing for the New York Rangers in the 1932–33 season. Cook tallied 50 points with 28 goals and 22 assists.

★ **MOST CAREER POINTS—U.S. ICE HOCKEY (FEMALE)** Cammi Granato (U.S.A.) is the leading career scorer among U.S.A. Women's team members with 343 points (186 goals, 157 assists) through January 2006. Granato captained the Americans to the first Olympic women's hockey gold medal in 1998 and to silver in 2002.

★ **FIRST PERSON TO SCORE ON A PENALTY SHOT IN STANLEY CUP FINALS** Chris Pronger (Canada) of the Edmonton Oilers (Canada) was the first player to score on a penalty shot in the Stanley Cup finals, beating goaltender Cam Ward (Canada) of the Carolina Hurricanes (U.S.A.) in Game 1 of the Stanley Cup finals on June 6, 2006. It was the ninth penalty shot attempt in Stanley Cup finals history.

★ **MOST SEASONS IN THE STANLEY CUP PLAYOFFS BY A PLAYER** Chris Chelios (U.S.A.), playing for the Montreal Canadiens (Canada), Chicago Blackhawks, and Detroit Red Wings, has played in the Stanley Cup playoffs on 22 occasions since 1984, missing only two seasons as an NHL player.

★ FIRST NHL REGULAR SEASON GAME PLAYED IN EUROPE The first National Hockey League (NHL) regular season games played in Europe were contested between the Los Angeles Kings and the Anaheim Ducks (both U.S.A.) at the 02 Arena in London, UK, on September 29 and 30, 2007. The Kings won the first game 4–1, and the Ducks won the second by the same score. The NHL has opened its season outside North America three other times: in Japan in 1997, 1998, and 2000, but this was the first league game played in Europe.

Most points scored by an individual in a pro ice hockey game

Two Canadians share the record for the most points scored in a game, with 10 points each: Jim Harrison (three goals, seven assists) for Alberta, later Edmonton Oilers (Canada), in a World Hockey Association game in Edmonton, Canada, on January 30, 1973; and Darryl Sittler (six goals, four assists) for the Toronto Maple Leafs (Canada) vs. Boston Bruins (U.S.A.) in an NHL game in Toronto, Canada, on February 7, 1976.

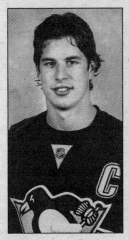

SIDNEY CROSBY Ice hockey sensation Sidney Crosby (Canada, b. August 7, 1987) has been breaking records with ease since his first professional NHL game for the Pittsburgh Penguins (U.S.A.) on October 5, 2005. Aged 18 years 253 days, Crosby scored his 100th point of the season in a game against the New York Islanders in Pittsburgh on April 17, 2006, becoming the ☆ **youngest player in NHL history to produce 100 points in a season.** Crosby finished the 2005/06 season with 102 points.

At 19 years 245 days old, Crosby became the ★ **youngest player in NHL history to win a league scoring title** when the final game of the 2006/07 season was played on April 9, 2007. And just 52 days later, aged 19 years 297 days, Crosby became the ★ **youngest player in NHL history to be named team captain.**

★ **Most playoff games consecutively started by a goaltender** The New Jersey Devils (U.S.A.) goaltender Martin Brodeur (Canada) started in a record 137 straight playoff games through the 2007 Stanley Cup playoffs.

☆ **Largest ice hockey tournament by players** With 510 teams taking part from eight countries—and a total of 8,145 players—the largest ice hockey tournament ever was the Bell Capital Cup held in Ottawa, Ontario, Canada, from December 28, 2006, to January 1, 2007. Over 1,000 games were played during this festival of ice hockey.

★ **Most matches played in an NHL career** Gordie Howe (Canada) played 1,767 games for the Detroit Red Wings and Hartford Whalers (U.S.A.) between 1946 and 1980, an all-time NHL record. *See photo on pg. 370 for more on the record-breaking Gordie Howe.*

MARTIAL ARTS

Heaviest living athlete Sumo wrestler Emmanuel "Manny" Yarborough, of Rahway, New Jersey, U.S.A., stands 6 ft. 8 in. (2.03 m) tall and weighs a colossal 704 lb. (319.3 kg). He was introduced to Sumo by his judo coach and went on to become ranked No. 1 in the Open Sumo Wrestling category for amateurs.

★ **MOST WINS OF THE UFC LIGHT HEAVYWEIGHT CHAMPIONSHIPS** Tito Ortiz (U.S.A., left) won six Ultimate Fighting Championship (UFC) light heavyweight championship bouts between 2000 and 2002.

☆**MOST UFC HEAVYWEIGHT CHAMPIONSHIPS** Randy Couture (U.S.A., above) won six UFC heavyweight championship bouts between 1997 and 2007—the most by an individual fighter.

☆**Heaviest UFC fighter** The record for the heaviest Ultimate Fighting Championship contestant is shared by five fighters: Sean Gannon, Gan McGee, Tim Sylvia, Scott Junk, and Brock Lesnar (all U.S.A.), all weighing in at 265 lb. (120 kg).

The ☆**lightest Ultimate Fighting Championship contestants** are Thiago Alves (Brazil), Jeff Curran, and Jens Pulver (both U.S.A.), all of whom weigh in at 145 lb. (63.5 kg).

★**Most sumo matches won in a career** *Yokozuna* Mitsugu Akimoto (Japan), alias Chiyonofuji Mitsugu, holds the record for the most wins throughout his professional career, with 1,045 between September 1970 and May 1991. He has also won the most *Makunouchi* (top division) matches, with 807 victories.

DID YOU KNOW?

In 2001, the World Wildlife Fund sued the World Wrestling Federation over the use of the initials WWF. The trial led to the wrestling organization rebranding itself to WWE (World Wrestling Entertainment) in 2002.

☆ **MOST PEOPLE IN A WWE ROYAL RUMBLE COMPETITION** On two occasions, 30 wrestlers have been entered into a World Wrestling Entertainment Royal Rumble competition. The first occasion was on January 28, 2007, in San Antonio, Texas, U.S.A., in a contest won by The Undertaker (U.S.A.). The second time, on January 27, 2008, in New York City, U.S.A., the contest was won by John Cena (U.S.A.).

WWE championship Bruno Sammartino (Italy) was World Wrestling Entertainment (WWE) champion for 2,803 days from May 17, 1963, to January 18, 1971, the ★ **longest WWE Championship reign.**

André the Giant (France) was the WWE Champion with the ★ **shortest WWE Championship reign**—just 45 seconds on February 5, 1988. He defeated Hulk Hogan in controversial circumstances, but immediately sold the title to fellow wrestler Ted Dibiase. World Wrestling Federation (WWF) president Jack Tunney promptly nullified the transaction and the title was vacated.

Most martial arts kicks in one minute (using both legs) In 1989, on the set of *Record Breakers* in London, UK, 14-year-old Scott Reave (UK) completed 218 kicks successfully in one minute. He alternated legs during the attempt, starting and finishing on his right side.

TEAM KATA WORLD CHAMPIONSHIPS The ★ **most women's Team Kata Karate World Championships won by a national team is seven,** by Japan, between 1988 and 2004.

The ☆ **most men's Team Kata Karate World Championships won by a national team is eight,** again by Japan, between 1986 and 2002.

☆ **MOST WORLD JUDO TITLES (WOMEN)** Japanese martial artist Ryoko Tani (born Tamura) won seven women's World Judo Championship titles in the 48 kg category between 1993 and 2007.

Most martial arts throws in one hour Dale Moore and Nigel Townsend (both UK) completed 3,786 judo throws in one hour at Esporta Health Club, Chiswick Park, London, UK, on February 23, 2002.

☆ **WORLD JUDO CHAMPIONSHIPS** Four *judoka* have won four World Judo Championship titles: Naoya Ogawa (Japan), between 1987 and 1991; Shozo Fujii (Japan), between 1971 and 1979; Yasuhiro Yamashita (Japan), between 1979 and 1983; and David Douillet (France, above), between 1993 and 1997.

★Fastest 1,000 martial arts sword cuts Isao Machii (Japan) completed a total of 1,000 cuts through rolled straw mats with a sword in 36 min. 4 sec. on September 19, 2007. The record-breaking feat took place on the set of *The Best House 123* in Tokyo, Japan.

Highest martial arts kick Jessie Frankson (U.S.A.) performed a 9-ft. 8-in.-high (2.94 m) kick on the set of *Guinness World Records Primetime,* Los Angeles, U.S.A., on December 21, 2000.

RUGBY

RUGBY UNION

★Most appearances in the Five Nations Championship by a player Mike Gibson (Ireland) played 56 times for Ireland in the Five Nations Championship between 1964 and 1979. (The Five Nations became the Six Nations in 2000.)

☆Most appearances in English Premiership matches by a player Neal Hatley (UK) played 193 times in English Premiership matches between 1998 and 2007 for his team London Irish. The Premiership (currently known as the Guinness Premiership) is the top division of the English rugby union system.

★Most international rugby union tests refereed Derek Bevan (UK) refereed 44 international rugby union matches in a career that lasted from 1985 to 2000.

★Most points in a Tri-Nations career Andrew Mehrtens (New Zealand) scored 328 points playing for the All Blacks (the New Zealand national team) in the Tri-Nations championship between 1995 and 2004.

★MOST NRL TITLES The Brisbane Broncos have won the National Rugby League (NRL) title three times, in 1998, 2000, and 2006. The NRL, which is Australia's premier rugby league competition, was instituted in 1998.

☆**MOST INTERNATIONAL APPEARANCES IN RUGBY UNION** George Gregan (Australia, b. Zambia) has made 139 appearances for the Australian national rugby union team between 1994 and 2007, more international appearances than any other player.

☆**Most IRB Sevens World Series titles** The International Rugby Board (IRB) Sevens World Series, which began in 1999, has been won seven times by New Zealand, in 1999–2000, 2000–01, 2001–02, 2002–03, 2003–04, 2004–05, and 2006–07. Fiji broke New Zealand's dominance to claim its first title in 2005–06.

RUGBY LEAGUE

☆**Most World Club Trophy wins** Two teams have won the World Club Challenge Trophy on three occasions: Wigan (UK) in 1987, 1991, and 1994; and Bradford Bulls (UK) in 2002, 2004, and 2006. The World Club Challenge Trophy is contested each year by the winners of the Super League (Europe) and National Rugby League (Australia).

DID YOU KNOW?

With two titles each, Australia (in 1991 and 1999) and South Africa (in 1995 and 2007) share the record for **most Rugby Union World Cup final victories.**

★ **MOST TRIES IN A SUPER RUGBY CAREER** Doug Howlett (New Zealand, above) scored a total of 58 tries in Super Rugby playing for the Auckland Blues between 1998 and 2007.

   Playing for the Canterbury Crusaders from 1996 to 2005, Andrew Mehrtens (New Zealand) scored 981 points—the most points scored by an individual player in a Super Rugby career.

★ **Most tries scored in a National Rugby League career** Ken Irvine (Australia) scored 212 tries between 1958 and 1973, playing for the North Sydney Bears and the Manly-Warringah Sea Eagles—the most tries scored by an individual player in the National Rugby League.

☆ **MOST RUGBY LEAGUE STATE OF ORIGIN SERIES WINS** Queensland has won Australia's rugby league State of Origin series on 16 occasions between 1980 and 2007.

★ **MOST TRIES IN A RUGBY WORLD CUP TOURNAMENT** In the history of the Rugby World Cup, two players have scored a record eight tries in the finals stage of the tournament. Jonah Lomu (New Zealand) achieved the feat in 1999 and Bryan Habana (South Africa, left) equalled Jonah's achievement during the 2007 competition.

☆ **Most points scored in a National Rugby League career** Andrew Johns (Australia) scored 2,176 points in the National Rugby League between 1993 and 2007, playing for the Newcastle Knights.

RUGBY RECORD MACHINE England fly-half Jonny Wilkinson (UK, above) has scored 1,099 points in 75 matches for England (1,032 points in 69 matches) and the British and Irish Lions (67 points in 6 matches) from April 4, 1998, to March 8, 2008—the ☆ **greatest number of points scored in a rugby union international career.**

Wilkinson has scored 249 points in 15 World Cup matches between 1999 and 2007, making him the ☆ **leading scorer in World Cup matches,** and he is the ★ **only person to score in two World Cup Final matches** (2003 and 2007).

His glittering career has also seen him score the ☆ **most points in a Five/Six Nations Championship career,** with 443 in matches between 1998 and 2008. And when he kicked a drop goal against France in the 2008 Six Nations Championship on February 23, 2008, he had kicked 29 drop goals in Test rugby—the ★ **most Test drop goals ever.**

☆ **MOST TRI-NATIONS TITLES** The Tri-Nations—an international rugby union competition inaugurated in 1996 and played annually between Australia, New Zealand, and South Africa—has been won a record eight times by New Zealand, in 1996–97, 1999, 2002–03, and 2005–07.

Fastest try Lee Jackson (UK) scored after nine seconds for Hull against Sheffield Eagles in a Yorkshire Cup semifinal at Don Valley Stadium, Sheffield, UK, on October 6, 1992.

TENNIS & RACKET SPORTS

TENNIS

★**Oldest seeded Wimbledon players** The ★**oldest seeded Wimbledon male competitor** is Ricardo Gonzalez (U.S.A., b. May 9, 1928), who was 41 years 45 days old when he played at the championships in 1969. The ★**oldest seeded Wimbledon female competitor** is Billie Jean King (U.S.A., b. November 22, 1943), who was aged 39 years 210 days when she played at the championships in 1983.

FACT

The ★ **shortest tennis player to play at the Wimbledon Championships** is Gem Hoahing (UK), who was 4 ft. 9.5 in. (1.46 m) tall when she took part in the 1937 competition.

★TALLEST PLAYER AT WIMBLEDON Ivo Karlovic (Croatia) measured 6 ft. 10 in. (2.08 m) at the 2003 Wimbledon Championships.

☆HIGHEST EARNINGS IN A TENNIS SEASON Tennis star Roger Federer (Switzerland, pictured) won an unprecedented $10,130,620 in prize money during the 2007 season.

★ **MOST WINS OF THE WHEELCHAIR TENNIS WORLD CHAMPIONSHIPS BY AN INDIVIDUAL (FEMALE)** Esther Vergeer (Netherlands) won the International Tennis Federation (ITF) Wheelchair Tennis World Championships eight times between 2000 and 2007.

TITANS OF TENNIS

Most Wimbledon men's singles titles: seven, by W. C. Renshaw (UK) in 1881–86 and 1889, and Peter Sampras (U.S.A.) in 1993–95 and 1997–2000.

Most Wimbledon ladies' singles titles: nine, by Martina Navratilova (U.S.A.) in 1978–79, 1982–87, and 1990.

Grand Slam pioneers: The **first man to achieve the tennis grand slam** (winning all four of the world's major tennis singles championships—Wimbledon, the U.S. Open, the Australian Open, and the French Open) was Fred Perry (UK), after he won the French title in 1935.

Maureen Connolly (U.S.A.) was the **first woman to achieve the tennis grand slam,** in 1953. She went on to win six successive grand slam tournaments.

★LONGEST GRAND SLAM DOUBLES MATCH The Wimbledon quarterfinal match between Daniel Nestor (Canada) and Mark Knowles (Bahamas) and Simon Aspelin (Sweden) and Todd Perry (Australia), on July 4–5, 2006, lasted 6 hr. 9 min. Knowles and Nestor won 5–7, 6–3, 6–7, 6–3, 23–21.

★LATEST FINISH TO A GRAND SLAM SINGLES MATCH An Australian Open match between Lleyton Hewitt (Australia, pictured above) and Marcos Baghdatis (Cyprus), played in Melbourne, Australia, on January 19–20, 2008, finished at 4:33 a.m. Hewitt finally won 4–6, 7–5, 7–5, 6–7, (4–7), 6–3.

TABLE TENNIS

☆Most world championship wins by a team (men) China has won the Swaythling Cup 16 times, in 1961, 1963, 1965, 1971, 1975, 1977, 1981, 1983, 1985, 1987, 1995, 1997, 2001, 2004, and 2006–07.

Most table tennis Olympic golds (women) Deng Yaping (China) won four Olympic golds: the women's singles in 1992 and 1996, and the women's doubles (both with Qiao Hang) in 1992 and 1996.

SQUASH

Most World Open titles Jansher Khan (Pakistan) won eight World Open titles: in 1987, 1989, and 1990; and from 1992 to 1996.

The **most women's World Open titles** is five, by Sarah Fitzgerald (Australia) in 1996–98 and 2001–02.

★**Most mixed doubles world championships** Rachael Grinham (Australia) has won two Mixed Doubles World Squash Championships, playing with David Palmer (Australia) in 2004 and Joe Kneipp (Australia) in 2006. The Mixed Doubles World Squash Championships have been held on three occasions, in 1997, 2004, and 2006.

★**Most Pro Squash Association Super Series titles** Peter Nicol (UK) won three Professional Squash Association Super Series titles consecutively, in 1999–2001.

BADMINTON

☆**Most wins of the Sudirman Cup** China has won the mixed World Team Badminton Championships for the Sudirman Cup (instituted in 1989) on six occasions, in 1995, 1997, 1999, 2001, 2005, and 2007.

The ★**most consecutive wins of the Sudirman Cup,** for the mixed World Team Badminton Championships, is four, again by China, from 1995 to 2001.

☆**Most wins of the Uber Cup (women)** China has won the women's World Team Badminton Championships for the Uber Cup (instituted 1956) 10 times, in 1984, 1986, 1988, 1990, 1992, 1998, 2000, 2002, 2004, and 2006.

MOST WINS OF THE THOMAS CUP Indonesia has won the men's World Team Badminton Championships for the Thomas Cup (instituted 1948) 13 times, in 1958, 1961, 1964, 1970, 1973, 1976, 1979, 1984, 1994, 1996, 1998, 2000, and 2002.

WATERSPORTS

DIVING

★**Deepest scuba dive** On June 10, 2005, Nuno Gomes (South Africa) dived to a depth of 1,044 ft. (318.25 m) in the Red Sea off Dahab, Egypt.

Diving world championships Greg Louganis (U.S.A.) won five world titles—in highboard (1978), and in both highboard and springboard (1982 and 1986)—the **most diving world championship wins.** Orlando Duque (Colombia) has won the World High Diving Federation World Championships three times (2000, 2001, and 2002), the **most high diving world championship wins.**

★**MOST WINS OF THE FINA DIVING GRAND PRIX WOMEN'S SPRINGBOARD (3 M) TITLES** Guo Jingjing (China, above) has won three Fédération Internationale de Natation (FINA) Diving Grand Prix Springboard titles, in 1999–2000 and 2006.

★ **MOST WINS OF THE FINA DIVING GRAND PRIX MEN'S SPRINGBOARD TITLES** Dmitri Sautin (Russia, above) has won seven FINA Diving Grand Prix Springboard titles, in 1995–2001.

ROWING

☆ **Fastest 2,000 m by an eight (men)** On August 15, 2004, a U.S. team rowed 2,000 m in 5 min. 19.85 sec. at the World Championships in Athens, Greece.

☆ **Fastest 2,000 m, single sculls (female)** Rumyana Neykova (Bulgaria) rowed 2,000 m in a time of 7 min. 7.71 sec. in Seville, Spain, on September 21, 2002.

★ **Fastest double sculls, lightweight class (men)** Mads Rasmussen and Rasmus Quist (both Denmark) recorded a time of 6 min. 10.02 sec. in Amsterdam, the Netherlands, on June 23, 2007.

☆ **Most university boat race wins** The first boat race between Oxford and Cambridge universities (both UK), which Oxford won, was staged on June 10, 1829. In the 154 races to 2008, Cambridge had won 79 times, Oxford 74 times, and there was a dead heat on March 24, 1877.

SWIMMING

Most individual Olympic gold medals Krisztina Egerszegi (Hungary) has won five swimming gold medals, in 100 m backstroke (1992), 200 m backstroke (1988, 1992, and 1996) and 400 m medley (1992).

☆**FASTEST SWIM SHORT COURSE 800 M FREESTYLE (FEMALE)** Kate Ziegler (U.S.A.) swam the women's short course 800 m freestyle in 8 min. 9.68 sec. in Essen, Germany, on October 12, 2007.

Six swimmers share the record for the **most Olympic swimming gold medals won by a man,** with four each: Charles Meldrum Daniels (U.S.A.) in 100 m freestyle (1906 and 1908), 220 yd. freestyle (1904), and 440 yd. freestyle (1904); Roland Matthes (GDR) in 100 m and 200 m backstroke (1968 and 1972); Mark Spitz (U.S.A.) in 100 m and 200 m freestyle, 100 m and 200 m butterfly (1972); Tamás Daryni (Hungary) in 200 m and 400 m medley (1988 and 1992); Aleksandr Popov (Russia) in 50 m and 100 m freestyle (1992 and 1996); and Michael Phelps (U.S.A.) in 100 m and 200 m butterfly and 200 m and 400 m medley (2004).

Most Olympic medals Jenny Thompson (U.S.A.) won 12 Olympic medals in 1992–2004; eight golds, three silvers, and a bronze.

Most world records Ragnhild Hveger (Denmark) set 42 swimming world records from 1936 to 1942.

WATER POLO

Most international goals Debbie Handley scored 13 goals for Australia (16) v. Canada (10) at the World Championship in Guayaquil, Ecuador, in 1982.

Olympic water polo The record for the **most Olympic gold medals in water polo** is shared by five players, each of whom have won three golds: George Wilkinson (UK) in 1900, 1908, and 1912; Paulo "Paul" Radmilovic and Charles Sidney Smith (both UK) in 1908, 1912, and 1920; and Desz

MOST OLYMPIC WATER POLO TITLES (WOMEN) Since women's water polo was introduced at the 2000 Olympic Games, two countries have won the title: Australia in 2000 and Italy in 2004. Pictured left are Alexandra Araujo of Italy and Georgia Lara of Greece during the Olympic gold medal match in Athens, Greece, in 2004.

Gyarmati and Gyorgy Karpati (both Hungary), both of whom won gold medals in 1952, 1956, and 1964.

Hungary holds the record for the **most Olympic water polo titles (men),** with eight victories, in 1932, 1936, 1952, 1956, 1964, 1976, 2000, and 2004.

WATERSKIING

Fastest speed Christopher Michael Massey (Australia) waterskied at a speed of 143.08 mph (230.26 km/h) on the Hawkesbury River, Windsor, New South Wales, Australia, on March 6, 1983.

Dawna Patterson Brice (U.S.A.) waterskied at 111.11 mph (178.8 km/h) in Long Beach, California, U.S.A., on August 21, 1977, the **fastest speed by a female waterskier.**

★Fastest speed (barefoot) Scott Michael Pellaton (U.S.A.) reached 135.74 mph (218.44 km/h) over a course in Chandler, Arizona, California, U.S.A., in November 1989.

☆ **FARTHEST WATERSKI JUMP** Freddy Krueger (U.S.A., above) performed a waterski jump measuring 243 ft. 5 in. (74.2 m) in Seffner, Florida, U.S.A., on November 5, 2005.

Elena Milakova (Russia) set the record for the **farthest water-ski jump by a woman,** with a leap of 186 ft. (56.6 m) in Rio Linda, California, U.S.A., on July 21, 2002.

"I would have a tough time saying anyone has a better job than I have. I get a salary to go surf around the world!"

Kelly Slater, surfing's top earner

☆**HIGHEST SURFING CAREER EARNINGS** At the end of the 2007 season, Kelly Slater (U.S.A.) had earned $1,587,805 from professional surfing.

Layne Beachley (Australia, above) had earned a total of $605,035 by the end of the same season, the ☆**highest career earnings for a female surfer.**

★ SURFING ★

NAME/NATIONALITY	RECORD	NUMBER OF WINS
Nat Young (Australia)	★ Most wins of ASP* Tour Longboard World Championship	Four (1986, 1988–90)
Layne Beachley (Australia)	Most wins of ASP Tour World Championship (female)	Seven (1998–2003, 2006)
Kelly Slater (U.S.A.)	Most wins of Pro Surfing World Championships (male)	Eight (1992, 1994–98, 2005–06)
Michael Novakov (Australia)	Most World Amateur Surfing Championships	Three (1982, 1984, 1986)

*Association for Surfing Professionals

WHEEL SKILLS

SKATEBOARD

☆ **LONGEST 50-50 RAIL GRIND Rob Dyrdek (U.S.A.)** achieved a 100-ft. 5.75-in. (30.62-m) 50-50 skateboard rail grind on MTV's *The Rob & Big Show* in Los Angeles, California, U.S.A., on September 17, 2007. This also represents the ☆ **longest board slide.**

★ **Longest one-wheeled wheelie** Brent Kronmueller (U.S.A.) covered 134 ft. (40.84 m) while performing a one-wheeled wheelie on MTV's *The Rob & Big Show* in Los Angeles, California, U.S.A., on September 17, 2007.

☆ **Most 360 kickflips (one minute)** The greatest number of 360 degree kickflips performed in a minute is 23, by Kristos Andrews (U.S.A.) at the X Games in Los Angeles, California, U.S.A., on August 4, 2007.

★ **Most skateboard tricks invented** Widely regarded as the most influential skater of all time, Rodney Mullen (U.S.A.) invented a total of 30 skateboard tricks between 1997 and 2008.

UNICYCLE

☆ **Most skips (one minute)** Daiki Izumida (Japan), a.k.a. Shiojyari, jumped over a skipping rope on his unicycle 214 times in one minute at New Town Plaza in Hong Kong, China, on August 12, 2007.

★ **Most stairs climbed (30 seconds)** The most stairs climbed on a unicycle in 30 seconds is 56, achieved by Peter Rosendahl (Sweden) at the Millennium Monument in Beijing, China, on November 1, 2007.

LONGEST JUMP ON A UNICYCLE David Weichenberger (Austria) jumped 9 ft. 8 in. (2.95 m) on his unicycle during the Vienna Recordia event in Vienna, Austria, on September 16, 2006.

★ **Most stairs climbed** Benjamin Guiraud (France), a.k.a. Yoggi, climbed 670 stairs on a unicycle without his feet or any part of his body touching the ground, in 22 min. 32 sec. at the Eiffel Tower in Paris, France, on November 20, 2006.

MOTORCYCLE

★ **LONGEST NO-HANDS MOTORCYCLE WHEELIE** AC Farias (Netherlands) performed an 292-ft. (89 m) wheelie without using his hands in Amsterdam, the Netherlands, on October 22, 2004. Farias propels the bike on to its back wheel in the usual manner and, once it is balanced, he then lets go of the handlebars and continues to ride.

★ **Most donuts (one minute)** Axel Winterhoff (Germany) achieved 21 donuts in one minute in Cologne, Germany, on November 23, 2007. A donut is performed by locking the front wheel with the brake and accelerating the rear so that the bike spins around in a tight circle at high speed.

Longest wheelie Yasuyuki Kudo (Japan) covered 205 miles (331 km) nonstop on the rear wheel of his Honda TLM220R at the Japan Automobile Research Institute proving ground, Tsukuba, Japan, on May 5, 1991.

FACT

David Weichenberger (see top photo) was born in 1985 and has been unicycling since 1995. His competitive successes include 2006 Downhill World Champion, 2006 Street World Bronze Medalist, 2004 Long Jump World Champion, 2004 World Silver Medalist in Downhill, and Bronze in Trials.

LONGEST DISTANCE TWO-WHEEL DRIVING IN A CAR Sven-Eric Söderman (Sweden) covered 214.7 miles (345.6 km) on just two wheels of his car at Mora Siljan Airport, Dalarna, Sweden, on September 25, 1999. In an event lasting 10 hr. 38 min. he covered 108 laps of a circuit 1.9 miles (3.2 km) long.

★ **KARTING—GREATEST DISTANCE IN 24 HOURS (OUTDOOR)** Team Equipe Vitesse covered 1,277.97 miles (2,056.7 km) in 24 hours at Teesside Karting's track at the Redcar & Cleveland Offroad Centre, Middlesbrough, UK, on September 20–21, 2007.

★**FASTEST TIME TO CHANGE A WHEEL ON A SPINNING CAR** The record for the fastest time to change a wheel on a spinning car is 3 min. 47 sec., achieved by Terry Grant (UK) at Santa Pod Raceway, Wellingborough, Northamptonshire, UK, on October 3, 2007.

☆**Largest simultaneous burnout** The record for the largest motorcycle burnout is 213, set by the team Harleystunts and Smokey Mountain Harley-Davidson in Maryville, Tennessee, U.S.A., on August 26, 2006.

BICYCLE

☆**Most pinky squeaks (one minute)** Andreas Lindqvist (Sweden) achieved 57 pinky squeaks, in one minute on his BMX in Gothenburg, Sweden, on November 24, 2007.

★**Longest distance front-wheel wheelie (feet off pedals)** The longest distance for a front-wheel wheelie without the feet touching the bike's pedals is 506 ft. 10 in. (154.5 m), set by Andreas Lindqvist (Sweden) in Stockholm, Sweden, on November 2, 2007.

HOW HE DOES IT...

To raise the car as he drives, Terry Grant (see photo) deploys a jack that passes through the car floor and anchors it to the ground. The car spins around the jack, similar to a motorcycle performing a donut, when the car is raised. With the car in motion, Terry balances on the runningboard to get access to the wheel nuts. He also jumps off the car, leaving it spinning, to pick up tools. When the wheel is changed, Terry retracts the jack and drives off.

WORLD'S STRONGEST MAN

★ **Most reps of an overhead safe lift** In the overhead safe lift, competitors strive to lift two safes that have been clamped together, weighing 275 lb. (125 kg) in total. On the third day of the 2007 World's Strongest Man competition in Anaheim, California, U.S.A., Sebastian Wenta (Poland) achieved an incredible 19 repetitions (reps) in this event.

★ **Country with the most wins** The competition has traveled to many locations—Zambia, Iceland, Mauritius, Malaysia, Morocco, and China, to name a few—and entrants also represent a wide range of countries. But since the competition started, Iceland has provided the winner for a record eight times (1984, 1986, 1988, 1990, 1991, 1994, 1995, 1996). The last Icelandic winner, more than a decade ago, was four-times winner Magnús Ver Magnússon.

★ **Most finals reached** Magnus Samuelsson (Norway) reached the final round of a record 10 World's Strongest Man competitions in the 13 years between 1995 and 2007. He won the title once, in 1998.

★ **Oldest entrant** Odd Haugen (Norway, b. January 16, 1960) was 46 years and 241 days old at the championship in Sanya, China, in September 2006.

★ **Youngest entrant** Kevin Nee (U.S.A., b. August 21, 1985) was just 20 years 1 month and 6 days old at the start of the WSM event held in Chengdu, China, on September 27, 2005. Although he failed to qualify in his first two years of competing, in 2007 in Anaheim, California, U.S.A., he was placed a credible 6th in the final ranking.

★ **Shortest winner of the championship** Welsh weightlifter and bodybuilder Gary Taylor (UK) was named the World's Strongest Man in 1993. His height at the time was 5 ft. 11.5 in. (1.82 m). Taylor's career came to a premature end in 1997 when his legs were crushed during a tractor tire flipping event.

★ **MOST CONSECUTIVE WINS**
Two heavyweights have won the prestigious WSM title three years in a row: Bill Kazmaier (U.S.A.) won from 1980 to 1982 and Magnús Ver Magnússon (Iceland, pictured at the 1995 event) held the title from 1994 to 1996.

> *"The World's Strongest Man competition is pure jaw-dropping entertainment . . . Last man standing, no-way-I-can-do-that, primitive stuff."*
>
> **Jay Weiner, MinnPost**

★ **Tallest winner of the championship** Ted van der Parre (Netherlands) was 7 ft. (2.13 m) tall when he won the World's Strongest Man championship in 1992. He was also the **heaviest ever winner,** at 350 lb. (159 kg) and the only winner from the Netherlands. The Dutch champion had the lowest WSM body mass index (BMI) of 35. (BMI is a statistical measure of weight in relation to height, to give an approximate total body fat level.)

★ **Largest margin of victory** In the 1980 World's Strongest Man championship, Bill Kazmaier (U.S.A.) finished a record 23.5 points ahead of his nearest rival, Lars Hedlund (Sweden). Kazmaier won the WSM title three times, in 1980, 1981, and 1982. His final WSM appearance was in 1989.

★ **MOST WINS OF THE WORLD'S STRONGEST MAN TITLE** Three competitors share the record for the most overall wins of this championship. Mariusz Pudzianowski (Poland, pictured) won in 2002, 2003, 2005, and 2007. Sharing the record with him is Jón Páll Sigmarsson (Iceland, 1984, 1986, 1988, 1990) and Magnús Ver Magnússon (Iceland, 1991, 1994, 1995, 1996).

★ **SMALLEST MARGIN OF VICTORY** In the 1990 World's Strongest Man championship, only a half point separated the winner, Jón Páll Sigmarsson (Iceland), from the runner-up, O.D. Wilson (U.S.A.). Pictured is Sigmarsson in the truck-pulling event in 1984.

STRONG STUFF

The first World's Strongest Man (WSM) championships took place in 1977. It is an annual contest, and since 2001 the World's Strongest Woman has been held alongside the men's competition.

Among the events featured in these competitions of strength are the following:

• Farmer's Walk	• Tug of War
• Yoke Walk/Fridge Carry	• Duck Walk
• Husafell Stone	• Crucifix
• Truck Pulling	• Dead Lift
• Overhead Press	• Loading
• Log Throw/Caber Toss	• Car Carry
• Decapitation Punch	• Keg Toss
• Carry and Drag	• Pole Pushing
• Fingal's Fingers	• Squat Lift
• Hercules Hold	• Plane Pulling
• Power Stairs	• Atlas Stones

★**HEAVIEST OBJECT PULLED AT THE WSM COMPETITION** An aircraft weighing approximately 154,323 lb. (70 metric tons), plus 661 lb. (300 kg) of anchors and chains, is the heaviest single challenge facing competitors in the World's Strongest Man competition. Athletes have just 75 seconds to pull the plane 98 ft. 5 in. (30 m), the winner being either the fastest to complete the course or he who covers the greatest distance in 30 seconds. Pictured is 1997 and 1999 champion Jouko Ahola (Finland).

★**FASTEST TIME TO COMPLETE FINGAL'S FINGERS** On the last day of the 2007 World's Strongest Man event in Anaheim, California, U.S.A., Sebastian Wenta (Poland) became the first person to complete the Fingal's Fingers event in under 31 seconds, with a time of 30.92 seconds. Fingal's Fingers are an ever-lengthening series of five wooden poles weighing from 441 to 661 lb. (200 to 300 kg) hinged at ground level; the aim is to flip over each finger 180 degrees in as fast a time as possible. Sebastian Wenta is pictured above left.

X GAMES

SUMMER

Highest attendance for an action sports event The ESPN X Games 5, held in San Francisco, California, U.S.A., was attended by 268,390 visitors over its 10-day duration in 1999.

Most gold medals won The individual with the most ESPN X Games gold medals is Dave Mirra (U.S.A.) with 14 wins as of 2007.

First "900" on a skateboard Skateboard legend Tony Hawk (U.S.A.) became the first person to achieve a "900" in competition at the ESPN X Games 5 in San Francisco, California, U.S.A., on June 27, 1999. The "900" (named after the fact that the skater spins two and a half rotations, or 900°) is regarded as one of the most difficult tricks in vert skateboarding.

Longest BMX 360 ramp jump Mike Escamilla (U.S.A., a.k.a. "Rooftop") completed a 50-ft. 6 in. (15.39 m) BMX 360 degree ramp jump on the Mega Ramp at X Games 11 in Los Angeles, California, U.S.A., on August 3, 2005.

YOUNGEST GOLD MEDAL HOLDER Ryan Sheckler (U.S.A.), b. December 30, 1989) was 13 years 230 days old when he won the Skateboard Park gold medal at ESPN X Games 9 in Los Angeles, California, U.S.A., on August 17, 2003.

"They're so much faster and so much less under control."

Shaun White on why skateboards are tougher than snowboards.

MOST SKATEBOARD MEDALS WON Both Tony Hawk (U.S.A.) and Andy Macdonald (U.S.A., pictured) have earned 16 Summer X Games Skateboard medals.

MOST MEDALS WON BY AN INDIVIDUAL Dave Mirra (U.S.A.), who competes in BMX Freestyle, has won 21 medals in the ESPN X Games.

MOST WAKEBOARDING MEDALS WON Darin Shapiro (pictured), Dallas Friday, and Tara Hamilton (all U.S.A.) have each earned six X Games medals in the sport of wakeboarding.

☆**LONGEST SKATEBOARD RAMP JUMP** Professional skateboarder Danny Way (U.S.A.) achieved a 79-ft. (24 m) 360 degree air on his Mega Ramp at X Games 10 in Los Angeles, California, U.S.A., on August 8, 2004.

X-REF

Danny Way (pictured above) won his third X Games Big Air gold medal at the 2006 X Games. For more incredible skateboard records, including kickflips and rail grinds, as well as other exploits on four, two, and one wheels, take a look at **Wheel Skills** on pp. 392–395.

MOST AGGRESSIVE IN-LINE SKATE MEDALS Fabiola da Silva (Brazil) has won eight medals for Aggressive In-line Skating at the X Games, seven of which are gold.

FIRST MOTORCYCLE DOUBLE BACKFLIP Travis Pastrana (U.S.A.) completed the first successful double backflip on a motorcycle at X Games 12 in Los Angeles, California, U.S.A., on August 4, 2006.

Most Moto X medals won Travis Pastrana (U.S.A.) has won the most medals for Moto X at the X Games, with 11 as of ESPN X Games 12—held in Los Angeles, California, U.S.A., from August 3 to 6, 2006.

Pastrana won gold for Freestyle every year from 1999 to 2005; silver for Step Up in 2001; and for Best Trick he won bronze in 2004, silver in 2005, and gold in 2006.

WINTER

Most gold medals Shaun Palmer and Shaun White (both U.S.A.) have each won six gold medals at the Winter X Games. Palmer earned gold in Skier X Men's in 2000, Snowboarder X Men's from 1997 to 1999, Snow Mountain Biking in 1997, and UltraCross in 2001. White won his golds in Snowboard Superpipe Men's in 2003 and 2006 and Slopestyle Men's from 2003 to 2006.

Most skiing slopestyle medals Tanner Hall (U.S.A.) and Jon Olsson (Sweden) have each earned four medals for Skiing Slopestyle. Hall took gold from 2002 to 2004 and silver in 2005. Olsson took bronze from 2002 to 2005.

Most skiing superpipe men's medals The most medals won in ESPN Winter X Games competitions in the Skiing SuperPipe Men's discipline is four by Jon Olsson (Sweden), Tanner Hall, and Simon Dumont (both

MOST SNOWBOARDER X WOMEN'S MEDALS WON Lindsey Jacobellis (U.S.A.) has won four medals for Snowboarder X Women's at ESPN Winter X Games competitions. Jacobellis won gold from 2003 to 2005 and silver at ESPN Winter X Games 10 in Aspen/Snowmass, Colorado, U.S.A., in January 2007.

U.S.A.). Olsson took gold in 2002, silver in 2004, and bronze in 2003 and 2005; Hall won golds in 2006 and 2007 and silvers in 2003 and 2005; and Dumont earned two golds in 2004 and 2005, bronze in 2006, and silver in 2007.

Most snowboard slopestyle women's medals Two women have each won five medals for Snowboard Slopestyle Women's in ESPN Winter X Games competitions—Barrett Christy and Janna Meyen (both U.S.A.). Christy won gold in 1997, silver in 1998 and 1999, and bronze in 2000 and 2002; Meyen earned four golds from 2003 to 2006 and silver in 2002.

Most snowboard superpipe men's medals Danny Kass and Shaun White (both U.S.A.) have each won four medals in the Snowboard Super-Pipe Men's discipline of the ESPN Winter X Games. Kass won gold in 2001, silver in 2003 and 2004, and bronze in 2005; White won gold in 2003 and 2006 and silver in 2002 and 2007.

Most snowboarding medals won Barrett Christy and Shaun White (both U.S.A.) have each won 10 individual Winter X Games medals for snowboarding.

X GAMES OLDIE

The **oldest athlete to compete in the X Games** is Angelika Casteneda (U.S.A.), who was 53 years old when she competed in the X Venture Race in 1996. Angelika was part of a three-person team (also including John Howard and Keith Murray, both U.S.A.) that won the six-day event, making her the **oldest X Games gold medalist**.

MOST SNOCROSS MEDALS Blair Morgan (Canada) has won eight SnoCross medals: gold from 2001 to 2003, 2005, and 2006, silver in 1999 and 2000, and bronze in 2004. SnoCross has featured at the Winter X Games since 1998.

Christy won gold in 1997, silver in 1998 and 1999, and bronze in 2000 and 2002 for Slopestyle Women's; in Big Air, she won gold in 1997 and 1999, silver in 1998, and 2001, and she earned a silver for SuperPipe Women's in 2000.

In the Slopestyle Men's event, White won silver in 2002, golds from 2003 to 2006, and bronze in 2007. In the SuperPipe Men's, he won silver in 2002 and 2007 and gold in 2003 and 2006.

Most snowboard superpipe women's medals won Kelly Clark (U.S.A.) has earned four Snowboard SuperPipe Women's medals: gold in 2002 and 2006 as well as silver in 2003 and 2004.

SPORTS REFERENCE

★ TRACK & FIELD—OUTDOOR TRACK EVENTS ★

MEN	TIME/DISTANCE	NAME & NATIONALITY
100 m	9.72	Usain Bolt (Jamaica)
200 m	19.32	Michael Johnson (U.S.A.)
400 m	43.18	Michael Johnson (U.S.A.)
800 m	1:41.11	Wilson Kipketer (Denmark)
1,000 m	2:11.96	Noah Ngeny (Kenya)
1,500 m	3:26.00	Hicham El Guerrouj (Morocco)
1 mile	3:43.13	Hicham El Guerrouj (Morocco)
2,000 m	4:44.79	Hicham El Guerrouj (Morocco)
3,000 m	7:20.67	Daniel Komen (Kenya)
5,000 m	12:37.35	Kenenisa Bekele (Ethiopia)
10,000 m	26:17.53	Kenenisa Bekele (Ethiopia)
20,000 m	56:26.00	Haile Gebrselassie (Ethiopia)
1 hour	21,285 m	Haile Gebrselassie (Ethiopia)
25,000 m	1:13:55.80	Toshihiko Seko (Japan)
30,000 m	1:29:18.80	Toshihiko Seko (Japan)
3,000 m steeplechase	7:53.63	Saif Saaeed Shaheen (Qatar)
110 m hurdles	12.88	Xiang Liu (China)
400 m hurdles	46.78	Kevin Young (U.S.A.)
4 × 100 m relay	37.40	U.S.A. (Michael Marsh, Leroy Burrell, Dennis Mitchell, Carl Lewis)
	37.40	U.S.A. (John Drummond Jr., Andre Cason, Dennis Mitchell, Leroy Burrell)
4 × 200 m relay	1:18.68	Santa Monica Track Club, U.S.A. (Michael Marsh, Leroy Burrell, Floyd Heard, Carl Lewis)
4 × 400 m relay	2:54.20	U.S.A. (Jerome Young, Antonio Pettigrew, Tyree Washington, Michael Johnson)
4 × 800 m relay	7:02.43	Kenya (Joseph Mutua, William Yiampoy, Ismael Kombich, Wilfred Bungei)
4 × 1,500 m relay	14:38.80	West Germany (Thomas Wessinghage, Harald Hudak, Michael Lederer, Karl Fleschen)

WOMEN	TIME/DISTANCE	NAME & NATIONALITY
100 m	10.49	Florence Griffith-Joyner (U.S.A.)
200 m	21.34	Florence Griffith-Joyner (U.S.A.)
400 m	47.60	Marita Koch (GDR)
800 m	1:53.28	Jarmila Kratochvílová (Czechoslovakia)
1,000 m	2:28.98	Svetlana Masterkova (Russia)
1,500 m	3:50.46	Qu Yunxia (China)
1 mile	4:12.56	Svetlana Masterkova (Russia)
2,000 m	5:25.36	Sonia O'Sullivan (Ireland)
3,000 m	8:06.11	Wang Junxia (China)
5,000 m	14:16.63	Meseret Defar (Ethiopia)

PLACE	DATE
New York, U.S.A.	May 31, 2008
Atlanta, U.S.A.	Aug. 1, 1996
Seville, Spain	Aug. 26, 1999
Cologne, Germany	Aug. 24, 1997
Rieti, Italy	Sep. 5, 1999
Rome, Italy	Jul. 14, 1998
Rome, Italy	Jul. 7, 1999
Berlin, Germany	Sep. 7, 1999
Rieti, Italy	Sep. 1, 1996
Hengelo, Netherlands	May 31, 2004
Brussels, Belgium	Aug. 26, 2005
Ostrava, Czech Republic	Jun. 26, 2007
Ostrava, Czech Republic	Jun. 27, 2007
Christchurch, New Zealand	Mar. 22, 1981
Christchurch, New Zealand	Mar. 22, 1981
Brussels, Belgium	Sep. 3, 2004
Lausanne, Switzerland	Jul. 11, 2006
Barcelona, Spain	Aug. 6, 1992
Barcelona, Spain	Aug. 8, 1992
Stuttgart, Germany	Aug. 21, 1993
Walnut, U.S.A.	Apr. 17, 1994
Uniondale, U.S.A.	Jul. 22, 1998
Brussels, Belgium	Aug. 25, 2006
Cologne, Germany	Aug. 17, 1977

MEN'S 2,000 M Morocco's **Hicham El Guerrouj** wins the 2,000 m in Berlin, Germany, in 4 min. 44.79 sec. (see left).

PLACE	DATE
Indianapolis, U.S.A.	Jul. 16, 1988
Seoul, South Korea	Sep. 29, 1988
Canberra, Australia	Oct. 6, 1985
Munich, Germany	Jul. 26, 1983
Brussels, Belgium	Aug. 23, 1996
Beijing, China	Sep. 11, 1993
Zürich, Switzerland	Aug. 14, 1996
Edinburgh, UK	Jul. 8, 1994
Beijing, China	Sep. 13, 1993
Oslo, Norway	Jun. 15, 2007

☆ **WOMEN'S 5,000 M** On June 15, 2007, at the Golden League Bislett Games in Oslo, Norway, **Meseret Defar** (Ethiopia) ran the outdoor 5,000 m in 14 min. 16.63 sec.

WOMEN	TIME/DISTANCE	NAME & NATIONALITY
10,000 m	29:31.78	Wang Junxia (China)
20,000 m	1:05:26.60	Tegla Loroupe (Kenya)
1 hour	18,340 m	Tegla Loroupe (Kenya)
25,000 m	1:27:05.90	Tegla Loroupe (Kenya)
30,000 m	1:45:50.00	Tegla Loroupe (Kenya)
3,000 m steeplechase	9:01.59	Gulnara Samitova-Galkina (Russia)
100 m hurdles	12.21	Yordanka Donkova (Bulgaria)
400 m hurdles	52.34	Yuliya Pechonkina (Russia)
4 × 100 m relay	41.37	GDR (Silke Gladisch, Sabine Rieger, Ingrid Auerswald, Marlies Göhr)
4 × 200 m relay	1:27.46	United States "Blue" (LaTasha Jenkins, LaTasha Colander-Richardson, Nanceen Perry, Marion Jones)
4 × 400 m relay	3:15.17	USSR (Tatyana Ledovskaya, Olga Nazarova, Maria Pinigina, Olga Bryzgina)
4 × 800 m relay	7:50.17	USSR (Nadezhda Olizarenko, Lyubov Gurina, Lyudmila Borisova, Irina Podyalovskaya)

★ TRACK & FIELD—INDOOR TRACK EVENTS ★

MEN	TIME	NAME & NATIONALITY
50 m	5.56	Donovan Bailey (Canada)
	5.56	Maurice Greene (U.S.A.)
60 m	6.39	Maurice Greene (U.S.A.)
	6.39	Maurice Greene (U.S.A.)
200 m	19.92	Frankie Fredericks (Namibia)
400 m	44.57	Kerron Clement (U.S.A.)
800 m	1:42.67	Wilson Kipketer (Denmark)
1,000 m	2:14.96	Wilson Kipketer (Denmark)
1,500 m	3:31.18	Hicham El Guerrouj (Morocco)
1 mile	3:48.45	Hicham El Guerrouj (Morocco)
3,000 m	7:24.90	Daniel Komen (Kenya)
5,000 m	12:49.60	Kenenisa Bekele (Ethiopia)
50 m hurdles	6.25	Mark McKoy (Canada)
60 m hurdles	7.30	Colin Jackson (GB)
4 × 200 m relay	1:22.11	Great Britain & N. Ireland (Linford Christie, Darren Braithwaite, Ade Mafe, John Regis)
4 × 400 m relay	3:02.83	U.S.A. (A. Morris, D. Johnson, D. Minor, M. Campbell)
4 × 800 m relay	7:13.94	Global Athletics & Marketing, U.S.A. (Joey Woody, Karl Paranya, Rich Kenah, David Krummenacker)
5,000 m walk	18:07.08	Mikhail Shchennikov (Russia)

MEN'S 800 M Two indoor world records belong to Wilson Kipketer (Denmark): 800 m and 1,000 m. Pictured is Kipketer after running the outdoor 800 m in a record 1 min. 41.11 sec. at the International Track and Field meeting in Cologne, Germany, on August 24, 1997.

★ TRACK & FIELD—INDOOR TRACK EVENTS ★

WOMEN	TIME	NAME & NATIONALITY
50 m	5.96	Irina Privalova (Russia)
60 m	6.92	Irina Privalova (Russia)
	6.92	Irina Privalova (Russia)
200 m	21.87	Merlene Ottey (Jamaica)
400 m	49.59	Jarmila Kratochvílová (Czechoslovakia)
800 m	1:55.82	Jolanda Ceplak (Slovenia)
1,000 m	2:30.94	Maria de Lurdes Mutola (Mozambique)
1,500 m	3:57.71	Yelena Soboleva (Russia)
1 mile	4:17.14	Doina Melinte (Romania)
3,000 m	8:23.72	Meseret Defar (Ethiopia)
5,000 m	14:27.42	Tirunesh Dibaba (Ethiopia)
50 m hurdles	6.58	Cornelia Oschkenat (GDR)
60 m hurdles	7.68	Susanna Kallur (Sweden)
4 × 200 m relay	1:32.41	Russia (Yekaterina Kondratyeva, Irina Khabarova, Yuliva Pechonkina, Yulia Gushchina)
4 × 400 m relay	3:23.37	Russia (Yulia Gushchina, Olga Kotlyarova, Olga Zaytseva, Olesya Krasnomovets)
4 × 800 m relay	8:18.54	Moskovskaya Region (Anna Balakshina, Natalya Pantelyeva, Anna Emashova, Olesya Chumakova)
3,000 m walk	11:40.33	Claudia Stef (Romania)

★ TRACK & FIELD—ULTRA-LONG DISTANCE [TRACK] ★

MEN	TIME/DISTANCE	NAME & NATIONALITY
50 km	2:48:06	Jeff Norman (GB)
100 km	6:10:20	Donald Ritchie (GB)
100 miles	11:28:03	Oleg Kharitonov (Russia)
1,000 miles	11 days 13:54:58	Peter Silkinas (Lithuania)
24 hours	188.46 miles (303.306 km)	Yiannis Kouros (Greece)
48 hours	294.21 miles (473.495 km)	Yiannis Kouros (Greece)
6 days	635.78 miles (1,023.2 km)	Yiannis Kouros (Greece)

WOMEN	TIME/DISTANCE	NAME & NATIONALITY
50 km	3:18:52	Carolyn Hunter-Rowe (GB)
100 km	7:14:06	Norimi Sakurai (Japan)
100 miles	14:25:45	Edit Berces (Hungary)
1,000 miles	13 days 1:54:02	Eleanor Robinson (GB)
24 hours	155.40 miles (250.106 km)	Edit Berces (Hungary)
48 hours	234.81 miles (377.892 km)	Sue Ellen Trapp (U.S.A.)
6 days	549.06 miles (883.631 km)	Sandra Barwick (New Zealand)

PLACE	DATE
Madrid, Spain	Feb. 9, 1995
Madrid, Spain	Feb. 11, 1993
Madrid, Spain	Feb. 9, 1995
Liévin, France	Feb. 13, 1993
Milan, Italy	Mar. 7, 1982
Vienna, Austria	Mar. 3, 2002
Stockholm, Sweden	Feb. 25, 1999
Valencia, Spain	Mar. 9, 2008
East Rutherford, U.S.A.	Feb. 9, 1990
Stuttgart, Germany	Feb. 3, 2007
Boston, U.S.A.	Jan. 27, 2007
Berlin, Germany	Feb. 20, 1988
Karlsruhe, Germany	Feb. 10, 2008
Glasgow, UK	Jan. 29, 2005
Glasgow, UK	Jan. 28, 2006
Volgograd, Russia	Feb. 11, 2007
Bucharest, Romania	Jan. 30, 1999

☆ **WOMEN'S 1,500 M** Yelena Soboleva (Russia) celebrates winning gold in the women's indoor 1,500 m. She competed at the 12th IAAF World Indoor Championships in Valencia, Spain, on March 9, 2008, securing a new world record time of 3 min. 57.71 sec.

PLACE	DATE
Timperley, UK	Jun. 7, 1980
London, UK	Oct. 28, 1978
London, UK	Oct. 2, 2002
Nanango, Australia	Mar. 11–23, 1998
Adelaide, Australia	Oct. 4–5, 1997
Surgères, France	May 3–5, 1996
Colac, Australia	Nov. 26–Dec. 2, 1984

PLACE	DATE
Barry, South Wales, UK	Mar. 3, 1996
Verona, Italy	Sep. 27, 2003
Verona, Italy	Sep. 21–22, 2002
Nanango, Australia	Mar. 11–23, 1998
Verona, Italy	Sep. 21–22, 2002
Surgères, France	May 2–4, 1997
Campbelltown, Australia	Nov. 18–24, 1990

OFFICIAL WEBSITES

ATHLETICS:
www.iaaf.org

ULTRARUNNING:
www.iau.org.tw

★ TRACK & FIELD—ROAD RACE ★

MEN	TIME	NAME & NATIONALITY
10 km	27:02	Haile Gebrselassie (Ethiopia)
15 km	41:29	Felix Limo (Kenya)
20 km	55:48	Haile Gebrselassie (Ethiopia)
Half marathon	58:33	Samuel Wanjiru (Kenya)
25 km	1:12:45	Paul Malakwen Kosgei (Kenya)
30 km	1:28:00	Takayuki Matsumiya (Japan)
Marathon	2:04:26	Haile Gebrselassie (Ethiopia)
100 km	6:13:33	Takahiro Sunada (Japan)
Road relay	1:57:06	Kenya (Josephat Ndambiri, Martin Mathathi, Daniel Mwangi, Mekubo Mogusu, Onesmus Nyerere, John Kariuki)

WOMEN	TIME	NAME & NATIONALITY
10 km	30:21	Paula Radcliffe (GB)
15 km	46:55	Kayoko Fukushi (Japan)
20 km	1:02:57	Lornah Kiplagat (Netherlands)
Half marathon	1:06:25	Lornah Kiplagat (Netherlands)
25 km	1:22:13	Mizuki Noguchi (Japan)
30 km	1:38:49	Mizuki Noguchi (Japan)
Marathon	2:15:25	Paula Radcliffe (GB)
100 km	6:33:11	Tomoe Abe (Japan)
Road relay	2:11:41	China (Jiang Bo, Dong Yanmei, Zhao Fengdi, Ma Zaijie, Lan Lixin, Li Na)

★ TRACK & FIELD—RACE WALKING ★

MEN	TIME	NAME & NATIONALITY
20,000 m	1:17:25.6	Bernardo Segura (Mexico)
20 km (road)	1:17:16	Vladimir Kanaykin (Russia)
30,000 m	2:01:44.1	Maurizio Damilano (Italy)
50,000 m	3:40:57.9	Thierry Toutain (France)
50 km (road)	3:35:47	Nathan Deakes (Australia)

WOMEN	TIME	NAME & NATIONALITY
10,000 m	41:56.23	Nadezhda Ryashkina (USSR)
20,000 m	1:26:52.3	Olimpiada Ivanova (Russia)
20 km (road)	1:25:41	Olimpiada Ivanova (Russia)

OFFICIAL WEBSITES

TRACK & FIELD
& RACEWALKING:
www.iaaf.org

CYCLING:
www.uci.ch

PLACE	DATE
Doha, Qatar	Dec. 11, 2002
Nijmegen, the Netherlands	Nov. 11, 2001
Phoenix, U.S.A.	Jan. 15, 2006
The Hague, the Netherlands	Mar. 17, 2007
Berlin, Germany	May 9, 2004
Kumamoto, Japan	Feb. 27, 2005
Berlin, Germany	Sep. 30, 2007
Tokoro, Japan	Jun. 21, 1998
Chiba, Japan	Nov. 23, 2005

PLACE	DATE
San Juan, Puerto Rico	Feb. 23, 2003
Marugame, Japan	Feb. 5, 2006
Udine, Italy	Oct. 14, 2007
Udine, Italy	Oct. 14, 2007
Berlin, Germany	Sep. 25, 2005
Berlin, Germany	Sep. 25, 2005.
London, UK	Apr. 13, 2003
Tokoro, Japan	Jun. 25, 2000
Beijing, China	Feb. 28, 1998

☆ MEN'S HALF MARATHON Samuel Wanjiru (Kenya) competes at the Great North Run in Newcastle-Upon-Tyne, UK, on September 30, 2007. Earlier the same year, he broke the half marathon world record with a time of 58 min. 33 sec.

PLACE	DATE
Bergen, Norway	May 7, 1994
Saransk, Russia	Sep. 29, 2007
Cuneo, Italy	Oct. 3, 1992
Héricourt, France	Sep. 29, 1996
Geelong, Australia	Dec. 2, 2006

PLACE	DATE
Seattle, U.S.A.	Jul. 24, 1990
Brisbane, Australia	Sep. 6, 2001
Helsinki, Finland	Aug. 7, 2005

☆ MEN'S 20 KM RACE WALK (ROAD) Vladimir Kanaykin (Russia) celebrates after crossing the finishing line as the winner of the men's 10 km race walk at the IAAF Junior Athletics World Championships at the National Stadium in Kingston, Jamaica, in July 2002. Kanaykin broke the 20 km men's record on September 29, 2007, in Saransk, Russia, when he achieved a time of 1 hr. 17 min. 16 sec.

★ TRACK & FIELD—OUTDOOR FIELD EVENTS ★

MEN	RECORD	NAME & NATIONALITY
High jump	2.45 m (8 ft. 0.45 in.)	Javier Sotomayor (Cuba)
Pole vault	6.14 m (20 ft. 1.73 in.)	Sergei Bubka (Ukraine)
Long jump	8.95 m (29 ft. 4.36 in.)	Mike Powell (U.S.A.)
Triple jump	18.29 m (60 ft. 0.78 in.)	Jonathan Edwards (GB)
Shot put	23.12 m (75 ft. 10.23 in.)	Randy Barnes (U.S.A.)
Discus	74.08 m (243 ft. 0.53 in.)	Jürgen Schult (GDR)
Hammer	86.74 m (284 ft. 7 in.)	Yuriy Sedykh (USSR)
Javelin	98.48 m (323 ft. 1.16 in.)	Jan Železný (Czech Republic)
Decathlon*	9,026 points	Roman Sebrle (Czech Republic)

*100 m 10.64 seconds; long jump 8.11 m; shot put 15.33 m; high jump 2.12 m; 400 m 47.79 seconds; 110 m hurdles 13.92 seconds; discus 47.92 m; pole vault 4.80 m; javelin 70.16 m; 1,500 m 4 min. 21.98 sec.

WOMEN	RECORD	NAME & NATIONALITY
High jump	2.09 m (6 ft. 10.28 in.)	Stefka Kostadinova (Bulgaria)
Pole vault	5.01 m (16 ft. 5.24 in.)	Yelena Isinbayeva (Russia)
Long jump	7.52 m (24 ft. 8.06 in.)	Galina Chistyakova (USSR)
Triple jump	15.50 m (50 ft. 10.23 in.)	Inessa Kravets (Ukraine)
Shot put	22.63 m (74 ft. 2.94 in.)	Natalya Lisovskaya (USSR)
Discus	76.80 m (252 ft.)	Gabriele Reinsch (GDR)
Hammer	77.80 m (255 ft. 3 in.)	Tatyana Lysenko (Russia)
Javelin	71.70 m (235 ft. 2.83 in.)	Osleidys Menéndez (Cuba)
Heptathlon†	7,291 points	Jacqueline Joyner-Kersee (U.S.A.)
Decathlon**	8,358 points	Austra Skujyte (Lithuania)

†100 m hurdles 12.69 seconds; high jump 1.86 m; shot put 15.80 m; 200 m 22.56 seconds; long jump 7.27 m; javelin 45.66 m; 800 m 2 min. 8.51 sec.

**100 m 12.49 seconds; long jump 6.12 m; shot put 16.42 m; high jump 1.78 m; 400 m; 57.19 seconds; 100 m hurdles 14.22 seconds; discus 46.19 m; pole vault 3.10 m; javelin 48.78 m; 1,500 m 5 min. 15.86 sec.

★ TRACK & FIELD—INDOOR FIELD EVENTS ★

MEN	RECORD	NAME & NATIONALITY
High jump	2.43 m (7 ft. 11.66 in.)	Javier Sotomayor (Cuba)
Pole vault	6.15 m (20 ft. 2.12 in.)	Sergei Bubka (Ukraine)
Long jump	8.79 m (28 ft. 10.06 in.)	Carl Lewis (U.S.A.)
Triple jump	17.83 m (58 ft. 5.96 in.)	Aliecer Urrutia (Cuba)
	17.83 m (58 ft. 5.96 in.)	Christian Olsson (Sweden)
Shot put	22.66 m (74 ft. 4.12 in.)	Randy Barnes (U.S.A.)
Heptathlon*	6,476 points	Dan O'Brien (U.S.A.)

*60 m 6.67 seconds; long jump 7.84 m; shot put 16.02 m; high jump 2.13 m; 60 m hurdles 7.85 seconds; pole vault 5.20 m; 1,000 m 2 min. 57.96 sec.

PLACE	DATE
Salamanca, Spain	Jul. 27, 1993
Sestriere, Italy	Jul. 31, 1994
Tokyo, Japan	Aug. 30, 1991
Gothenburg, Sweden	Aug. 7, 1995
Los Angeles, U.S.A.	May 20, 1990
Neubrandenburg, Germany	Jun. 6, 1986
Stuttgart, Germany	Aug. 30, 1986
Jena, Germany	May 25, 1996
Götzis, Austria	May 27, 2001

PLACE	DATE
Rome, Italy	Aug. 30, 1987
Helsinki, Finland	Aug. 12, 2005
St. Petersburg, Russia	Jun. 11, 1988
Gothenburg, Sweden	Aug. 10, 1995
Moscow, Russia	Jun. 7, 1987
Neubrandenburg, Germany	Jul. 9, 1988
Tallinn, Estonia	Aug. 15, 2006
Helsinki, Finland	Aug. 14, 2005
Seoul, South Korea	Sep. 24, 1988
Columbia, U.S.A.	Apr. 15, 2005

PLACE	DATE
Budapest, Hungary	Mar. 4, 1989
Donetsk, Ukraine	Feb. 21, 1993
New York City, U.S.A.	Jan. 27, 1984
Sindelfingen, Germany	Mar. 1, 1997
Budapest, Hungary	Mar. 7, 2004
Los Angeles, U.S.A.	Jan. 20, 1989
Toronto, Canada	Mar. 14, 1993

★ TRACK & FIELD—INDOOR FIELD EVENTS ★

WOMEN	RECORD	NAME & NATIONALITY
High jump	2.08 m (6 ft. 9.8 in.)	Kajsa Bergqvist (Sweden)
Pole vault	4.95 m (16 ft. 2.9 in.)	Yelena Isinbayeva (Russia)
Long jump	7.37 m (24 ft. 2.15 in.)	Heike Drechsler (GDR)
Triple jump	15.36 m (50 ft. 4.72 in.)	Tatyana Lebedeva (Russia)
Shot put	22.50 m (73 ft. 9.82 in.)	Helena Fibingerová (Czechoslovakia)
Pentathlon†	4,991 points	Irina Belova (Russia)

†60 m hurdles 8.22 seconds; high jump 1.93 m; shot put 13.25 m; long jump 6.67 m; 800 m 2 min. 10.26 sec.

★ CYCLING [ABSOLUTE TRACK] ★

MEN	TIME/DISTANCE	NAME & NATIONALITY
200 m (flying start)	9.772	Theo Bos (Netherlands)
500 m (flying start)	24.758	Chris Hoy (UK)
1 km (standing start)	58.875	Arnaud Tournant (France)
4 km (standing start)	4:11.114	Christopher Boardman (UK)
Team 4 km (standing start)	3:56.610	Australia (Graeme Brown, Luke Roberts, Brett Lancasfer, Bradley McGee)
1 hour	49.7 km*	Ondrej Sosenka (Czech Republic)

WOMEN	TIME/DISTANCE	NAME & NATIONALITY
200 m (flying start)	10.831	Olga Slioussareva (Russia)
500 m (flying start)	29.655	Erika Salumäe (Estonia)
500 m (standing start)	33.588	Anna Meares (Australia)
3 km (standing start)	3:24.537	Sarah Ulmer (New Zealand)
1 hour	46.65 km*	Leontien Zijlaard-van Moorsel (Netherlands)

*Some athletes achieved better distances within an hour with bicycles that are no longer allowed by the Union Cycliste Internationale (UCI). The 1-hour records given here are in accordance with the new UCI rules

★ FREEDIVING ★

MEN'S DEPTH DISCIPLINES	DEPTH/TIME	NAME & NATIONALITY
Constant weight with fins	112 m (367 ft. 5 in.)	Herbert Nitsch (Austria)
Constant weight without fins	86 m (282 ft. 1 in.)	William Trubridge (New Zealand)
Variable weight	140 m (459 ft. 4 in.)	Carlos Coste (Venezuela)
No limit	214 m (702 ft.)	Herbert Nitsch (Austria)
Free immersion	108 m (354 ft. 4 in.)	William Trubridge (New Zealand)

PLACE	DATE
Arnstadt, Germany	Feb. 4, 2006
Donetsk, Ukraine	Feb. 16, 2008
Vienna, Austria	Feb. 13, 1988
Budapest, Hungary	Mar. 6, 2004
Jablonec, Czechoslovakia	Feb. 19, 1977
Berlin, Germany	Feb. 15, 1992

PLACE	DATE
Moscow, Russia	Dec. 16, 2006
La Paz, Bolivia	May 13, 2007
La Paz, Bolivia	Oct. 10, 2001
Manchester, UK	Aug. 29, 1996
Athens, Greece	Aug. 22, 2004
Moscow, Russia	Jul. 19, 2005

☆ WOMEN'S 500 M CYCLING Anna Meares (Australia), on her way to winning the women's 500 m time trial (standing start) in a record time of 33.588 seconds at the UCI Track Cycling World Championship in Palma de Mallorca, Spain, on March 31, 2007.

PLACE	DATE
Moscow, Russia	Apr. 25, 1993
Moscow, Russia	Aug. 6, 1987
Palma de Mallorca, Spain	Mar. 31, 2007
Athens, Greece	Aug. 22, 2004
Mexico City, Mexico	Oct. 1, 2003

PLACE	DATE
Sharm el Sheikh, Egypt	Nov. 1, 2007
Bahamas	Apr. 10, 2008
Sharm el Sheikh, Egypt	May 9, 2006
Spetses, Greece	Jun. 14, 2007
Bahamas	Apr. 11, 2008

★ FREEDIVING ★

MEN'S DYNAMIC APNEA

With fins	244 m (800 ft. 6 in.)	Dave Mullins (New Zealand)
Without fins	186 m (610 ft. 3 in.)	Stig Aavall Severinsen (Denmark)

MEN'S STATIC APNEA

Duration	9 min. 8 sec.	Tom Sietas (Germany)

WOMEN'S DEPTH DISCIPLINES

Constant weight with fins	90 m (295 ft. 3 in.)	Sara Campbell (UK)
Constant weight without fins	•57 m (187 ft.)	Natalya Avseenko (Russia)
Variable weight	122 m (400 ft. 3 in.)	Tanya Streeter (U.S.A.)
No limit	160 m (524 ft. 11 in.)	Tanya Streeter (U.S.A.)
Free immersion	81 m (265 ft. 9 in.)	Sara Campbell (UK)

•Please note that these records were still awaiting ratification at the time of going to press.

WOMEN'S DYNAMIC APNEA

With fins	205 m (662 ft. 6 in.)	Natalia Molchanova (Russia)
Without fins	149 m (488 ft. 10 in.)	Natalia Molchanova (Russia)

WOMEN'S STATIC APNEA

Duration	8 min. 0 sec.	Natalia Molchanova (Russia)

★ ROWING ★

MEN	TIME	NAME & NATIONALITY
Single sculls	6:35.40	Mahe Drysdale (New Zealand)
Double sculls	6:03.25	Jean-Baptiste Macquet, Adrien Hardy (France)
Quadruple sculls	5:37.31	Konrad Wasielewski, Marek Kolbowicz, Michal Jelinski, Adam Korol (Poland)
Coxless pairs	6:14.27	Matthew Pinsent, James Cracknell (GB)
Coxless fours	5:41.35	Sebastian Thormann, Paul Dienstbach, Philipp Stüer, Bernd Heidicker (Germany)

Wellington, New Zealand	Sep. 23, 2007
Maribor, Slovenia	Jul. 7, 2007

Hamburg, Germany	May 1, 2007

Dahab, Egypt	Oct. 20, 2007
Bahamas	Apr. 8, 2008
Turks and Caicos Islands	Jul. 19, 2003
Turks and Caicos Islands	Aug. 17, 2002
Dahab, Egypt	Oct. 19, 2007

Maribor, Slovenia	Jul. 5, 2007
Maribor, Slovenia	Jul. 7, 2007

Maribor, Slovenia	Jul. 6, 2007

REGATTA	DATE
Eton, UK	Aug. 26, 2006
Poznan, Poland	Jun. 17, 2006
Poznan, Poland	Jun. 17, 2006
Seville, Spain	Sep. 21, 2002
Seville, Spain	Sep. 21, 2002

OFFICIAL WEBSITES

FREEDIVING:
www.aida-international.org

ROWING:
www.worldrowing.com

SPEED SKATING:
www.isu.org

★ ROWING ★

MEN	TIME	NAME & NATIONALITY
Coxed pairs*	6:42.16	Igor Boraska, Tihomir Frankovic, Milan Razov (Croatia)
Coxed fours*	5:58.96	Matthias Ungemach, Armin Eichholz, Armin Weyrauch, Bahne Rabe, Jörg Dederding (Germany)
Coxed eights	5:19.85	Deakin, Beery, Hoopman, Volpenhein, Cipollone, Read, Allen, Ahrens, Hansen (U.S.A.)

LIGHTWEIGHT

Single sculls*	6:47.82	Zac Purchase (GB)
Double sculls	6:10.02	Mads Rasmussen and Rasmus Quist (Denmark)
Quadruple sculls*	5:45.18	Francesco Esposito, Massimo Lana, Michelangelo Crispi, Massimo Guglielmi (Italy)
Coxless pairs*	6:26.61	Tony O'Connor, Neville Maxwell (Ireland)
Coxless fours	5:45.60	Thomas Poulsen, Thomas Ebert, Eskild Ebbesen, Victor Feddersen (Denmark)
Coxed eights*	5:30.24	Altena, Dahlke, Kobor, Stomporowski, Melges, März, Buchheit, Von Warburg, Kaska (Germany)

WOMEN

Single sculls	7:07.71	Rumyana Neykova (Bulgaria)
Double sculls	6:38.78	Georgina and Caroline Evers-Swindell (New Zealand)
Quadruple sculls	6:10.80	Kathrin Boron, Katrin Rutschow-Stomporowski, Jana Sorgers, Kerstin Köppen (Germany)
Coxless pairs	6:53.80	Georgeta Andrunache, Viorica Susanu (Romania)
Coxless fours*	6:25.35	Robyn Selby Smith, Jo Lutz, Amber Bradley, Kate Hornsey (Australia)
Coxed eights	5:55.50	Mickelson, Whipple, Lind, Goodale, Sickler, Cooke, Shoop, Francia, Davies (U.S.A.)

LIGHTWEIGHT

Single sculls*	7:28.15	Constanta Pipota (Romania)
Double sculls	6:49.77	Dongxiang Xu, Shimin Yan (China)
Quadruple sculls*	6:23.96	Hua Yu, Haixia Chen, Xuefei Fan, Jing Liu (China)
Coxless pairs*	7:18.32	Eliza Blair, Justine Joyce (Australia)

*Denotes non-Olympic boat classes

REGATTA	DATE
Indianapolis, U.S.A.	Sep. 18, 1994
Vienna, Austria	Aug. 24, 1991
Athens, Greece	Aug. 15, 2004
Eton, UK	Aug. 26, 2006
Amsterdam, the Netherlands	Jun. 23, 2007
Montreal, Canada	1992
Paris, France	1994
Lucerne, Switzerland	Jul. 9, 1999
Montreal, Canada	1992
Seville, Spain	Sep. 21, 2002
Seville, Spain	Sep. 21, 2002
Duisburg, Germany	May 19, 1996
Seville, Spain	Sep. 21, 2002
Eton, UK	Aug. 26, 2006
Eton, UK	Aug. 27, 2006
Paris, France	Jun. 19, 1994
Poznan, Poland	Jun. 17, 2006
Eton, UK	Aug. 27, 2006
Aiguebelette-le-Lac, France	Sep. 7, 1997

★ SPEED SKATING—LONG TRACK ★

MEN

MEN	TIME/POINTS	NAME & NATIONALITY
500 m	34.03	Jeremy Wotherspoon (Canada)
2 × 500 m	68.31	Jeremy Wotherspoon (Canada)
1,000 m	1:07.00	Pekka Koskela (Finland)
1,500 m	1:42.01	Denny Morrison (Canada)
3,000 m	3:37.28	Eskil Ervik (Norway)
5,000 m	6:06.32	Sven Kramer (Netherlands)
10,000 m	12:41.69	Sven Kramer (Netherlands)
500/1,000/500/1,000 m	137,230 points	Jeremy Wotherspoon (Canada)
500/3,000/1,500/5,000 m	146,365 points	Erben Wennemars (Netherlands)
500/5,000/1,500/10,000 m	145,742 points	Shani Davis (U.S.A.)
Team pursuit (8 laps)	3:37.80	Netherlands (Sven Kramer, Carl Verheijen, Erben Wennemars)

WOMEN

WOMEN	TIME/POINTS	NAME & NATIONALITY
500 m	37.02	Jenny Wolf (Germany)
2 × 500 m	74.42	Jenny Wolf (Germany)
1,000 m	1:13.11	Cindy Klassen (Canada)
1,500 m	1:51.79	Cindy Klassen (Canada)
3,000 m	3:53.34	Cindy Klassen (Canada)
5,000 m	6:45.61	Martina Sáblíková (Czech Rebublic)
500/1,000/500/1,000 m	149,305 points	Monique Garbrecht-Enfeldt (Germany), Cindy Klassen (Canada)
500/1,500/1,000/3,000 m	155,576 points	Cindy Klassen (Canada)
500/3,000/1,500/5,000 m	154,580 points	Cindy Klassen (Canada)
Team pursuit (6 laps)	2:56.04	Germany (Daniela Anschütz, Anni Friesinger, Claudia Pechstein)

★ SPEED SKATING—SHORT TRACK ★

MEN

MEN	TIME	NAME & NATIONALITY
500 m	41.051	Sung Si-Bak (South Korea)
1,000 m	1:23.815	Michael Gilday (Canada)
1,500 m	2:10.639	Ahn Hyun-Soo (South Korea)
3,000 m	4:32.646	Ahn Hyun-Soo (South Korea)
5,000 m relay	6:39.990	Canada (Charles Hamelin, Steve Robillard, François-Louis Tremblay, Mathieu Turcotte)

WOMEN

WOMEN	TIME	NAME & NATIONALITY
500 m	43.216	Wang Meng (China)
1,000 m	1:29.495	Wang Meng (China)
1,500 m	2:16.729	Zhou Yang (China)
3,000 m	4:46.983	Jung Eun-Ju (South Korea)
3,000 m relay	4:09.938	South Korea (Jung Eun-Ju, Park Seung-Hi, Shin Sae-Bom, Yang Shin-Young)

PLACE	DATE
Salt Lake City, U.S.A.	Nov. 9, 2007
Calgary, Canada	Mar. 15, 2008
Salt Lake City, U.S.A.	Nov. 10, 2007
Calgary, Canada	Mar. 14, 2008
Calgary, Canada	Nov. 5, 2005
Calgary, Canada	Nov. 17, 2007
Salt Lake City, U.S.A.	Mar. 10, 2007
Calgary, Canada	Jan. 18–19, 2003
Calgary, Canada	Aug. 12–13, 2005
Calgary, Canada	Mar. 18–19, 2006
Salt Lake City, U.S.A.	Mar. 11, 2007

PLACE	DATE
Salt Lake City, U.S.A.	Nov. 16, 2007
Salt Lake City, U.S.A.	Mar. 10, 2007
Calgary, Canada	Mar. 25, 2006
Salt Lake City, U.S.A.	Nov. 20, 2005
Calgary, Canada	Mar. 18, 2006
Salt Lake City, U.S.A.	Mar. 11, 2007
Salt Lake City, U.S.A.	Jan. 11–12, 2003
Calgary, Canada	Mar. 24–25, 2006
Calgary, Canada	Mar. 15–17, 2001
Calgary, Canada	Mar. 18–19, 2006
Calgary, Canada	Nov. 13, 2005

☆ MEN'S LONG TRACK 1,500 M Denny Morrison (Canada) competing at the 2008 ISU Single Distances Speed Skating Championships in Nagano, Japan, on March 8, 2008. Only a few days later, on March 14, Morrison broke the world record long track event with a time of 1 min. 42.01 sec. back in his home country.

PLACE	DATE
Salt Lake City, U.S.A.	Feb. 2, 2008
Calgary, Canada	Oct. 14, 2007
Marquette, U.S.A.	Oct. 24, 2003
Beijing, China	Dec. 7, 2003
Beijing, China	Mar. 13, 2005

PLACE	DATE
Salt Lake City, U.S.A.	Feb. 9, 2008
Harbin, China	Mar. 15, 2008
Salt Lake City, U.S.A.	Feb. 9, 2008
Harbin, China	Mar. 15, 2008
Salt Lake City, U.S.A.	Feb. 10, 2008

☆ WOMEN'S SHORT TRACK 1,000 M Wang Meng (China) competes in the 1,000 m semifinals at the 2008 ISU World Short Track Speed Skating Championships on March 9, 2008, in Gangneung, South Korea. A few days later, on March 15, she broke the world record for the 1,000 m when she clocked 1 min. 29.495 sec. in Harbin, China.

★ SWIMMING—LONG COURSE [50 M POOL] ★

MEN	TIME	NAME & NATIONALITY
50 m freestyle	21.64	Alexander Popov (Russia)
100 m freestyle	47.84	Pieter van den Hoogenband (Netherlands)
200 m freestyle	1:43.86	Michael Phelps (U.S.A.)
400 m freestyle	3:40.08	Ian Thorpe (Australia)
800 m freestyle	7:38.65	Grant Hackett (Australia)
1,500 m freestyle	14:34.56	Grant Hackett (Australia)
4 × 100 m freestyle relay	3:12.46	U.S.A. (Michael Phelps, Neil Walker, Cullen Jones, Jason Lezak)
4 × 200 m freestyle relay	7:03.24	U.S.A. (Michael Phelps, Ryan Lochte, Klete Keller, Peter Vanderkaay)
50 m butterfly	22.96	Roland Schoeman (South Africa)
100 m butterfly	50.40	Ian Crocker (U.S.A.)
200 m butterfly	1:52.09	Michael Phelps (U.S.A.)
50 m backstroke	24.80	Thomas Rupprath (Germany)
100 m backstroke	52.98	Aaron Peirsol (U.S.A.)
200 m backstroke	1:54.32	Ryan Lochte (U.S.A.)
50 m breaststroke	27.18	Oleg Lisogor (Ukraine)
100 m breaststroke	59.13	Brendan Hansen (U.S.A.)
200 m breaststroke	2:08.50	Brendan Hansen (U.S.A.)
200 m medley	1:54.98	Michael Phelps (U.S.A.)
400 m medley	4:06.22	Michael Phelps (U.S.A.)
4 × 100 m medley relay	3:30.68	U.S.A. (Aaron Peirsol, Brendan Hansen, Ian Crocker, Jason Lezak)

WOMEN	TIME	NAME & NATIONALITY
50 m freestyle	24.13	Inge de Bruijn (Netherlands)
100 m freestyle	53.30	Britta Steffen (Germany)
200 m freestyle	1:55.52	Laure Manaudou (France)
400 m freestyle	4:02.13	Laure Manaudou (France)
800 m freestyle	8:16.22	Janet Evans (U.S.A.)
1,500 m freestyle	15:42.54	Kate Ziegler (U.S.A.)
4 × 100 m freestyle relay	3:35.22	Germany (Petra Dallmann, Daniella Goetz, Britta Steffen, Annika Liebs)
4 × 200 m freestyle relay	7:50.09	U.S.A. (Natalie Coughlin, Dana Vollmer, Lacey Nymeyer, Katie Hoff)
50 m butterfly	25.46	Therese Alshammar (Sweden)
100 m butterfly	56.61	Inge de Bruijn (Netherlands)
200 m butterfly	2:05.40	Jessicah Schipper (Australia)
50 m backstroke	28.09	Li Yang (China)
100 m backstroke	59.44	Natalie Coughlin (U.S.A.)
200 m backstroke	2:06.62	Krisztina Egerszegi (Hungary)
50 m breaststroke	30.31	Jade Edmistone (Australia)
100 m breaststroke	1:05.09	Leisel Jones (Australia)
200 m breaststroke	2:20.54	Leisel Jones (Australia)
200 m medley	2:09.72	Wu Yanyan (China)
400 m medley	4:32.89	Katie Hoff (U.S.A.)
4 × 100 m medley relay	3:55.74	Australia (Emily Seebohm, Leisel Jones, Jessicah Schipper, Lisbeth Lenton)

PLACE	DATE
Moscow, Russia	Jun. 16, 2000
Sydney, Australia	Sep. 19, 2000
Melbourne, Australia	Mar. 27, 2007
Manchester, UK	Jul. 30, 2002
Montreal, Canada	Jul. 27, 2005
Fukuoka, Japan	Jul. 29, 2001
Victoria, Canada	Aug. 19, 2006
Melbourne, Australia	Mar. 30, 2007
Montreal, Canada	Jul. 25, 2005
Montreal, Canada	Jul. 30, 2005
Melbourne, Australia	Mar. 28, 2007
Barcelona, Spain	Jul. 27, 2003
Melbourne, Australia	Mar. 27, 2007
Melbourne, Australia	Mar. 30, 2007
Berlin, Germany	Aug. 2, 2002
Irvine, U.S.A.	Aug. 1, 2006
Victoria, Canada	Aug. 20, 2006
Melbourne, Australia	Mar. 29, 2007
Melbourne, Australia	Apr. 1, 2007
Athens, Greece	Aug. 21, 2004

MEN'S 800 M FREESTYLE Grant Hackett (Australia) won the gold medal in a time of 7 min. 38.65 sec. for the 800 m long course freestyle during the XI FINA World Championships in Montreal, Quebec, Canada, on July 27, 2005. Hackett also holds the 1,500 m freestyle record.

PLACE	DATE
Sydney, Australia	Sep. 22, 2000
Budapest, Hungary	Aug. 2, 2006
Melbourne, Australia	Mar. 28, 2007
Budapest, Hungary	Aug. 6, 2006
Tokyo, Japan	Aug. 20, 1989
Mission Viejo, U.S.A.	Jun. 17, 2007
Budapest, Hungary	Jul. 31, 2006
Melbourne, Australia	Mar. 29, 2007
Barcelona, Spain	Jun. 13, 2007
Sydney, Australia	Sep. 17, 2000
Victoria, Canada	Aug. 17, 2006
Hyderabad, India	Oct. 19, 2007
Melbourne, Australia	Mar. 27, 2007
Athens, Greece	Aug. 25, 1991
Melbourne, Australia	Jan. 30, 2006
Melbourne, Australia	Mar. 20, 2006
Melbourne, Australia	Feb. 21, 2006
Shanghai, China	Oct. 17, 2004
Melbourne, Australia	Apr. 1, 2007
Melbourne, Australia	Mar. 31, 2007

☆ **WOMEN'S 50 M BUTTERFLY** Therese Alshammar (Sweden) swam the 50 m long course butterfly in 25.46 seconds during the second leg of Europe's Mare Nostrum Series in Barcelona, Spain, on June 13, 2007.

★ SWIMMING—SHORT COURSE [25 M POOL] ★

MEN	TIME	NAME & NATIONALITY
50 m freestyle	20.93	Stefan Nystrand (Sweden)
100 m freestyle	45.83	Stefan Nystrand (Sweden)
200 m freestyle	1:41.10	Ian Thorpe (Australia)
400 m freestyle	3:34.58	Grant Hackett (Australia)
800 m freestyle	7:25.28	Grant Hackett (Australia)
1,500 m freestyle	14:10.10	Grant Hackett (Australia)
4 × 100 m freestyle relay	3:09.57	Sweden (Johan Nyström, Lars Frölander, Mattias Ohlin, Stefan Nystrand)
4 × 200 m freestyle relay	6:52.66	Australia (Kirk Palmer, Grant Hackett, Grant Brits, Kenrick Monk)
50 m butterfly	22.60	Kaio Almeida (Brazil)
100 m butterfly	49.07	Ian Crocker (U.S.A.)
200 m butterfly	1:50.73	Franck Esposito (France)
50 m backstroke	23.27	Thomas Rupprath (Germany)
100 m backstroke	49.99	Ryan Lochte (U.S.A.)
200 m backstroke	1:49.05	Ryan Lochte (U.S.A.)
50 m breaststroke	26.17	Oleg Lisogor (Ukraine)
100 m breaststroke	57.47	Ed Moses (U.S.A.)
200 m breaststroke	2:02.92	Ed Moses (U.S.A.)
200 m medley	1:52.99	Laszlo Cseh (Hungary)
400 m medley	3:59.33	Laszlo Cseh (Hungary)
4 × 100 m medley relay	3:25.09	U.S.A. (Aaron Peirsol, Brendan Hansen, Ian Crocker, Jason Lezak)

WOMEN	TIME	NAME & NATIONALITY
50 m freestyle	23.58	Marleen Veldhuis (Netherlands)
100 m freestyle	51.70	Lisbeth Lenton (Australia)
200 m freestyle	1:53.29	Lisbeth Lenton (Australia)
400 m freestyle	3:56.09	Laure Manaudou (France)
800 m freestyle	8:08.00	Kate Ziegler (U.S.A.)
1,500 m freestyle	15:32.90	Kate Ziegler (U.S.A.)
4 × 100 m freestyle relay	3:30.85	Netherlands (Hinkelien Schreuder, Femke Heemskerk, Ranomi Kranowidjojo, Marleen Veldhuis)
4 × 200 m freestyle relay	7:46.30	China (Xu Yanvei, Zhu Yingven, Tang Jingzhi, Yang Yu)
50 m butterfly	25.33	Anne-Karin Kammerling (Sweden)
100 m butterfly	55.95	Lisbeth Lenton (Australia)
200 m butterfly	2:03.53	Otylia Jedrzejczak (Poland)
50 m backstroke	26.50	Sanja Jovanovic (Croatia)
100 m backstroke	56.51	Natalie Coughlin (U.S.A.)
200 m backstroke	2:03.62	Natalie Coughlin (U.S.A.)
50 m breaststroke	29.90	Jade Edmistone (Australia)
100 m breaststroke	1:03.86	Leisel Jones (Australia)
200 m breaststroke	2:17.75	Leisel Jones (Australia)
200 m medley	2:07.79	Allison Wagner (U.S.A.)
400 m medley	4:27.83	Yana Klochkova (Ukraine)
4 × 100 m medley relay	3:51.84	Australia (Tayliah Zimmer, Jade Edmistone, Jessicah Schipper, Lisbeth Lenton)

PLACE	DATE
Berlin, Germany	Nov. 18, 2007
Berlin, Germany	Nov. 18, 2007
Berlin, Germany	Feb. 6, 2000
Sydney, Australia	Jul. 18, 2002
Perth, Australia	Aug. 3, 2001
Perth, Australia	Aug. 7, 2001
Athens, Greece	Mar. 16, 2000
Melbourne, Australia	Aug. 31, 2007
Santos, Brazil	Dec. 17, 2005
New York City, U.S.A.	Mar. 26, 2004
Antibes, France	Dec. 8, 2002
Vienna, Austria	Dec. 10, 2004
Shanghai, China	Apr. 9, 2006
Shanghai, China	Apr. 9, 2006
Berlin, Germany	Jan. 21, 2006
Stockholm, Sweden	Jan. 23, 2002
Berlin, Germany	Jan. 17, 2004
Debrecen, Hungary	Dec. 13, 2007
Debrecen, Hungary	Dec. 14, 2007
Indianapolis, U.S.A.	Oct. 11, 2004

PLACE	DATE
Berlin, Germany	Nov. 18, 2007
Melbourne, Australia	Aug. 9, 2005
Sydney, Australia	Nov. 19, 2005
Helsinki, Finland	Dec. 9, 2006
Essen, Germany	Oct. 14, 2007
Essen, Germany	Oct. 12, 2007
Eindhoven, Netherlands	Dec. 9, 2007
Moscow, Russia	Apr. 3, 2002
Gothenburg, Sweden	Mar. 12, 2005
Hobart, Australia	Aug. 28, 2006
Debrecen, Hungary	Dec. 13, 2007
Debrecen, Hungary	Dec. 15, 2007
Singapore	Oct. 28, 2007
New York City, U.S.A.	Nov. 27, 2001
Brisbane, Australia	Sep. 26, 2004
Hobart, Australia	Aug. 28, 2006
Melbourne, Australia	Nov. 29, 2003
Palma de Mallorca, Spain	Dec. 5, 1993
Paris, France	Jan. 19, 2002
Shanghai, China	Apr. 7, 2006

☆ MEN'S 200 M & 400 M MEDLEYS Laszlo Cseh (Hungary) broke his own 400 m medley record with a time of 3 min. 59.33 sec. on December 14, 2007, during the European Short Course Swimming Championships. The previous day, he set a new record in the 200 m relay of 1 min. 52.99 sec.

☆ WOMEN'S 200 M BUTTERFLY Otylia Jedrzejczak (Poland) won the 200 m butterfly at the European Short Track Swimming Championships in Debrecen, Hungary, on December 13, 2007. She swam in a record time of 2 min. 3.53 sec.

OFFICIAL WEBSITE

SWIMMING:
www.fina.org

MEN	CATEGORY	WEIGHT LIFTED	NAME & NATIONALITY
56 kg	Snatch	138 kg	Halil Mutlu (Turkey)
	Clean & jerk	168 kg	Halil Mutlu (Turkey)
	Total	305 kg	Halil Mutlu (Turkey)
62 kg	Snatch	153 kg	Shi Zhiyong (China)
	Clean & jerk	182 kg	Le Maosheng (China)
	Total	325 kg	World Standard*
69 kg	Snatch	165 kg	Georgi Markov (Bulgaria)
	Clean & jerk	197 kg	Zhang Guozheng (China)
	Total	357 kg	Galabin Boevski (Bulgaria)
77 kg	Snatch	173 kg	Sergey Filimonov (Kazakhstan)
	Clean & jerk	210 kg	Oleg Perepetchenov (Russia)
	Total	377 kg	Plamen Zhelyazkov (Bulgaria)
85 kg	Snatch	187 kg	Andrei Rybakou (Belarus)
	Clean & jerk	218 kg	Zhang Yong (China)
	Total	395 kg	World Standard*
94 kg	Snatch	188 kg	Akakios Kakhiasvilis (Greece)
	Clean & jerk	232 kg	Szymon Kolecki (Poland)
	Total	417 kg	World Standard*
105 kg	Snatch	199 kg	Marcin Dolega (Poland)
	Clean & jerk	242 kg	World Standard*
	Total	440 kg	World Standard*
+105 kg	Snatch	213 kg	Hossein Rezazadeh (Iran)
	Clean & jerk	263 kg	Hossein Rezazadeh (Iran)
	Total	472 kg	Hossein Rezazadeh (Iran)

*From January 1, 1998, the International Weightlifting Federation (IWF) introduced modified bodyweight categories, thereby making the then-world records redundant. This is the new listing with the world standards for the new bodyweight categories. Results achieved at IWF-approved competitions exceeding the world standards by a minimum of **1 kg** will be recognized as world records.

OFFICIAL WEBSITES

WEIGHTLIFTING:
www.iwf.net

WATERSKIING:
www.iwsf.com

PLACE	DATE
Antalya, Turkey	Nov. 4, 2001
Trencín, Slovakia	Apr. 24, 2001
Sydney, Australia	Sep. 16, 2000
Izmir, Turkey	Jun. 28, 2002
Busan, South Korea	Oct. 2, 2002
Sydney, Australia	Sep. 20, 2000
Qinhuangdao, China	Sep. 11, 2003
Athens, Greece	Nov. 24, 1999
Almaty, Kazakhstan	Apr. 9, 2004
Trencín, Slovakia	Apr. 27, 2001
Doha, Qatar	Mar. 27, 2002
Chiang Mai, Thailand	Sep. 22, 2007
Ramat Gan, Israel	Apr. 25, 1998
Athens, Greece	Nov. 27, 1999
Sofia, Bulgaria	Apr. 29, 2000
Wladyslawowo, Poland	May 7, 2006
Qinhuangdao, China	Sep. 14, 2003
Athens, Greece	Aug. 25, 2004
Sydney, Australia	Sep. 26, 2000

☆ MEN'S 85 KG SNATCH
Andrei Rybakou (Belarus) lifts the bar to break the world record in the men's 85 kg snatch at the weightlifting world championships in Chiang Mai, Thailand, on September 22, 2007. He succeeded in lifting 187 kg.

★ WEIGHTLIFTING ★

WOMEN	CATEGORY	WEIGHT LIFTED	NAME & NATIONALITY
48 kg	Snatch	98 kg	Yang Lian (China)
	Clean & jerk	120 kg	Chen Xiexia (China)
	Total	217 kg	Yang Lian (China)
53 kg	Snatch	102 kg	Ri Song-Hui (North Korea)
	Clean & jerk	129 kg	Li Ping (China)
	Total	226 kg	Qiu Hongxia (China)
58 kg	Snatch	111 kg	Chen Yanqing (China)
	Clean & jerk	141 kg	Qiu Hongmei (China)
	Total	251 kg	Chen Yanqing (China)
63 kg	Snatch	116 kg	Pawina Thongsuk (Thailand)
	Clean & jerk	142 kg	Pawina Thongsuk (Thailand)
	Total	257 kg	Liu Haixia (China)
69 kg	Snatch	123 kg	Oxana Slivenko (Russia)
	Clean & jerk	157 kg	Zarema Kasaeva (Russia)
	Total	276 kg	Oxana Slivenko (Russia)
75 kg	Snatch	131 kg	Natalia Zabolotnaia (Russia)
	Clean & jerk	159 kg	Liu Chunhong (China)
	Total	286 kg	Svetlana Podobedova (Russia)
+75 kg	Snatch	139 kg	Mu Shuangshuang (China)
	Clean & jerk	182 kg	Gonghong Tang (China)
	Total	319 kg	Mu Shuangshuang (China)

★ WATERSKIING ★

MEN	RECORD	NAME & NATIONALITY
Slalom	1.5 buoy/9.75-m line	Chris Parrish (U.S.A.)
Barefoot slalom	20.6 crossings of wake in 15 seconds	Keith St. Onge (U.S.A.)
Tricks	12,400 points	Nicolas Le Forestier (France)
Barefoot tricks	10,880 points	Keith St. Onge (U.S.A.)
Jump	243 ft. 5 in. (74.2 m)	Freddy Krueger (U.S.A.)
Barefoot jump	89 ft. 11 in. (27.4 m)	David Small (GB)
Ski fly	298 ft. 10 in. (91.1 m)	Jaret Llewellyn (Canada)
Overall	2,818.01 points*	Jaret Llewellyn (Canada)

*5@11.25 m, 10,730 tricks, 71.7 m jump

WOMEN	RECORD	NAME & NATIONALITY
Slalom	1 buoy/10.25-m line	Kristi Overton Johnson (U.S.A.)
Barefoot slalom	17.0 crossings of wake in 15 seconds	Nadine de Villiers (South Africa)
Tricks	8,740 points	Mandy Nightingale (U.S.A.)
Barefoot tricks	4,400 points	Nadine de Villiers (South Africa)
Jump	186 ft. (56.6 m)	Elena Milakova (Russia)
Barefoot jump	67 ft. 7 in. (20.6 m)	Nadine de Villiers (South Africa)
Ski fly	227 ft. 8.2 in. (69.4 m)	Elena Milakova (Russia)
Overall	2,850.11 points**	Clementine Lucine (France)

**4@11.25 m, 8,680 tricks, 52.1 m jump; calculated with the 2006 scoring method

PLACE	DATE
Santo Domingo, Dominican Republic	Oct. 1, 2006
Taian City, China	Apr. 21, 2007
Santo Domingo, Dominican Republic	Oct. 1, 2006
Busan, South Korea	Oct. 1, 2002
Taian City, China	Apr. 22, 2007
Santo Domingo, Dominican Republic	Oct. 2, 2006
Doha, Qatar	Dec. 3, 2006
Taian City, China	Apr. 23, 2007
Doha, Qatar	Dec. 3, 2006
Doha, Qatar	Nov. 12, 2005
Doha, Qatar	Dec. 4, 2006
Chiang Mai, Thailand	Sep. 23, 2007
Santo Domingo, Dominican Republic	Oct. 4, 2006
Doha, Qatar	Apr. 25, 1998
Chiang Mai, Thailand	Sep. 24, 2007
Chiang Mai, Thailand	Sep. 25, 2007
Doha, Qatar	Nov. 13, 2005
Hangzhou, China	Jun. 2, 2006
Doha, Qatar	Dec. 6, 2006
Athens, Greece	Aug. 21, 2004
Chiang Mai, Thailand	Sep. 26, 2007

☆ WOMEN'S 75 KG SNATCH
Natalia Zabolotnaia (Russia)
lifts the bar to win the gold
medal in the women's 75 kg
snatch at the weightlifting
world championships in
Chiang Mai, Thailand, on
September 25, 2007. She
lifted 131 kg.

PLACE	DATE
Trophy Lakes, U.S.A.	Aug. 28, 2005
Bronkhorstspruit, South Africa	Jan. 6, 2006
Lac de Joux, Switzerland	Sep. 4, 2005
Adna, U.S.A.	Sep. 17, 2006
Seffner, U.S.A.	Nov. 5, 2006
Mulwala, Australia	Feb. 8, 2004
Orlando, U.S.A.	May 14, 2000
Seffner, U.S.A.	Sep. 29, 2002

PLACE	DATE
West Palm Beach, U.S.A.	Sep. 14, 1996
Witbank, South Africa	Jan. 5, 2001
Santa Rosa, U.S.A.	Jun. 10, 2006
Witbank, South Africa	Jan. 5, 2001
Rio Linda, U.S.A.	Jul. 21, 2002
Pretoria, South Africa	Mar. 4, 2000
Pine Mountain, U.S.A.	May 26, 2002
Lacanau, France	Jul. 9, 2006

☆ MEN'S WATERSKI JUMP
Freddy Krueger (U.S.A.)
jumped a record 243 ft. 5 in.
(74.2 m) on November 5,
2006, in Seffner, U.S.A.

★ LONGEST SPORTS MARATHONS ★

SPORT	TIME	NAME & NATIONALITY
★Aerobics	24 hours	Duberney Trujillo (Colombia)
Archery	27 hours	Michael Henri Dames (South Africa)
☆Baseball	32 hr. 29 min. 25 sec.	St. Louis Chapter of the Men's Senior Baseball League (U.S.A.)
☆Basketball	72 hours	Students of Holy Trinity Church of England Secondary School (UK)
Basketball (wheelchair)	26 hr. 3 min.	University of Omaha students and staff (U.S.A.)
Bowling	120 hours	Andy Milne (Canada)
Lawn bowling (indoor)	36 hours	Arnos Bowling Club (UK)
Lawn bowling (outdoor)	105 hours	Lloyd Hotel Bowling Club (UK)
☆Cricket	35 hours	Chestfield CC and Oakwood Homes (UK)
☆Curling	40 hr. 23 min.	B. Huston, C. McCarthy, G. Poole, K. McCarthy, K. Martin, M. Witherspoon, R. Martin, T. Gouldie, T. Teskey, W. From (Canada)
☆Darts (doubles)	25 hr. 34 min.	Richard Saunders, Derek Fox, Paul Taylor, Andrew Brymer (UK)
☆Darts (singles)	26 hr. 22 min.	Chris Nessling and Mick Dundee (UK)
★Fistball (indoor)	24 hours	TG 1855 Neustadt bei Coburg e.V. (Germany)
★Floorball	24 hr. 15 min.	TRM Floorball and Hornets Regio Moosseedorf Worblental (Switzerland)
Soccer	30 hr. 10 min.	FC Edo Simme and FC Spiez (Germany)
★Soccer (five per side)	24 hr. 30 min.	Rossendale Mavericks and the Fearns Community Sports College (UK)
Futsal (indoors)	30 hours	Max Cosi/Quinny and Keo teams (Cyprus)
Handball	70 hours	HV Mighty/Stevo team (Netherlands)
Hockey (ice)	240 hours	Brent Saik and friends (Canada)
☆Hockey (indoor)	32 hours	TF Farm Industries and Sandyhill teams (Canada)
Hockey (inline/roller)	24 hours	8K Roller Hockey League (U.S.A.)
☆Hockey (street)	100 hr. 2 min.	Blacks and Reds, Face-off for a Cure (Canada)
Korfball	26 hr. 2 min.	Korfball Club de Vinken (Netherlands)
☆Netball	56 hours	Airborne Netball Club (UK)
Parasailing	24 hr. 10 min.	Berne Persson (Sweden)
Pétanque (boules)	40 hr. 9 min.	Bevenser Boule-Freunde (Germany)
★Pool (singles)	50 hr. 2 min.	Alan Skerritt and Mike Tunnell (UK)
Skiing	202 hr. 1 min.	Nick Willey (Australia)
Snowboarding	180 hr. 34 min.	Bernhard Mair (Austria)
☆Spinning (static cycling)	175 hr. 50 min.	Joey Motsay (U.S.A.)
☆Table football	40 hr. 30 min.	Volker Lewedey, Karsten Link, Jakob Polzer and Christian Röhrer (Germany)
Table tennis (doubles)	101 hr. 1 min. 11 sec.	Lance, Phil and Mark Warren and Bill Weir (U.S.A.)
Table tennis (singles)	132 hr. 31 min.	Danny Price and Randy Nunes (U.S.A.)
☆Tai chi	25 hr. 5 min.	Ken Dickenson and Kevin Bartolo (Australia)

PLACE	DATE
Dosquebradas, Colombia	Feb. 26–27, 2005
Grahamstown, South Africa	Aug. 8–9, 2005
O'Fallon, Missouri, U.S.A.	Oct. 13–14, 2007
Crawley, West Sussex, UK	Jul. 13–16, 2007
Omaha, Nebraska, U.S.A.	Sep. 24–25, 2004
Mississauga, Ontario, Canada	Oct. 24–29, 2005
Southgate, UK	Apr. 20–21, 2002
Manchester, UK	Oct. 14–18, 2006
Chestfield, UK	Sep. 8–9, 2007
Brandon, Manitoba, Canada	Mar. 9–10, 2007
Hurst, Berkshire, UK	Jan. 12–13, 2007
Hurst, Berkshire, UK	Jan. 12–13, 2007
Frankehalle, Neustadt, Germany	Apr. 16–17, 2005
Zollikofen, Switzerland	Apr. 27–28, 2007
Erlenbach, Switzerland	Jul. 8–9, 2006
Waterfoot Rossendale, UK	Nov. 23–24, 2007
Limassol, Cyprus	Nov. 19–20, 2005 •
Tubbergen, the Netherlands	Aug. 30–Sep. 2, 2001
Strathcona, Alberta, Canada	Feb. 11–21, 2005
Taber, Alberta, Canada	Aug. 17–18, 2007
Eastpointe, Michigan, U.S.A.	Sep. 13–14, 2002
Winnipeg, Manitoba, Canada	May 13–17, 2007
Vinkeveen, the Netherlands	May 23–24, 2001
Bristol, UK	May 26–28, 2007
Lake Graningesjön, Sweden	Jul. 19–20, 2002
Bad Bevensen, Germany	Jul. 22–23, 2006
Stockton-on-Tees, UK	Mar. 22–24, 2006
Thredbo, NSW, Australia	Sep. 2–10, 2005
Bad Kleinkirchheim, Austria	Jan. 9–16, 2004
Greensboro, North Carolina, U.S.A.	Sep. 22–29, 2007
Spaichingen, Germany	Jul. 14–15, 2007
Sacramento, California, U.S.A.	Apr. 9–13, 1979
Cherry Hill, New Jersey, U.S.A.	Aug. 20–26, 1978
Sutherland, NSW, Australia	Mar. 17–18, 2006

★ LONGEST SPORTS MARATHONS ★

SPORT	TIME	NAME & NATIONALITY
Tennis (doubles match)	48 hr. 15 min.	Brian Jahrsdoerfer, Michel Lavoie, Peter Okpokpo, Warner Tse (U.S.A.)
☆ Tennis (singles match)	26 hr. 26 min. 26 sec.	Rinie Loeffen and Ton Dollevoet (Netherlands)
Tobogganing (steel)	56 hours	Michael Kinzel (Germany)
☆ Volleyball (indoor)	55 hr. 3 min.	OBEY (U.S.A.)
Wakeboarding	6 hr. 17 min.	Ian Taylor (UK)

PLEASE NOTE: GWR sports marathon guidelines are constantly updated—please contact us for information before you attempt a record.

PLACE	DATE
Houston, Texas, U.S.A.	Apr. 13–15, 2006
Macharen, the Netherlands	Jun. 23–24, 2007
Kirchhundem, Germany	May 4–6, 2002
Lexington, Kentucky, U.S.A.	Jul. 30–Aug. 1, 2007
Milton Keynes, UK	Sep. 1, 2004

HOLLYWOOD HALL OF FAME

DANIEL DAY-LEWIS
Most Best Actor
Oscar wins (2)*

MERYL STREEP Most
Oscar-nominated
actress (14)

ANGELINA JOLIE
Most powerful
actress in Hollywood

JACK NICHOLSON
Most Oscar-
nominated actor (12)

BRAD PITT Most
powerful actor in
Hollywood

Most Best Actor
Oscar wins (2)*

SAMUEL L. JACKSON
Highest-grossing
actor ($7.42 bn)†

*Record shared with Tom Hanks, Dustin Hoffman, Frederic March, Gary Cooper, Marlon Brando and Spencer Tracey, Daniel Day-Lewis awarded Oscars for *My Left Foot: The Story of Christie Brown* (1990) and *There Will Be Blood* (2008); Jack Nicholson awarded Oscars for *Terms of Endearment* (1983) and *As Good As It Gets* (1998).

†Based on 68 movies including *Star Wars: Episodes I, II & III, Jurassic Park, The Incredibles, Patriot Games, S.W.A.T.* and *Pulp Fiction.* The Guinness World Records movie power ratings are calculated using a combination of earnings, box office takings, awards, web impressions and p.r. & media exposure between May 1, 2007 and April 30, 2008.

> *"There's 300 to 400 films every year. Five of them get that phone call, and I've gotten it 18 times. . . . I really feel fortunate."*
>
> *Kevin O'Connell, interviewed in 2006*

MOST OSCAR NOMINATIONS WITHOUT A WIN Sound mixer Kevin O'Connell (U.S.A.) has received 20 Oscar nominations for sound, starting with *Terms of Endearment* (U.S.A., 1983) in 1984 and most recently with *Transformers* (U.S.A., 2007) in 2008—the longest losing streak in Oscar history! He is pictured below at his mantlepiece, where his Oscar statue will eventually go!

★ **MOST LUCRATIVE MOVIE PARTNERSHIP** In terms of total box-office gross, the most successful partnership in Hollywood—not including sequels—is that of director Tim Burton (above left) and actor Johnny Depp (above right). Together, the duo have grossed $986.89 million from six movies: *Edward Scissorhands, Ed Wood, Sleepy Hollow, Charlie and the Chocolate Factory, The Corpse Bride,* and *Sweeney Todd* (pictured).

> *"I hate film premieres. The one thing I never do at them is smile—neither does Johnny Depp or Tim Burton. It's so phony."*
>
> Christopher Lee

CHRISTOPHER LEE

This veteran actor has recorded the most screen credits by a Hollywood actor (244 acknowledged film and TV movie roles out of at least 358 screen credits) and the most sword fights in a movie career (17). We asked the screen legend how it feels to be a Guinness World Record holder.

Well, the word "survival" comes to mind! Survival and privilege. Sometimes when I look at all the things I've done, I don't realize it was me. I was going through a list of everyone in this business that I've worked with—or even just met—and I worked out that I've met just about everyone you would have heard of—from the Golden Era, at least—everyone except [Greta] Garbo.

Who's the greatest actor you've ever worked with? The greatest *actress* I've worked with was Bette Davis [in *Return from Witch Mountain* (U.S.A., 1978)], and the French actor Jean Reno [in *Crimson Rivers 2: Angels of the Apocalypse* (U.S.A., 2004)] was terrific—such a generous man. The best *young* actor I can think of is [Leonardo] DiCaprio. I met him, and he was very nice, very quiet. Oh, and Viggo Mortensen is a wonderful actor, isn't he? And Johnny Depp—he's brilliant, and a good friend of mine.

Are you happy to have played the bad guy so often? Well, they're much more interesting to play! But I haven't made what they refer to as—and I dislike, as did [co-star] Boris Karloff—a "horror" film since 1975. I was typecast for a while, but not anymore.

Any advice for up-and-coming actors? Don't expect to be a megastar overnight. I've always said that it takes ten years to become an actor. Far too many actors are far too young to handle major roles.

THE MAGIC OF HARRY POTTER

HARRY MAGIC

★ **Largest order of forestry-certified paper** Almost two-thirds of the initial 36.8 million lbs. (16,700 metric tons) of paper needed to print *Deathly Hallows* in the U.S.A. was certified by the Forest Stewardship Council (FSC), the global body responsible for forest management.

☆ **Fastest-selling fiction book (24 hrs.)** *Deathly Hallows* sold 8.3 million copies in the first 24 hours (or 345,833 books per hour) following its release in the U.S.A. on July 21, 2007.

★ HARRY POTTER AND THE . . . ★

TITLE	BOOK SALES	MOVIE GROSS	MOVIE OPENING
Philosopher's/ Sorcerer's Stone	120 million	$317,575,550	$90,294,621
Chamber of Secrets	77 million	$261,988,482	$88,357,488
Prisoner of Azkaban	61 million	$249,541,069	$93,687,367
Goblet of Fire	66 million	$290,013,036	$102,685,961
Order of the Phoenix	55 million	$292,004,738	$77,108,414
Half-Blood Prince	65 million	n/a	n/a
Deathly Hallows	75 million	n/a	n/a

HALLOWED VOICES In April 2007, actor Jim Dale (UK) created and recorded 146 different and distinguishable character voices for the U.S. audiobook *Harry Potter and the Deathly Hallows*—the ★most voices by an individual in an audiobook. He shares the record with Stephen Fry (UK), narrator of the UK edition.

Largest first-edition print run The release of *Order of the Phoenix* in June 2003 marked the largest first-edition print run ever, at 8.5 million copies.

Most advance orders *Goblet of Fire* received record advance orders of 5.3 million copies from around the world.

J. K. ROWLING

The Harry Potter series has sold 400 million copies worldwide and made its creator one of the wealthiest people in the world. We wanted to know which was her favorite book of the series.... *Deathly Hallows* remains my favorite book of the series. I hope that, even if it is not yours, you understand at least, that this was where the story was leading; it was the ending I had planned for 17 years, and there was more satisfaction than you can possibly imagine in finally sharing it with my readers.

Now that it's all over, how would you describe your relationship with Harry? It's been one of the longest relationships of my adult life: my rock through bereavement, marriage and divorce, single motherhood, changes of country; and also one of joy—on the day Bloomsbury decided to publish it.

You support many notable charities. Why did you decide to start your own? The Children's High Level Group was founded by, among others, Emma Nicholson and myself when we were deeply moved by the poverty, sickness, and maltreatment of children. The Children's Voice campaign wants to make life better for young people in care around the world.

The Magic of Harry Potter

MONEY MAGIC GWR's entertainment consultant Thomasina Gibson spoke to the Hogwarts high flying trio and heard how they spend some of their hard-earned sickles and knuts.

Rupert Grint "Oh, I bought a proper Mr. Whippy-type ice-cream van! It's really cool. It's got it all. Whipped ice-cream, treats, toppings—everything!"

Daniel Radcliffe "I'm quite interested in artwork and things like that, but I've never been into cars so I don't think I'm going to rush out and buy an exotic car any time soon like people expect me to."

Emma Watson "I guess my biggest thing was I bought myself an Apple Mac, my little laptop, which I love. It's my pride and joy."

DANIEL RADCLIFFE

Daniel Radcliffe talked to GWR about playing Harry Potter and the advice his parents gave him about handling his fame:
My mom and dad have just told me to enjoy it. There are a lot worse things that could happen than just being recognized.

What was the most memorable part of movie making, and the most nerve-wracking? I'm not just saying this, but one of the best parts was working with Chris [Columbus], because he's a total inspiration. He really enjoys what he does, and it's a real honor working with him. The most nerve-wracking thing was the first day, because before that it had just been me, Rupert [Grint], Emma [Watson], and Chris rehearsing in Chris's office. I got the call sheet for the first day, I looked under the cast and it said "Daniel Radcliffe, Emma Watson, and Rupert Grint." So I thought, fine, I'm used to that. Then I turned over the page and it said: "Extras, 150." At that moment, I got quite scared. . . .

HARRY SPELLS MAGIC FOR WARNER BROS. The Harry Potter franchise has proved a highly successful one for Warner Bros. (U.S.A.). Today, all five Harry Potter movies feature in Warners' Top 10 most successful films ever. In 2005, the studio's gross profits came to $1.37 billion, giving them the record at the time for the highest-grossing studio (though this has since been broken). The studio's most successful movie of the year was *Harry Potter and the Goblet of Fire* ($290 million), followed by *Charlie and the Chocolate Factory* ($206 million) and *Batman Begins* ($205 million).

Fastest-selling DVD ever The *Goblet of Fire* DVD sold more than six copies per second on the day of release in the UK on March 20, 2006, and has continued to sell more than three copies per second since. It also sold more than 5 million copies on the first day of release in the U.S.A., on March 7, 2006.

Largest reading J. K. Rowling was one of three authors who read excerpts from their works to a record audience of 20,264 at Toronto's Sky-Dome stadium (Canada) on October 24, 2000. Rowling read from *Harry Potter and the Goblet of Fire;* readings were also given by Kenneth Oppel and Tim Wynne-Jones (both Canada).

RECORD-BREAKING CAST & CREW

The Harry Potter film franchise is among the most successful ever, grossing an average of $890 million per movie and attracting the cream of British and American talent both in front of the cameras and behind. Among those who brought the books alive are a selection of record holders:

Robbie Coltrane (Hagrid): Robbie Coltrane (UK, right) earned himself a record for the **most consecutive Best Actor BAFTA wins**, with three, playing criminal psychologist Eddie "Fitz" Fitzgerald in *Cracker* in 1994, 1995, and 1996.

Michael Gambon (Dumbledore, left): Equaling Coltrane's record for the **most consecutive Best Actor BAFTA wins** is Michael Gambon (UK), who won BAFTA gongs for *Wives and Daughters* (1999), *Longitude* (2000), and *Perfect Strangers* (2001).

Emma Thompson (Sybil Trelawney): In 1993, Emma Thompson (UK) won a Best Actress Oscar for her role in *Howards End* (UK, 1991) and was awarded Best Screenplay Written Directly for the Screen for *Sense and Sensibility* (U.S.A./UK, 1995) in 1996, making her the **first person to win Oscars for both acting and writing**.

Julie Walters (Molly Weasley, below): The record for the **most Best Actress BAFTA wins** is three, shared by four British actresses, one of whom is Julie Walters (UK). She won for *My Beautiful Son* (UK/U.S.A., 2001), *Murder* (UK, 2002), and *The Canterbury Tales* (UK, 2003). She also shares with Helen Mirren (UK) a record for **most consecutive Best Actress wins**.

John Williams (composer): Maestro Williams (U.S.A.) has had 45 Academy Award nominations from 1968 to 2006, making him the **most Oscar-nominated living person**. His first nomination was for Best Music, Scoring of Music, Adaptation or Treatment for *Valley of the Dolls* (U.S.A., 1967), with his most recent for Best Achievement in Music Written for Motion Pictures, Original Score at the 2006 Oscar ceremony for both *Munich* and *Memoirs of a Geisha* (both U.S.A., 2005).

HE PINGPING

MEET HE PINGPING He's from China and he's the ☆ **shortest (mobile) living man** to be officially authenticated by Guinness World Records. The minuscule 19-year-old from Inner Mongolia, China, measures just 2 ft. 5.37 in. (74.61 cm).

Read on to discover more about this incredible new record breaker.

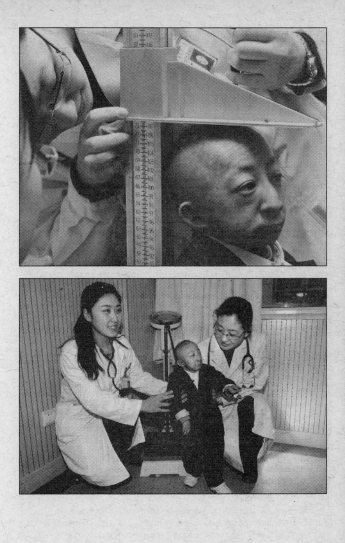

SIZE MATTERS To fully ratify any height-related claims, Guinness World Records insists on taking six measurements of the claimant three times in one day—in the morning, afternoon, and evening—both lying down and standing up. The final height is the average of the six figures.

There are, however, people who cannot be as thoroughly measured, due to medical reasons. For example, sufferers of severe osteogenesis imperfecta, or OI ("imperfect bone formation")—a crippling genetic disorder characterized by congenital brittle bones, are unable to stand or lie flat.

Linn Yih-Chih of Taiwan (above right) is technically the world's **shortest living man** at 27 in. (67.5 cm), but he is immobilized by OI, as is Madge Bester (South Africa, pictured being kissed), the **shortest living woman** at 26 in. (65 cm).

DEFINING HEIGHTS

When Pingping was born, his brother-in-law told us, he was no bigger than his father's palm. Doctors at the time diagnosed osteogenesis imperfecta (see "Size Matters" above). However, his mobility now suggests that this is not the case. There is no doubt that he has a dwarfism, but there are around 200 different types of that condition—so which one is it?

• Primordial dwarfism (PD) is a profound growth retardation that begins in the womb and continues after birth. There are many subtypes, which can be difficult to diagnose, but the umbrella term means "small from the beginning of life."

• Pingping also displays "proportionate dwarfism," as his legs, arms, head, and body are the same size in relation to one other. The medical definition for this used to be "midget," although this is no longer considered an acceptable term; "person of short stature" or simply "little person" are now preferred. (The most common dwarfism is achondroplasia, which accounts for 70% of cases and results in shortened limbs or a shortened trunk.)

ADULTS ONLY! The average Chinese adult measures between 5 ft. 5 in.–5 ft. 7 in. (165 and 170 cm), but Pingping's height is equivalent to that of a one-year-old child. For this reason, it is important that we confirmed his age, as only people who are over 18 years old are eligible for this record. Pingping proved his age with his identity card (held by everyone in China over the age of 16, see picture below), confirming that he reached adulthood.

EYEWITNESS TESTIMONY To verify He Pingping's final height, Guinness World Records' Editor-in-Chief Craig Glenday personally oversaw the six-step measuring process in a hospital in Hohhot, the capital city of Inner Mongolia. "The tallest and smallest human categories are among the most important records," he said. "Nothing should be left to chance or doubt."

NO TALL TALES He Pingping lives in Huade County in Wulanchabu Meng, which is part of China's Inner Mongolia Autonomous Region. Incredibly, he lives close to Chifung, the home of Xi Shun (China), who is officially recognized as the world's **tallest man** (at 7 ft. 8.95 in.; 2.361 m)! Despite the close proximity, the two men only met for the first time in July 2007 when Xi Shun married Xia Shujian (China) and invited Pingping to the formal Mongolian wedding ceremony!

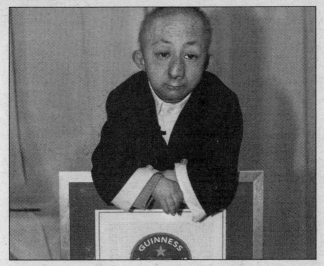

RECORD HOLDER! After repeated visits to the hospital for measurements and having satisfied all the other criteria, Pingping finally earned his Guinness World Records certificate. The average measurement takes into account the shrinking of the spine during a typical day—the spongy discs between the vertebrae become more compact, which is why you go to bed shorter than when you wake up!—but in Pingping's case, the variation was minimal. Welcome to the GWR family!

NELSON DE LA ROSA The title of **shortest (mobile) living man** (see above) passes to Pingping from Nelson de la Rosa (Dominican Republic), who measured 28.3 in. (72 cm). Before his death at the age of 38 in October 2006, this colorful character had carved out a successful media career for himself, including a role in *The Island of Dr. Moreau* (U.S.A., 1996).

GAZETTEER

CONTENTS

U.S.A.

★**Largest mammal exploded** The largest mammal ever exploded was the 16,000-lb. (7.25-metric ton), 45-ft.-long (13.7-m) carcass of a sperm whale that washed up south of Florence, Oregon. On November 12, 1970, the Oregon State Highway Division placed 1,000 lb. (half a metric ton) of dynamite around the decomposing, foul-smelling whale and detonated it. The dynamite was far more powerful than required and huge chunks of whale meat rained down on spectators. One 3 × 5-ft. (0.9 × 1.5-m) lump of whale crushed the roof of a Buick car 0.25 mile (0.4 km) away!

AT A GLANCE • **AREA**: 3,794,083 miles² (9,826,630 km²)
• **POPULATION**: 301.1 million
• **DENSITY**: 79 people/mile² (30 people/km²)
• **KEY FACTS**: The U.S.A. is the world's **most powerful nation-state**, with a per capita gross domestic product (GDP) of $46,000. The U.S.A. spends more than any other country on **health**—$5,274 per person in 2002, **foreign aid,** and the **military**; it is also home to the **most billionaires** (419 of the world's 946 total). U.S. citizens are the **greatest consumers of calories** (3,774.1 a day) and watch the **most TV** (4 hr. 32 min. per person per day). They own the **most guns** (40% of homes have them) and **downloaded singles** (98% of singles were bought online in 2005). The U.S.A. also has the **highest national debt**: as of 22 April 2008, it was $9,372,485,723,263.83.

A great sports nation, the U.S.A. has also won the **most Olympic medals** (975 from summer and winter games); and, in golf, the **most Walker** (34), **Solheim** (7), and **Ryder** (24) cups.

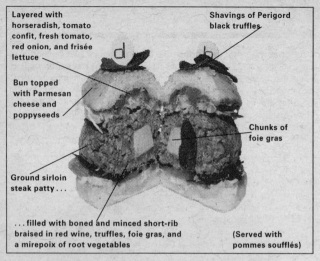

Layered with horseradish, tomato confit, fresh tomato, red onion, and frisée lettuce

Shavings of Perigord black truffles

Bun topped with Parmesan cheese and poppyseeds

Chunks of foie gras

Ground sirloin steak patty...

...filled with boned and minced short-rib braised in red wine, truffles, foie gras, and a mirepoix of root vegetables

(Served with pommes soufflés)

☆ **MOST EXPENSIVE HAMBURGER** The most expensive burger commercially available is the db Double Truffle Burger, created by Chef Daniel Boulud (France) and available on the menu of db Bistro Moderne in New York City for $120.

★ **Largest liquor store** The largest liquor store is Daveco Liquors, owned by Henry Sawaged (U.S.A.) and located in Thornton, Colorado. The store covers an area of 100,073 ft.^{2} (9,297.13 m^2)—enough to accommodate 35 tennis courts!—and was opened on November 18, 2006.

☆ **Fastest rap MC** The fastest rap MC is Rebel XD (a.k.a. Seandale Price, U.S.A.), who rapped 852 syllables in 42 seconds in Chicago, Illinois, on July 27, 2007.

Fastest run up the Empire State Building At the 26th Annual Empire State Building Run-Up in New York, U.S.A., on February 4, 2003, the fastest time, achieved by Paul Crake, (Australia) was 9 min. 33 sec. The **fastest woman to run up the Empire State Building** was Belinda Soszyn (Australia) in 1996, with a time of 12 min. 19 sec. The course covers 1,576 steps up to the 86th floor.

☆ **Highest annual gambling revenue (city)** In the year 2000, the casinos and entertainment complexes of Las Vegas, Nevada, generated an unprecedented $7,673,134,286 in gambling revenue.

☆ **Largest line dance** A total of 17,000 participants performed the *Cupid Shuffle* line dance for eight minutes at the Ebony Black Family Reunion Tour in Atlanta, Georgia, on August 25, 2007.

LARGEST LAND GORGE The Grand Canyon, created over millions of years by the Colorado River in north-central Arizona, extends from Marble Gorge to the Grand Wash Cliffs over a distance of 277 miles (446 km). It reaches a depth of 1 mile (1.6 km), while its width ranges from 0.3–18 miles (0.5 km to 29 km).

☆ **Longest road network** According to the most recent figures (2007), the U.S.A. has 3,997,449 miles (6,433,272 km) of graded roads—enough to circle the Earth at least 160 times!

☆ **Largest corn maze (temporary)** The world's largest temporary corn maze measured an amazing 40.489 acres (16.385 ha) when opened to the public in September 2007 at Coolpatch Pumpkins in Dixon, California. This mammoth project was organized by Mark Cooley (U.S.A.).

Most RIAA certificates ever The recording artist with the greatest number of Recording Industry Association of America (RIAA) certificates is Elvis Presley (U.S.A.), with 262 certified titles (148 gold, 82 platinum, 32 multiplatinum) for both albums and singles.

Greatest prize money won at a rodeo The most prize money won at a single rodeo is $124,821 by Ty Murray (U.S.A.) at the National Finals Rodeo in Las Vegas, Nevada, in 1993.

Greatest range for a light The lights with the greatest range are those 1,089 ft. (332 m) above the ground on the Empire State Building in New York City. Each of the four-arc mercury bulbs is visible 80 miles (130 km) away on the ground and 300 miles (490 km) away from aircraft.

Highest annual sports earnings Football: In 2005, the Atlanta Falcons' quarterback Michael Vick (U.S.A.) earned $37.5 million. Vick signed

LARGEST INFLATABLE PARADE Macy's Annual Thanksgiving Day Parade in New York City is the world's largest inflatable parade, seen by millions of spectators lining the streets and watching on television. On November 22, 2001, the famous parade celebrated its 75th anniversary with 30 larger-than-life balloon characters.

a 10-year, $130-million deal on December 23, 2004, which included a $27 million signing bonus.

Basketball: The Miami Heat's Shaquille O'Neal earned an estimated $33.4 million in 2005.

MOST HIT SINGLES (U.S. CHART) Elvis Presley (U.S.A.) had a record 151 hit singles on the Billboard Hot 100 from 1956 to 2003.

FACT

More than 2.5 million people line the streets of New York City to see the Macy's parade each year. An additional 44 million tune in to watch it on TV.

HEAVIEST STATUE *Liberty Lighting the World,* a.k.a. the Statue of Liberty on Liberty Island, New York City, was presented to the United States by France in 1886 to commemorate liberty and friendship between the nations. The 305-ft. 1-in.-tall (92.99-m) statue weighs a total of 54.3 million lb. (24,635 metric tons), of which 61,729 lb. (28 metric tons) are copper, 250,000 lb. (113 metric tons) are steel, and 53.9 million lb. (24,493 metric tons) are the concrete in the pedestal.

MEXICO

AT A GLANCE •AREA: 761,605 miles² (1,972,550 km²)
•POPULATION: 108,700,891
•DENSITY: 142 people/mile²; (55 people/km²)
•KEY FACTS: Mexico cradles the Gulf of Mexico, the world's **largest gulf,** at 596,000 miles² (1,544,000 km²) and with a shoreline of 3,100 miles (5,000 km). The 1,933-mile (3,110-km) border the country shares with the U.S.A is the world's **most crossed border:** in 2000, more than 290 million people crossed from Mexico into the U.S.A. Just over 10 years ago, Mexico City, the capital, was the largest conurbation in the world, with a population of 16,908,000. Today, this record is held by Tokyo. *(See p. 524.)*

MOST DEATHS CAUSED BY SCORPION STINGS In 1946, a total of 1,933 people died in Mexico as a result of scorpion stings—more than in any other country in a single year. As many as 1,000 people, mostly children, still die every year.

Shortest presidency Pedro Lascurain (Mexico) governed his country for one hour on February 18, 1913, as successor to Francisco Madero (Mexico), who was murdered on February 13, 1913. The vice-president of Mexico was disqualified as he was under arrest at the time and thus Lascurain was sworn in, appointed general Victoriano Huerta (Mexico) as his successor, then resigned.

LARGEST COLONY OF MAMMALS The black-tailed prairie dog (*Cynomys ludovicianus*), a rodent of the family Sciuridae found in the western U.S.A. and northern Mexico, builds large colonies. One single "town" discovered in 1901 contained about 400 million individuals and was estimated to cover 23,705 miles^2 (61,400 km^2)—almost the size of Ireland—making it the largest colony of mammals ever recorded.

LARGEST PYRAMID In terms of volume, the largest monument ever constructed, and the largest pyramid, is the Quetzalcóatl Pyramid at Cholula de Rivadavia, 63 miles (101 km) southeast of Mexico City. It is 177 ft. (54 m) tall, and its base covers nearly 45 acres (18.2 ha). Its total volume is an estimated 166.5 million ft.³ (3.3 million m³).

★**Largest taco** A taco weighing 1,654 lb. (750 kg) was made by the city of Mexicali and Cocinex SA de CV, in Baja California on March 8, 2003. A taco is a traditional Mexican dish: a rolled maize tortilla with a filling.

FASTEST LAND MAMMAL (LONG DISTANCE) The pronghorn (*Antilocapra americana*) is the fastest land animal over long distances. These antelope-like ungulates have been observed traveling at 35 mph (56 km/h) for up to 4 miles (6 km). They are found in the western U.S.A., southwestern Canada, and parts of northern Mexico. (*For the fastest mammal on land over short distances, see p. 57.*)

CENTRAL AMERICA & THE CARIBBEAN

Shortest snake The very rare thread snake (*Leptotyphlops bilineata*), known only from Martinique, Barbados, and St. Lucia, has such a matchstick-thin body that it could enter the hole left in a standard pencil after the lead has been removed. The longest known specimen measured only 4.25 in. (10.8 cm).

Longest cigar A cigar measuring 135 ft. 2 in. (41.2 m) was hand-rolled by Patricio Peña (Puerto Rico) and his team from Don Ray Cigars in Fort Buchanan, Puerto Rico, from February 13 to 15, 2007.

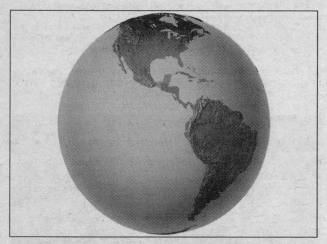

AT A GLANCE •**AREA**: Central America: 202,232 mile² (523,780 km²); Caribbean: 49,325 mile² (127,753 km²)
•**POPULATION**: C. America: 44,934,014; Caribbean: 22,636,621 (2007 est.)
•**DENSITY**: 268 people/mile²; 103 people/km²
•**COUNTRIES**: C. America: Belize, Costa Rica, El Salvador, Guatemala, Honduras, Nicaragua, Panama; Caribbean: Anguila, Antigua and Barbuda, Aruba, The Bahamas, Barbados, British Virgin Is., Cayman Is., Cuba, Dominica, Dominican Republic, Grenada, Guadeloupe, Haiti, Jamaica, Martinique, Montserrat, Netherlands Antilles, Puerto Rico, St. Barthélemy, Kitts & Nevis, St. Lucia, St. Martin, St. Vincent & the Grenadines, Trinidad & Tobago, Turks & Caicos, U.S. Virgin Islands.

Fidel Castro (Cuba), president of Cuba's Council of State, is the longest-serving non-royal head of state. He was Cuba's unchallenged revolutionary and political leader from July 26, 1959 (when his guerrilla movement, led by Latin American revolutionary Che Guevara, overthrew the island-state's military dictatorship), until his announced retirement on February 19, 2008—a total of 48 years 208 days. (Castro became president of Cuba when the post of premier was abolished in 1976.) Castro is also known for the **longest UN speech.** On September 26, 1960, he addressed the United Nations for 4 hr. 29 min.

In 2006, Fabian Escalante (Cuba), a bodyguard assigned to protect Castro, announced that the president had survived 638 assassination attempts— **the most failed assassinations** on the life of any person.

Most intense rainfall While rainfall readings for very short periods are difficult to collect, the figure of 1.5 in. (38.1 mm) in one minute at Basse Terre, Guadeloupe on November 26, 1970, is regarded as the most intense recorded using modern methods.

DEEPEST BLUE HOLE Dean's Blue Hole is a 250-ft.-wide (76-m) vertical shaft that plunges 663 ft. (202 m) at Turtle Cove near Clarence Town on the Atlantic edge of The Bahamas. Lying just a few steps offshore, it contains 11.8 million ft.³ (1.1 million m³) of water and is the second largest water-filled cavern on the planet. Blue holes are found at or just below sea level and were once caves that filled with water as the icecaps melted and the water levels rose during the last ice age.

★ OLDEST BRIDES & GROOMS Of the 2,628 marriages in The Bahamas in 1996, 73.9% of the brides were aged 30 or over, as were 86% of the bridegrooms.

Oldest artist to have a million-seller Cuban singer/guitarist Compay Segundo sold over one million albums around the world after his 88th birthday in 1995. He first recorded in the 1930s, but found new fame as a member of the Buena Vista Social Club in 1996.

RAREST LIZARD The Jamaican iguana (*Cyclura collei*) is a critically endangered species, only rediscovered in 1990. With no more than 100 adult specimens existing, it is clinging to survival in southern Jamaica's remote Hellshire Hills—the only sizable area of primary dry forest remaining on the island, but under threat from charcoal burners.

SOUTH AMERICA

★**Fastest guitar player** José del Rio (Chile) played "Dueling Banjos" on the guitar at a speed of 250 beats per minute in Las Condes, Santiago, Chile, on April 9, 2006.

☆**Highest altitude concert on land** Musikkapelle Roggenzell—a group of 10 musicians from Germany and Bolivia—successfully staged the highest concert on land when they played at 19,911 ft. (6,069 m) on Mount Acotango, Bolivia, on August 6, 2007.

☆**Largest swimming pool by area** The San Alfonso del Mar seawater pool in Algarrobo, Chile, is 3,324 ft. (1,013 m) long and has an area of 19.77 acres (8 ha)—larger than 15 American football fields!

Largest attendance at a stadium A crowd of 199,854 attended the Brazil vs. Uruguay World Cup Final match in the Maracanã Municipal Stadium, Rio de Janeiro, Brazil, on July 16, 1950. Uruguay won 2–1.

AT A GLANCE •AREA: 6,888,062 miles² (17,840,000 km²)
•POPULATION: 371 million
•DENSITY: 53.8 people/mile² (20.8 people/km²)
•KEY FACTS: The South American continent (which does *not* include Central America) covers 3.5% of our planet's surface.
•COUNTRIES: Argentina; Bolivia (home of the world's **largest land-locked navy,** with 4,800 personnel as of 2006); Brazil (the largest country in the continent, the world's **most forested country,** and the only Portuguese-speaking country in the Americas); Chile; Colombia (infamously the country with the **highest rates of kidnapping** and the **largest producer of cocaine**); Ecuador (☆**highest murder rate**); French Guiana; Guyana; Paraguay; Peru; Suriname; Uruguay; and Venezuela (**most wins of the Miss World beauty competition**).

HIGHEST FOOD CONSUMPTION
According to the latest figures published in the Britannica Yearbook 2000, Argentina has the highest food consumption with each citizen consuming 183% of the United Nations Food and Agriculture Organization's (FAO) recommended requirements. This figure was recorded in 1996.

☆**Largest bingo hall** A game of bingo involving 70,080 participants took place at an event organized by Almacenes Exito S.A. in Bogotá, Colombia, on December 2, 2006.

Fewest theaters per population Suriname, with a population of 436,494, has only one movie theater, which is located in the capital, Paramaribo. In 1997, this theater saw a total of 103,626 admissions.

Highest and longest passenger cable car The Teleférico Mérida, in Venezuela, travels from Mérida City, at 5,379 ft. (1,639.5 m) above sea level, to the summit of Pico Espejo, at 15,629 ft. (4,763.7 m), a rise of 10,250 ft. (3,124 m).

☆**Longest reading aloud marathon (team)** A team comprising Milton Nan, Silvina Carbone, Yolanda Baptista, Carlos Antón, Edit Díaz, and

WORST DESTRUCTION OF THE NATURAL ENVIRONMENT BY FIRE Deliberately started forest fires made 1997 the worst year in recorded history for the destruction of the natural environment. The largest and most numerous were in Brazil, where they raged on a 1,000-mile (1,600-km) front.

DRIEST PLACE For the period between 1964 and 2001, the average annual rainfall for the meteorological station in Quillagua, in the Atacama Desert, Chile, was just 0.5 mm. This discovery was made during the making of the documentary series *Going to Extremes*, by Keo Films, in 2001.

Natalie Dantaz (all Uruguay) read aloud for 224 hours at Mac Center Shopping, Paysandú, Uruguay, between September 13 and 22, 2007.

★**Most dangerous road** The road considered by many to be the most lethal in the world is the North Yungas Road that runs for 43 miles (69 km) from La Paz to Coroico in Bolivia. It is responsible for up to 300 deaths annually, which works out at 6.9 deaths per mile (4.3 per km). For the majority of the stretch, the single-lane mud road (with two-way traffic) has an unbarricaded vertical drop measuring 15,420 ft. (4,700 m) at its highest. Not surprisingly, the road is at its most deadly during the rainy season!

Most southerly birth At the time of his birth, Emilio Marcos Palma (Argentina), born January 7, 1978, at the Sargento Cabral Base, Antarctica,

☆ **MOST SURFERS RIDING THE SAME WAVE SIMULTANEOUSLY** Rico de Souza (Brazil) led 84 surfers riding the same wave simultaneously at Santos Beach in Santos, Sao Paulo, Brazil, on September 2, 2007.

★ **FIRST PERSON SHOT BY A GUN IN THE AMERICAS** A young Inca, who is believed to have been shot by a Spanish conquistador during the siege of Lima (in present-day Peru) in 1536, is the earliest-known victim of a gunshot wound in the New World. (*See box below.*)

could claim to be the first and only child to be born on the icy southern continent.

Most southerly village Puerto Williams (pop. 1,600 in 1996) on the north coast of Isla Navarino, in Tierra del Fuego, Chile, is 677 miles (1,090 km) north of Antarctica.

Most successful lawyer Sir Lionel Luckhoo (b. March 2, 1914), senior partner of Luckhoo and Luckhoo of Georgetown, Guyana, succeeded in getting 245 successive murder-charge acquittals between 1940 and 1985.

Tree bearing most different fruit species In 2000, Luis H. Carrasco E. of Lo Barnechea, Santiago, Chile, grafted five different fruit species onto a single prune tree. The tree later successfully produced apricots, cherries, nectarines, plums, and peaches.

Fastest goal in a world cup finals by a substitute Uruguay's Richard Morales scored just 18 seconds after coming on against Senegal at the 2002 World Cup in Suwon, South Korea, on June 11, 2002.

Widest road The Monumental Axis runs for 1.8 miles (2.4 km) through Brasilia, Brazil. The six-lane boulevard was opened in April 1960 and is 820 ft. 2 in. (250 m) wide.

UNEARTHING THE VICTIM

Excavation work by archeologists in Puruchuco, Lima, Peru, led by Guillermo Cock (Peru), unearthed the body of the young Inca with 71 others in a mass grave. Close forensic examination of the victim discovered traces of iron on the edges of two round holes in the skull, which was believed to be the iron of a musket ball, a weapon widely used by the conquistadors. Exit damage was also found in the face where the bullet left the head. The skeleton was discovered in 2004 and announced by *National Geographic* in June 2007.

★ MOST ENDANGERED TRIBES
According to a report published in August 2003 by Survival International, the worldwide organization supporting tribal peoples, the three tribes currently facing the greatest threat to their survival are the Ayoreo-Totobiegosode (pop. 5,000) of western Paraguay (pictured), the Gana and Gwi "Bushmen" (pop. 100,000) in Botswana, and the Jarawa tribe (pop. 200–300) from the Andaman Islands in the Indian Ocean.

LARGEST LAGOON Lagoa dos Patos, located along the seashore in Rio Grande do Sul, southernmost Brazil, is 174 miles (280 km) long and extends over 3,803 miles² (9,850 km²). It is separated from the Atlantic Ocean by long sand strips, and has a maximum width of 44 miles (70 km).

CANADA

Largest shopping mall The enormous West Edmonton Mall in Alberta covers 5.3 million ft.² (492,386 m²)—the equivalent of 48 city blocks or 115 football fields—and cost CAN$1.2 billion ($92 million) to build. It features more than 800 stores and 110 food outlets.

The mall opened on September 15, 1981. Parking for over 20,000 vehicles (plus an overflow capacity for another 10,000) is provided in the world's

AT A GLANCE •AREA: 3,855,102 miles² (9,984,670 km²)
•POPULATION: 33,390,141
•DENSITY: 8.6 people/mile² (3.3 people/km²)
•KEY FACTS: Canada is the world's second-largest country and one of the most sparsely populated—only about half of the country is developed, with the north still an untouched wilderness. Hudson Bay is the largest bay in the world, with a shoreline of 7,623 miles (12,268 km) and covering an area of about 476,000 miles² (1,233,000 km²), and the Davis Strait between Baffin Island in Canada and Greenland is, at 210 miles (388 km), the world's widest strait. Beyond its natural wonders, Canada boasts the world's largest shopping center—the West Edmonton Mall, with over 800 stores (see p. 467)—and the CN Tower, the largest freestanding tower (see p. 471).

largest parking lot. The mall also includes Galaxyland, the largest indoor amusement park, which at 400,000 ft.² (37,200 m²) holds 30 skill games and 27 rides and attractions, including *Mindbender*, a 14-story, triple-loop roller coaster, and *Drop of Doom*, a 13-story free-fall ride.

★Longest winter road The "Wapusk Trail" road is 467 miles (752 km) in length and is constructed each year between Gillam, Manitoba, and Peawanuk, Ontario. It gives road access for a few weeks to remote settlements around Hudson Bay until warmer March weather forces its closure. These settlements are normally only accessible by air.

☆Largest smoothie The largest smoothie contained 155 gallons (681.92 liters) of bananas, strawberries, sorbet, ice, and fruit juice, and was made by Frank and Simon Voisin (Canada) of Booster Juice juice and smoothie bar, London, Ontario, on July 22, 2006.

LARGEST ISLAND MADE BY HUMAN INTERVENTION The largest island
created as a result of human action is the Ile Rene-Lavasseur in
Manicouagan Reservoir, Quebec. It measures 780 mile^2 (2,020 km^2) in
size, so the whole of New York City could fit onto it 2.5 times. It was
formed after a river was dammed, flooding a 210-million-year-old
meteor crater. The central uplift of the meteor crater forms the island.

MOST ART ROSS TROPHIES The Art Ross Trophy is awarded each year
to the player who has scored the most points in National Hockey
League regular season play. Wayne Gretzky (Canada) won an
unprecedented 10 Art Ross Trophies between 1981 and 1994.

LONGEST BOUNDARY The boundary between Canada and the United States, when including the Great Lakes boundaries, extends for 3,986 miles (6,416 km), but excludes the frontier of 1,582 miles (2,547 km) with Alaska. If the Alaskan boundary is added, the Canada–U.S.A. boundary is 5,568 miles (8,963 km) long in total.

LARGEST NATURALLY FROZEN ICE RINK The Rideau Canal Skateway in Ottawa, Ontario, is 4.8 miles (7.8 km) long and has a total maintained surface area of 1.782 million ft.² (165,621 m²), which is equivalent to 90 Olympic-size skating rinks.

★ **Most consecutive renditions of a national anthem** The Canadian national anthem was performed 607 times consecutively by members of Magic Feet Canada at Harborfront Center, Toronto, Ontario, on July 1, 2000.

Largest admission ticket The largest admission ticket is 56 × 19 in. (142 × 50 cm) and was created by Canada's National Arts Centre for entrance to the Hope and Glory concert in Ottawa on February 8, 2007.

★ **Fastest run across Canada by a woman** Ann Keane (Canada) ran across the country from St. John's, Newfoundland, to Tofino, British Columbia, in 143 days between April 17 and September 8, 2002. She covered a total of 4,866 miles (7,831 km).

FACT

Officially known as the International Boundary, the Canada–U.S.A. border must be kept clear of brush and vegetation for 20 ft. (6 m)—or 10 ft. (3 m) on both sides of the line—as seen above.

TALLEST FREESTANDING TOWER
The CN Tower in Toronto rises to a height of 1,815 ft. 5 in. (553.34 m). Excavation for work on the 286,600-lb. (130,000-metric ton), reinforced, post-tensioned concrete structure began in February 1973, and it was finally "topped out" on April 2, 1975.

CN Tower—visitor's guide

- *The Tower took 40 months to complete, finally opening to the public in June 1976. In total, 1,537 workers labored five days a week, 24 hours a day, to get the job done.*
- *It can survive an earthquake of 8.5 on the Richter scale, and the upper reaches can withstand winds of up to 260 mph (418 km/h).*
- *On a clear day, visitors can see for more than 100 miles (160 km) from the observation deck—all the way to Niagara Falls and across to New York State.*
- *The 360 Restaurant, situated around two-thirds of the way up, makes a complete rotation every 72 minutes.*
- *The CN Tower is double the height of the iconic Eiffel Tower in Paris, France!*

TOWER TREATS

The lofty CN Tower has hosted many record-breaking attempts over the years. The **longest descent down the side of a building** was one of 1,465 ft. (446.5 m), by two teams of 12. All 24 people rappelled from the Space Deck of the Tower to the ground on July 1, 1992. The world's **highest wine cellar** is the Tower's "Cellar in the Sky," located 1,151 ft. (351 m) above Toronto. Lastly, the **fastest time to pogo-stick jump up the CN Tower** is 57 min. 51 sec., achieved by Ashrita Furman (U.S.A.) on July 23, 1999.

☆**Fastest marathon skipping** The record for the fastest marathon run while skipping with a rope is 4 hr. 28 min. 48 sec. and was set by Chris Baron (Canada) at the ING Ottawa Marathon, Ontario, on May 27, 2007.

Highest tide ever A tide range of 54 ft. 6 in. (16.6 m) was recorded at springs in Leaf Basin in Ungava Bay, Quebec, in 1953.

UK & IRELAND

★**Largest Highland dance** The largest Highland dance involved 1,453 participants from five schools in the Nairn region of Scotland, UK. They danced the *Dashing White Sergeant* for an event organized by Nairn Associated Schools Group to celebrate the Highland Year of Culture 2007 at Nairn Links, Scotland, on June 22, 2007.

AT A GLANCE • AREA: UK 94,525 miles² (244,820 km²); **Ireland** 27,135 miles² (70,280 km²)
•**POPULATION: UK** 60.7 million; **Ireland** 4.1 million
•**DENSITY: UK** 643 people/mile² (248 people/km²); **Ireland** 9 people/mile² (3.5 people/km²)
•**KEY FACTS: The United Kingdom** comprises Great Britain (England, Scotland, and Wales) and Northern Ireland (occupying one-sixth of the island of Ireland). The country of **Ireland** (or Eire, to use its local short form) occupies five-sixths of the island of Ireland.
   The British Empire was the **largest empire** of all time, covering 14.1 million miles² (36.6 million km²)—about a quarter of the Earth's surface—at the height of its power (1917–22).

★Largest morris dance A morris dance involving 88 participants was organized by The Moreton-in-Marsh Show in Gloucestershire, UK, on September 1, 2007.

☆Most movies seen Gwilym Hughes (UK) of Gwynedd, Wales, saw his first movie, *King Solomon's Mines* (U.S.A., 1950), in 1953. Since then, he has kept a diary of all the movies he has seen, and has logged a total of 28,074 different movies as of March 13, 2008.

★Largest bowl of porridge A bowl of porridge weighing 179 lb. 14 oz. (81.6 kg) was served at the Edinburgh Farmers' Market in Edinburgh, Scotland, UK, on September 15, 2007.

★Most expensive antique car sold at auction An anonymous British collector paid £3,521,500 ($7,242,916) for the world's oldest surviving Rolls-Royce, numbered 20154, making it the most expensive antique (pre-1905) car. The two-seater, 10-hp automobile, manufactured in Manchester, UK, in 1904, was sold by Bonhams in London, UK, on December 3, 2007.

Most tornadoes (area) Incredibly, the UK is the world's tornado hotspot, hit by a record of one tornado per 2,856 mile² (7,397 km²). The equivalent figure for the U.S.A. is one tornado per 3,345 mile² (8,663 km²).

★Largest same-name gathering (last name) On September 9, 2007, a total of 1,488 people who all shared the surname Gallagher gathered together in Letterkenny, Ireland.

★LONGEST REIGN (LIVING QUEEN) The longest-reigning living queen is Her Majesty Queen Elizabeth II (b. April 21, 1926), who succeeded to the throne on February 6, 1952, on the death of her father, King George VI. Elizabeth II is queen of the UK and head of the Commonwealth.

FASTEST TAP DANCE The fastest rate ever measured for tap dancing is 38 taps per second, by James Devine of Ardnacrusha, County Clare, Ireland, on May 25, 1998. Devine beat the record of 35 taps per second by "Lord of the Dance" Michael Flatley (U.S.A.).

★**Tallest windmill** St. Patrick's Distillery Mill in Dublin, Ireland, has the tallest windmill in the world. Now without sails, the mill is 150 ft. (45.7 m) tall.

☆**Longest Riverdance line** The world record for the longest "Riverdance" line was 216, achieved by CLRG Dance Schools, Leinster Province, at St. Stephens Green, Dublin, Ireland, on November 8 in the celebrations for Guinness World Records Day 2007.

Smallest crystal bowl A crystal bowl made by Jim Irish (Ireland), a former master cutter at Waterford Crystal, measured 0.33 in. (8.55 mm) wide, 0.18 in. (4.6 mm) tall, 0.08 in. (2.1 mm) thick, and was made with 208 cuts.

Longest dance party Unique Events Limited (Ireland) organized a dance party at the Quay Front, Wexford, Ireland, that began on October 27, 2006, at midday with 40 dancers, and finished 55 hours later with 31 exhausted dancers still on their feet!

FASTEST TIME TO PLUCK A TURKEY Vincent Pilkington of Cootehill, County Cavan, Ireland, plucked a turkey in 1 min. 30 sec. on RTE television in Dublin, Ireland, on November 17, 1980. Despite the 29 years that have passed since Vincent set this record, his achievement has yet to be bettered.

★ **FIRST FEMALE BEEFEATER** The first female Beefeater is Moira Cameron (UK), who was appointed as Yeoman Warder of Her Majesty's Royal Palace and Fortress the Tower of London, UK, in January 2007. Historically a male role, Beefeaters are ceremonial guardians of the Tower of London, whose traditional purpose was to oversee prisoners being held there and to safeguard the British crown jewels. Today, however, Yeoman Warder Cameron's duties include the Ceremony of the Keys (the nightly locking of the gates) and knowing the 1,000-year history of the tower so she can conduct Beefeater tours.

☆ **MOST PUBS VISITED** As of December 9, 2006, Bruce Masters (UK) had visited 40,000 pubs and bars since 1960, sampling the local brew where available.

DID YOU KNOW?

Bruce made his 40,000th pub visit at the Bull's Head in Ranmoor, Sheffield, UK. The picture above was taken at The Red Lion pub in Hernhill, Kent, UK.

LARGEST TRILITHONS Stonehenge on Salisbury Plain, UK, has the world's largest trilithons (structures made from two large vertical stones supporting a third stone set across the top), with a series of sarsen blocks weighing over 99,208 lb. (45 metric tons) each. The tallest upright stone in the prehistoric monument is 22 ft. (6.7 m) high, with another 8 ft. (2.4 m) below ground. The first stage in the stone circle has been dated to 2950 B.C.

FRANCE

First manned flight Frenchman François Pilâtre de Rozier is regarded as the first person to have flown. On October 15, 1783, he rose 84 ft. (26 m) into the air in a tethered hot-air balloon built by the inventors Joseph and Jacques Montgolfier (France).

☆ **MOST NATIONALITIES SERVING IN ONE MILITARY FORCE** As of July 2007, the French Foreign Legion had 7,655 men serving in its ranks, with a diverse range of nationalities from 136 countries.

AT A GLANCE •AREA: 211,209 miles² (547,030 km²)
•**POPULATION:** 60.8 million
•**DENSITY:** 287 people/mile² (111 people/km²)
•**KEY FACTS:** France is the world's **most popular tourist
destination**, attracting 79.1 million international visitors in 2006. A
total of 49,733 people applied for asylum in France in 2005, the ☆ **most
applications received for political asylum by one country.**

France is a nation of wine lovers, so it is perhaps unsurprising that
the **most expensive commercially available wine** is French—the
Chateau d'Yquem Sauternes of 1787, a sweet dessert wine from
Bordeaux, priced at an average of $60,000.

And the **most expensive wine per glass?** Again, it's French: Robert
Denby (UK) paid FF8,600 ($1,382.80) for the first glass of Beaujolais
Nouveau 1993, released in Beaune (from Maison Jaffelin), in the wine
region of Burgundy, France. It was purchased at Pickwick's, a British
pub in Beaune, on November 18, 1993.

First cinema The Cinématographe Lumière at the Salon Indien—a former billiard hall in the Grand Café, 14 Boulevard de Capucines, Paris,
opened on December 28, 1895.

Heaviest chocolate truffle On November 30, 2001, Alain Benier
(France) presented a chocolate truffle weighing 220.4 lb. (100 kg) on the set
of *L'Émission des Records* in Paris.

DID YOU KNOW?

The **highest average speed by a train over a distance of 1,000 km** (621
miles) is 306.37 km/h (190.37 mph), by an unmodified SNCF TGV train
between Calais and Marseille on May 26, 2001.

☆ **FASTEST TRAIN ON A NATIONAL RAILWAY** A French SNCF modified version of the TGV called V150 (with larger wheels than usual and two engines) reached a speed of 574.8 km/h (357.2 mph) on April 3, 2007.

★ **MOST EXPENSIVE WEAPON SOLD AT AUCTION** A sword used by the Emperor Napoléon Bonaparte secured the sum of €4.8 million ($6.5 million) at an auction held in Fontainebleau on June 10, 2007.

★ **Fastest moving walkway** A high-speed moving walkway (or travelator) at Montparnasse metro station in Paris, moves commuters at 5.6 mph (9 km/h), around three times as fast as regular moving sidewalks. The 590-ft.-long (180-m) walkway was installed in 2003.

ITALY

★ **Largest pancetta** The Commune de Ponte dell'Olio and the Piacenza Chamber of Commerce, Piacenza, created a pancetta (a cured pork belly roll) weighing 331 lb. 12 oz. (150.5 kg). It was displayed at the Pancetta Festival in Ponte dell'Olio on June 23, 2002.

AT A GLANCE •**AREA**: 116,305 miles² (301,230 km²)
•**POPULATION**: 58.1 million
•**DENSITY**: 499 people/mile² (192 people/km²)
•**KEY FACTS**: It's no surprise that Italy holds the record for the
★**longest pizza**. A team of chefs led by Umberto Mosti (Italy), owner
of the Pizzeria Fornaretto in Massa, Italy, created a 1,329-ft. 11-in.
(407.37-m) pizza on October 4, 2007. *Il bel paese* is also home to Mt.
Stromboli, in the Tyrrhenian Sea, the **longest continuously erupting
volcano**, which has undergone continuous eruptions since at least the
7th century B.C. Its regular mild explosions of gas and lava—usually
several each hour—have earned it the nickname "Lighthouse of the
Mediterranean."

Most F1 Grand Prix wins by a manufacturer The greatest number of
grand prix wins in Formula One by a constructor is 201 by Ferrari (Italy) between 1951 and 2007.

Fastest goal in a Champions League final Paolo Maldini (Italy)
scored a goal for AC Milan against Liverpool in just 52 seconds in the
Champions League final on May 25, 2005.

LARGEST AMPHITHEATER The
Flavian amphitheater or
Colosseum of Rome,
completed in A.D. 80, covers an
area of 5 acres (2 ha) and has a
capacity of 87,000. It has a
maximum length of 612 ft.
(187 m) and a maximum width
of 515 ft. (157 m).

★ LARGEST CAZŌLA A cazōla is a traditional Italian dish much like a stew, comprising pork ribs, bacon, sausages, and vegetables. The largest cazōla was created by 10 volunteers from the town of Ossona, and weighed 2,053 lb. 6 oz. (931.46 kg). It was displayed at the Piazza Litta, Ossona, on August 24, 2002.

☆ **Largest soccer shirt** A soccer shirt measuring 224 ft. 8 in. × 232 ft. 11 in. (68.50 × 71 m) was created by ERREA for KONAMI to mark the launch of ProEvolution Soccer 2008 in an event organized by Brand2Live at the Arena Civica, in Milan on December 18, 2007.

OLDEST SCOOTER MANUFACTURER Piaggio of Italy is the producer of the famous Vespa. The prototype Vespa scooter was tested and approved in December 1945, with production beginning in April 1946.

Best-selling classical music album *In Concert*—recorded by José Carreras, Placido Domingo, and Luciano Pavarotti (all Italy) in Rome on July 7, 1990, during the 1990 World Cup Finals held in Italy—has registered global sales of 10.5 million copies to date.

☆**Longest radio DJ marathon** Stefano Venneri (Italy) DJ'd for 135 hours on Radio BBSI in Alessandria from April 21 to 26, 2007.

SPAIN

☆**Largest commercial jigsaw puzzle** EDUCA of Barcelona makes a puzzle consisting of 24,000 pieces.

AT A GLANCE •**AREA**: 194,897 miles² (504,782 km²)
•**POPULATION**: 40,448,191
•**DENSITY**: 207 people/mile² (80 people/km²)
•**KEY FACTS**: Spain is the world's **leading cultivator of olives,** producing a grand total of 2.1 billion lb. (970,000 metric tons) a year. Principal olive-producing regions are Catalonia and Andalusia, Spain and Italy together account for 54% of the total amount of olive oil produced worldwide.

The Casa Botín, in Madrid, Spain, is regarded as the **oldest restaurant** in the world. It has been in operation continuously since it opened in 1725.

Continuing the food theme, Spain holds the record for the **largest paella.** Juan Carlos Galbis (Spain) and a team of helpers created a paella measuring 65 ft. 7 in. (20 m) in diameter in Valencia, on March 8, 1992. It was eaten by 100,000 people.

LARGEST FOOD FIGHT On the last Wednesday in August, the town of Buñol, near Valencia, holds its annual tomato festival, La Tomatina. In 2004, 38,000 people spent one hour at this giant food fight, throwing about 275,500 lb. (125 metric tons) of tomatoes at each other. Now a tourist attraction in its own right, the festival attracts over three times the town's population of 9,000.

★**Longest chorizo** A 361-ft. 4-in.-long (110.15-m) chorizo was created by mayor Manuel Alberto Pardellas Álvarez and the Concello de Melón, in Melón, Ourense, on February 25, 2007.

☆**Largest French press** Salzillo Tea and Coffee (Spain) created a French press 7 ft. 6 in. (230 cm) tall and 2 ft. 4 in. (72 cm) in diameter in Murcia in February 2007.

Largest castanet dance (JOTA) A total of 157 mixed couples performed the traditional folk dance *The Jota of Aragon* for eight minutes in Zaragoza on May 18, 2003.

Largest nightclub Privilege nightclub in San Rafael, Ibiza can hold up to 10,000 people and covers an area of 69,940 ft.^{2} (6,500 m^2).

★**Most botijos** Jesús Gil-Gilbernau del Río of Logroño has collected more than 3,000 botijos (traditional Spanish drinking vessels with two spouts and a handle).

FACT

La Tomatina has been held every year since 1944. After the battle, participants walk to the riverbank, where makeshift public showers are provided.

★ MOST PARTICIPANTS IN A ROLE-PLAYING GAME A total of 483 people from the Irmandiños a Revolta group took part in a massive role-playing game in Monterrei, from October 5 to 7, 2007.

☆ LARGEST SAND PAINTING A sand painting measuring 9,250 ft.² (859 m²) was created in the town square of La Oratava, Tenerife, for its patron saint day festivities on June 13, 2007.

☆ LARGEST WATER-PISTOL FIGHT A record 2,671 participants took a soaking in the world's largest water-pistol fight. The event was organized by the Coordinadora de Peñas de Valladolid in Valladolid on September 14, 2007, as part of the annual celebrations for the patron of Valladolid, the capital of Spain's largest province, Castile-Leon.

PORTUGAL

★**Largest pocketknife** Designed by Telmo Cadavez and handmade by Virgílio, Raúl, and Manuel Pires (all Portugal), the largest pocketknife measures 12 ft. 8 in. (3.9 m) when open, and weighs 268 lb. 14 oz. (122 kg).

☆**Largest car mosaic** Realizar S.A. and Smart Advertising (both Portugal) co-produced a car mosaic comprising of 253 Smart cars at Mundo Dakar on December 9, 2007. The event was organized by Euro RSCG for Jogos Santa Casa in Lisbon.

☆**Longest Mexican wave** On August 12, 2007, a Mexican wave involving 8,453 participants was organized by Realizar Impact Marketing at the Parque das Nações in Lisbon.

Largest acoustic guitar The largest playable acoustic guitar measures 59 ft. 11 in. (16.75 m) long, 24 ft. 10 in. (7.57 m) wide, and 8 ft. 9 in.

AT A GLANCE •AREA: 35,672 miles² (92,391 km²)
•**POPULATION**: 10,642,836
•**DENSITY**: 298 people/mile² (115 people/km²)
•**KEY FACTS**: With 7,711 ft. (2,351 m) above the sea's surface and 20,000 ft. (6,098 m) below, Monte Pico in Portugal's Azores Islands is the world's **highest underwater mountain**.
  Crown Prince Luis Filipe of Portugal was technically king of Portugal (Dom Luis III) for approximately 20 minutes on February 1, 1908. His father was shot dead in the streets of Lisbon, and the crown prince was mortally wounded at the same time. Although it would have been little consolation, this gave him the record for the **shortest reign ever.**

MOST CORK FOREST At 1,791,514 acres (725,000 ha), Portugal's cork-oak forests account for 33% of the world total. This represents 51% of global cork production.

(2.67 m) deep. The instrument was built by Realizar Eventos Especiais and weighs 8,818 lb. (4 metric tons).

Largest patchwork quilt The world's largest patchwork quilt measures an impressive 270,174 ft.² (25,100 m²) and is called *Manta da Cultura* (*Patchwork for Culture*). The project was carried out by Realizar Eventos Especiais of Parque da Cidade, Porto, and was completed on June 18, 2000.

Largest fireworks display Macedo's Pirotecnia Lda, presented a fireworks display consisting of 66,326 fireworks in Funchal, Madeira, on December 31, 2006.

☆ **Most paper aircraft launched simultaneously** A total of 12,672 paper aircraft were launched simultaneously on November 2, 2007, at an event organized by Realizar Impact Marketing and FC Porto at the Dragao Stadium in Porto.

MOST WIDELY SUPPORTED FOOTBALL CLUB Sport Lisboa e Benfica, Portugal, has 160,398 paid-up members. The record was acknowledged on November 9, 2006 during celebrations for Guinness World Records Day.

☆ **OLDEST MOVIE DIRECTOR** Manoel de Oliveira (Portugal, b. December 1908), who began directing movies in 1931, made his most recent film, *Cristóvão Colombo—O Enigma* (Portugal, 2007), at the age of 99 years 2 days.

NORDIC COUNTRIES

★ **Longest-lived animal** The oldest known (noncolonial) animal was a quahog clam (*Arctica islandica*) that had been living on the seabed off the north coast of Iceland until it was dredged by researchers from Bangor University's School of Ocean Sciences, UK, in 2006. On October 28, 2007, sclerochronologists from the university declared that the clam was 405–410 years old.

The clam was nicknamed "Ming," for the Chinese dynasty that was in power when it was born.

Most victories at Le Mans The greatest number of wins by an individual at the Le Mans 24-hour race is seven by Tom Kristensen (Denmark) in 1997 and 2000–05.

Highest annual movie attendance Iceland registers greater movie attendance per capita than any other country, with 5.45 visits per person in 2004. The country has 46 theaters, which in 2003 saw 1,531,000 admissions.

AT A GLANCE
SWEDEN
- **AREA**: 173,732 miles^2 (449,964 km^2)
- **POPULATION**: 9 million
- **DENSITY**: 51 people/mile^2 (20 people/km^2)

FINLAND
- **AREA**: 130,558 miles^2 (338,145 km^2)
- **POPULATION**: 5.2 million
- **DENSITY**: 39 people/mile^2 (15 people/km^2)

NORWAY
- **AREA**: 125,020 miles^2 (323,802 km^2)
- **POPULATION**: 4.6 million
- **DENSITY**: 36 people/mile^2 (14 people/km^2)

ICELAND
- **AREA**: 39,768 miles^2 (103,000 km^2)
- **POPULATION**: 304,367
- **DENSITY**: 7.5 people/mile^2 (2.9 people/km^2)

DENMARK
- **AREA**: 16,638 miles^2 (43,094 km^2)
- **POPULATION**: 5.4 million
- **DENSITY**: 324 people/mile^2 (125 people/km^2)

Most Formula One fastest laps in a season Mika Hakkinen (Finland) scored a total of nine fastest lap times in the 2000 Formula One season.

DID YOU KNOW?

Iceland is the country with the **lowest military spending per capita.**
According to the *CIA World Factbook,* Iceland spent $0 (£0) on the military as of 2005.

MOST NORTHERLY CAPITAL CITY The most northerly city—and the northernmost national capital—is Reykjavik, Iceland (64°08'N), which had a population of 113,387 in 2003.

The most northerly capital of a dependency is Nuuk (formerly Godthåb), Greenland (64°15'N). Its population was 15,047 in 2007.

Most Olympic athletics medals (male) Paavo Nurmi (Finland) won a total of 12 athletics medals (nine gold and three silver) at the Olympic Games of 1920, 1924 and 1928.

Largest permanent tree maze Designed by Erik and Karen Poulsen (both Denmark), The Samso Labyrinten on the island of Samso in Denmark opened to the public on May 6, 2000 and has an area of 645,835 ft.^{2} (60,000 m^2).

MOST CONCURRENT MUSICAL PRODUCTIONS As of February 2005, 12 productions of *Mamma Mia!* (music and lyrics by Benny Andersson and Björn Ulvaeus, both Sweden) were playing at one time: nine resident productions (London, UK; Las Vegas, U.S.A.; New York City, U.S.A.; Madrid, Spain; Osaka, Japan; Stockholm, Sweden; Stuttgart, Germany; Toronto, Canada and Utrecht, Holland) and three tours in Europe, South Africa, and the U.S.A.

☆**LARGEST CONSUMERS OF ENERGY** This photograph of the Earth at night is assembled from several satellite shots and shows the major conurbations of the world, clearly indicated by street lights.

The world's greatest consumer of electricity is the United States, which used 3.717 trillion kW per hour in 2005. This figure is almost a quarter of the total net electricity consumption of the whole world, which in 2005 came to 16.282 trillion kW per hour.

The ☆**greatest consumer of electricity per person** is Iceland, where 26,101 kW per hour per person were used in 2005. In the United States, 12,343 kW per hour per person were consumed over the same period. Seven of the 10 countries that use the lowest amounts of electricity are located in Africa.

KEY FACTS

•**LARGEST ICE VILLAGE:** A village of 140 igloos was built near the famous Icehotel at Jukkasjärvi, Sweden, to accommodate 700 employees of Tetra Pak International during a conference at the hotel in December 2002.

•**LARGEST WOODEN CHURCH:** The Kerimäki church in Kerimäki, Finland, is 147 ft. 7 in. (45 m) long, 137 ft. 9 in. (42 m) wide, and 88 ft. 6 in. (27 m) high. Its dome is 121 ft. 4 in. (37 m) tall. It can accommodate 3,000 people seated or 5,000 standing.

•★ **LARGEST FOREIGN AID DONATIONS (AS A PERCENTAGE OF GDP):** According to the Organization for Economic Cooperation and Development (OECD), Norway donated $2.2 billion, or 0.9% of its gross domestic product (GDP), to poorer countries in 2004.

•**COUNTRY WITH THE HIGHEST TAX:** In Denmark, the highest rate of personal income tax was 62.9% as of June 2003.

•**LARGEST HOT SPRINGS:** The largest boiling river flows from alkaline hot springs at Deildartunguhver, north of Reykjavik, Iceland, at a rate of 65 gallons (245 liters) of boiling water per second.

☆**LARGEST UKULELE ENSEMBLE** "Ukulele 07," staged on Långholmen Island in Stockholm, Sweden, on August 18, 2007, heard a ukulele ensemble comprising 401 participants.

Oldest continuously used national flag The current design of the Danish flag—a white Scandinavian cross on a red background—was adopted in 1625, and its square shape assumed in 1748. In Denmark, it is called the "Dannebrog," or "Danish cloth."

★**FASTEST DRIVE ON ICE** Four-time World Rally champion Juha Kankkunen (Finland) drove a Bentley Continental GT at 199.86 mph (321.65 km/h) on the frozen Gulf of Bothnia in Kuivaniemi, Finland, on February 20, 2007.

☆ **HIGHEST CONCERT** Norwegian band Magnet (aka Even Johansen) celebrated the launch of a new album, *The Simple Life!*, by performing at an altitude of 40,000 ft. (12,192 m) on a flight from Oslo, Norway, to Reykjavik, Iceland, on March 27, 2007.

☆ **Longest knitted scarf** Over a 23-year period, Helge Johansen (Norway) knitted an 11,363-ft. 11-in-long (3,463.73-m) scarf, finishing it in Oslo, Norway, on November 10, 2006.

★ **Deepest underground concert** Finnish group Agonizer performed a concert 4,169 ft. 11 in. (1,271 m) below sea level in the Pyhäsalmi Mine Oy, Pyhäjärvi, Finland, on August 4, 2007.

★ **Largest coffee morning (single venue)** On June 6, 2007, a group of 2,620 people gathered for a coffee morning at the Diocesan Festival in Kalmar, Sweden.

Most Olympic medals for alpine skiing (male) Kjetil André Aamodt (Norway) won a total of eight medals (four gold, two silver, and two bronze) at Olympic Games between 1992 and 2006.

★ **MOST DOLLAR MILLIONAIRES** One in every 86 Norwegians claims a net worth of over $1 million (NOK5.8 million)—excluding the value of their primary residences—according to a report by CapGemini and Merrill Lynch in July 2007.

GERMANY

★**Largest dirndl dress** On June 21, 2003, Gabriele Hein-Fischer (Germany) unveiled a dirndl dress that was an exact, scaled-up replica of the traditional Bavarian style, with the skirt measuring 9.5 ft. (2.9 m) long and 29.5 ft. (9 m) in diameter. Completing the look is a bodice and 4.9-ft.-long (1.5-m) sleeves!

☆**Largest Black Forest gateau** On July 16, 2006, Hans-Dieter Busch of the K&U Bakery in Rust made a Black Forest (cherry) gateau weighing 6,532 lb. (2,963 kg).

★**Highest cold-water geyser** Geysir Andernach in Andernach blows water to heights of 98–196 ft. (30–60 m). Unlike naturally occurring hot-

AT A GLANCE •**AREA**: 137,846 miles² (357,021 km²)
•**POPULATION**: 82.4 million
•**DENSITY**: 597 people/mile² (230 people/km²)
•**KEY FACTS**: Germany was home to the **first public electric railroad,** which opened on May 12, 1881, in Lichtervelde near Berlin. The Germans are also the **biggest spending tourists** while abroad; in 2004, they spent $71 billion when on vacation in foreign countries. The fall of the Berlin Wall in 1989 (which separated West Berlin from the rest of East Germany for 28 years between 1961 and 1989) caused the world's **largest traffic jam,** as 18 million cars became gridlocked on the border. Lastly, Germany holds the record for the **highest paper recycling rate**—it recycles between 70% and 80% of its paper and cardboard per year.

★ **NARROWEST STREET**
Spreuerhofstrasse in
Reutlingen is 1 ft. (31 cm) at
its narrowest and 1 ft. 8 in.
(50 cm) at its widest. It was
measured in February 2006.

water geysers, so-called "cold-water" geysers are formed by cold ground-water dissolving large amounts of carbon dioxide (released through cracks from the Earth's upper mantle) that effectively "charge" the water; this charged underground water then erupts from a drilled well.

The Andernach well is 1,148 ft. (350 m) deep and was re-drilled in 2001, following its closure in 1957 due to war damage. The highest recorded height, on September 19, 2002, was 201 ft. 9 in. (61.5 m). The average volume of water ejected per eruption is 2,064 gal. (7,800 liters).

★ **LONGEST STRUDEL** A 209-ft. 4-in. (63.81-m) strudel was made in
Bitburg on September 1, 2007, by the two companies Freunde der Bütt
and Bakery Flesch.

★**FARTHEST-LEANING TOWER**
The bell tower of the Protestant church in Suurhusen was found to be leaning at an angle of inclination of 5.1939 degrees when measured on January 17, 2007. It therefore claims the record previously held by the more famous Leaning Tower of Pisa in Italy—which tilts just 3.97 degrees.

★**Longest time flying an airship** In November 1928, Hugo Eckener (Germany) flew the Graf Zeppelin for 71 hours and 3,967 miles (6,384.5 km), between Lakehurst, New Jersey, U.S.A., and Friedrichshafen, Germany.

THE NETHERLANDS

AT A GLANCE •**AREA**: 16,033 miles² (41,526 km²)
•**POPULATION**: 16.5 million
•**DENSITY**: 1,033 people/mile² (399 people/km²)
•**KEY FACTS**: The Netherlands is famed for its beer brewing, and it celebrates this fact with the record for the **most people in a beer race**—there were 928 participants in a beer race, a kind of beer drinking game, in Wageningen, Gelderland, on February 1, 2007. The city of Amsterdam is home to the world's **oldest stock exchange**. Founded in 1602, it printed stocks for the United East India Company of the Netherlands.

☆ MOST DOMINOS TOPPLED BY A GROUP After hundreds of builders from 13 countries worked for several weeks to install a total of 4,079,381 dominos, they were toppled on November 17, 2006, at Domino Day 2006 in Leeuwarden, Friesland.

Tallest working windmill De Noord Molen in Schiedam stands 109 ft. 4 in. (33.33 m) high.

★ **Largest haystack** On July 6, 2006, at the Flaeijel Festival in Friesland, Frisia, a haystack was built measuring 31 ft. 2 in. tall (9.51 m) and with a diameter of 55 ft. 9 in. (17 m).

☆ LONGEST FLOTILLA OF TUGBOATS On June 16, 2007, De Binnenvaart Association of Inland Shipping boasted a flotilla of 148 tugboats in Dordrecht, South Holland. They covered a distance of more than 1.86 miles (3 km).

★**LARGEST GLASSES** The largest pair of spectacles were manufactured in December 2004 by Errold Jessurun (Netherlands), who is employed by Jess Optiek of Weesp, North Holland. The total width was 6 ft. 4.25 in. (1.94 m), with each lens 2 ft. 2.75 in. (68 cm) wide.

☆**Largest broom** On September 12, 2006, members of Kreateam 2006 made a huge broom in Sint-Annaland, Zeeland. The broom itself was 107 ft. 1 in. (32.65 m) long and the handle was an amazing 68 ft. 5 in. (20.85 m).

★**Most people spinning plates simultaneously** At the official opening of the Sportcampus in Utrecht, Ronstad, on September 25, 2007, 1,026 people spun plates at the same time.

Largest clog dance A group of 475 people took part in a clog dance at the Spuiplein in The Hague, the Netherlands, on July 8, 2006.

☆**Fastest half marathon barefoot on ice/snow** Wim Hof (Netherlands) ran a half marathon barefoot in 2 hr. 16 min. 34 sec. near Oulu, Finland, on January 26, 2007.

Fastest champions league goal Roy Makaay (Netherlands) scored the opening goal for Bayern Munich against Real Madrid in just 10 seconds in Munich, Germany, on March 7, 2007.

EASTERN & CENTRAL EUROPE

★**Largest honeycomb** A honeycomb weighing 22 lb. 14 oz. (10.4 kg)—as heavy as a two-year-old child—was extracted from a beehive owned by Argirios Koskos (Greece) on August 30, 2007.

AT A GLANCE •AREA: 1,372,220 miles² (3,554,034 km²)
•POPULATION: 438 million
•DENSITY: 319 people/mile² (123 people/km²)
•COUNTRIES: Central Europe: Austria (highest proportion of
organic farming, where 10% of land is farmed organically), Czech
Republic (largest consumers of beer, at 42.4 gallons; 160.5 liters per
person), Germany (see p. 492), Hungary (most goals scored in a
soccer World Cup tournament: 27 in 1954), Liechtenstein, Poland
(home of the oldest movie theater in operation, the Pionier, which
opened in 1909), Slovakia (largest collection of napkins: 30,300
owned by Antónia Kozáková), Slovenia (deepest natural shaft:
Vrtiglavica (meaning "vertigo") runs 2,110 ft. (643 m) deep through
Monte Kanin), and Switzerland.

Eastern Europe: Belarus, Estonia, Latvia (largest shortage of
men: 53.97% of the population are female and 46.03% male), Lithuania,
Moldova, (largest dog shelter: Ute Langenkamp can comfortably
house up to 3,000 dogs), and Ukraine.

Southeastern Europe: Albania, Bulgaria, Bosnia and Herzegovina,
Croatia, Greece (first dictionary (compiled by Protagoras of Abdera,
5th century B.C.), first Olympic Games: 776 B.C.), Macedonia,
Montenegro, Romania, Serbia, Kosovo, and part of Turkey.

Heaviest building The Palace of the Parliament in Bucharest, Romania,
is constructed from 1.5 billion lb. (700,000 metric tons) of steel and bronze,
35 million ft.³ (1 million m³) of marble, 7.7 million lb. (3,500 metric tons) of
crystal glass, and 31.7 million ft.³ (900,000 m³) of wood.

☆**Largest gathering of test-tube children** The largest gathering of
children born as a result of artificial insemination was 1,180 at the ISCARE
IVF Assisted Reproduction Centre in Prague, Czech Republic, on September 15, 2007.

☆ **MOST COUPLES KISSING SIMULTANEOUSLY** The greatest number of couples kissing simultaneously was 6,980 (13,960 participants) at an event organized by Radio Kameleon in Tuzla, Bosnia and Herzegovina, on September 1, 2007.

☆ **Smallest pub** The smallest permanent licensed bar is called the Smallest Whisky Bar on Earth and has a total floor area of 91.82 ft.² (8.53 m²). The bar, owned by Gunter Sommer (Switzerland), is in Sta. Maria, Graubünden, Switzerland, and was opened in 2006 and measured in July 2007.

★ **Largest matchstick** A matchstick measuring 20 ft. 5 in. (6.235 m) long, with a cross section of 10.8 in. (27.5 cm), was made by Estonian Match Ltd., and unveiled and struck at the Ugala Theater, Viljandi, Estonia, on November 27, 2004.

★ **Largest radiator** The largest radiator measured 19 ft. 9 in. (6.02 m) high and 19 ft. 7.4 in. (5.98 m) long. It was manufactured by CINI Co. and displayed in Cacak, Serbia, on April 23, 2007.

★ **Largest waltz** The largest waltz consisted of 115 pairs who danced in the Prater, Vienna, Austria. The record, organized by ORF Radio Wien, was set during the event Vienna Recordia in Vienna, on September 30, 2007.

★ **Longest chain of condoms** The record for the longest chain of condoms is 10,726 ft. 6 in. (3,269.46 m) and was achieved by PSI Romania on Unirii Boulevard, Bucharest, Romania, on October 28, 2007.

HIGHEST DENOMINATION CURRENCY NOTE The currency note with the highest denomination in the world is the Hungarian 100 million B-pengó (100,000,000,000,000,000,000 pengó). It was introduced on January 1, 1946, and withdrawn on July 31, 1946, when it was worth approximately $0.20.

★HIGHEST PERCENTAGE OF FEMALE WORKFORCE (COUNTRY) The
country with the highest percentage of women in the workforce is
Belarus, where 53.3% of workers are female. (In contrast, Pakistan has
the **★highest percentage of men in the workforce**: 83.9% of
workers there are male.)

☆**Longest ocean swim** The longest distance ever swum without flippers in open sea is 139.8 miles (225 km) by Veljko Rogosic (Croatia) across
the Adriatic Sea from Grado to Riccinoe (both Italy) from August 29 to 31,
2006.

**MOST POINTS IN A DECATHLON
(FEMALE)** Austra Skujyte
(Lithuania) scored a total of 8,358
points in the decathlon in
Columbia, Missouri, U.S.A. on April
14–15, 2005. She bettered the
previous record of 8,150
established by Marie Collonvillé
(France) in the previous year.

☆ **LONGEST WEDDING-DRESS TRAIN** The longest wedding-dress train measured an incredible 4,468 ft. 5 in. (1,362 m) and was created by Andreas Evstratiou (Cyprus) for the bridal shop Green Leaf in Paphos, Cyprus, on February 18, 2007. When laid flat, the train stretches as long as 20 jumbo jets end to end!

Longest motorcycle wedding procession Motorcycle enthusiasts Peter Schmidl and Anna Turceková (both Slovakia) had a wedding procession of 597 motorcycles when they tied the knot in Bratislava, Slovakia, on May 6, 2000. The event coincided with the Chopper Show 2000, which the majority of procession members were attending.

YOUNGEST CHESS GRAND MASTER Sergey Karjakin (Ukraine, b. January 12, 1990) became the youngest individual to qualify as an International Grand Master on August 12, 2002, aged 12 years 212 days.

LOWEST ROAD FATALITY RATE Malta has the lowest fatality rate in road traffic accidents, with just 1.6 deaths per 100,000 population in 1996, according to the latest figures available. (The highest rate is in Mauritius, with 43.9 per 100,000.)

RUSSIA

AT A GLANCE •**AREA**: 6,592,771 miles² (17,075,200 km²)
•**POPULATION**: 141.3 million
•**DENSITY**: 21.4 people/mile² (8.2 people/km²)
•**KEY FACTS**: Russia is the **largest country,** representing 11.5% of the world's total land area. It is also home to the **largest reservoir by volume,** the Bratskoye reservoir, which has a volume of 40.6 miles³ (169.3 km³).

OLDEST LAKE Lake Baikal in Siberia is 20–25 million years old and formed as a result of a tectonic rift in the Earth's crust. It holds more water than North America's Great Lakes combined and is host to the world's only freshwater seal.

Largest Russian nesting dolls (matrioshka) The largest set of Russian dolls is a 51-piece set hand-painted by Youlia Bereznitskaia (Russia). The largest doll measures 1 ft. 9.25 in. (53.97 cm) tall and the smallest 0.125 in. (0.31 cm) height. The set was completed on April 25, 2003.

Most TV stations Russia had a staggering 7,306 television stations in 1998!

Greatest flood Roughly 18,000 years ago, an ancient lake in Siberia about 75 miles (120 km) long ruptured, causing the greatest freshwater flood in history. Research suggests the catastrophe unleashed waters 1,600 ft. (490 m) deep and traveling at 100 mph (160 km/h). Scientists revealed the discovery in 1993.

Most orbits of the earth Russian cosmonaut Sergei Avdeyev completed 11,968 orbits of the Earth during his career. From

MOST GOALS SCORED IN A WORLD CUP FINALS MATCH Oleg Salenko scored five goals for Russia v. Cameroon in a World Cup finals match at Stanford Stadium, California, U.S.A., on June 28, 1994.

LONGEST UNINTERRUPTED TRAIN JOURNEY The longest rail journey with no change of trains extends 6,346 miles (10,214 km) from Moscow, Russia, to Pyongyang, North Korea. One train a week travels the route, using parts of the Trans-Siberian line.

July 1992 to July 1999, he spent 747 days 14 hr. 22 min. in space on three missions to the *Mir* space station.

Longest-operating nuclear power station The nuclear reactor in Obninsk operated from June 27, 1954, until it was decommissioned on April 30, 2002. It was the **first nuclear reactor** in the world.

FIRST MANNED SPACEFLIGHT The earliest manned spaceflight was by Cosmonaut Flight Major (later Col.) Yuri Alekseyevich Gagarin (USSR) in *Vostok 1* on April 12, 1961. The takeoff was from the Baikonur Cosmodrome, Kazakhstan, at 6:07 a.m. GMT and the landing at Smelovka, near Engels, in the Saratov region of Russia, 115 minutes later. Gagarin parachuted to the ground separately from his spacecraft, landing 118 minutes after launch.

ISRAEL

Largest mezuzah A standard mezuzah consists of two excerpts taken from Deuteronomy in the Old Testament, hand written in Hebrew on a single piece of parchment, rolled up, and placed in a container on the door frames of Jewish homes. The largest mezuzah parchment measured 3 ft. 1 in. (94 cm) long and 2 ft. 6 in. (76 cm) wide, and its container measured 3 ft. 7.3 in. (110 cm) long on May 19, 2004. It was created by Avraham-Hersh Borshevsky (Israel).

Oldest active fighter pilot Uri Gil (Israel; b. April 9, 1943), a brigadier general in the Israeli Air Force, was a fighter pilot from 1964 to June 20, 2003, when he was 60 years 72 days old.

Oldest synagogue A synagogue dating back to between 50 and 75 years B.C. was unearthed by archeologist Ehud Netzer's team in 1998. The remains of the synagogue were discovered beneath the ruins of the Hasmonean

AT A GLANCE •AREA: 8,019 miles² (20,770 km²)
•POPULATION: 6.4 million
•DENSITY: 798 people/mile² (308 people/km²)
•KEY FACTS: Israel is the country with the highest consumption of protein, according to the United Nations, with an average of 4.53 oz. (128.6 g) of protein per person per day. The world average is 2.65 oz. (75.3 g).
  Israel is also the country with the highest military expenditure per capita, with $1,429.03 spent per person as of the latest figures available in 2005.

☆**LARGEST DANCE BY COUPLES** A dance featuring 552 couples took place on May 9, 2008 at Sportek Park in Tel Aviv, Israel; the participants performed Israeli folk dances for 30 minutes. The event was organized by Eddy Hassid and Gadi Bittonk and took six months to plan.

★**LARGEST BANNER** On December 23, 2007, in Bar Yeuda, Massada, Grace Galindez-Gupana (Philippines)—President of HalleluYAH Prophetic Global Foundation Philippines—unveiled the largest banner, which combined the flags of Israel, the Philippines, North Korea, and South Korea, and measured 586,103 ft.² (54,451 m²). The record attempt was organized by Sar-El Tours.

The industrious Ms. Galindez-Gupana has also achieved several other world records, including the one for the ☆**longest drawing** (16,428 ft. 3.76 in.; 5,007.36 m).

DID YOU KNOW?

The Dead Sea on the Israel–Jordan border is the **lowest exposed body of water,** at an average of around 1,312 ft. (400 m) below sea level. It is 50 miles (80 km) long and measures 11 miles (18 km) at its widest point.

Israel

winter palace, built by King Herod. The synagogue was destroyed by an earthquake in 31 B.C.

Longest siege The longest recorded siege was that of Azotus (now Ashdod). According to the Greek historian Herodotus, it was besieged by Psamtik I of Egypt for 29 years in the period 664–610 B.C.

Least extensive subway system The shortest operating underground system is the Carmelit, in Haifa; it opened in 1959 and is 1 mile 626 ft. (1,800 m) long. The only subway/metro in Israel, the Carmelit is a funicular running at a gradient of 12 degrees and has six stations.

Longest time to spin a soccer ball on one finger Raphael Harris (Israel) spun a regulation-size soccer ball on one finger continuously for 4 min. 21 sec. in Jerusalem on October 27, 2000.

Oldest plant cultivated for food In June 2006, researchers from Harvard University (U.S.A.) and Israel's Bar-Ilan University reported the discovery of nine carbonized figs, dated as 11,200–11,400 years old, in an early Neolithic village called Gilgal I, near Jericho.

THE MIDDLE EAST

FIRST . . .

Autographs Autographs made by scribes on cuneiform clay tablets from Tell Abu Salābikh, Iraq, have been dated to the early Dynastic III A period, ca. 2600 B.C. On one of these tablets, a scribe named "a-du" added "dubsar" after his name, thus translating to "Adu, scribe." The earliest surviving signature on a papyrus is that of a scribe named Amen'aa. It has been dated back to the Egyptian middle kingdom, which began ca. 2130 B.C.

Castle Gomdan, or Gumdan, Castle, in the old city of Sana'a, Yemen, was built before A.D. 200 and once had 20 stories.

SANDIEST DESERT The Arabian Desert covers nearly 1 million miles² (2,600,000 km²), of which about one-third is covered in sand. The desert occupies Saudi Arabia, Jordan, Iraq, Kuwait, Qatar, the United Arab Emirates, Oman, and Yemen.

AT A GLANCE
- **AREA**: 2,763,954 miles² (7,158,624 km²)
- **POPULATION**: 334 million
- **DENSITY**: 120 people/mile² (46 people/km²)
- **KEY FACTS**: The **earliest coins** date from the reign of King Gyges of Lydia, Turkey, *ca.* 630 B.C. The **sovereign countries with the least personal income tax** are Bahrain and Qatar, where the rate is zero. Iran is the country with the **youngest voting age**—just 15 years old.
- **COUNTRIES**: Bahrain, Egypt, Iran, Iraq, Jordan, Kuwait, Lebanon, Oman, Qatar, Saudi Arabia, Syria, Turkey, United Arab Emirates (UAE), Yemen.

(NB: Since the Middle East is not a strickly definable region, we have opted to include the Gulf states here. For Israel, see p. 504.)

Zoo The earliest known collection of animals was established at modern-day Puzurish, Iraq, by Shulgi, a third-dynasty ruler of Ur from 2097 B.C. to 2094 B.C.

OLDEST . . .

Church An ancient church unearthed in the Jordanian coastal town of Aqaba by archeologists from North Carolina State University is dated to between A.D. 290 and A.D. 300, making it the world's oldest purpose-built church.

Datable bridge The slab-stone, single-arch bridge over the Meles River in Izmir (formerly Smyrna), Turkey, dates from *ca.* 850 B.C. Remnants of Mycenaean bridges dated *ca.* 1600 B.C. exist in the region of Mycenae, Greece, over the Havos River.

☆**OLDEST WALLED TOWN** Following radiocarbon dating on specimens from the lowest levels of the town of Jericho, on the West Bank, archeologists have revealed that a community of more than 2,000 people lived there as early as 7800 B.C.

Love song An Assyrian love song to an Ugaritic god has been dated to *ca.* 1800 B.C. It was reconstructed from a tablet of notation for an 11-string lyre at the University of California, Berkeley, U.S.A., on March 6, 1974.

★**Shipwreck** A shipwreck located off Uluburun near Kas, southern Turkey, has been dated to the 14th century B.C.

LARGEST...

☆**Bed** On January 30, 2007, the Dubai Shopping Festival and Intercoil International created a bed measuring 45 ft. 11 in. (14 m) long, 39 ft. 4 in. (12 m) wide, and 6 ft. 10 in. (2.10 m) tall in Dubai, UAE.

Chandelier Made from Swarovski crystal, the largest chandelier hangs in the Sultan Qaboos Grand Mosque in Muscat, Oman, and is 46 ft. (14.1 m) tall, 26 ft. (8 m) in diameter, with 1,114 bulbs. Weighing around 18,740 lb. (8,500 kg), it was built by Kurt Faustig SAS of Munich, Germany, in April 2000.

LARGEST PERCENTAGE OF POPULATION AT A FUNERAL Official Iranian estimates report the size of the crowds lining the 20-mile (32-km) route to Tehran's Behesht-e Zahra cemetery for the funeral of Ayatollah Ruhollah Khomeini on June 11, 1989, as 10,200,000 people—or one-sixth of Iran's population.

☆ **LARGEST KITE FLOWN**
Abdulrahman Al Farsi and Faris Al Farsi (both Kuwait) made a kite with a lifting area of 10,226 ft.^{2} (950 m^2). When laid flat, it had a total area of 10,968 ft.^{2} (1,019 m^2)—approximately the same area as four tennis courts laid together. The kite was flown at the Kuwait Hala Festival in Flag Square, Kuwait City, Kuwait, on February 15, 2005.

TALLEST PYRAMID The pyramid of Khufu at Giza, Egypt, is the world's tallest. Also known as the Great Pyramid, it was 481 ft. 4 in. (146.7 m) high when completed around 4,500 years ago, but erosion and vandalism have reduced its height to 451 ft. 4 in. (137.5 m) today.

FACT

Ayatollah Khomeini actually had two funerals (see photo p. 508). The first was abandoned because the huge crowds damaged the wooden coffin in their eagerness to touch it. For the second funeral, security was boosted and the body was placed in a metal casket.

LARGEST ROYAL FAMILY The house of Al-Saud of Saudi Arabia had over 4,000 royal princes and 30,000 royal relatives in 2002. The kingdom was established in 1932 by the patriarch, King Abdul Aziz, who had 44 sons by 17 wives, four of whom have ruled the kingdom since the king's death in 1953.

Saudi Arabia is the country with the most siblings in government—a total of six. The king, Abdullah bin Abdulaziz Al-Saud, is also prime minister and commander of the Saudi National Guard. Between them, his five half-brothers hold the positions of crown prince, deputy prime minister, defense minister, interior minister, deputy minister of defense, governor of Riyadh, and deputy minister of the interior.

Gold ring The Najmat Taiba (which means "Star of Taiba") was created by Taiba for Gold and Jewelry Co., Ltd., of Saudi Arabia. The ring consists of 11 lb. 6 oz. (5.17 kg) of precious jewels set on a 129-lb. 6-oz. (58.686-kg) 21-carat gold ring. The total weight of the ring is 140 lb. 12 oz. (63.856 kg). It is 27.5 in. (70 cm) in diameter and took 55 workers 45 days to build.

★ Inflatable sculpture The largest inflatable sculpture took the shape of a bottle and had a volume of 52,972 ft.^{3} (1,500 m^3). It was 82 ft. (25 m) high and 39 ft. (11.9 m) wide, and was created by Vitaene C at the Dubai Shopping Festival in Dubai, UAE, on January 28, 2007.

AFRICA

☆**Highest birth and fertility rates** Based on estimates for 2005–10, Niger is among the world's fastest-growing countries, with a predicted population increase of 41 million from 12 million (2004) to 53 million (2050). The country has the highest fertility rate, with 7.19 children per woman.

Niger also had 50.16 births per 1,000 population as of November 2007.

Tallest tribe Young adult males belonging to the Tutsi (also known as the Watussi) of Rwanda and Burundi, central Africa, average a height of 6 ft. (1.83 m).

AT A GLANCE
- **AREA**: 12,010,859 miles^2 (31,107,983 km^2)
- **POPULATION**: 930 million
- **DENSITY**: 77 people/mile^2 (30 people/km^2)
- **COUNTRIES**: Algeria, Angola, Benin, Botswana, Burkina Faso, Burundi, Cameroon, Cape Verde, Central African Republic, Chad, Comoros, Côte d'Ivoire, Democratic Republic of the Congo, Djibouti, Egypt, Equatorial Guinea, Eritrea, Ethiopia, Gabon, the Gambia, Ghana, Guinea, Guinea-Bissau, Kenya, Lesotho, Liberia, Libya, Madagascar, Malawi, Mali, Mauritania, Mauritius, Morocco, Mozambique, Namibia, Niger, Nigeria, Republic of the Congo, Réunion, Rwanda, Saint Helena, São Tomé and Príncipe, Senegal, Seychelles, Sierra Leone, Somalia, South Africa, Sudan, Swaziland, Tanzania, Togo, Tunisia, Uganda, Zambia, Zimbabwe.

RAREST CANID There are believed to be fewer than 450 specimens of the Ethiopian wolf (*Canis simiensis*) alive. This endangered species is very vulnerable to the threat of rabies—indeed, at least 38 Ethiopian wolves have díed from rabies since September 2003 in the Bale Mountains, Ethiopia, which is home to 300 individuals.

★**Largest bowl of couscous** The world's largest bowl of couscous was displayed at the International Fair of Algiers, Algeria, on June 3, 2004. It weighed 13,315 lb. (6.04 metric tons) and was made by Semoulerie Industrielle de la Mitidja.

Largest pink lake Retba Lake, better known as Lac Rose (Pink Lake), is the world's largest pink body of water, measuring about 0.9 × 3 miles (1.5 × 5 km) at low water. A shallow lagoon, located 18 miles (30 km) north of Dakar, Senegal, the lake's unusual color is the result of microorganisms and a strong concentration of minerals.

Longest rift system The East African Rift System is approximately 4,000 miles (6,400 km) long with an average width of 30–40 miles (50–65 km). The escarpments around the edge of the valley have an average height of 2,000–3,000 ft. (600–900 m). It begins in Jordan and extends to Mozambique in east Africa. This extensive rift system has been gradually forming for about 30 million years, as the Arabian Peninsula has separated from Africa.

Most venomous scorpion The Tunisian fat-tailed scorpion (*Androctonus australis*) is responsible for 80% of stings and 90% of deaths from scorpion stings in north Africa.

TALLEST MINARET The minaret of the Great Hassan II Mosque in Casablanca, Morocco, measures 656 ft. (200 m). The total construction cost of the mosque was 5 billion dirhams ($513.5 million). The mosque can accommodate 25,000 worshippers in its prayer hall, which has a retractable roof, and a further 80,000 outside.

SOUTH AFRICA

Largest diamond A 3,106-carat diamond was found on January 26, 1905, at the Premier Diamond Mine near Pretoria, South Africa, and was presented to the reigning British monarch, Edward VII. Named The Cullinan, it was cut into 106 polished diamonds.

YOUNGEST PERSON TO WIN THE MAN BOOKER PRIZE Ben Okri (Nigeria) was 32 when he won the Man Booker Prize in 1991 for his novel *The Famished Road.*
 The record for the **most Man Booker Prize wins** is shared by South African author J. M. Coetzee and Peter Carey (Australia), both of whom have won this prestigious prize twice.

FASTEST LAVA FLOW
Nyiragongo is a volcano in the Virunga Mountains in the Democratic Republic of Congo. When it erupted on January 10, 1977, the lava burst through fissures on the volcano's flank, traveling at speeds of almost 40 mph (60 km/h). Up to 2,000 people were killed when the flow inundated the nearby city of Goma.

Largest marimba ensemble On October 29, 2004, at Bishops Diocesan College, Cape Town, South Africa, an ensemble of 78 musicians played the marimba (a percussion instrument similar to the xylophone) for over 10 minutes.

☆**Deepest mine** The Savuka Mine in South Africa is the largest gold mine, operating at a depth of 12,391 ft. (3,777 m) as of 2005. At this depth, miners are able to extract rock containing some 1.2 in.³ (20 cm³) of gold in approximately each cubic yard (1 m³). The mine is in the Witwatersrand Basin, the world's **largest gold reserve,** which has produced over 1.5 billion ounces (42.5 billion grams) of gold since 1886.

LARGEST . . .

Bird The flightless elephant bird, or vouron patra (*Aepyornis maximus*), from Madagascar, died out about 1,000 years ago (although sightings were

LARGEST DESERT Nearly an eighth of the world's land surface is arid, with rainfall of less than 10 in. (25 cm) per annum. The Sahara in north Africa is the largest hot desert in the world—it is larger than all of Australia. At its greatest length, it is 3,200 miles (5,150 km) from east to west. From north to south, it is between 800 and 1,400 miles (1,280–2,250 km). The area covered by the desert is about 3.5 million miles² (9.1 million km²).

On September 13, 1922, the **highest recorded temperature**—136°F (58°C)—was registered in the shade at Al'Aziziyah in the Sahara Desert, Libya.

LARGEST POPULATION OF CHILDREN Uganda had the highest population of children, with 50.8% aged between 0 and 14 years old, in 2003. The picture above shows children waiting for the arrival of Prince Charles, the Prince of Wales (UK), in Kawempe Slum, Kampala, Uganda, on November 23, 2007.

reported up to 1658). It grew to around 10–11 ft. (3–3.3 m) tall and weighed approximately 1,100 lb. (500 kg). (*For the **tallest bird ever,** see p. 531.*)

Elephant relocation In August 1993, the charity Care For The Wild International (CFTWI) moved more than 500 elephants in family groups some 155 miles (250 km) across Zimbabwe, from Gonarezhou National Park to the Save Valley Conservancy.

CENTRAL & SOUTHERN ASIA

Oldest Koran The Holy Koran Mushaf of Othman, owned by the Muslim Board of Uzbekistan, once belonged to Caliph Othman (*ca.* A.D. 588–656), third successor to the Prophet Mohammed. Only about half of the original 706 pages survive.

★**Largest chapati** An Indian bread weighing 141.07 lb. (63.99 kg) was made by the Shree Jalarm Mandir Jirnodhar Samitee organization at Jamnagar, India, on January 15, 2005.

Largest landlocked country The largest country with no border access to the open ocean is Kazakhstan. It covers an area of 1,052,100 miles² (2,724,900 km²) and is bordered by Russia, China, Kyrgystan, Uzbekistan, Turkmenistan, and the land-locked Caspian Sea. In terms of area, Kazakhstan is the ninth largest country in the world, and had a population of 15.2 million in 2007.

AT A GLANCE
- **AREA:** 1,390,080 miles² (3,600,292 km²)
- **POPULATION:** 1.5 billion
- **DENSITY:** 1,079 people mile² (416 people/km²)
- **KEY FACTS:** Home to the **largest sea** (the Caspian, at 371,000 km²; 143,244 miles²) and Mount Everest, the **highest mountain** at 8,828 m (29,028 ft.), located on the Nepal–China border.
- **COUNTRIES:** Afghanistan, Bangladesh, Bhutan, British Indian Ocean Territories, India, Kazakhstan, Kyrgyzstan, Maldives **(flattest country; highest divorce rate, at 10.97 per 1,000 per year)**, Nepal, Sri Lanka **(★ most cabinet ministers, with 52)**, Pakistan, Tajikistan, Turkmenistan, and Uzbekistan.

(Iran is considered south Asian only by the UN. The G8 regards it as part of the Greater Middle East—and so does GWR! For Middle Eastern records, please turn to pp. 506–510.)

☆ **MOST REFUGEES** According to the United Nations High Commission for Refugees (UNHCR), Pakistan had received 1,085,000 refugees by January 1, 2006, more than any other country. This excludes Afghan refugees who live outside the UNHCR refugee camps, estimated at a further 1.5 million in 2005.

HIGHEST RAINFALL Mawsynram in Meghalaya, India, has an annual rainfall of 467 in. (11,873 mm). The second rainiest place, at 450 in. (11,430 mm) per year, is Cherrapunji, also in the state of Meghalaya. Most of the rain occurs during the monsoon season (May to September). Pictured is a Khasi woman taking her children to school on the outskirts of Shillong city.

Largest delta The Ganges river delta (also called the Bengal delta or Green delta) created by the Ganges and Brahmaputra rivers in Bangladesh and West Bengal, India, covers an area of 30,000 miles^2 (75,000 km^2). It is one of the most fertile areas on Earth.

BOLLYWOOD BASICS

• Lalita Pawar (India) was the **actress with the longest Bollywood** career. She made her debut at the age of 12 and appeared in more than 700 films over the next 70 years.

P. Jairaj (India), who made his acting debut in 1929, had a career spanning 300 films and more than 70 years—the **longest career for a Bollywood actor.**

• The **most expensive Bollywood film** in history is *Devdas* (India, 2002), which cost an estimated 500 million rupees ($11.2 million) to make.

• *Hum Aapke Hain Koun . . . !* (India, 1994), starring Madhuri Dixit and Salman Khan, is the **highest grossing Bollywood film**. It took in over $63.8 million in its first year, breaking the record set by the curry western *Sholay* in 1975.

Central & Southern Asia

☆**CHEAPEST PRODUCTION CAR** The Tata Nano, a four-door, five-seater family car with a 33-bhp, 623-cc rear engine (capable of 43 mph, or 70 km/h) was launched by Tata Motors at the Ninth Auto Expo in New Delhi, India, on January 10, 2008. Chairman Ratan Tata (India) hopes that, with a price tag of just 100,000 rupees ($2,521), it will make car ownership a reality for millions across the developing world.

☆**Youngest professional artist** Arushi Bhatnagar (India, b. June 1, 2002) had her first solo exhibition at the Kalidasa Akademi in Ujjain, India, on May 11, 2003, when she was 344 days (or 11 months) old.

☆**Largest school by pupils** The City Montessori School in Lucknow, India, had a record enrolment of 32,114 pupils on February 5, 2008 for the 2007–2008 academic year.

★**Highest botanical gardens** The Pamir Botanical Gardens near Khorog, Tajikistan, are located at an elevation of 6,889–11,483 ft. (2,100–3,500 m) above sea level. The 29.6-acre (12-ha) site features more than 2,000 species of flora.

HIGHEST ROAD The highest road in the world is in the Khardungla pass, at an altitude of 18,640 ft. (5,682 m). It is one of the three passes of the Leh–Manali road in Kashmir, completed in 1976 by the Border Roads Organization, New Delhi, India. Motor vehicles have been able to use it since 1988.

★ **LARGEST HINDU TEMPLE** BAPS Swaminarayan Akshardham in New Delhi, India, has a total area of 86,342 ft.² (8,021 m²). The temple was built within five years by 11,000 artisans. It is 356 ft. (108.5 m) long, 316 ft. (96.3 m) wide, and 141 ft. (42.9 m) tall.

BAPS Swaminarayan
Akshardham — visitor's guide

- Consecrated November 2005, GWR certificate presented to His Holiness Pramukh Swami Maharaj in December 2007.
- Constructed in just five years entirely from Rajasthani pink sandstone and Italian Carrara sandstone — absolutely no steel or concrete allowed!
- Houses an 85 x 65 ft (26 x 20 m) IMAX movie theater!

- You can take a 12-minute boat ride through 10,000 years of Indian history.
- Don't miss the giant stone musical fountain!
- Walk through 60 acres of lawns and gardens and see bronze statues of prominent figures from Indian history.
- Audio-animatronics and a light/sound diorama is used to tell the story of Bhagwan Swaminarayan.

SOUTHEAST ASIA

☆ **Largest Batik** A batik painting called *The Batik On The Road* measuring 12,916 ft.² (1,200 m²) was created by 1,000 participants on behalf of the Pekalongan Batik Community in Pekalongan City, Indonesia, on September 16, 2005.

AT A GLANCE
- **AREA:** 1,735,742 miles² (4,495,553 km²)
- **POPULATION:** 574 million
- **DENSITY:** 330 people/mile² (128 people/km²)
- **COUNTRIES:** Brunei (boasting the **largest residential palace** in the world, with 1,788 rooms and 257 lavatories), Burma (home to the Padaung tribe, whose females have the **longest necks,** stretching up to 15.75 in.; 40 cm), Cambodia, Indonesia (**largest Muslim population,** at 203 million), Laos (**most bombed country,** with 5 billion lb.; 2.2 million metric tons; of bombs dropped between 1964 and 1973 during the Vietnam War), Malaysia (home to the 1,482-ft. [451.9-m] Petronas Towers, the **tallest twin towers**), the Philippines, Singapore, Thailand (capital city Bangkok is the **longest place name** at 175 letters*), and Vietnam.

☆**Largest shoe** Measuring 17.35 ft. (5.29 m) long, 7 ft. 8 in. (2.37 m) wide, and 6 ft. 7 in. (2.03 m) high, the world's largest shoe was created by the Marikina Colossal Footwear Team on October 21, 2002, in Marikina City, the Philippines.

☆**Most trees planted simultaneously** In an event organized by Nurturers of the Earth, Children for Breastfeeding, and the Department of Environment and Natural Resources (all the Philippines), 516,137 people planted 653,143 trees simultaneously along the National Highway of the Philippines on August 25, 2006.

★**Largest Tet cake** The world's largest Tet cake weighed 3,858 lb. (1.75 metric tons) and was made by Saigontourist at Dam Sen Cultural Park, Ho Chi Minh City, Vietnam from January 18 to 21, 2004.

*The shortened, 111-letter, six-word version of Bangkok is krungthephphramahanakhon bowonratanakosin mahintharayuthaya mahadilokphiphobnovpharad radchataniburirom udomsantisug.

LARGEST ANIMAL ORCHESTRA The 12-piece Thai Elephant Orchestra at the Thai Elephant Conservation Center in Lampang, Thailand, was founded by Richard Lair and David Soldier (both U.S.A.) in 2000, to help conserve the Asiatic elephant species.

Heaviest bell in use The Mingun bell in Mandalay, Burma, weighs 202,825 lb. (92 metric tons) with a diameter of 16 ft. 8 in. (5.09 m) at the lip. The bell is struck by a teak boom from the outside. It was cast at Mingun, late in the reign of King Bodawpaya (1782–1819).

Loudest noise When the island-volcano Krakatoa in the Sunda Strait between Sumatra and Java, Indonesia, exploded in an eruption on August 27, 1883, the sound was heard 3,100 miles (5,000 km) away. The noise is estimated to have been heard over 8% of the Earth's surface and to have had 26 times the power of the largest ever H-bomb test.

Longest alphabet The language using the most letters is Khmer (Cambodian), with 74 (including some without any current use).

Largest fountain The Suntec City Fountain of Wealth in Singapore has a cast bronze superstructure weighing 187,393 lb. (85 metric tons) and stands 46 ft. (14 m) high, while the base of the fountain has a total area of 18,117 ft.^{2} (1,683.07 m^2). It cost an estimated $6 million to build in 1997.

Largest religious structure The Angkor Wat (City Temple) encloses 401 acres (162.6 ha) in Cambodia, making it the largest religious structure ever constructed. It was built to the Hindu god Vishnu by the Khmer King Suryavarman II in the period 1113–1150. Its curtain wall measures 4,200 ft. (1,280 m) and its population, before it was abandoned in 1432, was estimated to have reached 80,000. The temple forms part of a complex of 72 major monuments, begun *ca.* A.D. 900, that extends over 15.4 miles (24.8 km).

WORST MONSOON Monsoons that raged throughout Thailand from September to December 1983 resulted in the deaths of 10,000 people. Up to 100,000 victims contracted waterborne diseases and 15,000 people were evacuated. More than $400 million worth of damage was caused.

LARGEST BUDDHIST TEMPLE The largest Buddhist temple is Borobudur, near Yogyakarta, central Java, Indonesia, constructed between A.D. 750 and A.D. 842. The 2,118,880-ft.^{3} (60,000-m^3) stone structure is 113 ft. (34.5 m) tall and its base measures 403 × 403 ft. (123 × 123 m). Having fallen into disrepair from the 14th century onward, Borobudur was rediscovered by Sir Thomas Stamford Raffles in 1814, while he was British governor of Java.

FACT

Monsoon rains also caused flooding in India's Bengal state during September 1978. With 15 million out of a population of 44 million made homeless, it is the world's **worst flood disaster** in terms of homes lost.

The world's most populous island is Java, Indonesia, which had a population of 121,352,608 according to the 2000 census, all living in an area of 49,254 miles² (127,569 km²). That's more that 2,463 people per mile² (936 people per km²)

LARGEST GILDED BUILDING The cone-shaped Shwe Dagon Pagoda in Rangoon, Burma, is 325 ft. (99 m) tall, measures 450 ft. (137 m) across at its base, and is covered in gold plating. The Buddhist shrine has been rebuilt many times, but there is thought to have been a stupa (Buddhist monument) there for more than 2,000 years.

FAR EAST

☆**Densest network of roads** Macau, a Special Administrative Region of China, has 21.3 km (13.2 miles) of road per km² (0.38 miles²) of land area, according to *The Economist* in 2008.

☆**Most heavily used network of roads** With 5,565,600 km (3,458,300 miles) being driven for every kilometer (0.62 miles) of its road network each year, Hong Kong's roads are the most heavily used in the world.

AT A GLANCE •**AREA:** 4,554,087 miles² (11,795,031 km²)
•**POPULATION:** 1.55 billion
•**DENSITY:** 341 people/mile² (132 people/km²)
•**COUNTRIES:** China (**the most populated country**, with 1,323,345,000 citizens in 2005; also includes Special Administrative Regions [SARs] of Hong Kong and Macau).

Other countries: Japan (**largest population of centenarians**, with 25,606 people aged over 100 years old as of 2005), North Korea (**the most militarized country** per capita, with nearly 5% of the population in the military), Mongolia (**the most sparsely populated country**, with 4.1 people per mile², or 1.6 people per km²), South Korea (boasting the **hardest-working citizens**, averaging 2,423 hours per person per year), and Taiwan (home to the world's **tallest building**, Taipei 101, at 1,666 ft.; 508 m).

★**Longest boom (truck-mounted)** Made by SANY Heavy Industry Co., Ltd. (China), the longest truck-mounted boom is 216 ft. 6 in. (66 m) long. The multistage extensible arm is used in large-scale engineering projects.

☆**Highest city population** By 2007, Greater Tokyo, Japan, had a population of over 35 million, making it Asia's largest conurbation and the world's most populous urban agglomeration.

DID YOU KNOW?

The ★ **longest dancing dragon** was 16,587 ft. (5,056 m) in length and was also made for the 25th Luoyang Peony Festival (see photo p. 525) of Henan Province, China, on April 10, 2007.

LARGEST GATHERING OF DANCING DRAGONS A total of 55 dancing dragons assembled to take part in the opening ceremony of the 25th Luoyang Peony Festival of Henan Province, China, on April 10, 2007.

★**Largest gymnastics display** The record for the largest gymnastics display involved 100,090 participants in May Day Stadium, Pyongyang, Democratic People's Republic of Korea, on August 14, 2007. The event was organized by Grand Mass Gymnastic and Artistic Performance "Arirang" State Preparing Committee of Democratic People's Republic of Korea.

☆**Largest parade of bicycles** A parade of 2,152 bicycles was organized by Da Jia Jenn Lann Temple, Taichung County Government, and Volvic Taiwan, in Taichung, Taiwan, on March 1, 2008.

★**Largest rice cake** A rice cake made by Kwak Sungho and staff of Han Bbang (South Korea) at the 12th World Rice Food Festival, Dongjin-gun, Chungnam, South Korea, on October 7, 2007, weighed 8,113 lb. (3.68 metric tons).

★**Longest noodle** On March 24, 2007, Hiroshi Kuroda (Japan) made a noodle 1,800 ft. 2 in. (548.7 m) long and 0.1 in. (3.3 mm) in diameter in Nasu, Tochigi, Japan.

★**LARGEST EMPIRE** The largest connected empire that ever existed was the Mongol Empire of 1206–1367, run by the Khan Dynasty. At its most powerful in 1279 under Kublai Khan, the empire ruled over 100 million people living across an area of 13.8 million miles^2 (35.7 million km^2)—including areas in the present-day countries of China, Russia, Mongolia, central Asia, the Middle East, and the Korean Peninsula.

★ **MOST PANDAS BORN IN ONE YEAR** The most remarkable year for panda births was 2006, during which 30 cubs were born into captivity, some of which are shown here. Most of the cubs were born at Wolong Panda Research Center in southwest China. The 30th cub was born at Adventure World, Wakayama, Japan, on December 23, 2006.

☆ **Longest sushi roll** The Liaison Council of Japanese Postal Workers' Union in Gunma Prefecture, Maebashi City, Japan, created a 6,671-ft.-long (2,033.3-m) sushi roll on April 22, 2007.

★ **Largest kadomatsu** A kadomatsu is a traditional Japanese decoration of the New Year placed in front of homes to welcome ancestral spirits. Two kadomatsu measuring 32 ft. 3 in. (9.866 m) each were completed in the Tachibana Park, Chijiwa-Nagasaki, Japan, on December 18, 2000. Sixty moso bamboos were used to create them.

★ **LARGEST KICK-BOXING CLASS** A total of 986 people attended a kickboxing class at an event organized by the charity HER fund at the MacPherson playground, Mongkok, Kowloon, Hong Kong, China, on March 4, 2007.

★LARGEST DISPLAY OF LANTERNS On February 24, 2008, Tainan County Government organized a display of 47,759 lanterns at Solar City in the "Prayer for Peace" area of Tainan Science Park, Tainan, Taiwan—the greatest lantern display in a single venue.

The total area covered was 820 ft. 2 in. × 328 ft. 1 in. or 269,096.68 ft.² (250 × 100 m, or 25,000 m²). Seen from above, the completed arrangement of lanterns spelled out the words "Taiwan Peace" in Mandarin and English.

LARGEST PIGGY BANK A golden piggy bank made by Zhong Xing Shenyang Commercial Building Co., Ltd., was unveiled in Shenyang, China, on May 2, 2007. It is 18 ft. 4 in. (5.6 m) long, 12 ft. 11 in. (3.96 m) tall, and has a circumference of 47 ft. 10 in. (14.6 m). It weighs about 6,000 lb. (3 metric tons).

AUSTRALIA

★**Most people fire-eating** A total of 171 members of the Chilli Club International (Australia) performed *Fire Storm Crossing Australi'* at the opening ceremony of the Sydney Olympic Games, on September 15, 2000.

Most venomous land snake The small-scaled snake *Oxyuranus microlepidotus* measures 5 ft. 7 in. (1.7 m) and is found mainly in the Diamantina River and Cooper Creek drainage basins of Queensland and western New South Wales. The average venom yield after milking is 0.00155 oz. (44 mg), but one male specimen yielded 0.00385 oz. (110 mg), enough to kill 250,000 mice or 125 men. Fortunately, *O. microlepidotus* lives only in the arid deserts of central eastern Australia and no human death has been reported from its bite.

☆**Most jokes told in an hour** Anthony Lehmann (Australia) told a total of 549 jokes in one hour at the Rhino Room club, Adelaide, South Australia, on May 25, 2005.

☆**Loudest drummer** Col Hatchman (Australia) hit a peak reading of 137.2 decibels during a gig with his band, Dirty Skanks, at the Northern Star Hotel, Hamilton, New South Wales, on August 4, 2006.

AT A GLANCE
- **AREA:** 2,967,909 miles² (7,686,850 km²)
- **POPULATION:** 20.4 million
- **DENSITY:** 6.9 people/mile² (2.6 people/km²)

★ **LARGEST BOTTLE OF WINE** At 6 ft. 5 in. (1.95 m) tall, the world's largest bottle of wine contained 76.72 gallons (290 liters) of red wine. The production of the bottle was organized by North Road Liquor (Australia), and it was filled at Plantagenet Wines (Australia) on May 29, 2006.

Largest producer of natural diamonds Australia provides about 34% of the world's annual production of 110 million carats of natural diamonds.

★ **LONGEST PINBALL-PLAYING MARATHON** Alessandro Parisi (Australia) played pinball for 28 hours at the Westland Shopping Centre in Whyalla, on January 22–23, 2007.

LONGEST REEF The Great Barrier Reef, located off the coast of Queensland, is 1,260 miles (2,027 km) in length. It is not actually a single entity but consists of thousands of separate reefs. On three occasions—between 1962 and 1971, 1979 and 1991, and 1995 to the present day—corals in large areas of the central section of the reef have been devastated by the crown-of-thorns starfish (*Acanthaster planci*).

★**LARGEST MARRIAGE-VOW RENEWAL CEREMONY** In an event organized by Virgin Money of Australia, 272 married couples took part in the largest marriage-vow renewal ceremony in Centennial Park, Sydney, New South Wales. The ceremony took place on September 16, 2007, and was presided over by Angela Miller.

NEW ZEALAND

★**Most participants in a snowboard race** A record 88 participants took part in a snowboard race at an event organized by The Rock FM and Mount Hutt at Mount Hutt in Christchurch, New Zealand, on October 6, 2007.

★**Longest handshake** The longest time two people have shaken hands without interruption is 9 hr. 19 min., achieved by Alastair Galpin and Jesse van Keken (both New Zealand) at Aotea Square Events Centre, Auckland, on November 11, 2006.

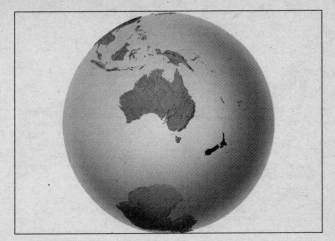

AT A GLANCE
- **AREA**: 103,737 miles² (268,680 km²)
- **POPULATION**: 4.1 million
- **DENSITY**: 39.5 people/mile² (15.3 people/km²)
- **KEY FACTS**: Research presented to the World Economic Forum in January 2006 revealed that the country with the best environmental performance was New Zealand. It is also home to the world's tallest recorded geyser, the Waimangu geyser, which erupted to a height in excess of 1,500 ft. (460 m) in 1903.

TALLEST EXTINCT BIRD The *Dinornis maximus*—a species of moa (flightless birds native to New Zealand)—is believed to have attained a height of 12 ft. (3.6 m) and weighed about 500 lb. (227 kg). It had no wings, was ostrich-like, and died out less than 10,000 years ago.

★ LARGEST SPECIES OF WETA Belonging to the order Orthoptera (grasshoppers and crickets) and confined entirely to New Zealand, the 70 species of weta include some of the world's most intimidating insects. The largest species of weta is the Little Barrier Island giant weta *Deinacrida heteracantha,* with a maximum recorded length of 4.4 in. (11 cm) and a leg-span of over 7 in. (17.5 cm).

★ **Most people fire-walking** At an event organized by the New Zealand International Fire Festival, a total of 350 people attempted a fire-walk consecutively in a time of 1 hr. 20 min. in Dunedin, South Island, on July 11, 2004.

Most southerly vineyard Westons Reserve Winery is located in Dunedin, South Island, south of Lat. 45°51´S, and is the world's most southerly commercial vineyard.

★ MOST SOUTHERLY CAPITAL CITY Wellington, North Island, with an estimated 2001 population of 165,278, is the southernmost capital city of an independent country (41°17'S). The world's southernmost capital of a dependent territory is Port Stanley, Falkland Islands (51°43'S), with a population of 1,989 (excluding service personnel) in 2001.

INDEX

This year's index is organized into two parts: by subject and by superlative. Bold entries in the subject index indicate a main entry on a topic, and entries in BOLD CAPITALS indicate an entire chapter. Neither index lists personal names.

SUBJECT

falcons, 62
Far East, 523-527
farming, 497
fashion, 214-218
fasting, 63, 67
feats of strength, 144-148
feet, 83
ferns, 47
fertility rates, 511
FIFA, 358, 359
fights: custard pie, 153; food, 482; water
    pistol, 483
Fingal's Fingers, 399
fingernails, 102
fire: bonfires, 250; tunnel of, 139; wall of,
    139
fire breathing, 139, 140
fire eating, 528
fire walking, 139, 532
fireworks, 485
fish, 29-31, 33-35, 59, 67
fishcakes, 203
fistball, 432-433
fitness, 98-101
flags, 570
flies, 45, 46
flights, 476; aircraft, 177; balloons, 177;
    transatlantic, 265
floods, 502, 522
floorball, 432-433
flower: structures, xxiv
flowers, 63; altitude, 59; space, 69
flukes, 71, 72
food: consumption, 464; fights, 482;
    plants, 506
football, 298
football, 314-319; Australian, 334,
    336; Canadian, 333, 335; Gaelic,
    335
foreign aid, 489
forensics, 223
forests: cork, 485; deforestation, 52
Formula One, 479, 487
fountains, 259, 521; champagne, 197;
    Mentos-and-soda, 198
four-leafed clovers, 193
France, 476-478
fraud, 222
freediving, 416-419
freefalling, 311, 312
French Foreign Legion, 476
frog jumping, 158
fruit, 46, 466; mosaic, 278
fudge, 203
fund-raising, 149, 150
funerals, 508
fungi, 48, 209
fur, 36
futsal, 432-433

G

Gaelic football, 335
galactic jets, 7
galaxies & nebulas, 6-9
gambling, 454
games, 241
Gangkar Punsum, Bhutan, 188
garden gnomes, 252
garden greats, 205-209
gardens, 518
garlic, 203, 206
Gazeteer, 451-532
genetics, 237-241
geodesic domes, 42
Germany, 492-494
geysers, 10, 492, 531
giant clams, 38
giant kelp, 35
giant pandas, 58
giant sequoias, 47, 49
Gila monster, 40
gingerbread houses, 251
gingerbread men, 203
ginseng, 207
giraffes, 56
glasses, 496
gliding, 312
gloves, 156
glue, 137
goalkeepers (soccer), 359
goals and field goals
    basketball, 342, 344
    football, 315
    ice hockey, 370
    Korfball, 333
    soccer, 357, 358, 362, 479, 496, 497, 502
    water polo, 389
gold
    coins, 251
    rings, 510
Gold Glove, 337
Gold Glove award, 337
golden oldies, 106-110
golf
    age, 129, 132, 366
    holes-in-one, 132, 133, 366
    on Moon, 120
    underwater, 366
golf, 366-369
golf courses, 366, 367
golf driving ranges, 367
Gomdan Castle, Yemen, 506
Google, 244
gorges, 455
gourds, 206, 207
government, 510, 516
GPS, 24, 247
graffiti, 162
grafting, 466
Grammy Awards, 287
Grand Canyon, Arizona, 455

Q

quarantine, 211
Quebec Bridge, Canada, 257
quilts, 485

R

rabbits, 211
race walking, 412-413
radiation, 224
radiators, 498
radio DJs, 481
railways
  electric, 492
  high-speed, 255
  networks, 257
  tunnels, 257
  underground, 254
rain dances, 165
rainfall, 461, 517
rainforests, 51-54
rap MCs, 454
rappeling (abseiling), 471
rats, 52
rattlesnakes, 46, 111, 137
ravioli, 203
reading, 464
recycling, 492
red dwarfs, 3
red supergiants, 4
reefs, 530
referees, umpires, and officials
  cricket, 350
  ice hockey, 371
  rugby, 378
refugees, 516
reigns, 484
rescuers, 151-152
reservoir, 501
restaurants, 259, 481
retirement, 110
Rhea (moon), 13
rheas, 55
rice, 196
rice cakes, 525
rift systems, 512
Rigel (star), 4
rings
  gold, 510
  planetary, 11, 13
Rinspeed sQuba car, 261
rivers, 32, 34
rivers, lakes, & ponds, 32-35
road cycling, 353-355
road racing, 412-413
road running, 322, 412-413
roads, 465, 466, 518, 523
  deaths, 500
  tunnels, 255
robots, 236
rock jocks, 288-292

rockets, 121, 126
rodents, 43
rodeo riding, 129, 133
rodeos, 455
rogue trading, 222
role-playing games, 483
roots, 69
rosaries, 194
rotation, chaotic, 13
rotations
  power drill, 139
rotations:
  rope, 98
roundworms, 72
rowing, 388
  sports reference, 418-421
  ocean crossings, 173, 175
royal family, 510
Royal Navy, 269, 271
rubber bands, 156
rubber ducks, 251
Rubik's cubes, 143
rugby, 378-382
  league, 379-382
  sevens, 379
  union, 378-379
running, 101, 135, 149, 150
  cross-country, 323
  marathons, 324-328, 430-432
  road, 322, 412-413
  track events, 320-322, 324
  ultra-long distance, 410-411
runs (cricket), 352
Russia, 270, 501-503
Ryder Cup (golf), 453

S

Saemangeum Seawall, South Korea, 254
Sahara Desert, 514
sailing, 169, 172, 176
salad, 203, 204
salamanders, 32, 54
salami, 203
Salvation Army, 150
sand paintings, 483
sandcastles, 253
sandwiches, 201
Santa Claus, 194
Sargasso Sea, 29
saris, 217
satellites, 24
Saturn, 8, 11
Saturn V rocket, 121, 126
scarecrows, 165
scarves, 491
school reunions, 164
schools, 518
SCIENCE & ENGINEERING, 231-272
science frontiers, 233-236
scissors, 93, 253
scooters, 480

Index

545

Index

Index

Index

ACKNOWLEDGMENTS/CREDITS

Guinness World Records would like to thank the following individuals, companies, groups, websites, societies, and universities for their help in the creation of the 2009 edition:

Pedro Adrega (Fédération Internationale de Natation), American Paper Optics (John Jerit), BAPS Swaminarayan Akshardham, Bender Media Services (Susan and Sally), Betsy Baker, Luke and Joseph Boatfield, Ceri, Olivia Boulton, Katie & Georgie Boulton, Alfie Boulton-Fay, Box Office Mojo, Julie Bradshaw & The Channel Swimming Association (The CSA), Sir Richard Branson, Nikki Brin, Carlsberg, Stockholm, Peter Cassidy (Race Walking Association), The Cavalry & Guards Club, London, CCTV (Guo Tong and Wang Xuechun), Gene Cernan, ChartTrack, Edd & Imogen China, Ian Coburn, Paulo Coelho, Edouard Cointreau, The Costume Studio, London, Kenneth & Tatiana Crutchlow (ORS), Stacey Cusack, Elaine Davidson, Ceri Davis, Davis Media, Debbie De Groot, David Donnelly, Terry Doyle, James Ellerker, Louis Epstein, ESPN X Games—Kelly Robshaw, Katie Moses Swope, Deb McKinnis, Europroducciones Spain and Italy (Stefano, Marco, Maria, Gabriella et al), Explorersweb, Factiva, Fall Out Boy (Andy Hurley, Patrick Stump, Joe Trohman, Pete Wentz, plus Bob Mclynn, Henry Bordeaux, Kyle Chirnside, Brian Diaz), Famitsu, Adam Fenton, Ian Fisk, Flix (Tam, Nic, and Sharan), Forbes, Marion Gallimore (Fédération Internationale des Sociétés d'Aviron), The GFK Group, Brett Gold, Golden Tulip Hotel, Luxembourg, Google/YouTube (Theo), Louise Grant, Bexier Group, Jordan, Ryan and Brandon Greenwood, Debby de Groot, Kristopher Growcott, AJ Hackett, Tim Haines, Impossible Pictures, Peter Harper, Ray Harper, Andy Harris (International Water Skiing Federation), Stuart Hendry, Gavin Hennessy, Gill Hill (International Water Skiing Federation), Nigel Hobbs, Homewood School, Tenterden, Hospital Xanit Internacional, Malaga, Hotel Arts, Barcelona, Hotel Guadalpin, Marbella, ICM (Greg Lipstone, Heather Grayson), The Infamous Grouse and Sir Les (Jack Brockbank, Robert Dimery, Craig Glenday, Kaoru Ishikawa, Lucia Sinigagliesi, Nick Watson), Internet Movie Database, Tan Jun, Cathy & Bob Jung, Jefferson County Fairgrounds, Colorado, Jon Jeritt, Jon Adam Fashion Group, Joost (Alexandra and Symon), Mark Karges, Dr. Haydn Kelly, Dr. Theo Kreouzis, Department of Physics, Queen Mary University of London, Orla and Thea Langton, Christopher Lee, Lingfield Racecourse, Surrey, Helen Livingstone, Carey Low, Canadian Manda Group, Lula-Bell, Mad Max III (Claire Bygrave, Carol & Maureen Kane, Sam Malone, David Moncur), Manda, Canada, Mediazone (Gary), Clare Merryfield, Mora Siljan Airport, Sweden, MTV (Ritesh Guptah, James Montgomery), Derek Musso, National Geographic Kids magazine (Rachel Buchholz, Eleanor Shannah), NBA Entertainment (Patrick Sullivan, Karen Barberan, Jason Iodato, NBC (Craig Plestis, Jenny

Ellis), Aniko Nemeth Mora (International Weightlifting Federation), Nation-master, Liam Nesbitt, Norddeich TV Germany (Ollie, Melanie, Claudia, Jan et al.), NPD Group, OANDA, Ocean Rowing Society, Michael Oram & CS&PF, Alberto Parise, Clara Piccirillo, Professor Theodore W. Pietsch, University of Washington, La Porte des Indes Restaurant, London, Fabrice Prahin (International Skating Union), He Pingping and family, Rob Pullar, Keith Pullin, La Quatre-Cats restaurant, Barcelona, R et G Productions, France (Stefan, Jerome, David, Jean-Francois, Julien et al.), Red Lion Public House, Hernhill, Lee Redmond, Brian Reinert, Martyn Richards, Martyn Richards Research, Richmond Theatre, Surrey, RTL (Sascha, Tom, Sandra, Sebastian, Jennifer, Julia, et al.), Rebecca Saponiere, Tom Sergeant, Robyn Sheppard, Julien Stauffer (Union Cycliste Internationale), Bethan Muir Tame, Greenfield Media, Texperts (Tom, Sarah, Rhod, and Paul), True Enter-tainment (Stephen Weinstock, Glenda Hersh, Bryan Hale, Shari Solomon Cedar), TSA/MAX Entertainment (Marcus, Belle, Alex, Christy, Ery, et al.), Twin Galaxies (Walter Day, Pete Bouvier), Jan Vandendriessche (Interna-tional Association of Ultra Runners), Veoh (Emilia), VG Chartz, Jessica and Isabel Way, Carina Weirauch, Fran Wheelen, Royal Bath & West Show, Nor-man Wilson (International Association of Ultra Runners), Wookey Hole Caves, Somerset, YouTube.

In memoriam...
Art Arfons, former land speed record holder; Bernie Barker, **Oldest male stripper;** Chris Bishop, GWR's military consultant; Hal Fishman, **Longest career as a newsreader;** Moses Aleksandrovich Feigin, **Oldest profes-sional artist;** Steve Fossett, **Longest non-stop flight,** *inter alia;* Bertha Fry (b. December 1, 1893), third oldest person in the world at time of death; Wally Herbert, **First crossing of the Arctic;** Sir Edmund Hillary, **First as-cent of Mt. Everest;** Sarah Jeanmougin, **Oldest living twin;** Verity Lam-bert, founding producer of *Dr. Who,* the **longest running sci-fi show on television;** Humphrey Lyttelton, organizer of the **Largest kazoo ensemble;** Eddie "Bozo" Miller, competitive eater; Yone Minegawa, **Oldest living woman** (and **person**) at time of death; Ellen Isabela Robertson, one of the **Oldest living female twins;** Charles Wright, **Oldest music teacher.**

PICTURE CREDITS

ix–xi: (U.S.) Gary C. Knapp/AP/PA; (U.S.) Lisa Colvin; xi: (U.S.) Yesikka Vivancos; (U.S.) Hannah Foslien/Minnesota Twins; (U.S.) Shane Nickerson; xii: (U.S.) Matthew Simmons/Getty Images; (U.S.) Joe Murphy/NBAE/Getty Images; xiii–xv: (U.S.) Brian Ach/Getty Images; (U.S.) Larry F. Griffiths; xvi: (CAN) Koichi Kamoshida/Getty Images; xvii: (CAN) Martin Jardine; xviii–xx: (CAN) John Wright/GWR; xxi: John Wright/GWR; xxii: Andy Paradise/GWR; xxiii–xxv: Paul Michael Hughes/GWR; xxvi–xxix: The Art Archive; akg-images; Getty Images; PA; xxx: Rex Features; Stan Honda/Getty Images; NASA; Jack Smith/AP/PA; Emiliano Grillotti/Getty Images; 1: NASA; 4: Mark Garlick/SPL; Harvard-Smithsonian Center for Astrophysics; Mark Garlick/SPL; 5–6: NASA; NASA/MAXPPP; 7–8: Luke Dodd/SPL; NASA; 9–11: NASA; SPL; NASA; 12–15: NASA; SPL; Dept. of Geological Sciences, Dallas; 16: ESA/DLR/FU Berlin (G. Neukum); SPL; Kees Veenenbos/SPL; 17–18: NASA; NASA; Gordon Garradd/SPL; 19: Detlev Van Ravenswaay/SPL; NASA; 20: David Steele; 21: Alan Dawson/Alamy; Santiago Ferrero; Joe Sohm/Photolibrary; 22–23: Dave Lewis/Rex Features; European Space Agency; NASA; 24–25: NASA/SPL; NASA; NASA/AP/PA; 27: Photolibrary; 29: Valerie Taylor/Ardea; 30–32: FLPA; G Douwma/Getty Images; Doc White/Nature PL; 33–36: Fred Hirschmann/Getty Images; George Grall/Getty Images; Mary Plage/Photolibrary; 37–38: Mike Linley/Getty Images; Mark Carwardine/Nature PL; 39–40: Richard Herrmann/Photolibrary; Steven David Miller/Nature PL; Jim Watt/Photolibrary; 41–42: Tim Laman/Getty Images; Richard Manuel/Photolibrary; Alamy; 43–44: Joe & Mary McDonald/Alamy; Eric Francis/Getty Images; FLPA; 45–47: Samuel Aranda/Getty Images; Maximilian Weinzierl/Alamy; Peter Chadwick/SPL; Reuters; 48–49: David Courtenay/Photolibrary; FLPA; J & A Scott/Getty Images; 50–51: Bobby Haas/Getty Images; Frank Greenaway/Getty Images; Alamy; 52–53: Duncan Shaw/SPL; Terry Whittaker/Alamy; Alamy; 54: John Dransfield/Kew Gardens; Tony Craddock/SPL; Gerald Cubitt/NHPA; 55–57: Bruce Beehler/AP/PA; Twan Leenders; Mark Carwardine/Nature PL; 58–60: FLPA; FLPA; 61: Martin Harvey/NHPA; FLPA; 62–63: Daryl Balfour/NHPA; Ranald Mackechnie/GWR; 64: Roy Toft/Getty Images; Nature PL; Rex Features; Andreas Lander/Corbis; 65: Murray Cooper/Nathan Muchhala; Andy Rouse/NHPA; 66: Alamy; Corbis; Corbis; Alamy; 67: Sam Chadwick/Alamy; Corbis; 68: Dietmar Nill/Nature Pl; Bruce Davidson/Nature PL; 69–70: Rex Features; Andrew Parkinson/Nature PL; 71: Ian Redmond/Nature PL; Matthias Breiter/Getty Images; David Scharf/Getty Images; 72: Kim Taylor/Nature PL; Hugo Willcox/Getty Images; 73: Ranald Mackechnie/GWR; 75: Mary Evans Picture Library; 76–77: Gray's Anatomy/Elsevier; 79–81: Ranald Mackechnie/GWR; Phil Meyers/AP/PA; 83–86: Sean Sexton/Getty Images; Tomas Bravo/GWR; 87–89: Ranald

Mackechnie/GWR; **90:** John Wright/GWR; Ranald Mackechnie/GWR; **91–94:** Manish Swarup/AP/PA; Paul Michael Hughes/GWR; Ranald Mackechnie/GWR; **95:** Li Zijun/Photoshot; Simon Smith/AP/PA; Ranald Mackechnie/GWR; **96–99:** Don Cravens/Getty Images; PA Photos; Daniel Berehulak/Getty Images; **100:** John Wright/GWR; **101–102:** Kiyoshi Ota/Reuters; **103:** Miguel Alvarez/Getty Images; Reuters; PA; **104:** Steve Dibblee/iStockphoto; Ranald Mackechnie/GWR; **105:** John Wright/GWR; RTL/Gregorowius; **106:** BBC Books/The Random House Group Ltd.; John Wright/GWR; Drew Gardner/GWR; **107:** Ranald Mackechnie/GWR; **108:** Ian Cook/Getty Images; MAXPPP; **109:** Barbara Laing/Getty Images; Tom Strickland/GWR; **110–114:** Erik G. Svensson; **115–116:** Richard Bradbury/GWR; Maxwells/GWR; **117–120:** BBC Books/The Random House Group Ltd.; Getty Images; **120–122:** Paul Michael Hughes/GWR; Corbis; NASA; **123–125:** NASA; NASA; NASA; NASA; NASA; NASA; Photolibrary; **126:** NASA/SPL; NASA; NASA/Getty Images; Dorling Kindersley; Moonpans.com; **129:** John Wright/GWR; **130–132:** Craig Ruttle/AP/PA; **133:** Thomas Mukoya/Reuters; Ned Redway; China Photos/Getty Images; **134:** Chet Gordon/Times Herald-Record; **135–136:** John Wright/GWR; Pali Rao/iStockphoto; **137:** John Wright/GWR; **138:** Ranald Mackechnie/GWR; **139–140:** Charles Rex Arbogast/AP/PA; Ranald Mackechnie/GWR; **141–142:** Richard Bradbury/GWR; John Wright/GWR; **143:** Ranald Mackechnie/GWR; **144–145:** Colin Young-Wolff/Alamy; AP/PA; Peter Macdiarmid/Getty Images; **146–153:** Alen Dobric/iStockphoto; Marek Szumlas/iStockphoto; Georges DeKeerle/Getty Images; Bob Landry/Getty Images; Mike Kipling/Alamy; **154–155:** Richard Bradbury/GWR; **156:** John Wright/GWR; John Wright/GWR; **157–159:** John Wright/GWR; John Wright/GWR; John Wright/GWR; **160–164:** John Wright/GWR; Sukree Sukplang/Reuters; John Wright/GWR; **165:** John Wright/GWR; Manish Swarup/AP/PA; **166:** WENN; WENN; Jeff Spicer/Alpha/Channel Four; **167:** Fredrik Schenholm/www.schenholm.se; **170:** Fred Tanneau/Getty Images; **171–172:** Vincent Kessler/Reuters; **173–177:** William Garnier/ORS; Wolfgang Rattay/Reuters; Filip Singer/Getty Images; Getty Images; **178–180:** Carl de Souza/Getty Images; David Dyson/Getty Images; **181–184:** PA; PA; AP/PA; **185–189:** Ira Block/NGS; Corbis; **190:** Hiroyuki Kuraoka/AP/PA; **191:** Richard Bradbury/GWR; **193–194:** Claro Cortes/Reuters; Richard Bradbury/GWR; **195–197:** Ranald Mackechnie/GWR; Paul Michael Hughes/GWR; WENN; Alamy; **198–200:** Richard Bradbury/GWR; Chip East/Reuters; **201–202:** Richard Bradbury/GWR; Jay Williams/GWR; **204–205:** Maximilian Weinzierl/Alamy; Richard Bradbury/GWR; **207:** Rex Features; Cosmopolitan & Venus Breeze; **209–213:** Mario Anzuoni/Reuters; **215–219:** Alberto Roque/Getty Images; Sean Sprague/Panos Pictures; Mustafa Deliormanli/iStockphoto; Norman Chan/iStockphoto; Luca Da Ros/4Corners Images; **220–223:** Philimon Bulawayo/Reuters; AP/PA; Reuters; **224–225:** Natasja Weitsz/Getty Images; Tariq Mahmood/Getty Images; Eyevine; **226:** AP/PA; Shannon Stapleton/Reuters; Paula Bronstein/Getty Images; Martin Bureau/Getty Images; **227:** Christopher Herwig/Reuters; Sandy Huffaker/Getty Images; Getty Images; **228:** Eyevine; Getty Images; David Manyua/Reuters;

231: Richard Bradbury/GWR; **233:** Yoshikazu Tsuno/Getty Images; **234:** CERN; **235–236:** Karl Shone/Getty Images; Randy Olson/Getty Images; Case Western Reserve University; **237:** David S. Holloway/Getty Images; Niels Bohr Institute; **238–240:** Swedish Institute; Corbis; Robert Galbraith/Reuters; **242–244:** Rex Features; Apple; DreamWorks Pictures (Paramount); **246–249:** WENN; Justin Sullivan/Getty Images; Apple/Rex Features; **250–251:** Roland Gladasch/GWR; Robert F. Bukaty/AP/PA; **252:** M. Roger/MAX PPP; **253–254:** James Davis/Alamy; Getty Images; **255–257:** Eitan Abramovich/Getty Images; Guang Niu/Getty Images; Adriana Lorete/Getty Images; **258:** Rabih Moghrabi/Getty Images; **259–264:** Rex Features; Kiyoshi Ota/Reuters; John Wright/GWR; **265:** Rex Features; **266:** Elaine Thompson/AP/PA; **267–269:** Georges Gobet/Getty Images; Jean-Bernard Gache; **270:** Getty Images; Reuters; **271–272:** Reuters; Reuters; Royal Navy; **273:** John Wright/GWR; **275–276:** Getty Images; David Burner/Rex Features; Rex Features; **277–278:** Chris Jackson/Getty Images; Francois Guillot/Getty Images; **279–281:** Photolibrary; National Park Service; Ronald Grant; Ronald Grant; Universal Pictures; Paramount Pictures; Columbia Pictures; **282–283:** Warner Bros/Kobal; Warner Bros/Ronald Grant; Universal Pictures/Ronald Grant; www.moviescreen shots.blogspot.com; Ronald Grant; Columbia Pictures; New Line Cinema; Paramount Pictures/Ronald Grant; **284–287:** Sony RCA; Alex Grimm/Reuters; Getty Images; Matt Cardy/Getty Images; **288–289:** Rick Diamond/Getty Images; Sony RCA; PA; **290:** Rex Features; Kevin Westenberg/Getty Images; Evan Agostini/AP/PA; **291:** Dave Benett/Getty Images; Gary He/AP/PA; John Wright/GWR; **292–293:** Cate Gillon/Getty Images; Mykel Nicolao/GWR; Chitose Suzuki/AP/PA; **294–295:** Manish Swarup/AP/PA; DC Comics; **296–300:** Frank Micelotta/Getty Images; NBC-TV/Rex Features; **301–302:** Hanna-Barbera; NBC-TV/Kobal; 20th Century Fox/Rex Features; **303:** Richard Bradbury/GWR; John Wright/GWR; **304–306:** John Wright/GWR; Hermann J. Knippertz/AP/PA; Francisco Bonilla/Reuters; Francisco Bonilla/Reuters; **307:** Rockstar Games; **309:** David Stluka/Getty Images; **311:** Ludovic Franco/RedBull; **312–314:** Richard Eaton/Max PPP; David Stluka/Getty Images; David Stluka/Getty Images; Kai Pfaffenbach/Reuters; **315–316:** Ben Liebenberg/Getty Images; Jamie Squire/Getty Images; **317–319:** Kai Pfaffenbach/Reuters; Emiliano Grillotti/Getty Images; Koichi Kamoshida/Getty Images; **320–324:** Alexander Hassenstein/Getty Images; Brian Snyder/Reuters; Alexander Hassenstein/Getty Images; Torsten Silz/Getty Images; **325–326:** Michael Steele/Getty Images; Andreas Rentz/Getty Images; **327–330:** Rusty Jarrett/Getty Images; Kim Kyung-Hoon/Reuters; J.P. Moczulski/Reuters; **331–332:** John Harrelson/Getty Images; Jonathan Ferrey/Getty Images; **333–335:** Tengku Bahar/Getty Images; Grigory Dukor/Reuters; Joe Bryksa/CP Picture Archive; **336:** Stephen Cooper/Newspix; Phil Walter/Getty Images; Dominic Ebenbichler/Reuters; **337:** Mike Fiala/Getty Images; Jim McIsaac/Getty Images; **338:** Al Bello/Getty Images; **339:** Ints Kalnins/Reuters; Fernando Medina/Getty Images; **340:** Jeffrey Bottari/Getty Images; Joe Murphy/Getty Images; Barry Gossage/Getty Images; **341:** Gregory Shamus, NBAE/Getty Images; Joe Murphy/NBAE/Getty Images; Joe Murphy/NBAE/Getty Images; **342–343:** Joe Murphy, NBAE/ Getty Images; Gregory Shamus/NBAE/Getty Images; **344:** Brendon Thorne/Getty Images; Paul Kane/Getty Images; Paul Kane/Getty Images; **345–347:** Craig Prentis/Getty Images; Lee Warren/Getty Images; Lee Warren/Getty Images; **348:** Yuruzu Sunada/Getty Images; Michael Steele/Getty Images; Jaime Reina/Getty Images; Yves Boucau/Getty Images; **349:** Jean Pierre Clatot/AFP; Samuel Golay/Gett Images; Getty Images; Getty Images; **350–351:** Carl De Souza/Getty Images; Carl De Souza/ Getty Images; Paco Serinelli/Getty Images; **352–353:** Clive Mason/Getty Images; PA; Felix Ordonez/Reuters; **354:** Ranald Mackechnie/GWR; John Wright/GWR; **355–356:** Ranald Mackechnie/GWR; John Wright/GWR; **357–358:** Yang Enuo/PA Photos; Anthony Devlin/PA Photos; Donald Miralle/Getty Images; **359–360:** Scott Halleran/Getty Images; Sam Greenwood/Getty Images; **361–365:** Chris Trotman/Getty Images; Dave Sandford/Getty Images; Steve Babineau/Getty Images; **366–371:** Gregory Shamus/Getty Images; Getty Images; **372–375:** Ricardo Moraes/AP/PA; Javier Sorano/AFP; Ed Mulholland/Getty Images; **376–377:** World Wrestling Entertainment, Inc.; Rex Features; Toshifumi Kitamura/AFP; **378–379:** Anthony Phelps/Reuters; JM Hervio/AI/Reuters; Cameron Spencer/Getty Images; **380–382:** Cameron Spencer/Getty Images; David Rogers/Getty Images; Cameron Spencer/Getty Images; Chris McGrath/ Getty Images; **383–384:** Brian Bahr/Getty Images; Odd Andersen/Getty Images; Clive Brunskill/Getty Images; Keith Hammet/AP/PA; **385–386:** Bobby Yip/Reuters; Cameron Spencer/Getty Images; Torsten Blackwood/ Getty Images; **387–388:** Adrees Latif/Reuters; Damir Sagolj/Reuters; Grant Ellis/Getty Images; Andy Clark/Reuters; **389–391:** Lucy Nicholson/ Reuters; **392–393:** Richard Bradbury/GWR; Ranald Mackechnie/GWR; **394–395:** IMG Media Ltd; IMG Media Ltd; **395–399:** IMG Media Ltd; IMG Media Ltd; Getty Images; **400–405:** David Callow/AP/PA; Tony Vu/ESPN; Jae C. Hong/AP/PA; Matt Morning/ESPN; Dom Cooley/ESPN; Tony Donaldson/ESPN; **407:** Jack Dempsey/AP/PA; Eric Lars Bakke/ ESPN; ESPN; Tony Vu/ESPN; **409:** Reuters; Michael Steele/Getty Images; **411:** Michael Steele/Getty Images; Roland Weihrauch/AP/PA; **413:** Matthew Lewis/Getty Images; Andy Lyons/Getty Images; **417:** Bryn Lennon/Getty Images; **423:** Junko Kimura/Getty Images; Chung Sung- Jun/Getty Images; **425:** Jonathan Ferrey/Getty Images; Albert Gea/Reuters; **427:** Giampiero Sposito/Reuters; Michael Sohn/AP/PA; **429:** Sukree Sukplang/Reuters; Sukree Sukplang/Reuters; **431:** Mark Dadswell/Getty Images; **436:** Paramount Pictures; Stefano Paltera/AP/PA; Ranald Mackechnie/GWR; **437:** David McNew/Getty Images; Kevin Winter/Getty Images; Vince Bucci/Getty Images; MJ Kim/Getty Images; **438:** David Fisher/Rex Features; Michael Buckner/Getty Images; **444–445:** Chen Jie/GWR; Chen Jie/GWR; Chen Jie/GWR; **446:** Reuters; Reuters; **447:** Chen Jie/GWR; Chen Jie/GWR; **448:** Rex Features; Chen Jie/GWR; **449:** Bloomsbury; Marco Secchi/Getty Images; **439–440:** Ranald Mackechnie/ GWR; Mario Anzuoni/Reuters; Warner Bros. Entertainment Inc.; **441–443:** Warner Bros. Entertainment Inc.; Dave M. Benett/Getty Images; Ronald Grant; Raine Vara/Alamy; **451:** NASA; **453:** Angelo Cavalli/Robert Hard-

ing; **454:** Hiroko Masuike/Getty Images; AP/PA; Getty Images; **455–456:**
Achim Prill/iStockphoto; Patricio Robles Gil/Getty Images; Gary Vestal/
Getty Images; Vladimir Pcholkin/Getty Images; **457:** Grey Villet/Getty Images; Adalberto Roque/Getty Images; Photolibrary; David McLain/Getty
Images; Alamy; **457:** NASA; Miguel Mendez/Getty Images; Joel Sartore/
Getty Images; **458–459:** Mauricio Lima/Getty Images; Elena Goycochea;
H. John Maier Jr./Getty Images; Reuters; **460:** Joe Raedle/Getty Images;
NASA; John Sylvester/Alamy; **461–462:** Reuters; Winston Fraser/Alamy;
463: Ranald Mackechnie/GWR; PA; iStockphoto; **464:** Ranald
Mackechnie/GWR; Shaun Curry/Getty Images; **465–466:** Francois
Nascimbeni/Getty Images; Remy de la Mauviniere/AP/PA; Stephane De
Satukin/Getty Images; **467–468:** OL Mazzatenta/Getty Images; AP/PA;
469–471: P Desmazes/Getty Images; Ricardo Suárez; Xan G. Muras;
472–474: Jose Manuel Ribeiro/Reuters; Clive Brunskill/Getty Images; Rex
Features; **474–476:** Mitchell Funk/Getty Images; Marcel Lelienhof;
477–479: Erlend Berge/Scanpix/PA; Gero Breloer/Corbis; **480:** Richard
Bradbury/GWR; **481–483:** HNJ Van Essen/Getty Images; **484–489:** Amel
Emric/AP/PA; Viktor Drachev/Getty Images; **490–492:** Michael
Steele/Getty Images; Hideo Kurihara/Alamy; PA; **493–494:** A Nemenov/
Getty Images; SPL; Stephen Dunn/Getty Images; Alamy; **495–497:** Bruno
Morandi/Getty Images; Duncan Ridgley/Rex Features; **498–502:** Thomas
Hartwell/Getty Images; Barry Lewis/Alamy; AA Rabbo/Getty Images;
503–506: Fred Derwal/Corbis; Anup Shah/Getty Images; Franck Guiziou/
Getty Images; **507–511:** George Mulala/Reuters; Chris Jackson/Getty Images; AP/PA; **512–517:** Corbis; Banaras Khan/Getty Images; **518–523:**
Saurabh Das/AP/PA; Angelo Cavalli/Tips Images; **524–527:** Zhang Jun/
Xinhua/WPN; Paula Bronstein/Getty Images; Ron Dahlquist/Getty Images;
528–529: Alex Bowie/Getty Images; Juliet Coombe/Lonely Planet; **530:**
AKG Images; Reuters; **531:** Jurgen Freund/Nature PL; **532:** Getty Images;
Mary Evans; FLPA; **570–571:** Michael Buckner/Getty Images; George
Burns/Harpo Productions; Paul Sanders; **572:** Rex Features; **573–574:** Gunnar Kullenberg/Rex Features

STOP PRESS

☆**Fastest ascent of Mount Kilimanjaro** Gerard Bavato (France) ran the 21.1 miles (34 km) from the base to the summit of Mount Kilimanjaro in 5 hr. 26 min. 40 sec. on October 26, 2007.

★**Youngest drummer** Tiger Onitsuka (Japan) was just 9 years 289 days old when his debut album—*Tiger*—was released on April 23, 2008. Tiger is a jazz drummer and is signed to the Columbia label.

☆**Youngest photographer** Zoe Fung Leung (Hong Kong, b. January 19, 2006) was 2 years 70 days old when she exhibited and sold her work at Plaza Hollywood, Kowloon, Hong Kong, on March 29–30, 2008, making her the youngest professional photographer.

☆**Largest flag draped** The largest flag draped measured 245,559.27 ft.^{2} (22,813.293 m^2) and was the national flag of the United Arab Emirates (UAE). It was created by Sedar Window Fashion (UAE) and presented, as a token of appreciation, to the government of Sharjah in Sharjah, UAE, on May 12, 2008.

★**Most accurate atomic clock** The world's most accurate atomic clock, as of July 2006, is a prototype mercury optical device which, if operated continually, would neither gain nor lose a second in approximately 400 million years. The clock has been built and developed by the National Institute of Standards and Technology (NIST) in Boulder, Colorado, U.S.A.

☆**LONGEST TIME TO HOLD ONE'S BREATH** David Blaine (U.S.A.) held his breath underwater for 17 min. 4.4 sec. on *The Oprah Winfrey Show* in Chicago, Illinois, U.S.A., on April 30, 2008.